Alzheimer's Disease and Other Dementias

Working with the needs of patients with Alzheimer's disease can be a major challenge for primary care physicians, psychiatrists, and other mental health professionals. Alzheimer's wreaks havoc on the patient, and its degenerative nature can create a protracted period of anguish and anxiety for the patient's family. Dr. Marc Agronin has put his years of experience as a geriatric psychiatrist to work to create an eminently useful resource for psychiatrists and others who treat patients suffering from Alzheimer's disease or other dementias. Now in its third edition, *Alzheimer's Disease and Other Dementias* uses concise and clear language to outline the symptoms, effects, and treatments used to combat the progress of Alzheimer's disease and other dementias likely to be suffered by older patients. Enriched by case studies from his own clinical practice, Dr. Agronin creates a volume full of humanity, insight, and knowledge that is sure to inform and improve the habits and methods of any clinician who deals with Alzheimer's disease and other forms of dementia.

Marc E. Agronin, MD, is a board-certified adult and geriatric psychiatrist; he serves as the medical director for mental health and clinical research at the Miami Jewish Health Systems and as an affiliate associate professor of psychiatry and neurology at the University of Miami Miller School of Medicine. He is the author of numerous articles and books in the field of psychiatry and a nationally known speaker and expert on Alzheimer's disease and other late-life psychiatric disorders. In 2008, Dr. Agronin was named "clinician of the year" by the American Association for Geriatric Psychiatry. He is the author of *How We Age: A Doctor's Journey into the Heart of Growing Old* and *Therapy with Older Clients: Key Strategies for Success*, as well as coeditor of *Principles and Practice of Geriatric Psychiatry*, second edition.

Alzheimer's Disease and Other Dementias

A Practical Guide

Third Edition

Marc E. Agronin

Routledge
Taylor & Francis Group

NEW YORK AND LONDON

Third edition published 2014
by Routledge
711 Third Avenue, New York, NY 10017

and by Routledge
27 Church Road, Hove, East Sussex BN3 2FA

Routledge is an imprint of the Taylor & Francis Group, an informa business

First edition published by Lippincott Williams & Wilkins 2004
Second edition published by Lippincott Williams & Wilkins 2007

Library of Congress Cataloging-in-Publication Data

Agronin, Marc E.
    Alzheimer's disease and other dementias : a practical guide / by Marc E. Agronin. — 3rd edition.
        pages cm
    Includes bibliographical references and index.
    1. Dementia—Handbooks, manuals, etc.   2. Dementia—Patients—Care—Handbooks, manuals, etc.   3. Caregivers—Handbooks, manuals, etc.   4. Geriatric psychiatry—Handbooks, manuals, etc.   I. Title.
    RC521.A377 2014
    616.8′3—dc23
    2013037410

ISBN: 978-0-415-85699-7 (hbk)
ISBN: 978-0-415-85700-0 (pbk)
ISBN: 978-0-203-70836-1 (ebk)

Typeset in Minion
by Apex CoVantage, LLC

MIX
Paper from
responsible sources
FSC® C014174

Printed and bound in the United States of America by Sheridan Books, Inc. (a Sheridan Group Company).

To the past . . .
The blessed memory of my grandparents,
Dr. Simon and Eva Cherkasky
and
Tany and Etta Agronin;

To the present . . .
The love and support of my wife, Robin;

To the future . . .
My sons, Jacob, Max, and Samuel

Contents

Foreword

Physicians often ask themselves, Why should I be interested in brain diseases such as dementias? In this third edition of *Alzheimer's Disease and Other Dementias, A Practical Guide*, Dr. Marc Agronin provides the answer. From the description of Alzheimer's disease by psychiatrist Alois Alzheimer to the current methods of diagnosis and treatment, clinicians have much to learn about and much to contribute to the assessment and management of both patients with this group of illnesses and their daily caregivers. In a direct, readable fashion, Dr. Agronin nicely addresses many of the questions raised by patients, caregivers, and clinicians. He does not oversimplify things, and he does acknowledge that, at times, physicians cannot be as specific as they would like to be. This practical guide is just what the title suggests—useful, succinct, and accessible to the busy practitioner.

Peter V. Rabins, MD, MPH
Professor, Department of Psychiatry
Johns Hopkins School of Medicine, Baltimore, Maryland

Acknowledgments

First, I thank Anna Moore for giving me the opportunity to revise this book in a third edition, as well as for her guidance, enthusiasm, and confidence; I also thank the staff members at Routledge who have been involved in producing and promoting this book.

My wife, Robin, provided the warmest environment imaginable in which to write and revise this book, as well as the love, support, and time to do so. My sons Jacob, Max, and Sam have always provided necessary distractions from my labors; my sincere hope is that one day they will pick up a copy of their father's book on dementia and react quizzically to all the time and effort I spent writing about a disease that has been eradicated in their lifetimes. I also acknowledge the support of my parents, Ronald and Belle Agronin; my siblings, Robin and Greg Druckman and Michael and Ellen Agronin; and my in-laws, Fred and Marlene Lippman. I owe special thanks to Dr. Alan Cherkasky, whose practice of medicine has always inspired me and whose practical approach has always challenged me to translate even the most complicated approaches into practical benefits for the patient.

Many colleagues at the Miami Jewish Health Systems (MJHS) have provided advice and have served as models of care for the book, including Dr. Mairelys Martinez, Niurka Colina, Dr. Amina Rivero, Jose Macias, Alex Gomez, Dr. Barbara Sparacino, and Dr. Brian Kiedrowski. I also acknowledge the inspiration of so many caregivers with whom I have worked, particularly the members of our caregiver support group, who embody the exemplary wisdom and dedication that is key to successful aging and coping.

The most important inspiration for this book comes from memories of spending time seeing patients with my grandfather Dr. Simon Cherkasky, who practiced medicine in the small town of Kaukauna, Wisconsin, for over 50 years. He taught me many of the invaluable lessons that pervade this book—to work up each and every patient thoroughly, to treat them completely, and to make medical decisions based on clinical need rather than on the availability of resources. This wisdom is crucial to the treatment of dementia. My grandmother Eva Cherkasky, his lifelong companion, provided from the warmth of her heart and her kitchen the true chicken soup for my soul. I hope that this book in a small way continues the educational and intellectual legacy of her own grandfather and my great-great grandfather, the beloved and well-respected teacher Rabbi Pesach Iser Gielczynski.

Introduction to the Third Edition

Do not cast me off in old age; when my strength fails, do not forsake me.

—Psalms 71:9

The diagnosis of dementia or even the possibility of such a diagnosis is often greeted with fear and trepidation by those affected. The ensuing fears of losing one's mind and capabilities and of being abandoned or "put away" in an institution are contemplated as fates worse than death. The disease stealthily encroaches in some individuals, robbing them of insight into their illness before they can truly appreciate what has happened. Others notice the changes building month to month and year to year but resign themselves to the process. Still others fight the changes or those around them who insist that they cut back on the activities that once meant independence and integrity but now carry the risk of disaster.

In its early stages, dementia is a disease that unifies patients, caregivers, and clinicians in a necessary alliance as patients try to cope with changes in cognition and function, caregivers attempt to adapt to these changes, and clinicians seek to provide both diagnosis and treatment for a disorder that is often incurable. The pitfalls in this alliance are clear: patients wrestle with fear and confusion that may sabotage their cooperation, caregivers struggle to overcome significant grief and exhaustion, and clinicians must remain engaged despite a tendency to develop a fatalistic complacency. Many of these factors are amplified as dementia progresses into moderate and severe stages, ultimately culminating in a terminal state.

With this in mind, a core theme underlying this book is to look for the human being behind the dementia. In practical terms, a clinician who masters every facet of dementia may be knowledgeable but not necessarily wise or caring. Every individual with dementia is more than a diseased brain; he or she is also an ailing human who is surrounded by grieving caregivers with good hearts but limited amounts of time and patience. A busy and harried clinician can easily lose sight of these factors when he or she is working with cognitively impaired individuals who can no longer express their own needs and wishes and who may be engaging in troubling behavioral problems.

Those clinicians who read and use this book will find sufficient information to teach them about nearly every facet of dementia—its forms, pathways, pitfalls, and treatments. The book is designed to be a practical guide that can be brought into the clinic when one is evaluating and treating patients. I have endeavored to provide case vignettes and clinical tips to help clinicians move beyond a simple book knowledge of dementia and to hone their practical skills in assessment and treatment. All of the new developments in Alzheimer's disease are detailed in the text, including amyloid-targeted neuroimaging, biomarkers, and anti-amyloid therapies. The diagnostic schemes for Alzheimer's disease and other dementias have been updated to conform with the fifth edition of the *Diagnostic and Statistical Manual of Mental Disorders* (DSM-5). I have chosen to retain the term *dementia* in this edition given its widespread use and familiarity, while acknowledging here that DSM-5's substitution of the term *neurocognitive disorders* is broader and likely more relevant. I hope that this newly revised work continues to serve as an invaluable guide and resource for all clinicians caring for individuals with dementia.

Part I

Clinical Assessment of Dementia

1 An Overview of Dementia

The term *dementia* has represented many different meanings and connotations over time. The word itself comes from Latin and literally means to be "without a mind." It is an ancient term that appears as both a disease state in Roman medical texts and a form of political sarcasm in the philosophical works of Cicero. In the past two centuries, dementia has been used to refer to a brain disease characterized by chronic intellectual impairment. In some of the first diagnostic schemes, dementia was referred to as an organic mental syndrome or an organic brain syndrome. The prefixes *presenile* and *senile* were frequently used to refer to disease states that developed before or after 65 years of age, respectively, and eventually the term *senility* became synonymous with dementia. Although dementia is still the most commonly used diagnostic term, revisions in the diagnostic nomenclature have replaced it with *neurocognitive disorder*. The term *dementia* will be retained in this book since it continues to be widely used and understood.

In the United States alone, rates of Alzheimer's disease (AD) and other dementias are at epidemic proportions, afflicting approximately 5.4 million individuals, with 96% being older than 65. Of this older group, 63% are female (Alzheimer's Association, 2012). The main risk factor for all forms of dementia is age, and with the number of older Americans projected to nearly double in the next 30 years, there will clearly be a tremendous surge in the number of dementia cases, barring any major advance in prevention or treatment. It is estimated that AD and other dementias afflict over 35 million people worldwide currently, with a projected increase to over 155 million people by 2050 (Alzheimer's Disease International, 2010). Most of the increase will take place in developing Southeast Asian countries such as China and India. The annual cost of treating dementia in the United States was estimated to be between $157 billion and $215 billion in 2010, eclipsing the costs of both heart disease and cancer (Hurd et al., 2013).

Case Study

Mr. R was a retired businessman who had immigrated to the United States at the age of 10 years and had spent most of his early life working in the garment industry in New York City. He later worked as a furrier, running his own business for more than 20 years. He was married for more than 60 years and had two grown daughters. Mr. R sold his business at the age of 75, and he and his wife moved to a retirement community. His wife passed away when he was 85, and Mr. R insisted on living by himself, despite his daughters' concern that his memory and physical strength had declined. Shortly after his 90th birthday, Mr. R fell and broke his hip. After the hip surgery, he was admitted to a long-term care facility for two months of rehabilitation, followed by permanent placement in a nursing home. Staff reported that Mr. R had significant cognitive impairment and symptoms of depression. He frequently spoke about his deceased wife, stating that he wished to join her. Six months after admission, Mr. R developed pneumonia, leading to his hospitalization. On his return to the facility, the staff noted that he was confused, paranoid, and agitated. The acute confusion resolved after approximately two weeks, but Mr. R's cognitive abilities appeared to be much worse. He continued to be quite depressed and even overtly suicidal, with paranoid ideation and episodes of agitation. These symptoms improved slowly after Mr. R was placed in a unit for residents with behavioral problems and was treated with psychotropic medications. Over the next few years, Mr. R's short-term memory continued to worsen, and he could not remember important facts about his life. He also began to have difficulty recognizing familiar family and friends. With time, he became more apathetic, and his language function worsened to the point where he was nearly mute. He stopped walking and relied on nursing staff for all of his daily needs.

Many details of this case—a slow, insidious course; comorbid medical problems that led to further decline; and associated psychiatric problems, including depression, psychosis, agitation, and delirium—are typical for dementia, especially AD. As this case illustrates, long-term care placement is a frequent result, since many individuals progress to a near vegetative state in which they are completely dependent on others for care.

Definitions and Diagnostic Criteria

According to the diagnostic classification in the *Diagnostic and Statistical Manual of Mental Disorders*, Fourth Edition, Text Revision, or DSM-IV-TR (American Psychiatric Association, 2000), dementia refers to the development of multiple cognitive or intellectual deficits that involve memory impairment of new or previously learned information and one or more of the following disturbances:

- aphasia, or language disturbance;
- apraxia, or impairment in carrying out skilled motor activities despite intact motor function;
- agnosia, or deficits in recognizing familiar persons or objects despite intact sensory function;
- executive dysfunction, or impairments in planning, initiating, organizing, and abstract reasoning.

These deficits result in significant impairment in both social and occupational functioning, and they represent a decline, often with an insidious onset and progressive course, from a previous level of functioning.

As noted, the revised diagnostic nomenclature for the *Diagnostic and Statistical Manual of Mental Disorders*, Fifth Edition, or DSM-5 (American Psychiatric Association, 2013) replaces the term *dementia* with *major or minor neurocognitive disorder* (NCD) to provide a broader definition. Whereas the DSM-IV-TR criteria for dementia are patterned after AD, the DSM-5 criteria encompass a variety of potential forms of dementia (in addition to delirium and amnestic disorders) and do not require memory impairment in all cases. Individuals can meet the criteria for major NCD if they have decline in one (and typically two or more) of the following cognitive domains:

- complex attention
- executive ability
- learning and memory
- language
- perceptual-motor
- social cognition.

These domains are detailed in Table 1.1. According to DSM-5 criteria for major NCD, the declines in these domains are acquired and not developmental, represent a decline from previous levels of functioning (preferably established by neuropsychological testing), interfere with independence in everyday activities, and are not associated with the cognitive deficits seen in other major mental disorders such as schizophrenia or bipolar disorder (American Psychiatric Association, 2013). The criteria for minor NCD (labeled "Cognitive Disorder, Not Otherwise Specified" in DSM-IV-TR) are similar to those for major NCD, although the degree of cognitive impairment is less, and it does not interfere entirely with independence in everyday activities. The diagnosis of mild cognitive impairment (MCI) is considered a prodromal state of dementia; it is described in Chapter 3. In DSM-5 it would be labeled as a mild NCD due to a specified cause, such as "mild NCD due to AD."

DSM-5 includes specifiers for severity (mild, moderate, and severe) and the presence (or absence) of behavioral disturbances, which may include psychosis, mood disturbances, agitation, apathy, and other unspecified behavioral symptoms.

Table 1.1 DSM-5 Neurocognitive Domains

Neurocognitive Domain	Description
Complex attention	Ability to attend to and process multiple stimuli
Executive function	Ability to plan, organize, and complete tasks and projects
Learning and memory	Acquiring, manipulating, and remembering items, facts, words (and their meanings), events, people, procedures, skills, and so on
Perceptual-motor	Identification and manipulation of figures, map, and items; motor tasks (e.g., drawing, copying, assembling, using tools, driving) and gestures; recognition of faces and colors
Social cognition	Socially appropriate behaviors and decision-making; empathy

Source: American Psychiatric Association (2013).

Classification

Many different ways exist for classifying dementia subtypes, including classification by etiology, anatomic location, course, and prognosis. The main subtypes of NCD in DSM-5 include the following:

- NCD due to Alzheimer's disease
- vascular NCD
- NCD with Lewy bodies
- NCD due to Parkinson's disease
- frontotemporal NCD
- NCD due to traumatic brain injury
- NCD due to HIV infection
- substance-/medication-induced NCD
- NCD due to Huntington's disease
- NCD due to prion disease
- NCD due to another medical condition
- NCD due to multiple etiologies
- unspecified NCD

Each of these categories has its own specific criteria, which will be detailed in the corresponding chapters in this text. NCD due to another medical condition specifies that there is evidence from the history, physical examination, or laboratory findings that the NCD is the "pathophysiological consequence" of a specified medical condition distinct from the categories already stated (American Psychiatric Association, 2013). An unspecified NCD involves a condition in which the symptoms meet general NCD criteria but not those for any specific disorder listed.

Of the DSM-5 categories, AD is the most common, accounting for 50% to 70% of all dementias, while vascular dementia and dementia due to Lewy body disease account for slightly more than 20% each (Chui, 2007; Rahkonen et al., 2003). All other types of dementia represent less than 10% of total cases. There is considerable overlap with AD and the other major types. For example, approximately 30% of patients with AD also have vascular dementia.

Clinical Tip

Many patients and caregivers confuse the terms *dementia* and *Alzheimer's disease*. One simple way to educate them is to explain that *dementia* is a general term, like *infection*, and there are different types. If a doctor told you that you had an infection, a natural question would be, "What type of infection do I have?" Similarly, patients and caregivers should always be told what type of dementia they may have based on existing symptoms. Remember that everyone who suffers from Alzheimer's disease has dementia, but not everyone with dementia has Alzheimer's disease.

Although DSM-IV-TR and DSM-5 describe the majority of dementias, they also obscure the great diversity of subtypes. The following section presents several general ways to classify the dementias; there is also a complete list in Table 1.2, grouped by etiology.

Table 1.2 Subtypes of Dementia, Grouped by Etiology

Etiology	Subtype

Primary cortical degeneration	• Alzheimer's disease
	• Dementia with Lewy bodies (cerebral involvement)
	• Frontotemporal dementia
	  ○ Frontal/behavioral variant
	  ○ Semantic dementia
	  ○ Progressive aphasia

Primary subcortical degeneration	• Dementia with Lewy bodies (brainstem involvement) • Parkinson's disease dementia • Corticobasal degeneration • Progressive supranuclear palsy • Argyrophilic grain disease
Cerebrovascular disease	Vascular dementia, due to • Large-vessel and small-vessel strokes • Multiple lacunar infarcts • Binswanger's disease • Cerebral autosomal dominant-arteriopathy with subcortical infarcts and leukoencephalopathy (CADASIL) • Cerebral amyloid angiopathy
Structural or traumatic injury	• Traumatic brain injury • Chronic traumatic encephalopathy/dementia pugilistica • Chronic subdural hematoma • Normal pressure hydrocephalus • Post-anoxic state • Postoperative cognitive dysfunction
Neoplasm	• Brain tumors (malignant or benign) • Paraneoplastic disease (e.g., limbic encephalitis)
Toxic exposure	• Substance-induced persisting dementia • Medication-induced dementia • Alcohol dementia • Marchiafava–Bignami disease (due to alcohol abuse) • Inhalant-induced dementia • Wernicke–Korsakoff syndrome • Toxic metal exposure (e.g., lead, mercury, manganese, arsenic) • Wilson's disease (copper poisoning) • Toxic gas exposure (carbon monoxide, carbon disulfide)
Nutritional deficiency	• Vitamin B12 deficiency • Subacute combined degeneration • Pernicious anemia • Folate deficiency • Niacin deficiency (pellagra) • Thiamine deficiency (beri, Wernicke–Korsakoff's syndrome)

(Continued)

Table 1.2 (Continued)

Etiology	Subtype

Infectious disease	• Bacterial
	  ○ Bacterial infection causing meningitis, encephalitis, or abscess
	  ○ Whipple's disease (Tropheryma whippelii)
	• Viral
	  ○ Viral meningitis or encephalitis
	  ○ Herpes simplex encephalitis
	  ○ Human immunodeficiency virus (HIV) associated dementia
	  ○ Progressive multifocal leukoencephalopathy
	  ○ Subacute sclerosing panencephalitis
	  ○ Encephalitis lethargica (sleeping sickness)
	• Spirochetal
	  ○ Neurosyphilis
	  ○ Lyme disease
	• Fungal infection causing meningitis (e.g., cryptococcal meningitis), encephalitis, or brain abscess
	• Parasitic diseases causing brain abscesses or cysts (e.g., neurocysticercosis)
	• Human Prion diseases (transmissible spongiform encephalopathy)
	  ○ Creutzfeldt–Jakob disease
	  ○ Variant Creutzfeldt–Jakob disease
	  ○ Kuru
	  ○ Gerstmann–Straüssler–Scheinker syndrome
	  ○ Fatal familial insomnia

Organ failure	• Uremic encephalopathy • Hepatic encephalopathy
Endocrine disease	• Diabetes mellitus • Hypothyroidism • Hyperparathyroidism (hypercalcemia) • Cushing's syndrome (hypercortisolemia) • Addison's disease (adrenocortical insufficiency)
Neurologic disorders	• Huntington's disease • Multiple sclerosis • Parkinson's disease
Metabolic disorders	• Inherited storage diseases • Adrenoleukodystrophy • Metachromatic leukodystrophy • Cerebrotendinous xanthomatosis

Inflammatory disease	• Collagen vascular diseases
	  ○ Behçet syndrome
	  ○ Sjögren syndrome
	  ○ Systemic lupus erythematosus
	• Vasculitides
	  ○ Granulomatous angiitis
	  ○ Lymphomatoid granulomatosis
	  ○ Polyarteritis nodosa
	  ○ Wegener's granulomatosis

Reversible Versus Irreversible

Approximately 10% of the presentations of dementia are potentially reversible when the underlying cause can be identified and treated; although in practice this does not often happen (Clarfield, 2003). A more accurate description would identify several subtypes of dementia under this heading as arrestable and modifiable because treatment of the cause may only ameliorate the course of the disease without stopping the pathologic process. An example of an arrestable dementia is normal pressure hydrocephalus; treatment can reduce the hydrocephalus and can arrest the progression of dementia, but it may not reverse the existing cognitive impairment to a significant degree. AD could be an example of a modifiable disease; treatment with currently available medications may temporarily improve or stabilize cognition without altering the fundamental pathologic process. The major reversible causes of dementia are discussed in Chapter 8, and these include structural or traumatic brain injury; the toxic effects of medications and other substances; vitamin deficiencies; infections; neurologic disorders; and neurologic sequelae of endocrine, metabolic, and inflammatory diseases.

Progressive Versus Nonprogressive

This distinction groups dementias based on their clinical course. Alzheimer's disease is the prime example of a progressive dementia, whereas dementia due to traumatic brain injury is a nonprogressive dementia as long as no more trauma occurs. A related distinction based on pathologic course is degenerative versus nondegenerative dementia. Degenerative dementias are associated with insidious pathologic processes that damage and kill brain cells, such as seen in Alzheimer's disease or Creutzfeldt–Jakob disease, or in specific progressive neurologic disorders such as multiple sclerosis or Parkinson's disease. Nondegenerative dementias result from episodes of brain injury, such as stroke or a traumatic injury, which are not necessarily recurrent events. However, this distinction can be subtle and subject to interpretation. For example, vascular dementia may appear to be an obvious form of nondegenerative dementia when it is clearly due to a single stroke. However, one could argue that the underlying atherosclerotic disease is actually a degenerative process. The goal of current research is to develop treatments to make all forms of dementia nonprogressive and ultimately curable diseases.

Cortical Versus Subcortical

This distinction refers to the anatomic location of the dementia's pathology, occurring in either the cerebral cortex or the cerebral subcortical regions, including the thalamus, basal ganglia, and brainstem regions. Basic differences between cortical and subcortical dementias are outlined in Table 1.3. Although these clinical differences provide some guidance for diagnosis, they are not absolute. The most common cortical dementia is Alzheimer's disease; however, it ultimately affects the subcortical regions as well. Similarly, subcortical dementias cause much of their cognitive impairment by damaging neural white matter pathways to the cortex (Menon & Kelley, 2009).

Table 1.3 Cortical Versus Subcortical Dementias

Feature	Cortical vs. Subcortical
Memory	Memory impairment is present in both but more prominent in cortical dementia.
Cognition	Aphasia, apraxia, and agnosia are cardinal features of cortical dementia, whereas slowed cognitive processing and disruptions in arousal and attention are more prominent in subcortical dementia.
Motor behavior	Prominent psychomotor retardation is seen in subcortical dementia, especially early in its course, and is often associated with dysarthric speech, gait disturbances, and parkinsonism; less prominent changes are seen in motor behavior in cortical dementia until later stages.
Motivation	Apathy tends to be more common in subcortical dementia.
Mood	Depression tends to be more common and prominent in subcortical dementia.
Pathology	Cortical dementia is associated with primary damage to the neocortex and hippocampus; subcortical dementia involves damage to the deep gray and white matter structures, including the thalamus, basal ganglia, brainstem nuclei, and frontal lobe projections.

Sources: Menon and Kelley (2009); Lavretsky and Chui (2011).

Differential Diagnosis

Having reviewed the basic classification and subtypes of dementia, the clinician must remember that not everything that looks like dementia is actually dementia. The differential diagnosis of dementia includes varying degrees of cognitive impairment that resemble, but do not equate to, early-stage dementia. Many medical and psychiatric disorders either mimic dementia or exist comorbidly with it (delirium is a good example), making a quick determination of a diagnosis extremely difficult. To clarify the differential diagnosis, the most important information is always the baseline memory and cognitive ability that predated any impairment. All comparisons begin there.

Age-Appropriate Versus Age-Inappropriate Cognitive Change

The effects of normal aging on cognitive function and memory are quite modest, and they are often never brought to clinical attention. Nonetheless, the context of aging and the common fear of dementia among many older individuals sometimes lead to great concern over occasional memory lapses, whimsically referred to as "senior moments." Such fears no doubt stem from the tendency seen throughout most of the past 100 years to equate aging with senility, suggesting that dementia is inevitable. The line between what is considered age-appropriate memory change and age-inappropriate change is quite blurry; it depends not only on subjective reports but also on diagnostic criteria, which are still being debated. Further complicating the picture (and the anxiety) is the new staging for AD, which recognizes a presymptomatic state. However, the advent of biomarkers for AD that can be measured in cerebrospinal fluid or on positron emission tomography (PET) scans is enabling clinicians to see pathologic changes ahead of time that can help to predict which individuals will go on to develop more severe symptoms.

A significant amount of research indicates that normal aging is associated with some deterioration in memory function and other cognitive skills (Schaie, 2005; Schaie, Willis, & Caskie, 2004). Deficits in attention and processing speed and accuracy can result in an overall decline in short-term (or immediate) memory. Although differences in performance generally favor younger subjects, these are small and they may be practically insignificant. In addition, factors such as environment (e.g., college versus retirement setting), testing familiarity, and expectations may affect test results, and many differences can be erased with training (Gross, Parisi, & Spira, 2012). Older subjects do perform better on some memory tests, an effect that may be attributed to increased overall knowledge.

Numerous terms have been used to describe memory loss that is greater than that which is seen with normal aging but less than that seen with true dementia. Early terms such as *benign senescent forgetfulness* and *age-associated memory impairment* are neither well-defined nor widely used but attempt to capture memory changes relative to normative adult performance. The term *mild cognitive impairment* (MCI) captures individuals with subjective complaints of cognitive impairment as well as objective decline relative to aged peers but without clear evidence of dementia. For many individuals, however, MCI represents a prodromal dementia. Current research efforts are attempting to identify those individuals with MCI who are at greatest risk of conversion to dementia. Diagnostic criteria and other characteristics of all of these conditions are highlighted in Chapter 3.

More Differential Diagnosis

When memory impairment is prominent but it is the only manifestation of cognitive impairment, a form of amnestic disorder may be the most appropriate diagnosis. An amnestic disorder was classified in DSM-IV-TR according to cause (e.g., head trauma, general medical condition, substance induced, not otherwise specified) and involves memory impairment for learning new information (anterograde) or recalling previously learned information (retrograde). It now falls under major NCD due to another medical condition (or due to traumatic brain injury, or unspecified) in DSM-5. When prominent symptoms of depression associated with cognitive impairment are present and when these symptoms improve with antidepressant therapy, the diagnosis of a pseudodementia ("fake" dementia), sometimes called a reversible dementia, would apply. The increased risk of developing a true dementia, given a history of pseudodementia, is discussed in Chapter 10.

Schizophrenia is often associated with some degree of cognitive impairment resulting from both the disorder itself and medication side effects (Bonner-Jackson, Grossman, Harrow, & Rosen, 2010). In older individuals with schizophrenia, more pronounced cognitive impairment may be related to characteristic changes in brain structure including cerebral atrophy and ventricular widening (Harvey, 2001). Symptom overlap between schizophrenia and dementia can be confusing because both are associated with psychosis, apathy, and social withdrawal. However, older individuals with schizophrenia have a history of chronic psychosis and declining social and occupational function that typically begins in younger adulthood.

Another key diagnosis that is critical to differentiate from dementia is delirium. The acute onset of mental status changes that characterize delirium should always prompt a thorough medical workup to establish an underlying etiology. Knowing a person's baseline cognitive status may help to distinguish dementia from delirium because dementia typically has a much longer and more insidious course. However, when such information is lacking, some clinical characteristics can be useful discriminators. These and other features of delirium are discussed in detail in Chapter 9.

References

Alzheimer's Association. (2012). *2012 Alzheimer's disease facts and figures.* Retrieved from www.alz.org/downloads/facts_figures_2012.pdf

Alzheimer's Disease International. (2010). *World Alzheimer's report 2010: The global economic impact of dementia.* London: Alzheimer's Disease International.

American Psychiatric Association. (2000). *Diagnostic and statistical manual of mental disorders* (4th ed., Text Rev.). Washington, DC: Author.

American Psychiatric Association. (2013). *Diagnostic and statistical manual of mental disorders* (5th ed.). Washington, DC: Author.

Bonner-Jackson, A., Grossman, L. S., Harrow, M., & Rosen, C. (2010). Neurocognition in schizophrenia: A 20-year multi-follow-up of the course of processing speed and stored knowledge. *Compr Psychiatry, 51*(5), 471–479.

Chui, H. C. (2007). Subcortical ischemic vascular dementia. *Neurol Clin, 25*(3), 717–740.

Clarfield, A. M. (2003). The decreasing prevalence of reversible dementias: An updated meta-analysis. *Arch Intern Med, 163*(18), 2219–2229.

Gross, A. L., Parisi, J. M., & Spira, A. P. (2012). Memory training interventions for older adults: A meta-analysis. *Aging Ment Health, 16*(6), 722–734. doi: 10.1080/13607863.2012.667783

Harvey, P. D. (2001). Cognitive impairment in elderly patients with schizophrenia: Age related changes. *Int J Geriatr Psychiatry, 16*(Suppl 1), S78–S85.

Hurd, M. D., Martorell, P., Delavande, A., et al. (2013). Monetary costs of dementia in the United States. *New England Journal of Medicine, 368*(14), 1326–1334.

Lavretsky, H., & Chui, H. (2011). Vascular dementia. In M. E. Agronin & G. J. Maletta (Eds.), *Principles and practice of geriatric psychiatry* (2nd ed., pp. 317–331). Philadelphia: Lippincott, Williams and Wilkins.

Menon, U., & Kelley, R. E. (2009). Subcortical ischemic cerebrovascular dementia. *Int Rev Neurobiol, 84*, 21–33.

Rahkonen, T., Eloniemi-Sulkava, U., Rissanen, S., et al. (2003). Dementia with Lewy bodies according to the consensus criteria in a general population aged 75 years or older. *J Neurol Neurosurg Psychiatry, 74*(6), 720–724.

Schaie, K. W. (2005). What can we learn from longitudinal studies of adult development? *Res Hum Dev, 2*(3): 133–158.

Schaie, K. W., Willis, S. L., & Caskie, G.I.L. (2004). The Seattle longitudinal study: Relationship between personality and cognition. *Neuropsychol Dev Cogn B Aging Neuropsychol Cogn, 11*(2–3), 304–324.

2   The Dementia Workup

In its early stages, dementia is not an obvious disorder. Every day, clinicians meet individuals in the community or see patients in clinical settings whom they would never guess have dementia. Casual conversation may not be revealing, and the friendly smile and graciousness of an older individual can easily cover up memory deficits, especially if a person's social skills are well preserved. In contrast, the stereotypical "demented" person is often imagined to be extremely frail and aged, and either stuporous or agitated. Further distorting the image of dementia is the use of the term *demented* in everyday language to connote craziness and sickness, and even perversion. This limited view of dementia can lead clinicians to ignore important symptoms in someone who does not look the part and to assume that everyone who appears frail or disoriented is demented.

Alarmingly, a high proportion of individuals with early-stage dementia are not diagnosed in a timely manner (Bradford et al., 2009). Without a proper diagnosis, there will be even greater delays in treatment. The gradual and insidious course of dementia enables many afflicted individuals and their family members to ignore, deny, cover up, and/or compensate for early deficits. Fear of Alzheimer's disease (AD) and related dementias can reinforce the denial of illness despite the presence of obvious signs. Insight into early cognitive changes may be poor due to the disease itself, hampering an individual's ability to recognize and then articulate the problem to loved ones.

The evaluation often occurs in the setting of a crisis when a medical illness or a major life stressor such as the death of a spouse or other close caregiver exposes the underlying cognitive impairment. Family members may express their alarm over the sudden change in their loved one's abilities, although frequently this change is not sudden. More likely, the physical, psychological, or social demands of a situation have overwhelmed the cognitively impaired individual's ability to hide his or her deficits. The increased family attention and scrutiny of an affected individual's behavior then reveal the deficits. The clinician must take all this into consideration when providing assessment, diagnosis, and education, and some degree of family counseling.

Case Study

Sonia was a 75-year-old woman with a lovely, affable demeanor. She was a retired teacher who had been widowed for five years. She had two daughters who both lived a plane ride away, and, for years, she had lived with her overprotective younger sister Rose in a retirement community. She was well-loved by her internist, especially because she would always bring a plate of freshly baked cookies to the office staff at each appointment. For several years, Sonia's daughters had noticed that she mixed up names and events when talking on the phone, although Rose would always be on the line to correct her. Once, one of the daughters accompanied Sonia to a checkup with her physician, who reviewed her high blood pressure and arthritis symptoms, and enjoyed wonderful chocolate chip cookies but did not raise any concerns about Sonia's memory. In response to the daughter's concerns, the doctor attributed the forgetfulness to "normal aging," characterizing it as "nothing out of the ordinary." Rose was suddenly hospitalized for congestive heart failure and died unexpectedly of complications. When Sonia's daughters arrived in town, they found that Sonia was disheveled, grossly confused, and dehydrated. They took Sonia to her internist, anxiously wondering what was wrong. A medical workup was unrevealing except for confirming mild dehydration. Sonia now seemed completely unable to care for herself, and the daughters had to look for a suitable nursing facility. They could not understand what had gone wrong.

What is the moral of this case? A thorough evaluation of Sonia's mental status months or even years before her sister Rose's death would have revealed significant cognitive deficits. Rose was a wonderful caregiver who had been able to keep Sonia well-groomed, fed, and organized. As a younger sister, she did not want to believe that Sonia, her older, wiser, and more mature sister, was impaired. Sonia's gracious personality and appearance obscured any problems when she visited her busy physician. Without Rose, Sonia was incapable of organizing even the most basic daily activities, such as hygiene, dressing appropriately, and cooking. The stress of losing the presence and support of Rose, compounded with poor fluid and food intake, led to dehydration and delirium within days. Sonia's daughters were seeing the logical consequences of dementia in the absence of proper caregiving.

Importance of Early Diagnosis

There are many reasons why early diagnosis is critical. It can enable the clinician to identify and treat any reversible medical causes of cognitive improvement. When a diagnosis is present, it can help to explain the presence of unusual, troublesome, and distressing behaviors not understood by concerned family members. Knowing that progressive decline is on the horizon will allow the individual to make critical life decisions while he or she still retains maximal decision-making capacity, including financial and estate planning, advanced medical directives, and life plans. Unfortunately, this capacity will fade as the dementia progresses. In many cases, early diagnosis will also allow clinicians to identify and treat associated psychiatric problems, particularly depression, agitation, and psychosis,

Table 2.1 Possible Early Signs and Symptoms of Dementia

Sign	Symptoms
Forgetfulness	Commonly manifested as short-term memory loss for recently learned names, appointments, purpose of activities, points of conversation, and completed tasks or errands. An individual may repeat questions or requests. The degree of forgetfulness begins to interfere with daily activities and responsibilities.
Disorientation	Episodic confusion regarding the exact day, date, or location.
Impaired performance on daily tasks	Difficulty performing everyday tasks such as preparing meals, running household appliances, cleaning, and hygiene (e.g., bathing, toileting, brushing teeth).
Impaired language	Increasing difficulty with selecting and using words. Sentences may become simpler or fragmented.
Impaired recognition	Diminished ability to remember or identify familiar faces, objects, sounds, and locations.
Impaired abstract thinking	Diminished ability to think clearly about or to discuss complex issues and to make logical connections between them, or to comprehend fully things that were previously understood.
Impaired judgment	Impairment in the ability to organize and plan and to make appropriate decisions or selections among several possibilities. A person may act in ways that were previously deemed uncharacteristic or inappropriate.
Changes in mood	Change in mood and behavior that may take many forms, including increased irritability, loss of emotional control (e.g., intense anger, frustration, tearfulness), abusive or inappropriate language, loss of pleasure in particular activities, and apathetic attitudes.
Changes in personality	The person may seem less sociable or more self-centered and may act out in disruptive or disinhibited ways. He or she may also seem more suspicious, fearful, or bothered by others, and reactions to everyday stress may be out of proportion.

thus preventing excessive impairment, hospitalization, and early long-term care placement. It will prompt caregivers to maximize safety and to avoid catastrophe by setting limits on activities, such as driving and hunting; using power tools, firearms, or heavy machinery; and caring for young children. Finally, early diagnosis allows for prompt intervention to prevent or slow the progression or to ameliorate the symptoms of the dementia, depending on the type. All of these goals will be outlined in more detail throughout the text. A guide to potential early symptoms of dementia can be found in Table 2.1.

The Dementia Interview

The diagnostic interview for dementia has two main goals. The first is to establish a rapport with the patient and informant. Mutual and friendly cooperation lays the basis for a successful clinician–patient relationship from which all information and clinical responsibilities will flow. The second goal is to obtain all relevant history to determine the baseline level of functioning and to establish whether dementia is present. The baseline, defined as the most recent, sustained level of cognition and function, is perhaps the most critical component of the differential diagnosis.

Two challenges immediately present themselves. First, depending on the degree of cognitive impairment already present, the patient may not understand the nature of the interview, and/or he or she may react to it with confusion, suspicion, indignation, denial, or resistance. The individual may not even have the capacity to consent to the interview. A second challenge is that the informant, if present, may demonstrate some of the same attitudes as the patient. These two challenges limit the ability of the interviewer to accomplish the basic goals of establishing a rapport and obtaining needed history. Out of these challenges, however, come the following principles for guiding the clinical interview:

- *Interview to the patient's capacity.* As the interviewer begins to know the cognitive strengths and weaknesses of the patient, the type and manner of questions should be adjusted to match his or her ability to provide responses.
- *Preserve the patient's dignity.* Always approach each patient, regardless of his or her known or assumed level of understanding, insight, or cognitive capacity, as if he or she is fully aware of the circumstances of the interview.
- *Obtain the patient's consent.* To the degree possible, the clinician should always seek permission from a patient to speak with him or her and should obtain consent to communicate with informants. One should avoid adopting an overly paternalistic attitude, which can foster disregard for such permission.
- *Respect boundaries.* Respect the patient's and the informant's right to set time limits on the interview, to refuse to answer questions, and to limit access to informants. This respect ultimately results in the best possible chance to obtain necessary information.

These principles may seem obvious, but they actually require constant vigilance in a busy clinical practice. Their role in building rapport and trust cannot be underestimated; guarding them carefully will enhance the principles of assessment and treatment discussed in this book.

A wide variety of patients will show up for dementia assessments, and the interview must account for all the special needs of these patients, including cognitive, sensory, and psychiatric impairments. Table 2.2 outlines the steps of a dementia interview for an older individual with potential cognitive impairment; it includes several handy tips for maximizing the factors just described.

Taking the History

It is no surprise that the author of the Sherlock Holmes mysteries, Sir Arthur Conan Doyle, was a physician because the search for a medical diagnosis is a process not unlike the search for clues in a great mystery. Similarly, the dementia workup can be viewed as a medical mystery in which clues must be gathered about aspects of an individual's physiological, psychological, and social functioning to determine a diagnosis. The well-organized approach described in this chapter will help clinicians to quickly identify the key diagnostic factors in otherwise complicated geriatric cases.

Table 2.2 Guide to the Dementia Interview

Preparation
- Before arrival, ensure that the patient is informed about the nature of the appointment, including the time, location, duration, types of questions, specialty of physician, and purpose.
- Ask an informant to accompany the patient, and request that he or she selects an appointment time that works well for the patient's daily routine.
- Make sure that the interview setting is quiet, private, and free of distractions that may disorient or upset the patient and impair his or her ability to participate.

Introduction
- Offer a formal introduction to the patient regardless of his or her potential cognitive limitations. This introduction should always include your name, title, specialty, and the purpose of the interview.
- Some patients may need more cues regarding the location and time of day, but be careful not to infantilize them or to overwhelm them with too much detail.

Sensory Check
- Always be aware of sensory impairment, especially hearing and visual loss.
- Do not assume that a nonverbal patient is aphasic—he or she just might not be able to hear you!
- When hearing impairment is a factor, always speak loudly into the better ear. Have an amplifying headset available for the patient.
- Use eye contact and gentle physical touches on a limb to maintain the patient's attention. Physical contact can also be useful for the visually impaired.

Rapport
To build rapport with patient and informant or caregiver, consider the following:
- smile frequently and broadly, and maintain good eye contact;
- use a soothing, yet audible, tone of voice;
- inquire about the patient's life history and family;
- interview each patient as a person with a rich life, rather than as another individual with dementia;
- speak to the informant or caregiver and inquire about his or her own experiences and stresses;
- find areas of common interest to discuss;
- listen to the patient in a relaxed manner, and make sure that, by the end of the interview, the informant knows how to get in touch with you if necessary;
- solicit questions and answer all of them.

For Severe Impairment
- Nonverbal behaviors may be the best (and only) information that the patient can provide.
- Use simply worded questions with a single idea (e.g., Do you feel sad? Are you afraid?).
- Questions may have to be yes or no rather than open ended.
- Do not rush questions. Be patient and wait for delayed responses.
- Provide language translation when necessary.

The first data gathered in any history are obviously the presenting problems and their history. Often, the clinician is unable to get a significant history from the dementia patient, so he or she has to rely on an informant and available medical records, which may themselves be limited. A description of the current behavior can range from subtle changes in daily functioning or personality to obvious and disruptive problems. The patient and informant should be asked to describe any current difficulties with memory or thinking, including how long they have lasted and whether they have progressed. If the responses lack focus,

Table 2.3 Common Medication Groups Associated with
            Cognitive Impairment

Anticholinergics (see Table 2.4)
Antidepressants
Antihistamines
Antipsychotics
Benzodiazepines
Corticosteroids
Narcotics
Sedative-hypnotics (i.e., sleeping pills)
Statins

---

the interviewer should ask more specific questions about episodes of forgetfulness, disorientation, misplacing objects, and getting lost in familiar settings, as well as difficulty recognizing familiar people or objects (agnosia), performing everyday tasks (apraxia), finding the correct words (aphasia), and planning or organizing activities (executive dysfunction).

The clinician should always determine whether any medical or psychiatric factors directly preceded the onset of symptoms or seemed to have worsened them. Several particularly relevant factors include a history of head injury, stroke, seizures, and major depression, as well as the use of medications with known side effects on the central nervous system. Head injury and strokes can themselves cause dementia or can serve as risk factors and even triggers for AD. Underlying vascular risk factors that should be identified include hypertension, high cholesterol, use of tobacco and alcohol, peripheral vascular disease, atherosclerotic heart disease, and transient ischemic attacks. Seizures may suggest an underlying metabolic disorder or brain lesion. Major depression can sometimes lead to severe but reversible cognitive changes that are reflected in a pseudodementia, or reversible dementia-like syndrome, which is associated with an increased risk of later developing an actual dementia. Other important psychiatric symptoms include agitation, depression, psychosis, anxiety, apathy, and personality changes, as well as any other behaviors that are unusual or uncharacteristic.

The use of medications with strong anticholinergic, antihistaminic, and other side effects can impair cognition and can precipitate depression, psychosis, or delirium. In the history, it is essential to obtain a list of all prescription, over-the-counter, and herbal medications that are currently being taken. Table 2.3 provides a list of some of the most commonly prescribed medication groups that are associated with cognitive impairment.

Clinical Tip

Anticholinergic effects may be the most worrisome medication side effects in the elderly because of their strong association with confusion and delirium (Campbell et al., 2009; Tune, Carr, Hoag, & Cooper, 1992). Anticholinergic effects oppose the actions of the neurotransmitter acetylcholine, which is critical to memory formation. Anticholinergic effects become especially deleterious when someone is taking an excessive dose of a single offending agent or several agents together, which then exert an additive effect. Commonly prescribed medications with anticholinergic properties are listed in Table 2.4.

Table 2.4 Medications with Anticholinergic Side Effects

Antipsychotics	Chlorpromazine, thioridazine, loxapine, clozapine, olanzapine
Antispasmodics	Oxybutynin, tolterodine
Cardiac medications	Nifedipine, digitalis, isosorbide
Diuretics	Triamterene, hydrochlorothiazide, furosemide
H$_2$-blockers	Cimetidine, ranitidine
Tricyclic antidepressants	Amitriptyline, imipramine, doxepin, clomipramine
Others	Codeine, prednisolone, captopril, dipyridamole, warfarin, theophylline

Source: Tune et al. (1992).

Social and Family History

The social history can establish a picture of premorbid social, occupational, and intellectual functioning that provides a context for change and enables comparisons with current deficits. For example, cognitive impairment relevant to mathematical skills (e.g., balancing a checkbook, paying for items at a store, performing calculations) will probably be more revealing in a college-educated individual who previously worked as an accountant. Similarly, apathy associated with dementia will be more revealing in a person who was always the life of the party or the perfect salesperson. A family history of dementia is rarely helpful in determining an exact diagnosis, but it may at least provide direction. For example, a history of cerebrovascular disease in first-degree relatives may suggest a higher likelihood of a vascular etiology for dementia. Family psychiatric history can be helpful in determining the individual's vulnerability to psychiatric symptoms, such as depression, anxiety, or mania.

Review of Systems

Each individual and informant should be questioned "from head to toe" to discern current symptoms and complaints that may be relevant to the patient's cognitive impairment. Reversible causes of dementia need to be identified, and the review of systems may offer clues to incipient problems that neither a routine medical history nor the physical examination is sufficient to identify.

The review of systems should also obtain information about sleep, appetite, and psychological stress. Major life events with the potential to induce strong adjustment reactions include retirement, financial loss, the death of a close family member or caregiver, relocation, family estrangement, and physical trauma. Individuals with dementia may overreact or react inappropriately to such major stresses or to minor events that frequently go unreported, such as a fight with a close friend, an embarrassing social indiscretion, or an episode of incontinence.

Medical Examination

After the dementia workup has obtained all relevant history, the next logical step is to examine the patient's medical status, which calls for a neurological examination, laboratory studies, neuroimaging, and electroencephalography. The main purpose of this examination is to identify potentially treatable factors that are causing or exacerbating the cognitive impairment. Sometimes a complete dementia workup requires the input from other clinical specialists in order to form the best diagnosis and treatment plan.

From the moment an individual walks into the office for an evaluation, the manifestations of brain impairment may already be present. Neurologic signs and symptoms are commonly associated with particular types of dementia, and their presence can help to narrow the differential diagnosis. Important symptoms to look for are listed in Table 2.5.

Table 2.5 Neurologic Findings Associated with Dementia

Extrapyramidal symptoms (e.g., slowed and rigid movements, tremors)
Gait disturbances
Hemiparesis
Frontal release signs
Myoclonus
Peripheral neuropathy
Gaze paralysis
Pseudobulbar palsy

Laboratory Tests

The essential laboratory tests in a standard dementia workup are listed in Table 2.6. These tests are especially important with cases of delirium, for which there is always a medical cause (see Chapter 9 for more information on delirium). A complete blood count and

Table 2.6 Standard Laboratory Tests in the Dementia Workup

Test	*Potential Causes of Cognitive Impairment*
Complete blood count	Infection, anemia
Electrolytes	Hyponatremia, SIADH
Glucose	Diabetes mellitus, hypoglycemia
Renal function (BUN, creatinine)	Renal failure (uremia)
Calcium	Hypocalcemia or hypercalcemia, parathyroid disease
Thyroid function tests	Hypothyroidism
Liver function tests	Hepatic encephalopathy
Vitamin B12, folate	Vitamin B12 or folate deficiency
Urinalysis	Urinary tract infection, urosepsis, renal disease

BUN = blood urea nitrogen; SIADH = syndrome of inappropriate secretion of antidiuretic hormone.

urinalysis can help rule out infection as an underlying factor in such cases. Other causes of both acute and more chronic cognitive impairment include abnormal electrolytes; abnormalities in renal, thyroid, or liver function; and hypocalcemic or hypercalcemic states. Fasting glucose and hemoglobin A1c are used to assess the impact and management of diabetes mellitus, a major cause of vascular dementia. Less common, but still important, causes of dementia that should be ruled out include deficiencies of vitamin B12 and folate.

Additional laboratory tests might be ordered when specific conditions are suspected (e.g., HIV, neurosyphilis) or the presentation of dementia has been precipitous; additionally, they may be ordered if the dementia is occurring in a young and/or otherwise healthy individual or if it is associated with an unusual presentation. Many of these conditions are described in Chapter 8. For example, individuals who work in the mining or chemical industry may have been exposed to some heavy metals, and they can be tested accordingly. A lumbar puncture is necessary for cerebrospinal fluid analysis when meningitis or encephalitis is suspected (see Table 2.7).

Table 2.7 Specialized Laboratory Tests

Test	Potential Causes of Cognitive Impairment
Drug screen	Substance abuse
Lyme titer	Lyme encephalopathy
Heavy metal screen	Mercury, lead, manganese, arsenic, cadmium, copper, and aluminum poisoning
HIV	HIV-associated dementia
Antinuclear antibody	Systemic lupus erythematosus
Cortisol	Adrenal disease (Addison's or Cushing's diseases)
Ceruloplasmin	Wilson's disease (abnormal copper metabolism)
ESR	Vasculitis, unspecified inflammatory or malignant process
Phosphorus	Parathyroid disease
Magnesium	Hypomagnesemia, alcohol dependence
Ammonia	Hepatic encephalopathy
RPR/FTA/VDRL	Neurosyphilis
Epstein–Barr virus	Viral encephalitis
Cytomegalovirus	Viral encephalitis
Long-chain fatty acids	Adrenoleukodystrophy
Arylsulfatase A	Metachromatic leukodystrophy
Porphobilinogen, ALA (24-hour urine)	Acute intermittent porphyria
Cerebrospinal fluid	CNS infection, multiple sclerosis

ALA = aminolevulinic acid; CNS = central nervous system; ESR = erythrocyte sedimentation rate; FTA = fluorescent treponemal antibody-absorption; RPR = rapid plasma reagent; VDRL = Venereal Disease Research Laboratory.

Neuroimaging

A structural brain scan is an essential feature of almost every dementia workup, since it serves to rule out the presence of anatomic lesions that may be causing cognitive impairment. In some circumstances, clinicians opt to order a computed tomography (CT) scan of the brain because it is the quickest, easiest, and cheapest examination, and it is readily able to reveal major strokes, bleeds, and masses. Conversely, magnetic resonance imaging (MRI) is superior to CT in revealing white matter lesions; smaller infarcts; subacute bleeding; and lesions in the brainstem, subcortical regions, and posterior fossa (Atiya et al., 2003). Unlike CT, MRI can distinguish between white and gray matter, and no radiation exposure is involved. However, MRI is more expensive and time-consuming, and it is not always well tolerated. With MRI, the signal reception can be altered to produce T1-weighted images with startling tissue resolution or T2-weighted images with greater tissue contrast to identify some pathologic changes (Margolin & Merrill, 2011).

Regardless of the type of structural scan, some of the following anatomic changes in the brain are inevitably encountered with aging: generalized cerebral atrophy, increased ventricular size, and the presence of periventricular and subcortical calcifications and nonspecific "spots." These spots have been given many names in the literature (e.g., hyperintensities [as seen on MRI], unidentified bright objects, leukomalacia, and leukoariosis), but all point to areas of likely neuronal injury due to one or more of the following factors: the effects of aging, chronic hypoperfusion, lacunar or atherosclerotic injury, gliosis, localized edema, and demyelination (Roman, 2004). The relevance of these spots to dementia is reviewed in Chapter 5 in the discussion of vascular dementia.

Of increasing importance to the dementia workup are functional brain scans, including positron emission tomography (PET) and single photon emission computed tomography (SPECT). Both PET and SPECT require the administration of radiolabeled isotopes to measure ongoing brain activity as a function of glucose metabolism or regional blood flow (de Leon et al., 1983). Medicare will currently pay for PET scans to differentiate Alzheimer's disease from frontotemporal dementia. In addition, newer techniques have been developed to use radiolabeled binding agents to measure the amount of pathologic entities such as beta-amyloid—previously only visualized through postmortem staining. Several newly developed radiotracers for PET scans can now identify the presence of amyloid plaques and neurofibrillary tangles (Vandenberghe et al., 2010; Wood et al., 2010). The ability to image for the presence of these pathologic hallmarks of AD could allow for much earlier diagnosis, which in turn could allow for implementation of effective treatments when they are developed.

Electroencephalography

Although an electroencephalography (EEG) is not a routine part of the dementia workup, it can be useful if the following questions cannot be answered with the available history and the examination:

- Does the patient have an underlying seizure disorder?
- Is the condition dementia or delirium?

Table 2.8 EEG Findings in Dementia and Associated Conditions

Condition	EEG Findings
Normal brain (birth to age 80)	Alpha rhythm (posterior dominant activity) predominates during wakeful states of relaxation, beta activity during concentration and when anxious, and theta and delta activity during deep sleep
Normal aging (age 80 and older)	Mild decrease in mean frequency of alpha activity with increased incidence of intermittent focal slowing. Some individuals have subclinical theta discharges.
Seizure disorders	Ictal epileptiform activity consists of rhythmic discharges distinct from interictal epileptiform activity, which consists of either normal patterns or spikes, slow waves, and spike-and-wave complexes.
Focal lesions	EEG shows focal slowing with periodic lateralized epileptiform discharges in acute presentations
Delirium	Diffuse slowing with intermittent episodes of further slowing; triphasic waves are seen in uremic and hepatic encephalopathy and postanoxic states
Alzheimer's disease	Background alpha activity slows and disorganizes as the disease progresses; increased presence of theta and delta activity
Vascular dementia	EEG changes resemble those in AD but appear unilateral or asymmetric, depending on the location of infarcts
Creutzfeldt–Jakob	Bursts of activity followed by minimal disease activity, called periodic complexes, associated with myoclonic jerks; bifrontal sharp waves or triphasic waves
Pseudodementia	EEG is normal, or it shows minimal slowing of posterior dominant rhythm compared with abnormal EEG in AD

EEG = electroencephalography.

Sources: Drazkowski (2008); Mancall (2011).

- Is the condition a true dementia or a pseudodementia (depression-associated dementia)?
- Does the individual have a sleep disorder?

In general, EEG activity in dementia is characterized by diffuse slowing of brain activity, with increased delta and theta frequency (Mancall, 2011). EEG findings associated with aging, dementia, and related conditions are summarized in Table 2.8.

Mental Status Examination

The mental status examination (MSE) is the heart of the dementia workup. As with the physical examination, the MSE begins the minute that the patient walks into the examination room, and it continues until the patient leaves. The basic components of a standard MSE include appearance, attitude and behavior, speech and language, affect and mood, thought process, thought content, and cognition. The following sections highlight several unique aspects of the MSE during dementia assessment.

Appearance, Attitude, and Behavior

The very appearance of the patient (grooming and dress, gait, motoric activity, and facial expression) coupled with his or her attitude toward the interviewer and interview content provides clues to the current situation and the diagnosis. For instance, a patient who is unkempt or malodorous may be suffering from incontinence associated with later stages of dementia and likely requires more assistance with hygiene. Lack of spontaneous motor movement may reflect apathy or parkinsonism, whereas motoric restlessness, such as wandering or pacing, may indicate agitation, agnosia (the patient does not recognize his or her surrounding and is exploring or attempting to leave), or akathisia. The facial expression may reflect underlying feelings of anxiety, depression, or agitation. Some individuals appear bewildered or impatient as part of their reaction to a sense of confusion or dislocation during an appointment. Other individuals may refuse to cooperate with the interview, or they may respond in a hostile manner, suggesting the presence of underlying fear or paranoia. The initial observations must be corroborated by further investigation.

Speech and Language

The characteristics of an individual's speech, including tone, volume, quality, and articulation, should be noted. In addition, the clinician should gauge the comprehension and expression of the patient's language—how thoughts are transformed into language and language into thoughts. The clinician must ensure that the patient can hear the interviewer's questions so that he or she can respond. The most important form of language impairment in most forms of dementia is aphasia, which is characterized by an underlying impairment in comprehension or expression, or both. Distinguishing aphasia from dysarthria and aprosody is important. Dysarthria is characterized by incoordination of the physical production of speech and is caused by damage to vocal muscles or nerves or to relevant control centers in the central nervous system, especially the cerebellum. Lack of emotional tone characterizes aprosodic speech, which can result from a stroke or head injury. Alterations or abnormalities in speech may also characterize some psychiatric conditions. For instance, loud and pressured speech occurs in disinhibited and manic states. In some individuals, severe depression may render a voice almost inaudible. Impairment in generating names of items is called anomia. Descriptions of the major forms of language impairment are listed in Table 2.9.

Affect and Mood

Affect refers to the emotional tone of a patient that is observed by the examiner, whereas mood refers to the patient's subjective description of his or her emotions. Affect has also been described as the current emotional state, whereas mood is the more enduring or characteristic emotional state. Dementia may damage the brain's limbic system, an important component in the generation and shaping of emotions, or the frontal lobes, which help to determine the selection and appropriateness of emotional expression. In later stages of dementia, affect becomes a more accurate indicator of emotional state than does self-reported mood.

Table 2.9 Speech and Language Disturbances Seen in Dementia

Disturbance	Comprehension	Expression
Hearing loss	Intact; only for what is heard	Intact
Dysarthria	Intact	Incoordinated or garbled articulation but language formation is intact
Aphasia (nonfluent/ Brocca's)	Intact	Impaired repetition, impaired grammar, telegraphic speech
Aphasia (fluent/ Wernicke)	Impaired	Impaired repetition; speech is fluent and melodic but not very intelligible due, in part, to multiple paraphasic errors (incorrect word choice or placement of word sounds)
Aphasia (conduction)	Intact	Impaired repetition; speech is fluent and intelligible but with paraphasic errors
Aphasia (global)	Impaired	Impaired, with some preservation of automatic speech

Source: McNutt and Armbruster (2008).

Clinical Tip

When you inquire about mood, a cooperative individual with severe dementia may sometimes provide direct but inaccurate responses, such as answering yes or no to every question. If you simply ask, "Are you sad?" and the patient answers, "Yes," do not immediately conclude that an element of depression is present; you may find that he or she also answers yes when you ask if he or she is happy. When you suspect such a response style, ask multiple questions repetitively and then ask the opposite in a similar fashion. An individual who responds yes to every question or who does not respond consistently when asked these questions a second time is obviously not a reliable historian.

Common affective changes in dementia include increased irritability, lability (i.e., rapid fluctuations), and apathy. The clinical challenge is to determine whether fluctuations in affect constitute an actual mood disorder. Consider the following clinical vignettes.

Clinical Vignettes

Mrs. W was an 81-year-old long-term care resident with a history of vascular dementia. During the day, she was noted to cry frequently without apparent reason. Sometimes she would begin sobbing after being startled by a loud noise. Nursing staff and family members expressed concern that she was severely depressed.

Mr. L, an 88-year-old man with subcortical dementia, lived at home with his wife of 65 years. He sat impassively in his wheelchair all day, staring at the television and never initiating any conversation. He made very little movement in his chair. Although he was agreeable to suggestions made by his wife, he answered her perfunctorily with yes-or-no responses.

In each case, correlating the current affect and mood with other parts of the history and examination is important. For example, Mrs. W had a history of frontal lobe and subcortical cerebral damage from strokes. She always denied feeling depressed, and she demonstrated good appetite and sleep. Her affect was more reflective of the neurologic syndrome pseudobulbar palsy (also known as emotional incontinence) than of depression or mania. Mr. L, conversely, was more apathetic than depressed because he did not demonstrate any symptoms of depression other than his affect, and he put up no resistance to his wife's efforts to encourage more involvement in activities. Chapter 10 describes in more detail how to differentiate among dementia, depression, and apathy.

Thought Process

Disruptions in thought process may be symptomatic of the dementia itself or of an associated psychosis or another psychiatric disorder. Regardless of the causes, impaired thought processes can be seen when an individual attempts to answer questions and to provide history. Individuals with severe memory impairment may confabulate, providing responses that either approximate or are not related to the question. They may overcompensate by providing a lot of extraneous or circumstantial information or marginally related or tangential information. When the frontal lobe circuits are damaged, an individual may perseverate—or present similar thoughts repeatedly— an occurrence that sometimes appears to reflect an obsession. As the patient's abstract thinking becomes more impaired, associations among ideas become looser or less logical. Ultimately, demented thought processes can become quite impoverished and even blocked by the inability to equate words with ideas (due to aphasia) or to recognize the subjects of the discussion (due to agnosia). These changes may manifest as significant response delay or latency, or even as muteness. The patient may, however, still be able to communicate when he or she is expressing automatic or overlearned forms of thought.

Psychotic Symptoms

Clinicians always need to identify whether there are psychotic symptoms such as delusions and hallucinations. Delusions are false, fixed ideas, and, in dementia, they typically consist of paranoid, grandiose, or bizarre types. Some of the most common delusions include paranoid beliefs that a spouse is being unfaithful, that medications are poisonous, or that caregivers are trying to inflict harm. Misidentification is another common form of delusion associated with dementia, in which an individual is convinced that a person is someone other than their true identity.

Hallucinations are false sensory perceptions that can be auditory, visual, and, less commonly, tactile or olfactory. Auditory hallucinations are the most common type of hallucination encountered in psychotic states, including psychosis associated with severe depression. Visual hallucinations and delusions are common side effects of medications used to treat Parkinson's disease. They are sometimes associated with visual impairment, such as occurs in the rare Charles Bonnet syndrome, in which an individual with no other psychiatric symptoms experiences vivid visual hallucinations (sometimes of small or Lilliputian people moving about) that typically cause little emotional distress. Tactile hallucinations are suggestive of substance withdrawal, whereas olfactory hallucinations are associated with temporal lobe seizures.

In the MSE of the dementia patient, it is important to distinguish between actual delusions or hallucinations and confused thoughts, as the following vignette illustrates.

Clinical Vignette

Mrs. D was a 90-year-old woman with moderate dementia. She told her doctor that her mother had come to visit her the other day. She began weeping, insisting that her mother told her that she was dying.

Was Mrs. D's experience a delusional belief that her mother had returned from the dead? Was it a delusion of misidentification, in which she believed that a visitor was actually her mother? Was she having hallucinations of seeing her mother? Was she merely confused by a recent visit by her daughter, who had always reminded her of her mother in looks and personality and who told her that she was not feeling well? All of these possibilities must be explored in the MSE. More information on the evaluation of psychosis can be found in Chapter 9.

Suicidal and Homicidal Thoughts

The clinician must inquire about suicidal and homicidal thoughts because individuals at high risk of dementia are also at high risk of committing suicide. In the United States, older white men with medical problems, chronic pain, and significant psychosocial losses represent the group at highest risk of completed suicide (American Association of Suicidality, 2010). This risk can increase during the early stages of dementia, when an individual may be reacting to increased cognitive impairment, especially if associated depression and/or impairment in judgment is present. Caregivers especially may be at risk of suicidal and even homicidal thoughts or behaviors directed toward an ailing spouse or parent. Although suicide-homicides in the elderly are rare, these are typically seen in a couple in which one spouse is quite ill and the other spouse (usually the husband) is overwhelmed by the burden of caregiving (Malphurs & Cohen, 2005).

Passive suicidal thoughts are the more common form of suicidal ideation that are seen in dementia, and they can take many forms. For example, an individual may express a sense of hopelessness or disgust about living. They may also not be concerned about waking up in the morning, dying soon, or being killed in some manner; they may even wish for these things to happen. On the borderline between passive and active suicidal ideation lie indirect life-threatening behaviors, such as a refusal to eat, to take medications, or to receive medical treatment.

Feelings of hopelessness, depression, or anger may drive active suicidal ideation, but an intact executive function is required for the suicidal ideation to pose a risk of being carried out. Consequently, such ideation will become more vague and less organized as dementia progresses. Some individuals in the early stages of dementia will confide their thoughts to family or clinicians, whereas others will make preparations without signaling their intentions to anyone. In later stages of dementia, individuals begin to lose the capacity to organize and carry out a plan; however, in rare cases, they may be assisted by family members.

Insight and Judgment

Insight depends on the following factors: memory function, intelligence, abstract thinking, and self-consciousness. These factors determine the extent to which individuals can remember insights from one day to the next; their understanding of the disease process and their ability to recognize a change in their condition; and the degree to which they are aware of their own changing self. All these cognitive abilities begin to deteriorate in progressive dementia, so that any degree of insight that is present early on in the disease process will eventually disappear. In the MSE, the assessment of insight determines an individual's awareness of his or her cognitive impairment; insight can be gauged through several simple questions:

- Are you having any memory problems?
- Do you have trouble thinking?
- Have you noticed anything wrong with your mind?

The degree of insight that an individual retains during the early stages of dementia can be a double-edged sword. Good insight into memory impairment can lead some individuals to be more cautious and to accept assistance; conversely, this insight can lead to anxiety, depression, and even panic in patients who react to their growing sense of confusion and difficulties in maintaining independence. Poor insight can also hamper an individual's level of cooperation with treatment.

Judgment describes an individual's ability to make appropriate decisions. It depends not only on an individual's abstract abilities but also on his or her ability to discriminate between safe and unsafe and right and wrong and to maintain an awareness of social etiquette. Impaired judgment can range from minor lapses to humiliating indiscretions to even dangerous miscalculations. Consider the examples presented in the following clinical vignettes.

Clinical Vignettes

Mr. C was a 68-year-old man with early-stage dementia. He was still driving, despite his daughter's warnings to stop. One day he was pulled over by the police for failing to stop behind a school bus with its lights flashing and the stop sign displayed. When confronted by the police officer, he appeared incredulous when he was informed that driving around the bus was illegal.

Mrs. G was a 78-year-old woman with moderate dementia who lived alone in an apartment. One evening, she came running out of her smoke-filled apartment screaming that there was a fire. Several neighbors rushed in to discover that she had turned on her oven with a cardboard box of food inside. When she was asked why she had done it, she seemed oblivious to the danger and began accusing her neighbors of being rude.

In both vignettes, an individual made a poor judgment that led to unfortunate consequences. These lapses in judgment reflect both a loss of knowledge of particular rules and a lapse in social etiquette. The best way to assess judgment in individuals with dementia is to ask family and staff about such incidents, rather than relying on specific screening questions.

The Use of a Cognitive Screen

The goal of the cognitive screen is to both qualify and quantify the presence of cognitive impairment that may already be suspected during the MSE. The ideal cognitive screen is quick, simple to use, and reliable; not impacted by examiner training, patient's age and educational level, and cultural factors; and has excellent sensitivity and specificity for dementia. Of course, such a test does not exist! However, several standardized instruments are available for use, and all focus to varying degrees on some of the following domains: short-term memory, attention, concentration, orientation, language skills, motor ability (praxis), word and object recognition, and visuospatial ability. If the examiner finds that a high index of suspicion for dementia exists after a screening, more comprehensive neuropsychological testing of the patient should be considered.

There are several brief and easily administered cognitive screens, including the Mini-Mental State Examination (MMSE) (Folstein, Folstein, & McHugh, 1975), the Mini-Cog (Borson et al., 2000), the Montreal Cognitive Assessment (MoCA) (Nasreddine et al., 2005), the St. Louis Test of Mental Status (SLUMS) (Tariq et al., 2006), and the Clock Drawing Test (CDT) (Rouleau et al., 1992). The MMSE is a 30-point screen with well-established norms that are adjusted by age and educational level (Crum, Anthony, Bassett, & Folstein, 1993). It is the most popular screen in use and provides an assessment of most cognitive domains in 5 to 10 minutes of administration. Scores in the range of 20 to 27 are consistent with mild impairment; 10 to 19, with moderate impairment; and below 10, with severe impairment (Folstein et al., 1975). The MMSE can be used to track people over time; scores for individuals with AD typically drop by 3 to 4 points per year (Doody, Massman, & Dunn, 2001). The disadvantages of the MMSE include its limited scope for frontal lobe (i.e., executive dysfunction) and right hemispheric impairment and the fact that differences in administration and scoring can lead to inconsistent results. In comparison, the MoCA takes about 10 minutes to administer and is less widely used, but it does incorporate measures of executive function. The SLUMS is similar to the MMSE but may be better at detecting milder cognitive impairment (Nasreddine et al., 2005). When time is more limited, the Mini-Cog, can be substituted since it only takes three to five minutes and provides excellent sensitivity and specificity (Borson et al., 2000).

Clinical Tip

The MMSE and other cognitive screens are meant to be used as screening tests and not gold standards for determining dementia. You are not seeking to make a specific diagnosis with it but rather to identify someone with potential deficits in one or more key areas of cognition. Initially, think of these screens as triage tools that help you to plot a course for evaluation. After a diagnosis has been established, these screens can then serve to track the patient's course.

Rapid cognitive assessment and triage are sometimes needed for outpatient or community memory screenings, or with medically compromised individuals in busy hospital, rehabilitation, or outpatient settings. The purpose of this evaluation is either for triage to a more comprehensive cognitive assessment or for determining decision-making capacity (see Chapter 11 for more details) or for assisting other clinicians or health care proxies with acute treatment planning. Such a "bedside" evaluation consists of a brief MSE followed by a cognitive screen. While the Mini-Cog is ideal for rapid screening in outpatient settings or at community memory screenings, the clinician might want a more complete picture of cognitive skills. In those circumstances, combining the MMSE with the CDT is practical, and additional information on specific cognitive skills such as executive function can be quickly obtained from the Trail-Making Test or the complex picture test, or other tests that a neuropsychologist can suggest. The MoCA already incorporates the CDT, a mini-version of the Trail-Making Test and other tests of executive function. Refer to Chapter 7 for more information on assessment of executive function. Table 2.10 illustrates how these cognitive screens can assess for the cognitive domains that are impaired in dementia.

Table 2.10 Rapid Assessment of Cognitive Domains

Domain	*Tests on Cognitive Screens*
Memory	• Immediate: repetition of several words • Recent: recall of three words • Remote: recall of past events
Language	• Comprehension: ability to follow simple commands • Expression: repetition of sentence; listen for missed or mispronounced words, nonsensical words • Naming: ask patient to identify common objects or pictures or to generate a word list based on a specific category
Praxis	• Constructional: ability to copy pentagons on MMSE, clock face on CDT and MoCA, or simple objects • Ideomotor: ability to demonstrate how to comb hair, brush teeth, or hammer a nail
Recognition	• Prosopagnosia: impaired recognition of familiar faces • Astereognosis: impaired recognition of familiar objects via tactile exploration

Executive function	• Ability to plan and sequence steps of drawing a clock • Ability to reproduce rhythm with finger tapped out by examiner • Ability to mimic sequence using same hand (Luria Hand Sequence): (1) slap fist on table, (2) open fist and slap side of hand on table, (3) slap palm on table • Trail making test on MoCA
Daily function	• Four IADL (Instrumental Activities of Daily Living Scale) score; ask caregiver whether patient needs assistance in these areas: (a) money management, (b) medication management, (c) telephone use, and (d) traveling • Suspect dementia with increased need for assistance

Neuropsychological Testing

Neuropsychological (NP) testing consists of the administration of a series of tests by a trained examiner to measure both the qualitative and quantitative aspects of a variety of cognitive skills. It builds on the mental status examination by providing greater detail across a broader range of cognitive domains. NP testing helps to characterize the patient's existing cognitive strengths and weaknesses, and it then correlates them with other aspects of brain structure and function. The resulting picture enables the clinician to construct the best possible diagnostic picture, and it provides a baseline against which the dementia can be tracked. The results also provide information on the individual's functional capacity in order to understand how his or her cognitive changes affect daily activities. This information can help the clinician sculpt the appropriate treatment interventions, including cognitive rehabilitation, counseling and psychotherapy, psychopharmacotherapy, and therapeutic activities. NP testing may also be part of a competency evaluation conducted to determine an individual's decision-making capacity.

Baseline NP testing should be ordered for most cases of early-stage and middle-stage dementia, as long as the patient can tolerate a two-hour to three-hour testing session. When the clinician is making a referral, he or she should always provide a summary of the dementia workup and should include diagnostic impressions and relevant questions to be answered by testing. For example, a clinician may want to rule out aphasia in a patient who has difficulty responding to questions in order to evaluate for apathy versus depression, or to seek evidence of frontal lobe impairment. Guided by these diagnostic hypotheses and questions, the examiner can determine the most appropriate tests to administer. The examiner can also adjust the battery of tests to account for sensory, physical, cognitive, and behavioral limitations. For accurate testing, administering the test in the individual's most familiar language is best. Because testing often requires several hours, the examiner must also have a sense of what the patient can tolerate; he or she may then decide to break the testing up into several sessions. Subsequent interviews with family members, the analysis of test results, and the preparation of a report can take an additional several hours; this underscores how labor-intensive NP testing can be.

Clinical Tip

Many clinicians postpone NP testing during the acute phase of a major depressive or psychotic episode. When the mood disorder or psychosis is more chronic, testing can actually serve a role in distinguishing impairment due to dementia from impairment secondary to the psychiatric condition.

Many neuropsychologists prefer to use a flexible approach to NP testing in which they select and modify tests from a variety of published batteries of tests. Subsections of the Wechsler Adult Intelligence Scale–Revised and the Wechsler Memory Scales–Revised form the foundation of most NP testing because both contain subtests that are relevant to a variety of cognitive functions. All NP testing involves one of the brief cognitive screens described earlier, of which the most popular choice is the MMSE. More specific tests for evaluating frontal lobe impairment include the Wisconsin Card Sorting Test and the Trail-Making Test, Parts A and B. Some examiners administer a fixed battery of standardized tests, such as the Halstead–Reitan Neuropsychological Battery (HRNB) or the Luria–Nebraska Neuropsychological Battery.

Functional Testing

NP assessment in dementia often includes functional testing, which attempts to identify how cognitive deficits translate into functional limitations that impact those skills often referred to as basic and instrumental activities of daily living (ADLs and IADLs). Examples of basic ADLs include dressing, grooming, and hygiene, while IADLs include food preparation, operating appliances, driving, shopping, making change with money, and writing checks. In addition to the neuropsychologist, a variety of clinicians may participate in making observations or conducting tests regarding daily function; such clinicians include occupational and physical therapists, social workers, and recreational therapists. An important advantage to functional testing is that it helps to engage both the patient and caregivers in a discussion of the patient's remaining strengths and weaknesses in the face of dementia.

Clinical Vignette

Mr. A was a 78-year-old farmer who lived in a rural area that was 100 miles away from the hospital he was sent to for a dementia workup. He was found to have a moderate degree of cognitive impairment, likely due to AD. Still, he insisted on driving, arguing that he could easily navigate the country roads. NP testing indicated deficits in the cognitive ability to switch focus between competing sets of instructions on a single task, known as "set shifting." Translated into practical terms, this deficit indicated that, although Mr. A may drive marginally well on a quiet country road during the middle of the day, he would be at much greater risk of having an accident or getting lost if he were driving on a busier road with competing stimuli, such as other cars, pedestrians, signal lights, and varying weather conditions. He was referred for a functional driving evaluation and performed poorly with reaction time, a finding consistent with other identified deficits.

Having to warn an individual of risky behaviors, especially driving, is never easy. Such information may pit family members or caregivers against the impaired individual or against each other—the last situation that any clinician wants to create. Functional testing can be helpful by clearly showing the family that the person's difficulties with particular tasks are real and not just theoretical. One of the most popular functional tests is the Instrumental Activities of Daily Living Scale (IADL). The IADL uses a care-giver interview to assess the following eight abilities, which are often impaired early in the course of dementia: handling the telephone, overseeing finances, shopping, pre-paring food, housekeeping, doing laundry, arranging transportation, and managing medication (Lawton & Brody, 1969). Other caregiver-rated functional tests include the Physical Self-Maintenance Scale, the Progressive Deterioration Scale, the Interview for Deterioration in Daily Living Activities in Dementia, and the Disability Assessment in Dementia Scale.

Dementia Staging

Both clinicians and researchers often use scales that rank an individual's dementia based on its stage of severity. Such a rating can serve several purposes: (1) in research, it can be used to compare individuals and cohorts at a given time or over time; (2) in the clinic, it may help to predict current function, the relative need for social supports, and the disease course; and, (3) in long-term care, it can help the clinician anticipate the individual's psychosocial and nursing needs, including roommate and floor placement, activity selection, and the utility of particular rehabilitative therapies. One of the most popular scales is the Global Deterioration Scale. It is clinician-rated and provides seven stages of decline ranging from none to severe; these are listed in Table 2.11 (Reisberg, Ferris, de Leon, & Crook, 1982). The Brief Cognitive Rating Scale is rated by the clinician based on a structured interview with the patient and caregiver, and it assesses dementia on five axes: orientation, concentration, memory (recent and past), and function (Reisberg & Ferris, 1988).

The Functional Assessment Staging is an extension of the function axis on the Brief Cognitive Rating Scale and provides a number of substages for individuals with more severe cognitive decline (Reisberg, 1988). Two other scales are the Functional Activities Questionnaire, a clinician-based instrument that assigns a stage from 1 (normal) to 7 (severely incapacitated in terms of ADL function), and the Clinical Dementia Rating Scale or CDR, a structured interview with both the patient and caregiver that rates individuals based on six cognitive and functional domains (Berg, 1984). CDR stages range from stages 0 (healthy), 0.5 (questionable dementia), and 1 (mild dementia), to ultimately stages 4 (profound) and 5 (terminal). CDR stage 0.5 is typically used in research studies to identify individuals with mild cognitive impair-ment (see Table 2.11).

Table 2.11 The Global Deterioration Scale

Stage	Description
Stage 1	Normal; no memory complaints and no evident cognitive impairment
Stage 2	Very mild; memory problem reported but not evident in clinical interview
Stage 3	Mild impairment in memory, concentration, and occupational performance
Stage 4	Moderate impairment in memory, knowledge retrieval, and complex tasks
Stage 5	Moderate to severe impairment in both recent and remote memory, frequent disorientation to time and place, and impairment in activities of daily living that indicates need for caregiver assistance
Stage 6	Severe cognitive impairment with inability to tend to activities of daily living without assistance
Stage 7	Very severe impairment in cognition, language, and motor skills, progressing to a less functional, vegetative state

Based on Reisberg et al. (1982).

Assessment of the Environment

Individuals with cognitive impairment can have an increased risk of self-injury, harming others, physical and mental abuse, neglect, and social and financial exploitation. Consider the following examples:

- A 79-year-old man with early-stage dementia signed over power of attorney to a daughter, who then promptly "borrowed" his remaining savings to finance her new house.
- An 84-year-old man with severe dementia was living in a filthy, vermin-ridden apartment without nursing assistance because his mildly demented and paranoid wife was not capable of home maintenance and personal hygiene and was afraid that the social service workers were trying to persecute them.

These troubling examples illustrate the need to gather information on both the care needs and the safety and adequacy of the social environment of the individual with dementia. The following questions can help:

- Does the home or other living environment provide adequate space, cleanliness, clothing, attention to hygiene, nutrition, and proper management of medications?
- Do bathrooms, stairs, kitchens, and other household locations account for the individual's physical limitations and sensory impairment?
- Does the individual receive adequate physical activity or therapy, sensory stimulation, and opportunities to engage in activities?
- Is the individual exposed to unsafe situations?
- Is the individual driving or using appliances or machinery against recommended advice?
- Does the individual need assistance taking medications?

The importance of these questions as part of the dementia workup should never be underestimated. The most brilliant workup and treatment plan becomes meaningless if the individual with dementia is returned to an unsafe environment. Chapter 12 contains information on educating caregivers on how to "dementia-proof" their home environment.

For individuals living in the community, their primary caregiver, commonly an elderly spouse or a daughter, is a vital part of assessment and treatment. If the caregiver is impaired, the individual with dementia can become excessively impaired. Ideally, the caregiver has a sufficient degree of trust in and comfort with the clinician to portray his or her situation accurately. The following questions can elicit information from caregivers:

- What is your understanding of the affected person's disorder?
- How do you feel about the situation? Depressed? Hopeless? Helpless? Resigned?
- What is most burdensome about the situation?
- What social supports do you have? How helpful are they?
- Do you have help with specific caregiving jobs like hygiene, cleaning, and meal preparation? Is the help sufficient?
- Do you have time to yourself? If so, how do you spend it? Is it adequate?
- Do you have any current medical or psychiatric problems? If so, are you getting help?
- Have you been in touch with the local Alzheimer's Association or a support group?
- How do you see the future?

The answers to these questions will provide clinicians with a sense of how much the caregiver really understands the disease process and how it affects his or her own life. Sometimes just asking these questions and showing concern can be therapeutic for the caregiver. For more information on working with caregivers across settings, see Chapter 12.

Presenting the Overall Findings

After the dementia workup is complete, the clinician must propose a diagnosis and a treatment plan. Presenting the results as clearly and consistently as possible and avoiding vague or conflicting diagnoses is important for both the patient and family. The last few paragraphs of the NP report usually suggest diagnoses that may or may not be in agreement with the clinician's thinking. If a discrepancy is present (i.e., the neuropsychologist suggests a diagnosis of AD, but the clinician is convinced it is dementia with Lewy bodies), a discussion with the examiner is warranted. NP test reports can sometimes be confusing; after all, without understanding the details of each test, including the normative scores, and the correlations between test results, brain function, and performance in the real world, incorporating the results into diagnostic impressions and recommendations can be difficult. Therefore, clinicians must have a rudimentary understanding of the purpose and nature of the tests, and they should communicate in person with the examiner to gain further insight into the selection of tests and the overall meaning of the results.

The clinician should take time to educate both the patient and family about the diagnosis and its expected course, emphasizing both the strengths and weaknesses of the patient's current state. Excessively technical or quantitative descriptions should be avoided, but the data should be used to support the diagnosis, and they should be translated into practical implications for daily functioning. Functional test results help in that regard. The clinician may recommend additional medical or psychiatric workups for residual questions if a reversible cause is suspected.

Practical treatment recommendations include preventive measures against further cognitive decline, attention to safety issues, treatment for a behavioral problem or psychiatric condition, assistance with daily functioning, increased therapeutic activities and social stimulation, better monitoring at home, or placement in a more structured setting. When these recommendations have been formulated, documented, and communicated to the patient, family, and caregivers, the dementia workup is complete. The next step is implementing the recommendations, which is covered throughout the remainder of the book.

References

American Association of Suicidality. (2010). *Elderly suicide fact sheet, based on 2010 data.* Retrieved from www.suicidology.org/c/document_library/get_file?folderId=262&name=DLFE-624.pdf

Atiya, M., Hyman, B. T., Albert, M. S., et al. (2003). Structural magnetic resonance imaging in established and prodromal Alzheimer disease: A review. *Alzheimer Disease & Associated Disorders, 17*(3), 177–195.

Berg, L. (1984). Clinical dementia rating. *British Journal of Psychiatry, 145,* 339.

Borson, S., Scanlan, J., Brush, M., et al. (2000). The Mini-Cog: A cognitive "vital signs" measure for dementia screening in multi-lingual elderly. *International Journal of Geriatric Psychiatry, 15,* 1021–1027.

Bradford, A., Kunik, M. E., Schulz, P., et al. (2009). Missed and delayed diagnosis of dementia in primary care: Prevalence and contributing factors. *Alzheimer Dis Assoc Disord, 23*(4), 306–314.

Campbell, N., Boustani, M., Limbil, T., et al. (2009). The cognitive impact of anticholinergics: A clinical review. *Clin Interv Aging, 4,* 225–233.

Crum, R. M., Anthony, J. C., Bassett, S. S., & Folstein, M. F. (1993). Population-based norms for the Mini-Mental State Examination by age and educational level. *JAMA, 269,* 2386–2691.

de Leon, M. J., Ferris, S. H., George, A. E., et al. (1983). Positron emission tomographic studies of aging and Alzheimer's disease. *Am J Neurorad, 4*(3), 568–571.

Doody, R. S., Massman, P., & Dunn, J. K. (2001). A method for estimating progression rates in Alzheimer disease. *Arch Neurol, 58,* 449–454.

Drazkowski, J. F. (2008). Diagnostic tests in the older adult: EEG. In J. I. Sirven & B. L. Malamut (Eds.), *Clinical neurology of the older adult* (2nd ed., pp. 25–32). Philadelphia: Lippincott, Williams and Wilkins.

Folstein, M. F., Folstein, S. E., & McHugh, P. R. (1975). "Mini-mental state": A practical method for grading the cognitive state of patients for the clinician. *J of Psychiatric Res, 12,* 189–198.

Lawton, M. P., & Brody, E. M. (1969). Assessment of older people: Self-maintaining and instrumental activities of daily living. *Gerontologist, 9,* 179–186.

Malphurs, J. E., & Cohen, D. (2005). A statewide case-control study of spousal homicide-suicide in older persons. *Am J Geriatr Psychiatry, 13*(3), 211–217.

Mancall, E. L. (2011). Neurological assessment of the elderly psychiatric patient. In M. E. Agronin & G. J. Maletta (Eds.), *Principles and practice of geriatric psychiatry* (2nd ed., pp. 77–92). Philadelphia: Lippincott, Williams and Wilkins.

Margolin, R., & Merrill, D. A. (2011). Neuroimaging in the geriatric patient. In M. E. Agronin & G. J. Maletta (Eds.), *Principles and practice of geriatric psychiatry* (2nd ed., pp. 93–118). Philadelphia: Lippincott, Williams and Wilkins.

McNutt, K. T., & Armbruster, A. P. (2008). Acquired disorders of swallowing, cognition, speech, and language in the older adult. In J. I. Sirven & B. L. Malamut (Eds.), *Clinical neurology of the older adult* (pp. 126–137). Philadelphia: Lippincott, Williams and Wilkins.

Nasreddine, Z. S., Phillips, N. A., Bédirian, V., et al. (2005). The Montreal Cognitive Assessment, MoCA: A brief screening tool for mild cognitive impairment. *JAGS, 53*, 695–699.

Reisberg, B. (1988). Functional assessment staging (FAST). *Psychopharmacol Bull, 24*, 653–659.

Reisberg, B., & Ferris, S. H. (1988). Brief cognitive rating scale (BCRS). *Psychopharmacol Bull, 24*(4), 629–636.

Reisberg, B., Ferris, S. H., de Leon, M. J., & Crook, T. (1982). The global deterioration scale for assessment of primary degenerative dementia. *Am J Psychiatry, 139*, 1136–1139.

Roman, G. C. (2004). Age-associated white matter lesion and dementia: Are these lesions causal or casual? *Arch Neurol., 61*(10), 1503–1504.

Rouleau, I., Salmon, D. P., Butters, N., et al. (1992). Quantitative and qualitative analyses of clock drawing in Alzheimer's disease and Huntington's disease. *Brain Cognition, 18*, 70–87.

Tariq, S. H., Tumona, N., Chibnall, J. T., et al. (2006). Comparison of the Saint Louis University Mental Status Examination and the Mini-Mental State Examination for detecting dementia and mild neurocognitive disorder: a pilot study. *Am J Geriatr Psychiatr, 14*, 900–910.

Tune, L., Carr, S., Hoag, E., & Cooper, T. (1992). Anticholinergic effects of drugs commonly prescribed for the elderly: Potential means for assessing risk of delirium. *Am J Psychiatry, 149*, 1393–1394.

Vandenberghe, R., Van Laere, K., Ivanoiu, A., et al. (2010). 18F-flutemetamol amyloid imaging in Alzheimer disease and mild cognitive impairment: A phase 2 trial. *Ann Neurol, 68*(3), 319–329.

Wood, D. F., Rosenberg, P. B., Zhou, Y., et al. (2010). In vivo imaging of amyloid deposition in Alzheimer disease using the radioligand 18F-AV-45 (florbetapir F-18). *J Nucl Med, 51*(6), 913–920.

Part II

Dementia Subtypes

3 Mild Cognitive Impairment

Most older individuals complain of occasional memory lapses, sometimes referred to colloquially as "senior moments" or "tip-of-the-tongue" experiences. Although these lapses are normal occurrences across the age span, they increase in frequency as a person ages (Brown & Nix, 1996). In fact, mild declines in memory processing speed and efficiency and other cognitive skills have been found to be *normal* age-associated changes (Schaie, 2005). Research has shown, however, that while such normal changes in memory may be noticeable and bothersome, they may have little practical effect on daily function. Older individuals can draw upon a knowledgebase of facts and experiences accumulated over a lifetime as part of their memory skills. They can also compensate for or even reverse mild declines in memory through the use of mnemonics (e.g., lists, calendars, memorizing techniques), mentally stimulating activities, and cognitive training (Ball et al., 2002; Willis et al., 2006). However, other aged individuals demonstrate more pronounced cognitive deficits, which are comprised in a syndrome known as mild cognitive impairment or MCI. Ongoing research emphasizes the importance of early screening and intervention for these individuals, since MCI may be for many of them a transitional state to Alzheimer's disease (AD) or other forms of dementia.

Case Study

Mr. N was a 79-year-old retired dentist. He worked as a tour guide at a local nature preserve. Both he and his wife noticed that he was more forgetful at times, but he was still able to carry out his usual daily routines without difficulty. He did need to rely more on his datebook to prompt his memory, and he remembered to check it on a daily basis. There were no changes in his language function or organizational ability, and he was still able to volunteer at the preserve without difficulty. A clinical workup noted the mild forgetfulness but was otherwise unremarkable. After a year without any change in his memory, he was given the diagnosis of amnestic mild cognitive impairment.

Definition and Diagnostic Criteria

Several clinical terms have been introduced over time to diagnose cognitive changes that occur in late life but do not constitute a formal dementia. *Benign senescent forgetfulness* is one such term, introduced by Kral in 1962 to describe the normal, mild, and nonprogressive forgetting in aged individuals of the details of events but not the events themselves (Kral, 1962). The term *age-associated memory impairment* or AAMI was introduced in 1986 by a workgroup from the National Institute of Mental Health. Diagnostic criteria for AAMI include an age of 50 years or older, subjective complaints of gradually developing memory failure that affects daily function, and a mean memory performance on neuropsychological testing that is at least one standard deviation less than that seen in younger adults (Crook et al., 1986). Overall, global intellectual function is intact, and neither a dementia diagnosis nor a condition known to produce cognitive impairment (e.g., stroke, brain trauma) is present. At the time this term was introduced, it was thought that as many as 50% of older individuals demonstrated AAMI. In addition, it was postulated that AAMI possibly represented a dementia prodrome because more than one-third of affected individuals later developed dementia. Other similar terms that have appeared in the scientific literature include *age-associated cognitive decline* (Levy, 1994) and *cognitive impairment no dementia* or CIND (Lyketsos et al., 2006).

Several clinical scales were developed to better describe the varying degrees of cognitive impairment represented by these terms and by various forms of dementia, including the Clinical Dementia Rating or CDR (Berg, 1988; Morris, 1993) and the Global Deterioration Scale or GDS (Reisberg, Ferris, de Leon, & Crook, 1982). The term *mild cognitive impairment* or MCI was coined by Barry Reisberg in 1982 to describe stage three of the GDS, detailed in Table 2.11 (Reisberg et al., 1982). Since that time, extensive research has refined the diagnosis of MCI, and it has increasingly become the most widely recognized and studied syndrome of cognitive decline that lies somewhere between normal age-associated cognitive changes and dementia (Geda & Nedelska, 2012). The tremendous growth in research on MCI stems from its role as a potential doorway into dementia. Its recognition allows researchers to look at the pathophysiological origins of AD and other forms of dementia, and holds the promise of identifying and treating individuals *before* they develop dementia.

The core diagnostic criteria for MCI as defined by Petersen and colleagues are as follows: (1) memory complaint, preferably corroborated by an informant; (2) objective memory impairment for age (ideally confirmed by neuropsychological testing); (3) normal general cognitive functioning; (4) normal activities of daily living; and (5) no dementia (Petersen et al., 1999). Criteria from an international working group on MCI have expanded these criteria to account for both subjective and objective *cognitive* deficits (instead of just *memory* deficits) that have no impact on basic activities of daily living but a potentially mild impact on more complex daily functions (Petersen, 2004).

Ongoing research has demonstrated that MCI is a heterogeneous syndrome with four subtypes: amnestic MCI, which involves only memory impairment (single domain) or memory impairment plus deficits in another cognitive domain such as language function, visuospatial skills, or executive function (multiple domain), and nonamnestic MCI, which involves discrete cognitive impairments in single or multiple domains other than memory function. A diagnostic flowchart can be found in Figure 3.1. A workgroup from the National Institute on Aging-Alzheimer's Association has also recognized a category of MCI due to AD as a predementia phase of AD, determined in part by amyloid and tau-based biomarkers from cerebrospinal fluid analysis and positron emission tomography or PET imaging (Albert et al., 2011). This stage would be termed *mild neurocognitive disorder due to AD* in DSM-5.

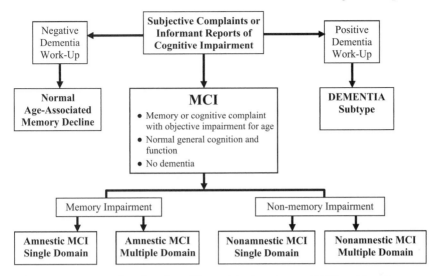

Figure 3.1 Diagnostic flowchart for mild cognitive impairment (MCI) and its subtypes

The prevalence of MCI in adults 65 years or older in the United States is estimated to range from 5.3% to 24.3% (Petersen et al., 2009). A review of prevalence studies indicates a range between 3% and 42% for MCI overall and 0.5% to 31.9% for amnestic MCI (Ward, Arrighi, Michels, & Cedarbaum, 2012). These rates will tend to be higher in clinical populations and in individuals with less than 12 years of education. Amnestic MCI is the most common subtype. Comorbid neuropsychiatric conditions including apathy, depression, anxiety, and irritability are seen in 35% to 85% of MCI patients over time, reflecting rates two to five times more common than in noncognitively impaired older individuals (Monastero et al., 2009).

Assessment

Because MCI is a heterogeneous disorder and may represent a prodromal syndrome for a variety of different dementia subtypes, clinical findings will vary. The clinical history should look for mild changes in memory function that have minimal impact on daily function and that are not associated with a known etiology such as a fall, head injury, or medical condition. Neuroimaging studies have found medial temporal lobe atrophy across MCI subtypes, which is associated with cognitive decline, especially in measures of delayed recall, as well as white matter hyperintensities, which have not correlated with the degree of cognitive impairment (van de Pol et al., 2009). Hippocampal atrophy is seen more often in those with the amnestic subtype, similar to that seen in AD (Becker et al., 2006).

Postmortem studies have found amyloid plaques, neurofibrillary tangles, small strokes, and Lewy bodies in the brains of MCI patients, with a predominance of neurofibrillary tangles in the hippocampus, amygdala, and entorhinal cortex (Markesbery, 2010). Studies of cerebrospinal fluid or CSF have also found evidence of amyloid and tau protein pathology in MCI patients, including elevated tau protein levels associated with worsening cognitive impairment. Newer positron emission tomography or PET scanning techniques using amyloid- and tau-specific ligands have begun to differentiate between AD patients and normal controls, as well as to identify MCI patients at greatest risk of further cognitive decline and eventual conversion to AD. Approximately 40% to 60% of MCI patients will show abnormal beta-amyloid deposition on these PET scans (Villemagne & Rowe, 2011). Genetic studies have looked at the frequency of the apolipoprotein E4 (APOE-4) allele (which confers an increased risk of AD) in MCI subtypes, finding its presence in approximately 31.4% of MCI patients compared to 19.2% of controls (DeCarli et al., 2001). Abnormalities in electroencephalogram readings have been seen in amnestic MCI patients, characterized by reductions in cortical alpha frequencies compared to age-matched controls (Koenig et al., 2005).

Clinical Course

A diagnosis of MCI brings with it a significantly increased risk of developing an actual dementia, typically AD. Roughly 12%–18% of MCI patients progress to AD each year, with a smaller percentage progressing to other forms of dementia, such as vascular dementia, frontotemporal dementia, or dementia with Lewy bodies. Over a three-year span, close to 35% of MCI patients will progress to dementia while more than half will remain stable (Petersen et al., 2009). In comparison, aged individuals without MCI have a 1%–2% annual risk of developing dementia. These rates will vary depending on the sample studied, the method of diagnosis, and the relative presence of the amnestic MCI subtype, which has been associated with a higher rate of eventual progression to AD.

Individuals with MCI who go on to develop AD have been found to have significantly elevated CSF levels of both total and phosphorylated tau protein, and lowered levels of beta-amyloid protein (Blennow, 2004). Other predictors of conversion to dementia include increased age, female gender, APOE-4 genotype, lower education, increased hippocampal and/or mesial temporal atrophy, slower gait, diabetes mellitus and other vascular risk factors, and the presence of neuropsychiatric symptoms such as depression (Lee et al., 2012; Velayudhan et al., 2010). In one study, MCI patients were divided into three groups based on having an AD biomarker pattern (abnormal CSF beta-amyloid and tau levels, temporoparietal hypometabolism on PET scans, and decreased hippocampal volume), a different biomarker pattern, or no biomarkers present. Followed over time, 100% of MCI patients with the AD biomarker pattern developed AD compared to 27% of those with another pattern and none of those with no biomarkers (Galluzzi et al., 2012).

Treatment

For most individuals with MCI, cognitive impairment will resolve in time or remain stable without any intervention. For others, formal cognitive training that teaches specific memory strategies has been shown to improve both subjective ratings and objective performance of memory function (Buschert et al., 2011; Hwang et al., 2012).

Prudent measures for all MCI patients include the control of vascular risk factors (e.g., hypertension); minimization or cessation of anticholinergic medications; increased mental, social, and physical stimulation; attention to comorbid medical conditions (e.g., hypothyroidism, diabetes); and aggressive treatment of depression and other psychiatric conditions that may negatively affect memory. Caregivers for MCI patients may also need therapeutic intervention (see Chapter 12).

There is no standard treatment for MCI, and no medication has been approved by the Food and Drug Administration. When working with MCI patients, clinicians should encourage any and all healthy lifestyle choices that protect the brain from injury and promote its stimulation. Vigilance must be maintained for signs that an actual dementia is developing through regular follow-ups two to three times a year. Patients and their loved ones should be made aware of the increased risks of dementia in a way that engages their participation in treatment without causing undue worry or panic. A brain-healthy lifestyle is summarized in Table 3.1 (Small & Vorgan, 2012).

Although studies of the three acetylcholinesterase inhibitors donepezil, rivastigmine, and galantamine in MCI patients have suggested potential benefits, they have not demonstrated consistent, statistically significant improvements in cognitive function, although there is some evidence that they may reduce the risk of conversion to AD (Dinitz et al., 2009; Loy & Schneider, 2006). One 24-week study of donepezil in amnestic MCI patients did not reveal improvement in memory but did show some benefit in measures of attention, concentration, and psychomotor speed (Salloway et al., 2004). Another three-year, placebo-controlled study looked at over 700 subjects with amnestic MCI treated with donepezil (10 mg/day) and high dose Vitamin E (2000 IU/day) (Petersen et al., 2005). The use of donepezil significantly slowed progression to AD over the first 18 months (approximately 12% on donepezil progressed to AD versus 20% on Vitamin E and 20% on placebo), although after three years the rates were roughly equivalent (25% on donepezil converted to AD versus 27% on Vitamin E and 28% on placebo).

Table 3.1 A Brain-Healthy Lifestyle

- Regular physical exercise (e.g., brisk walking for at least 30 minutes, 3–4 times a week)
- Low-fat diet rich with fruits and vegetables and a source of omega-3 fatty acids such as fish or nuts (e.g., Mediterranean diet)
- Regular mental and social stimulation (e.g., adult education, brain games, music, theater, hobbies, volunteer work, socializing with family and friends)
- Reduce impact of vascular risk factors (e.g., reduce risk of stroke via good control of blood pressure and glucose and lipid levels)
- Light alcohol intake (up to one drink per day of wine or alcohol) may reduce risk of dementia
- Avoid tobacco use
- Always use protective headgear when engaging in sports
- Minimize use of medications with negative effects on cognition (e.g., anticholinergics, antihistamines, and narcotics; see Tables 2.3 and 2.4)

Memantine has not been well-studied in MCI. One placebo-controlled study combining memantine 20 milligrams daily with galantamine 16 milligrams daily was interrupted before completion due to safety concerns arising from other studies with galantamine. Preliminary data did appear to indicate benefit from the combination therapy versus galantamine alone or placebo alone, but this change declined after medication discontinuation (Peters et al., 2012). However, the data was not complete and has not been corroborated.

References

Albert, M. S., DeKosky, S. T., Dickson, D., et al. (2011). The diagnosis of mild cognitive impairment due to Alzheimer's disease: recommendations from the National Institute on Aging-Alzheimer's Association workgroups on diagnostic guidelines for Alzheimer's disease. *Alz & Dem, 7*(3), 270–279.

Ball, K., Berch, D. B., Helmers, K. F., et al. (2002). Effects of cognitive training interventions with older adults: A randomized controlled trial. *JAMA, 288*(18), 2271–2281.

Becker, J. T., Davis, S. W., Hayashi, K. M., et al. (2006). Three-dimensional patterns of hippocampal atrophy in mild cognitive impairment. *Arch Neurol, 63*(1), 97.

Berg, L. (1988). Clinical Dementia Rating (CDR). *Psychopharmacol Bull, 24*, 637–639.

Blennow, K. (2004). CSF biomarkers for mild cognitive impairment. *J Int Med, 256*(3), 224–234.

Brown, A. S., & Nix, L. A. (1996). Age differences in the tip-of-the-tongue experience. *The Am J Psychol, 109*, 79–91.

Buschert, V. C., Friese, U., Teipel, S. J., et al. (2011). Effects of a newly developed cognitive intervention in amnestic mild cognitive impairment and mild Alzheimer's disease: A pilot study. *J Alz Dis, 25*(4), 679–694.

Crook, T., Bartus, R. T., Ferris, S. H., et al. (1986). Age-associated memory impairment: proposed diagnostic criteria and measures of clinical change—report of a National Institute of Mental Health work group. *Dev Neuropsychol, 2*, 261–276.

DeCarli, C., Miller, B. L., Swan, G. E., et al. (2001). Cerebrovascular and brain morphologic correlates of mild cognitive impairment in the National Heart, Lung, and Blood Institute Twin Study. *Arch Neurol, 58*(4), 643–647.

Dinitz, B. S., Pinto, J. A., Jr., Gonzega, M. I., et al. (2009). To treat or not to treat? A meta-analysis of the use of cholinesterase inhibitors in mild cognitive impairment for delaying progression to Alzheimer's disease. *Eur Arch Psychiatry Clin Neurosci, 259*(4), 248–256.

Galluzzi, S., Geroldi, C., Amicucci, G., et al., & the Translational Outpatient Memory Clinic Working Group. (2012, October 16). Supporting evidence for using biomarkers in the diagnosis of MCI due to AD. *J Neurol.*. Retrieved from www.ncbi.nlm.nih.gov/pubmed/23070466

Geda, Y. E., & Nedelska, Z. (2012). Mild cognitive impairment: a subset of minor neurocognitive disorder? *Am J Ger Psychiatry, 20*(10), 821–826.

Hwang, H. R., Choi, S. H., Yoon, D. H., et al. (2012). The effect of cognitive training in patients with mild cognitive impairment and early Alzheimer's disease: A preliminary study. *J Clin Neurol, 8*(3), 190–197.

Koenig, T., Prichep, L., Dierks, T., et al. (2005). Decreased EEG synchronization in Alzheimer's disease and mild cognitive impairment. *Neurobiology and Aging, 26*(2), 165–171.

Kral, V. (1962). Senescent forgetfulness: Benign and malignant. *Can Med Assoc J, 86*, 257–260.

Lee, G. J., Lu, P. H., Hua, X., et al., & the Alzheimer's Disease Neuroimaging Initiative. (2012). Depressive symptoms in mild cognitive impairment predict greater atrophy in Alzheimer's disease-related regions. *Biol Psychiatry, 71*(9), 814–821.

Levy, R. (1994). Age-associated cognitive decline. Working Party of the International Psychogeriatric Association in collaboration with the World Health Organization. *Int Psychogeriatrics, 6*, 63–68.

Loy, C., & Schneider, L. (2006, January 25). Galantamine for Alzheimer's disease and mild cognitive impairment. *Cochrane Database Syst Rev, (1)*, CD001747.

Lyketsos, C. G., Colenda, C. C., Beck, C., et al., & the Task Force of American Association for Geriatric Psychiatry. (2006). Position statement of the American Association for Geriatric Psychiatry regarding principles of care for patients with dementia resulting from Alzheimer disease. *Am J Geriatr Psychiatry, 14*(7), 561–572.

Markesbery, W. R. (2010). Neuropathologic alterations in mild cognitive impairment: A review. *J Alz Dis, 19*(1), 221–228.

Monastero, R., Mangialasche, F., Camarda, C., et al. (2009). A systematic review of neuropsychiatric symptoms in mild cognitive impairment. *J Alz Dis, 18*(1), 11–30.

Morris, J. C. (1993). The Clinical Dementia Rating (CDR): Current version and scoring rules. *Neurol, 43*, 2412–2414.

Peters, O., Lorenz, D., Fesche, A., et al. (2012). A combination of galantamine and memantine modifies cognitive function in subjects with amnestic MCI. *J Nut Health and Aging, 16*(6), 544–548.

Petersen, R. C. (2004). Mild cognitive impairment as a diagnostic entity. *J Int Med, 256*(3), 184–194.

Petersen, R. C., Roberts, R. O., Knopman, D. S., et al. (2009). Mild cognitive impairment: Ten years later. *Arch Neurol, 66*, 1447–1455.

Petersen, R. C., Smith, G. E. Waring, S. C., et al. (1999). Mild cognitive impairment: Clinical characterization and outcome. *Arch Neurol, 56*(3), 303–308.

Petersen, R. C., Thomas, R. G., Grundman, M., et al., & the Alzheimer's Disease Cooperative Study Group. (2005). Vitamin E and donepezil for the treatment of mild cognitive impairment. *N Eng J Med, 352*(23), 2379–2388.

Reisberg, B., Ferris, S. H., de Leon, M. J., & Crook, T. (1982). The global deterioration scale for assessment of primary degenerative dementia. *Am J Psychiatry, 139*, 1136–1139.

Salloway, S., Ferris, S., Kluger, A., et al. (2004). Efficacy of donepezil in mild cognitive impairment: A randomized placebo-controlled trial. *Neurology, 63*(4), 651–657.

Schaie, K. W. (2005). *Developmental influences on adult intelligence: The Seattle Longitudinal Study.* New York: Oxford University Press.

Small, G. W., & Vorgan, G. (2012). *The Alzheimer's Prevention Program: Keep your brain healthy for the rest of your life.* New York: Workman Publishing Company.

van de Pol, L. A., Verhey, F., Frisoni, G. B., et al. (2009). White matter hyperintensities and medial temporal lobe atrophy in clinical subtypes of mild cognitive impairment: The DESCRIPA study. *J Neurol Neurosurg Psychiatry, 80*(10), 1069–1074.

Velayudhan, L., Poppe, M., Archer, N., et al. (2010). Risk of developing dementia in people with diabetes and mild cognitive impairment. *Brit J Psychiatry, 196*(1), 36–40.

Villemagne, V. L., & Rowe, C. C. (2011). Amyloid imaging. *Int Psychogeriatrics* (Suppl. 2), S41–S49.

Ward, A., Arrighi, H. M., Michels, S., & Cedarbaum, J. M. (2012). Mild cognitive impairment: Disparity of incidence and prevalence estimates. *Alz Dem, 8*(1), 14–21.

Willis, S. E., Tennstedt, S. I., Marsiske, M., et al. (2006). Long-term effects of cognitive training on everyday functional outcomes in older adults. *JAMA, 296*, 2805–2814.

4   Alzheimer's Disease

Although the medical concept of dementia has existed for centuries, the modern-day knowledge of the most common form of dementia only began slightly more than 100 years ago. In late 1901, a 51-year-old woman in Germany was brought to a psychiatric hospital after a several-month history of progressive memory impairment and behavioral disturbances, including angry outbursts and paranoid ideation. For the next four years, she was followed by a psychiatrist who charted her downward course of increasing cognitive impairment and psychiatric disturbances, and, ultimately, a vegetative state before death. After her death, her psychiatrist, who had been unable to determine an exact diagnosis throughout her long course, was finally able to view the actual brain tissue. The results were startling—the brain cells were crowded and blotted out by brown-stained clumps of material, and the cells themselves were overrun by tangles of dark fibrils that appeared to have destroyed other cellular components. This dedicated and relentless physician, Dr. Alois Alzheimer, was looking at what clinicians now know as *plaques* and *tangles*, the pathologic hallmarks of the disease that he first wrote about and that today bears his name (Möller & Graeber, 1998).

At this time, AD is recognized as the most common form of dementia, and it accounts for, either alone or in part, as many as 60%–70% of all cases. According to the Alzheimer's Association, it afflicts an estimated 5–6 million individuals in the United States (Alzheimer's Association, 2012). After the age of 65, the prevalence rate doubles every five years such that, although fewer than 5% of individuals who are 65 years of age have AD, nearly 50% of individuals who are 85 years and older are affected (Alzheimer's Association, 2012). Because this most vulnerable age group is also one of the fastest growing segments of the population, AD will afflict between 11 and 16 million persons in the United States by the year 2050, barring any major advances in prevention of the disease (Hebert et al., 2003; Hebert, Weuve, Scherr, & Evans, 2013). It is estimated that AD affects over 35 million people worldwide currently, with a projected increase to over 155 million people by 2050 (Alzheimer's Disease International, 2010).

The realization that AD is the fourth leading cause of death in the United States is sobering. Not surprisingly, the social and economic burdens are staggering: the annual costs of AD to the United States economy are estimated to be as high as $400 billion (Alzheimer's Association, 2012), perhaps making it the mostly costly illness, even more than cancer and heart disease (Hurd, Martorelli, & Delavande, 2013). The annual caregiving costs per patient with AD in the United States is over $40,000, a figure that is three times greater than costs for someone without AD (Alzheimer's Association, 2012; Hurd et al., 2013).

Aside from these numbers, the most daunting aspect of AD lies in its very nature as a progressive and incurable disorder. In its earliest stages, it can be difficult to distinguish from normal age-related changes in memory or other benign causes of cognitive change. This uncertainty fuels denial of illness and likely accounts for the fact that it takes, on average, up to two years for an individual with symptoms to see a physician and up to one year to get a diagnosis (Balasa et al., 2011). More alarming is the fact that 20% of those individuals in the United States who have AD are never clinically diagnosed with the condition (Mok et al., 2004). This is true despite the fact that many obvious benefits to early diagnosis exist and that effective pharmacological treatments for the symptoms of AD have been on the market for over 15 years.

Case Study

Mrs. S was a 75-year-old retired real estate broker with a history of mild depression and migraine headaches. Her daughter began to notice some mild forgetfulness in her mother, such as not remembering the content of recent phone conversations. She also noticed that her mother was more irritable at times and that she was less sociable with her friends. She attributed this to increased depression and urged her mother to see her psychiatrist. Dr. B agreed that Mrs. S seemed depressed, and she restarted her on an antidepressant that had previously helped. Despite some improvement in her mood, Mrs. S continued to demonstrate forgetfulness and frequent bouts of disorientation when driving. She had to call her daughter on several occasions to get assistance in returning home. Twelve months after first noticing these changes, Mrs. S's daughter took her to her physician for a full medical workup, which was unrevealing. Mrs. S was referred to a memory clinic, where the evaluation suggested a probable diagnosis of AD.

Over the course of the next year, the symptoms progressed to the point that Mrs. S could no longer safely drive, and she was increasingly unable to balance her checkbook or manage her house. In the third year of illness, Mrs. S moved into an assisted-living facility where the additional structure and an aide for five hours every day allowed her to maintain some degree of independence.

Over the next two years, however, Mrs. S's memory continued to decline, as did her ability to orient herself in the facility and to recognize staff members. She became dependent on her daughter to manage all her affairs. She also demonstrated paranoid concerns that her aides were trying to steal from her, and on two occasions she barricaded herself in her apartment. Her psychiatrist increased her antidepressant and added an antipsychotic medication to calm her and to treat her paranoid delusions. In the sixth year of her illness, Mrs. S fell in her apartment and broke her hip. She became delirious after the hip replacement, and after some improvement in her mental status, she was admitted to a skilled nursing facility for rehabilitation. Because of her pronounced cognitive impairment and periods of combativeness towards staff, Mrs. S was transferred to a dementia unit at a long-term care facility instead of returning to the assisted-living facility.

By the seventh year of her illness, Mrs. S was able to recognize only her daughter, and she was unable to communicate well because of word-finding difficulty. By the eighth year, she was completely dependent on the staff for hygiene and dressing, although, with prompting, she could still feed herself. Over the course of the year, she fell several times, becoming wheelchair bound. Throughout the ninth year, Mrs. S spent most of her day sitting in her wheelchair or lying in bed, with minimal verbal communication. She no longer recognized her daughter. She began losing weight, and she became malnourished due to a poor appetite and mild dysphagia. In the 10th year, Mrs. S. developed an aspiration pneumonia and stopped eating. After two weeks in a vegetative state, she died.

The course of Mrs. S's illness illustrates the slow and progressive course of AD, which begins with memory dysfunction and evolves over time to involve the loss of multiple cognitive skills; changes in behavior and personality; and the loss of basic bodily functions; the disease ultimately culminates in death.

Definition and Diagnostic Criteria

AD is a cortical dementia characterized by a slow, progressive loss of cognitive function; it typically lasts for 8–12 years (with a range of 5–20 years) and culminates in a vegetative state and then death. The clinical signs of AD typically manifest in later life, although the pathologic features begin much earlier (Sperling et al., 2011). AD has been classified by age at onset (early or late) and by the presence or absence of an inheritance pattern (familial versus sporadic). Early-onset AD, which accounts for only 5%–10% of all cases of AD, presents before the age of 65 years and typically has a relatively rapid course. Late-onset AD, conversely, accounts for the other 90%–95% of cases and has an onset after the age of 65. All of the known cases of familial AD have had an early onset, and they have been traced to specific chromosomal mutations. Sporadic AD tends to have a later age at onset, and it is associated with some degree of genetic susceptibility. Further research may eventually identify patterns of inheritance in sporadic AD, but these patterns will be more difficult to recognize, and they will certainly entail an interaction between genetic and environmental factors. Genetic factors are reviewed in more detail in the section on AD etiology.

Although AD has been described in the literature for over 100 years, it wasn't until 1984 that the first diagnostic criteria were developed by the National Institute of Neurological and Communicative Disorders and Stroke (NINDS) and the Alzheimer's Disease and Related Disorders Association (ADRDA, also known as the Alzheimer's Association), commonly referred to as the NINDS-ADRDA criteria (McKhann et al., 1984). NINDS-ADRDA criteria and the *Diagnostic and Statistical Manual of Mental Disorders*, Fourth Edition, Text Revision (DSM-IV-TR) criteria were, until recently, the most commonly used (American Psychiatric Association, 2000). The critical aspect of AD present in both sets of criteria is the progressive and global nature of cognitive impairment. NINDS-ADRDA criteria also account for the probability of the diagnosis. As described in Chapter 1, the revised criteria for dementia in the *Diagnostic and Statistical Manual of Mental Disorders*, Fifth Edition (DSM-5) change "dementia" to "major neurocognitive disorder" and include AD as a subtype of this general term (American Psychiatric Association, 2013).

The most recent revision of the diagnostic criteria for AD was developed by the National Institute of Aging and the Alzheimer's Association (NIA-AA criteria). These organizations recognized the importance of progressive pathological changes underlying AD years before clinical presentation and thus established three stages: (1) preclinical AD (mainly a research construct); (2) mild cognitive impairment (MCI) due to AD; and (3) probable dementia due to AD (Albert et al., 2011; McKhann et al., 2011; Sperling et al., 2011). These stages are detailed in Table 4.1.

Table 4.1 The Stages of Alzheimer's Disease

Phase	Features
Preclinical AD	• Stage 1: asymptomatic but positive biomarkers for beta-amyloid in CSF or on amyloid-based PET scan • Stage 2: asymptomatic, positive biomarkers, and evidence of neuronal injury on MRI or on an FDG-based PET scan • Stage 3: positive biomarkers, evidence of neuronal injury, and evidence of subtle cognitive change
Mild cognitive impairment due to AD	• Meets criteria for MCI (see Chapter 3) • MCI due to AD (intermediate likelihood): positive biomarkers for beta-amyloid in CSF or on amyloid-based PET scan or evidence of neuronal injury on MRI or on an FDG-based PET scan • MCI due to AD (high likelihood): positive biomarkers and evidence of neuronal injury
Probable AD dementia	• Meets criteria for dementia (see Chapter 1) with (1) insidious onset over months to years; (2) clear history of worsening cognition based on report or observation; (3) impairment in learning and short-term recall (amnestic presentation) most common with impairment in language, visuospatial abilities, and executive function also present (and sometimes most prominent in nonamnestic presentations); and (4) no clear evidence of significant cerebrovascular disease or other likely causes of cognitive impairment • Possible AD: clinical evidence of AD but no biomarker evidence or atypical presentation or clinical symptoms of a non-AD dementia but positive biomarker evidence of AD • Probable AD: clinical presentation of AD with evidence of either biomarkers or neuronal injury (intermediate likelihood) or both (high likelihood) • Unlikely AD: dementia but without AD clinical presentation and/or there is evidence of an alternate form of dementia and/or negative biomarker evidence

PET = positron emission tomography; FDG = fluorodeoxyglucose; CSF = cerebrospinal fluid.

Course

AD typically begins with subtle changes in memory and orientation, including frequent forgetfulness, difficulty with complex daily tasks (e.g., balancing a checkbook, planning events or projects), challenges with word-finding, and lapses in the recognition of persons or places. This early stage may last several years, and it can be indistinguishable at times from the more mild states of cognitive impairment due to medication side effects; medical or psychiatric illness; or syndromes such as age-associated memory impairment or mild cognitive impairment (see Chapter 3). As AD progresses, the cognitive deficits worsen, becoming more global, and the incidences of comorbid psychiatric disturbances, such as anxiety, depression, apathy, agitation, and psychosis, increase. Individual function declines to the point where independent living becomes too hazardous, and individuals must rely on caregivers and structured living arrangements.

By 8–10 years into the illness, the early disturbances in memory, language (aphasia), motor abilities (apraxia), and recognition (agnosia) progress to severe states, rendering an individual totally dependent. In the terminal phase of AD, the afflicted individuals are usually incoherent or completely mute; they are unable to recognize their surroundings and close family members; and, ultimately, they are incapable of walking, feeding themselves, or participating in simple activities. The behavioral problems may begin to taper off, but those are overridden by a collapse of function and an increasing incidence of poor feeding, malnutrition, injuries from falls and unsafe behaviors, and pressure sores caused by inactivity. Death does not result from the pathologic effects of AD itself but rather from associated infection, dehydration, injury, or illness.

Etiology

With aging, every brain shows the same pathologic changes as those that cripple the brains of individuals with AD—the loss of neurons with subsequent shrinking or atrophy of brain tissue, widened ventricles, and pathologic collections of cellular debris known as neuritic plaques and neurofibrillary tangles. One age-related cause for this neuronal damage in both normal and AD brains may be oxidative stress, in which the accumulation of reactive oxygen species called free radicals damages the DNA and other cellular components. In AD, however, a dramatic acceleration and augmentation of this process occurs, producing the characteristic clinical symptoms as brain structure and function slowly and steadily erode.

Amyloid and Tau

Most scientists now believe that the story of AD begins with the buildup of an abnormal form of amyloid protein in the brain (Querfurth & LaFerla, 2010). This amyloid originates from part of a larger protein called the amyloid precursor protein (APP), which is normally found in the cell membranes of neurons throughout the brain. The exact role of APP has not yet been determined, although it appears to be involved in the formation and repair of synapses (Priller et al., 2006). APP is normally metabolized by a protease enzyme called alpha-secretase. In AD, however, the metabolism of APP is altered by two other enzymes, beta-secretase and gamma-secretase (also referred to as beta-site or gamma-site APP cleaving enzyme or BACE and GACE, respectively), which cleave APP, producing a protein fragment of 40 or 42 amino acids. This abnormal form of amyloid is referred to as *beta-amyloid* (denoted hereafter in the text as Aβ). The 40–amino acid variant (Aβ40) is more common, but the 42–amino acid variant (Aβ42) appears more pathologic, especially in early-stage AD. Once Aβ is formed, however, it self-aggregates into soluble oligomers consisting of two to six peptides (which may further group together) or into fibrils, which have a tendency to accumulate into insoluble beta-pleated sheets. These various forms of Aβ build up in the brain in the spaces between neurons and in small blood vessels (Walsh & Selkoe, 2007).

Both soluble and insoluble Aβ deposits are problematic in two ways. First, they are neurotoxic, leading to the death of surrounding neurons. Second, the Aβ deposits act as foreign bodies in the brain, inducing an inflammatory response that causes further neuronal damage and death. Activated leukocytes and microglial cells begin to release chemical mediators of inflammation, in turn activating the surrounding astrocyte cells. The pathologic result is a lesion or plaque—the infamous senile or neuritic plaque—consisting of a dense core of amyloid protein sheets surrounded by damaged and dead axons, dendrites, and glial cells (microglia and astrocytes). The *amyloid hypothesis* holds that this entire process is the primary trigger for the development of AD (Querfurth & LaFerla, 2010).

At the same time that plaques are forming, a parallel process inside the neuronal cell bodies is wreaking havoc by destroying the cell's main support structure (or cytoskeleton) and the transport system, which is composed of microtubules. A protein called tau, which stabilizes the microtubule architecture, becomes hyperphosphorylated, causing strands of it to wind around each other in what are called paired helical filaments. These filaments are unable to stabilize the microtubule system; instead, they begin to aggregate into clumps referred to as neurofibrillary tangles. Deprived of its inner structural support and system of intracellular communication, the cell body is no longer able to function normally.

As the plaques and tangles proliferate, a progressive loss of neurons and their supporting glial cells occurs, such that a gross examination of the AD brain reveals marked cortical atrophy with widened sulci and ventricles. In what is called the "trigger and bullet" hypothesis, this process is believed to result initially from Aβ buildup and then from tau hyperphosphorylation. In this model, the slow propagation of Aβ oligomers (the "trigger") induces the activation of three protein kinases that hyperphosphorylate tau (the "bullet"), which eventually leads the neurons to aberrantly enter the cell cycle, leading to slow death (Rapoport, Dawson, Binder, Vitek, & Ferreira, 2002; Varvel et al., 2008).

Research suggests that either intracellular hyperphosphorylated tau spreads cell-to-cell to induce pathology in the next cell or pathology in one cell induces pathology in neighboring cells without movement of tau from one to the next. In a transgenic mouse model followed over 22 months, abnormal tau spread along a linked anatomic pathway (Liu et al., 2012). On a larger level, close inspection of the brain tissue indicates that the following key brain regions are affected successively during the course of AD: the entorhinal cortex, the hippocampus, and the basal forebrain, and, eventually, general cortical regions. Both the entorhinal cortex and the hippocampus, which are located adjacent to one another in the temporal lobes, are critical to memory formation. Functional scanning has found that deterioration in these structures is an early indicator of AD.

STAGE I
Amyloid Precursor Protein (APP) is cleaved by β-Secretase and then
γ –Secretase into Aβ fragments and then the toxic Aβ42

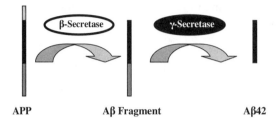

APP   Aβ Fragment   Aβ42

STAGE II
Aggregation of Aβ42 into oligomers, β-pleated sheets, and larger fibrils which
form the insoluble core of neuritic plaques

Aβ42   Aβ42 oligomers and fibrils   Neuritic plaque core

STAGE III
Inflammatory response with formation of neuritic plaques and subsequent
destruction of neurons

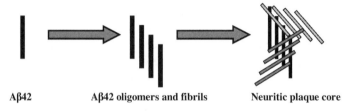

Activation of microglial cells   Neuritic plaques composed of insoluble
   and inflammatory response   Aβ42, microglial cells, dead and dying
                                        neurons and neuronal fragments

Figure 4.1 The Aβ pathway

The loss of neurons in these structures probably accounts for the early symptoms of
short-term memory impairment in AD. The abnormal Aβ and tau pathways are illustrated in Figures 4.1 and 4.2.

Other Pathological Processes

Early on in the disease course there is also progressive cerebral hypometabolism that
correlates with cognitive impairment, particularly in the cingulate gyrus and posterior
parietotemporal and prefrontal cortices (Bateman et al., 2012; Reiman et al., 2004). This

Tau is a soluble protein in axons that stabilizes and promotes microtubule assembly and transport.

STAGE I
Tau protein becomes hyperphosphorylated by kinase enzymes

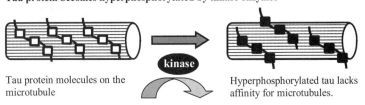

Tau protein molecules on the microtubule

Hyperphosphorylated tau lacks affinity for microtubules.

STAGE II
Hyperphosphorylated tau detaches from microtubules, which become destabilized and are no longer able to provide normal axonal transport and cell structural integrity. The detached tau proteins form paired helical filaments.

Tau protein molecules detach from the now destabilized microtubule

Detached hyperphosphorylated tau self-aggregates into paired helical filaments

STAGE III
Neurofibrillary tangles in the neurons are composed of insoluble aggregates of paired helical filaments of hyperphosphorylated tau protein

Neuronal body and axon

Neurofibrillary tangles clog the cytoplasm of the neuron and are cytotoxic, leading to loss of metabolic and structural integrity

Figure 4.2 The tau pathway

may be related to increased neuronal resistance to insulin signaling, which reduces glucose utilization and makes the cells less energy efficient (Messier & Teutenberg, 2005). Additional forces associated with brain damage in AD include synaptic loss, depletion of neurotrophins such as brain-derived neurotrophic factor or BDNF (Connor et al., 1997), mitochondrial dysfunction (Hauptmann et al., 2006), increased oxidative stress (Gibson & Huang, 2005), and inflammation mediated by microglial cells and astrocytes (Aisen, 2002). Neuronal damage in AD is also believed to result from excess release of glutamate—a key neurotransmitter for memory formation—into synapses, triggered in part by Aβ. This process causes neuronal damage through excessive calcium influx into the cells, as well as by increasing both Aβ production and tau hyperphosphorylation (Areosa, Sherriff, & McShane, 2005).

The basal forebrain, particularly the nucleus basalis of Meynert, contains numerous cell bodies that produce and transmit messages throughout the brain via the neurotransmitter acetylcholine. The cholinergic hypothesis suggests that the resultant deficiency in acetylcholine, and hence in cholinergic function, is responsible for the clinical symptoms of AD (Terry & Buccafusco, 2003). One experimental model supporting this hypothesis has demonstrated that the intravenous administration of anticholinergic drugs (e.g., scopolamine) can induce impairments in memory and cognitive function that are similar to the symptoms of AD. Other research has linked anticholinergic load in the body with an increased risk of delirium (Flacker et al., 1998).

As the disease progresses, the neuronal loss becomes more pronounced in the temporal, parietal, occipital, and frontal cortices. These changes account for the cardinal features of the disease—aphasia, apraxia, agnosia, and executive dysfunction. In addition, damage to the brain regions that regulate behavior, emotional expression, and neurovegetative function (e.g., sleeping, eating, motivation), including the amygdala, locus ceruleus, and raphe nucleus, occurs. The latter two nuclei regulate the synthesis and the release of the neurotransmitters norepinephrine and serotonin, respectively. Abnormal alterations in one or both chemicals in the brain may account for the high prevalence of depression and behavioral problems in AD.

Risk Factors

Numerous risk factors for AD exist, many of which can be tied into the pathologic scheme just described. General risk factors are summarized in Table 4.2. Given that prevalence rates double every five years after age 65 so that 40%–50% of the community older than 85 years is afflicted with AD, advanced age is the most dramatic risk factor for AD. Postmenopausal women appear to have a greater risk of developing AD, even after taking into account the fact that they live longer than men. This difference is most notable after the age of 85 (Fratiglioni et al., 2000). In terms of both race and ethnicity, there is no clear group that appears inherently more at risk for AD, since rates are remarkably stable across groups and countries (Manly & Mayeux, 2004). The fact that some studies have shown higher rates of AD in the United States in Blacks compared to non-Hispanic whites and Hispanics prior to age 75, and then in Hispanics after the age of 75, is likely attributable to the rates of the many other risk factors listed in this section (Gurland et al., 1999).

Brain-Related Risk Factors

Some research has suggested that individuals with smaller head circumferences and brain size, lower intelligence, and less formal education earlier in life have an increased risk for AD, especially when seen in combination with the apolipoprotein E or *APOE* ε4 allele. On the flipside, individuals with larger head circumferences and brain size, greater intelligence, and higher education early in life may have a reduced risk or delayed onset of AD, possibly because these factors confer upon them a greater, protective cognitive

Table 4.2 General Risk Factors for Alzheimer's Disease

Risk Factor	Findings That Affect the Risk of AD
Demographic factors	• Increasing age is the most significant risk factor for AD • Postmenopausal women have greater risk than men
Brain-related risk factors	AD risk may be *increased* by the following: • Smaller head circumference/brain volume • Lower intelligence • Fewer years of education, especially early in life • Traumatic brain injury
Medical and psychiatric risk factors	AD risk may be *increased* by the following: • Diabetes mellitus • Hypertension • Cerebro- and cardiovascular disease • Atrial fibrillation • Stroke • Hypercholesterolemia • Obesity • Elevated homocysteine levels • Chronic stress • Chronic depression
Lifestyle risk factors	AD risk may be *decreased* by the following: • Regular exercise • Mental stimulation • Active social relationships
Dietary risk factors	AD risk may be *decreased* by the following: • Low-fat, low-calorie diet • Omega-3 fatty acids/DHA • Regular fish consumption • Light to moderate use of alcohol • Intake of folate; Vitamins B12, C, and E; and niacin and antioxidants • Regular servings of fruits and vegetables • Mediterranean diet
Genetic risk factors	See Table 4.3

reserve (Mortimer, Snowdon, & Markesbery, 2003). Traumatic brain injury, even earlier in life, may increase the risk of AD by two to four times, depending on the severity of the injury (Mayeux, 2003). The belief is that brain injury may trigger the production of Aβ. In fact, several studies have found increased Aβ in the areas of previous cerebral trauma (Blennow, Hardy, & Zetterberg, 2012).

Medical and Psychiatric Risk Factors

Individuals suffering from a number of medical illnesses, including diabetes mellitus (DM), hypertension, obesity, cerebro- and cardiovascular disease, stroke, and hypercholesterolemia, have elevated rates of AD (Profenno, Porsteinsson, & Faraone, 2010; Reitz,

Brayne, & Mayeux, 2011). Elevated levels of both cholesterol and homocysteine confer an increased risk of AD, perhaps by increasing production of Aβ (Burns & Duff, 2002). Increased rates of AD have also been associated with chronic stress and depression, perhaps because these conditions are associated with persistently elevated levels of cortisol that can be toxic to neurons in the hippocampus (Köhler, van Boxtel, Jolles, & Verhey, 2011).

Lifestyle Risk Factors

An active lifestyle with physical exercise, such as engaging in brisk walking at least three times a week, may reduce the risk of AD (Ahlskog, Geda, Graff-Radford, & Petersen, 2011). One explanation may be that exercise reduces the risk of or blunts the effects of medical conditions such as obesity, hypertension, diabetes mellitus, hypercholesterolemia, and cerebro- and cardiovascular disease, all of which increase the risk of AD. Physical exercise may also increase the release of neural growth factors such as BDNF (Swardfager et al., 2011). Active social and mental stimulation has also been found to reduce the risk of AD, perhaps by increasing brain activity and the development of a greater cognitive reserve. It may be that a more active lifestyle helps to reduce both stress and depression, both of which can increase AD risk (Wang, Karp, Winblad, & Fratiglioni, 2002).

The use of tobacco products may confer variable risk; on the one hand, nicotine use has been found in some studies to actually reduce the risk of AD (given its positive effects on cholinergic function). On the other hand, smoking increases the risk of atherosclerosis, which in turn increases the risk of AD (Cataldo, Prochaska, & Glantz, 2010). On the balance, the health risks of tobacco use certainly outweigh any potential benefits in terms of AD risk reduction.

Dietary Risk Factors

There is some evidence that the following dietary factors may reduce the risk of AD: a lower fat and lower calorie diet, regular portions of fruits and vegetable (e.g., citrus, berries, broccoli, carrots, tomatoes), a source of omega-3 fatty acids such as docosahexaenoic acid (DHA) as found in fish oils and some nuts, and antioxidants such as Vitamins B12, C, and E, folate, and niacin, (Luchsinger, Tang, Shea, & Mayeux, 2003; Schaefer et al., 2006). Other research has not found clear benefits from antioxidants (Laurin et al., 2004). A Mediterranean diet incorporates many of these factors and has been found to potentially reduce the risk of AD (Scarmeas et al., 2006). Light to moderate alcohol intake, such as one glass of wine or one bottle of beer a day, may be protective in some individuals (Anstey, Mack, & Cherbuin, 2009).

Genetic Risk Factors

Genetic risk factors constitute some of the most widely studied aspects of AD, and these have proven to be the most informative in the search for a cause. First-degree relatives of individuals with AD have about twice the lifetime risk of late-onset AD (Green et al.,

2002). The risk is greatest if a sibling is affected, and it increases with the number of affected relatives. Identical (or monozygotic) twins have a 60%–80% concordance rate for late-onset AD (Gatz et al., 2006).

Early-onset AD, which includes all familial subtypes and represents 5%–10% of all cases of AD, has been traced to genetic mutations on chromosomes 1, 14, and 21, all of which are associated with the increased production of Aβ. The mode of inheritance in all three cases is autosomal dominant, meaning that a person needs only one copy of the gene from a parent to be affected (Reitz et al., 2011). Scientists have proposed that the presenilin 1 gene on chromosome 14 and the presenilin 2 gene on chromosome 1 may actually code for γ-secretase, one of the key enzymes responsible for creating Aβ in the first place (β-secretase may be coded for on chromosome 11).

Approximately 40% of early onset cases are linked to chromosome 14, whereas those cases linked to chromosome 1 are encountered in a small group of families whose members are the descendants of German immigrants from the Volga River Valley to the United States (Bertram & Tanzi, 2008). The other early onset genetic mutation has been traced to a gene on chromosome 21 that may code for APP. This may well explain why individuals with Down syndrome who have three copies of chromosome 21 (trisomy 21) face the inevitable development of AD pathology (although not necessarily its clinical symptoms) by their 40s (Menéndez, 2005).

Late-onset AD or LOAD, which encompasses the sporadic forms of the disease, has a more complex genetic picture than does early onset AD. Instead of being associated with specific genetic mutations that may cause the disease, LOAD is associated with a number of genetic factors that influence the susceptibility for developing the disease. The most important factor is the apolipoprotein E or *APOE* gene variants on chromosome 19. *APOE* is involved in the lipid metabolism that assists in myelination and neuronal membrane repair. It is found in both neurons and glial cells and in increased amounts in neuritic plaques (Reitz et al., 2011). The isoforms of *APOE* are encoded by three alleles, labeled ε2, ε3, and ε4; ε2 and ε3 may actually be protective against AD. The ε3/ε3 combination is the most common genotype, seen in 60% of the population (Corder et al., 1993).

The *APOE* ε4 allele confers a much higher risk of the disease, with a younger age at onset and a worse course (Raber, Huang, & Ashford, 2004). Overall, 50% of late-onset cases of AD have the ε4 allele; having one copy (heterozygote) increases the risk of developing AD by 2–3 times, whereas having two copies (homozygote) increases risk by 5–15 times, depending on age. By the age of 80, 90% of *APOE* ε4 homozygotes will have developed AD, compared with nearly 50% of *APOE* ε4 heterozygotes and 20% of individuals without an *APOE* ε4 allele (Corder et al., 1993). However, even having both *APOE* ε4 alleles does not guarantee that the individual will develop AD, a clear indication that other factors are involved.

Other genetic susceptibility factors for LOAD have been found on chromosomes 10, 11, and 12. These are listed in Table 4.3 and include the recently identified *SORL1* gene on chromosome 11, which may govern the distribution of APP inside neurons and has been associated with a tripling of the risk of LOAD in several select populations (Rogaeva et al., 2007). Despite extensive research, none of these factors has accumulated the amount of empirical support found with the *APOE* ε4 gene (Reitz et al., 2011).

Table 4.3 Genetic Risk Factors for Alzheimer Disease

Chromosome	Gene	Effects
Early Onset AD (5%–10% of All Cases)		
1	Presenilin 2	Increases Aβ by coding for γ-secretase
14	Presenilin 1	Increases Aβ by coding for γ-secretase
12	APP	Increases APP and Aβ production
Late Onset AD (90%–95% of All Cases)		
19	APOE	Apolipoprotein ε4 allele increases AD risk; ε2 and ε3 decreases risk
10	VR22	α–T catenin gene increases risk
10	PLAU	Plasminogen activator, urokinase gene increases risk
10	IDE	Insulin-degrading enzyme gene increases risk
10	DNMBP	Dynamin-binding protein gene may increase risk
10	SORL1	Sortilin-related receptor gene increases risk times three
11	GAPD	Glyceraldehydes-3-phosphate dehydrogenase gene increases risk
12	A2M	α–2–macroglobulin gene increases risk
Family History of AD		
Unclear	Unclear	Risk increases 3.5 times if a parent or sibling had AD

Assessment

Even without knowing anything about a given patient with dementia, clinicians do know through epidemiologic studies that 60%–70% of all cases involve AD. At present, however, the only way to make a diagnosis of AD with 100% certainty is to examine brain tissue for the presence of plaques and tangles. Obviously, this is not a realistic approach in the majority of patients. The diagnosis of AD, however, is by no means guesswork, and making a solid diagnosis with 90%–95% accuracy is possible. The growing development of AD biomarkers is helping to increase this certainty even more. The diagnostic workup for AD involves all the components outlined in Chapters 1 and 2; in this chapter, the focus is on several specific findings that help to distinguish AD from other types of dementia.

Clinical Tip

Patients and caregivers often, and not surprisingly, want as much diagnostic certainty as possible. You will be asked frequently, "Does he or she have Alzheimer's disease?" Although providing a clear answer to a family's question is important, do not rush to judgment. Many individuals may appear to have AD, but observation over time does not support the diagnosis. You do not want to provide a diagnosis with such a bleak course without having all of the available information. Conversely, do not cover up the possibility of AD and give false hope to patients and families. However, until a diagnosis for AD can be made with 100% certainty, you will always be in the position of having to make an educated guess. For more information on imparting diagnoses to both patients and caregivers, see Chapters 11 and 12.

History and Examination

The evolving history of cognitive changes is the first diagnostic clue; a slowly progressive decline in cognitive function, starting with memory impairment and increasingly involving aphasia, apraxia, agnosia, and executive dysfunction, almost always points to AD. If there is only focal impairment that persists over time, or noticeable improvement is observed, then the case is almost certainly not AD. The diagnosis can be more difficult when symptoms consistent with AD overlap with vascular risk factors; a history of stroke; or other diseases known to cause cognitive impairment, such as Parkinson's disease. Sometimes, early AD is associated with pronounced personality change, behavioral disturbances, depression, or psychosis.

Researchers have identified several variants of AD, confirming the fact that it is a heterogeneous disorder in terms of both pathology and clinical presentation. Whereas typical AD involves corticolimbic pathology and global cognitive decline, AD variants include hippocampal sparing with cortical dominant pathology, limbic predominant pathology, and posterior cortical atrophy (Murray et al., 2011). These variants have been associated with differences in age at onset, gender distribution, and the presence of atypical pathological features such as vascular lesions or Lewy bodies. For example, hippocampal-sparing AD has a lower age at onset, a lower percentage of female sufferers, and a lower percentage of both vascular features and Lewy bodies compared to typical and limbic predominant forms of AD (Murray et al., 2011).

Neuroimaging

Neuroimaging is used in the workup here to both identify common findings in AD as well as to rule out causative factors for other forms of dementia. In AD, structural computed tomography (CT) and magnetic resonance imaging (MRI) scans of the brain typically reveal progressive cerebral atrophy that is especially prominent in the hippocampus and entorhinal cortex. For this reason, the diagnostic scan should try to highlight and enlarge the hippocampus to determine the degree of atrophy (Mungas et al., 2005). It is also common in AD to see MRI evidence of vascular damage in the form of small lacunar infarcts and white matter hyperintensities. A mixed form of dementia (e.g., AD plus vascular dementia) would be diagnosed when there are multiple or larger lesions, especially in strategic locations in the brain, or other findings such as disproportionately dilated ventricles or tumors.

Imaging of AD patients using positron emission tomography (PET) has demonstrated consistent patterns of symmetric hypometabolism in the posterior cingulate and parietotemporal regions of the brain (Small et al., 2008). As noted earlier, reductions in cerebral glucose metabolism are characteristic of AD and can be visualized on PET scans using the tracer 18^F-fluorodeoxyglucose (18^F-FDG). Functional MRI scans can also show reductions in brain metabolism characteristic of AD (Sperling, 2011).

A newer diagnostic approach is to use PET tracers that bind to beta-amyloid plaques in the brain to reveal the relative pathologic load. Early developed compounds include Pittsburgh Compound B or PIB and 18^F-FDDNP (Morris et al., 2009). Newer compounds include florbetapir, flutemetamol, and florbetaben, all of which utilize the isotope fluorine 18 with a half-life of 100 minutes—compared to PIB, which uses carbon

11 with a half-life of only 20 minutes (Vallabhajosula, 2011). Florbetapir and flute-metamol are currently on the market and can be used in individuals with known or suspected AD to confirm the presence of beta-amyloid plaques (Wood et al., 2010).

Clinical Tip

Amyloid-based PET imaging promises to bring greater diagnostic direction. These scans are indicated for individuals who already have cognitive impairment or suspected AD, not for the concerned but cognitively normal individual. A positive scan indicates the presence of moderate to frequent amyloid neuritic plaques, as are present in patients with AD and other conditions (Clark et al., 2011). If someone presents with a clinical picture consistent with AD, a positive scan thus increases the likelihood that AD is the correct diagnosis. Keep in mind, however, that at least 20% of cognitively normal older adults have significant amyloid plaque (Aizenstein et al., 2008). A negative scan indicates sparse to no neuritic plaques and is inconsistent with a pathological diagnosis of AD; it should prompt more in-depth consideration of an alternate form of dementia. It is important to review this information with patients and caregivers and to be measured and accurate when presenting results. Education and counseling provided both before and after the scan must emphasize that regardless of the results, you are there to help them understand their symptoms and seek both answers and potential solutions. Evaluation of cognitive changes must be a process and not an event, guided all along by the clinical relationship you establish with patient and caregiver.

Biomarkers

A biomarker represents an anatomic or functional product of AD that can be sampled or measured to make a diagnosis. An ideal biomarker would have to be accurate, reliable, easily obtainable, and inexpensive. It would also have to improve the clinician's ability to identify individuals who actually have AD (sensitivity) and to distinguish AD from other diseases (specificity) over the current practice. Clinical diagnoses currently have a sensitivity between 85% and 90%, but biomarkers promise to provide a quicker, if not more certain, diagnosis. Many such tests have appeared and then receded over time because they did not meet the goals of the ideal biomarker.

The current focus is on using biomarkers that identify and track the presence of Aβ and hyperphosphorylated tau protein in the brain, along with corresponding neurodegeneration. Five important biomarkers are described in Table 4.4. These biomarkers are integrated into the new staging system for AD described at the beginning of the chapter. Changes in each of these biomarkers have been found to correspond to worsening clinical symptoms (Jack et al., 2010).

Table 4.4 Biomarkers for AD

Biomarker	Findings
Aβ in CSF	Decreased levels in CSF
Aβ in amyloid PET scan	Increased staining visible in scan
Tau in CSF	Increased levels in CSF
Cerebral glucose uptake on FDG-PET	Decreased glucose uptake, especially in bilateral posterior cingulate and parietotemporal regions
Brain structure on MRI	Atrophy, typically beginning in hippocampus and entorhinal cortex, then becoming more diffuse

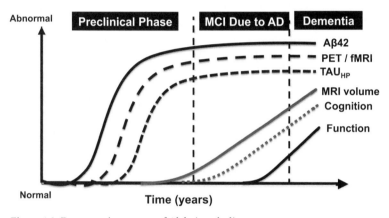

Figure 4.3 Degenerative course of Alzheimer's disease

Aβ42 = beta-amyloid 42 amino-acids; PET = positron emission tomography using fluorodeoxyglucose; MRI = magnetic resonance imaging; fMRI = functional MRI scan of brain; TAU$_{HP}$ = hyposphorylated tau protein. Based on Sperling et al. (2011).

A typical pattern seen in the cerebrospinal fluid (CSF) of patients with AD is a reduced level of Aβ42 (presumably because it is bound up in plaques) and an increase in tau protein. These findings, however, may also be encountered in other neurodegenerative conditions. Researchers now know that the build-up of Aβ and then hyperphosphorylated tau goes on for some time before there is apparent brain hypometabolism or atrophy. A schematic of the pathologic process of AD incorporating biomarkers is illustrated in Figure 4.3 (based on Sperling et al., 2011).

Neuropsychological Testing

Because AD affects the hippocampus early on, the first signs of impairment involve memory encoding. As a result, the most sensitive neuropsychological tests are usually those of verbal learning with delayed recall. In comparison, tests of digit span will usually be normal in early stages because immediate or working memory remains intact longer.

Tests of executive function and verbal fluency are impaired in the early to middle stages of AD, and the deficits in verbal fluency progress to more advanced degrees of aphasia throughout the course of the illness. In the middle to late stages of AD, neuropsychological testing reveals a profile of global cognitive impairment across a broad spectrum of individual tests (Koss, Attix, & Story, 2011).

Genetic Testing

Ideally, the purpose of genetic testing for AD is to detect the disease or to determine the relative chance of getting the disease before any symptoms appear. For an individual with early-onset AD before the age of 50 (fewer than 1% of all cases of AD), the most likely genetic cause would be a mutation on the presenilin 1 gene on chromosome 14 (Bertram & Tanzi, 2008). However, many possible mutations could occur on the gene, so a given genetic sequence may prove meaningless if it does not match the known abnormal sequences. For early-onset AD between the ages of 50 and 60, which represents fewer than 5% of all cases, genetic testing would have to completely sequence the genes for presenilins 1 and 2 on chromosomes 14 and 1, respectively, and for APP on chromosome 21 in the search for specific mutations. This testing would be expensive, and the yield would not be certain. Besides, most families with early-onset AD, especially of the autosomal dominant type, already know about their increased genetic risk.

For late-onset AD, the only available genetic testing is for the *APOE* ε4 allele. Although such information may improve diagnostic certainty for individuals with dementia, the existing test will not increase the confidence of the diagnosis being AD by more than 5%–10%. The combination of the history, examination, biomarkers, and neuropsychological testing may already be sufficient to make the diagnosis.

Clinical Tip

Although the cost of *APOE* testing has decreased considerably in recent years (and it is routine in AD clinical trials), it is not a recommended part of most diagnostic workups and is certainly not recommended for asymptomatic individuals who are worried about getting AD. Knowledge that a cognitively normal person is either hetero- or homozygous for the *APOE* ε4 allele is only indicative of an increased risk but brings no certainty of current or future diagnosis. It will have predictive value for clinical response to the medical food product caprylidene since *APOE* ε4+ individuals do not show improvement (Henderson et al., 2009). One downside to testing is that a positive result could unnecessarily increase the anxiety of those individuals who are concerned about getting AD, even though their chances are only slightly elevated. Plus, for asymptomatic individuals who test positive, there is no preventative treatment and little that they can do to reduce their risk other than adopting a brain-healthy lifestyle (see, in the previous chapter, Table 3.1).

Electroencephalography

Electroencephalography (EEG) is not commonly used to make a diagnosis of AD, but it may be recommended when delirium is strongly suspected in the differential diagnosis. Characteristic findings in AD include slower background alpha activity (8 Hz) that continues to slow and then disorganizes as the disease progresses. The increased presence of theta and delta activity is also observed (Drazkowski, 2008).

Treatment

Although AD remains an incurable disorder, it is not untreatable. Ideally, clinicians would like to prevent the disease from developing in the first place; the advent of biomarkers will enable better identification of individuals in the preclinical stage before symptoms appear, or in the very least when the symptoms are still quite mild. However, some individuals with a higher risk of AD can be identified, and there are a number of lifestyle and dietary factors that can reduce their risk (see Table 3.1 [in the previous chapter] and Table 4.2). There are many dietary supplements and other substances that have been proposed (and are being sold) to supposedly reduce the risk of AD, but there is little evidence that any of these make meaningful differences. Once clinical symptoms present, however, treatment approaches are more limited. There are several available United States Food and Drug Administration (FDA)–approved medications, including acetylcholinesterase inhibitors and the glutamate-receptor antagonist memantine, that can stabilize and/or improve the symptoms of AD. In addition, there are numerous treatments being studied to actually slow down the disease course, although without conclusive evidence to date, and none of these are yet available on the market. Still, there is reason for hope, based on preliminary research data.

Enhancing Cholinergic Function

As noted, the cholinergic hypothesis posits that a deficiency of acetylcholine (ACh) in the brain is primarily responsible for the cognitive impairment seen in AD. One approach to improving cognitive deficits in AD, then, is to increase levels of ACh in the brain. Increasing ACh by direct administration of physostigmine or by oral ingestion of acetycholine precursors such as lecithin (phosphatidylcholine) or l-acetyl-carnitine have not shown consistent benefit. The only strategy that has proven both efficacious and practical has been the use of acetylcholinesterase (AChE) inhibitors.

AChE inhibitors do not cure AD, but a wealth of data clearly shows that they can have important beneficial effects on the lives and the overall care of individuals with AD, including the following: (1) improvement and/or stabilization of cognition for 10–12 months, followed by a long-term decrease in the degree of symptomatic decline compared with placebo; (2) improvement and/or stabilization in function and behavior; (3) decreased caregiver stress and burden; and (4) overall cost savings, including delayed nursing home placement.

The three FDA-approved AChE inhibitors currently on the market include donepezil (indicated for mild, moderate, and severe AD; Rogers et al., 1998), rivastigmine

Table 4.5 FDA-Approved Medications for Alzheimer's Disease

Drug	Indications	Preparations	Dosing
Donepezil (Aricept, Aricept ODT)	Mild, moderate, and severe AD	• Tablets: 5 mg, 10 mg, 23 mg • Orally dissolving tablets: 5 mg, 10 mg • Oral solution	• Start at 5 mg QD or QHS • Increase to 10 mg after four weeks • After three months consider 23 mg dose
Rivastigmine (Exelon, Exelon Patch)	Mild, moderate, and severe AD Mild to moderate Parkinson's disease dementia	• Capsules: 1.5 mg, 3 mg, 4.5 mg, 6 mg • Oral solution • Transdermal patch: 4.6 mg, 9.5 mg, 13.3 mg	Capsules/Oral solution • Start at 1.5 mg BID with meals • Increase by 1.5 to 3 mg every three to four weeks to a range of 3 to 6 mg BID • Maximum daily dose: 12 mg Transdermal patch • Start at 4.6 mg/24 hours for 4 weeks, then increase to 9.5 mg/24 hours; after at least one month and if further decline is noted, increase to the 13.3 mg/24 hours
Galantamine (Razadyne extended release [ER], Razadyne immediate release [IR])	Mild to moderate AD	• IR tablets: 4 mg, 8 mg, 12 mg • ER capsules: 8 mg, 16 mg, 24 mg • Oral solution	• ER capsules: start at 8 mg QD with meals; increase to 16 mg QD after four weeks • IR tablets: start at 4 mg BID; increase to 8 mg BID after four weeks • Maximum daily dose: 24 mg for either preparation
Memantine (Namenda and Namenda extended release [XR])	Moderate to severe AD	• Tablets: 5 mg, 10 mg • XR capsules: 7 mg, 14 mg, 21 mg, 28 mg • Oral solution	• Tablets: start at 5 mg QD; increase to 5 mg BID after one week, 5 mg/10 mg after two weeks, and 10 mg BID after three weeks • ER capsules: if already on 10 mg BID, switch to 28 mg XR QD; if not on memantine already, start 7 mg XR QD for 7 days, then 14 mg for 7 days, then 21 mg for 7 days, then 28 mg QD
Caprylidene triglyceride (Axona)	Medical food for mild to moderate AD	• Packets of powder: 10 gm (in starter kit), 40 gm	• Start with 10 gm in 4–8 oz. of water or other liquid or soft food after breakfast or lunch, titrated every other day by 10 gm until 40 gm daily dose reached

QD = once daily; QHS = at bedtime; BID = twice daily.

(indicated for mild, moderate, and severe AD and mild to moderate Parkinson's disease dementia; Corey-Bloom, Anand, & Veach, 1998), and galantamine (indicated for mild to moderate AD; Raskind, Peskind, Wessel, & Yuan, 2000). All three AChE inhibitors are believed to work by increasing the levels of ACh in the brain. Indications and dosing strategies for the three commonly used AChE inhibitors are listed in Table 4.5.

Despite a significant body of data, some studies have called the benefits of AChE inhibitors into question, suggesting that the modest improvement, at best, is not worth the expense and side effects. One review of 22 double-blind, randomized controlled trials of AChE inhibitors versus placebo that appeared in the *British Medical Journal* found methodological flaws and small clinical benefits and suggested that these findings did not warrant a clear recommendation for their use (Kaduszkiewicz, Zimmermann, Beck-Bornholdt, & van den Bussche, 2005). On the other hand, a prospective study of 641 patients with probable AD followed over 20 years found that persistent use of AChE inhibitors and/or memantine was associated with significantly slower rates of decline on the average of one point on the MMSE per year, regardless of disease stage (Rountree et al., 2009).

Clinical Tip

When treating someone with an AChE inhibitor, avoid expectations for a cure or even for a dramatic change in the rate of decline. Such expectations are certain to leave you disappointed, perhaps leading you to withdraw the treatment prematurely. Consider the following analogy: your patient is sitting in a boat with a hole in the bottom, slowly sinking. You do not have a way to plug the hole to stop the water from coming in (i.e., there is no cure), but you can bail out water to keep him or her afloat for a longer period. In essence, this is what you are doing for your patient—keeping his or her cognitive abilities "afloat" longer than if he or she were not on any medication.

Because AChE inhibitors can increase ACh levels in the periphery, the potential side effects include the increased secretion of gastric acid, increased bronchial secretions, vagotonic effects on the heart that can exacerbate bradyarrhythmias, and the potentiation of the effects of succinylcholine in anesthesia. The most common are usually the gastrointestinal-related side effects, including nausea, vomiting, anorexia, and diarrhea (Corey-Bloom et al., 1998; Raskind et al., 2000; Rogers et al., 1998). Slow titration and administration with food can decrease the frequency and severity of these effects. Even when they do occur, the side effects tend to abate after several days as the individual's tolerance builds, or they may be relieved by temporary dose reduction. However, the initiation of treatment should be avoided in an individual with active peptic ulcer disease, unstable bradyarrthmyias, acute pulmonary disease, or congestive heart failure; AChE inhibitor treatment may be appropriate when these medical conditions have been stabilized.

Clinical Tip

Is one AChE inhibitor better than another? Research has not conclusively demonstrated that any one AChE inhibitor is superior to another. No clear basis exists, then, to recommend automatically switching someone from one AChE inhibitor to another to improve symptoms. However, if you do decide to switch for reasons of efficacy, make sure that you have pushed the first agent to the maximal recommended dose. If you still plan to change, a clean switch can be made by stopping the existing agent on Day 1 and starting the new agent at its starting dose on Day 2. If you are switching because of side effects, stop the original agent and allow the side effects to subside before starting the new agent.

Glutamate-Receptor Antagonism

Glutamate is the major excitatory neurotransmitter in the brain, present in approximately 40% of synapses. Along with ACh, glutamate is a particularly important neurotransmitter in neural pathways associated with learning and memory. In AD, however, it has been hypothesized that abnormal glutamate transmission termed *excitotoxicity* serves to both injure and kill neurons via excess cellular calcium influx (Wilcock, 2003). A logical therapeutic approach for AD, then, is to block this excitotoxicity with agents that act at the glutamate or NMDA (N-methyl-D-aspartate) receptor.

Memantine is currently the only FDA-approved glutamate- or NMDA-receptor antagonist for the treatment of AD. Memantine is a noncompetitive antagonist with low to moderate affinity for the NMDA-receptor calcium channel and serves to modulate glutaminergic transmission by blocking excess calcium influx into the neuron, while still allowing normal neurotransmission. Research studies have demonstrated that memantine is efficacious in treating cognitive, functional, and behavioral symptoms in moderately advanced AD sufferers compared to placebo and is well tolerated (Wilcock, 2003).

The most common side effects include sedation, confusion, headache, and constipation. Initial sedation and/or confusion tend to be mild and transient in many patients. There are minimal drug-drug interactions with memantine. Dosing is summarized in Table 4.5. Memantine can be used as monotherapy or can be safely combined with an AChE inhibitor. A 24-week study found significantly better stabilization of cognition and function above baseline in combination therapy with memantine and donepezil compared to donepezil plus placebo (Tariot et al., 2004). One interesting finding was that patients on combination therapy had fewer side effects than those on donepezil alone, particularly gastrointestinal side effects.

> **Clinical Tip**
>
> Standard of care is to combine memantine with an AChE inhibitor. There are no clear guidelines on which agent to start first, although typically an AChE inhibitor is started first in mild to moderate AD with memantine added later, and the reverse in moderate to severe AD. Keep in mind that these two types of agents have different mechanisms of action and so are complimentary.

Once an AChE inhibitor and/or memantine is started, it is reasonable to reassess efficacy after three to six months. In most cases, however, it makes sense to continue administering the cognitive enhancer indefinitely since longitudinal data clearly supports persistent benefits, even when they are difficult to detect clinically. Deciding when to stop one of these agents is difficult, since benefits can persist even into severe states of AD. Although it may be reasonable to consider tapering an individual off of the cognitive enhancing agent in the terminal phase of the illness, keep in mind that there can be precipitous losses of cognition, function, and behavioral control—even in quite advanced stages of AD—that can be difficult to reverse once the agent has been stopped.

Improving Cerebral Metabolism

As noted earlier, a well-recognized aspect of AD is the diminishment in cerebral glucose metabolism, perhaps related to insulin signaling dysfunction. This metabolic change is seen in PET scans of AD brains, even years before the onset of clinical symptoms (Reiman et al., 2004). One proposed way to circumvent this impairment is to provide an alternate source of fuel for neurons in the form of ketones, which provide a natural energy source for the body and brain during states of starvation. Ketogenic diets have also been used for weight loss and seizure control (Freeman, 2009). Caprylic triglyceride or caprylidene is an FDA-regulated medical food intended for the dietary management of AD. A medical food is a product prescribed by a physician with GRAS status ("generally recognized as safe") that has been demonstrated scientifically to help in the dietary management of a particular disease or condition. Carylidene is composed of a proprietary blend of medium-chain triglycerides, which are converted by the liver into ketone bodies; these in turn can cross the blood-brain barrier and boost the neuronal energy supply.

Caprylidene has been shown in a double-blind, randomized, placebo-controlled trial to provide statistically significant improvement in cognition for AD patients with mild to moderate impairment who are negative for the *APOE*-4 allele (Henderson et al., 2009). The main side effects include stomach upset, flatulence, and diarrhea, attributed in part to the load of medium-chain triglycerides entering the small intestine. Caprylidene can be combined with other cognitive enhancing medications since it has a different mechanism of action. Dosing strategies are summarized in Table 4.5.

Clinical Tip

When should you consider adding caprylidene to an individual's cognitive enhancing regimen? Most mild to moderate AD patients will be candidates unless they have baseline milk or soy allergies, or active GI disease. GI side effects often improve with time and can be mitigated to some degree by the following: (1) slowly titrating the caprylidene powder in 10-gram increments over a week; (2) slowly ingesting it over 30 minutes in a liquid or soft food (e.g., juice, nutritional drinks, yogurt, or oatmeal work best); and (3) ingesting it after eating breakfast or lunch (preferably containing some protein and fat), whichever meal is larger.

Anti-Amyloid Strategies

The next phase in the treatment of AD will be to actually target the disease process itself instead of just modulating its symptoms. To this end, numerous treatment strategies are being studied, including the following:

- preventing or interrupting the build-up of the toxic Aβ protein
- ridding the brain of Aβ once it is formed into oligomers, fibrils or plaques
- preventing the destabilization of tau protein or its aggregation into neurofibrillary tangles
- ridding the brain of tau once it has formed into neurofibrillary tangles
- reducing or preventing the neural damage resulting from Aβ or tau proteins.

To date, all of these strategies either remain in clinical trials or have failed to demonstrate efficacy. The key, it appears, is to be able to identify individuals with building pathology long before clinical symptoms have begun to take their toll. This approach depends on the development and refinement of early diagnostic techniques. Anti-amyloid strategies are summarized in Table 4.6.

Inhibiting Secretase Enzymes

Several agents have been developed to decrease the formation of Aβ42 by blocking β- or γ-secretase, the enzymes believed responsible for cleaving APP into Aβ42. The nonselective γ-secretase inhibitor semagacestat not only failed in clinical trials but also worsened symptoms in some subjects, perhaps because it inhibited the important Notch receptor (Imbimbo & Giardina, 2011). Active clinical trials are currently testing several new agents. An alternate approach to inhibiting the action of γ-secretase would be to modify its action sufficiently to lower Aβ42 production. Tarenflurbil is an allosteric modulator of γ-secretase that shifts APP cleavage away from producing the toxic Aβ42 and instead to producing less toxic protein fragments such as Aβ38. It was the first selective Aβ42 lowering agent in clinical trials but failed to show significant benefit for AD patients in a large Phase III trial (Imbimbo & Giardina, 2011).

Table 4.6 Anti-Amyloid Therapies

Mechanism	Agent(s)	Findings/Status
β-secretase inhibitors	LY2886721	In Phase II clinical trial
	E2609	Phase I trial complete
	MK-8931	In Phase II clinical trial
	RG7129	Phase I trial complete
	HPP854	In Phase I clinical trial
γ-secretase inhibitors	Semagacestat (LY450139)	Showed clinical decline in trials
	Avagacestat	Failed to meet outcome measures
	NIC5-15	In Phase II clinical trial
γ-secretase modulator	Tarenflurbil (Flurizan)	Failed to meet outcome measures
Anti-aggregation agents	Tramiprosate (homotaurine)	Failed to meet outcome measures
	Clioquinol (PBT1)	Failed to meet outcome measures
	PBT2	Showed benefit in Phase II trial
Anti-amyloid vaccines	AN-1792	Stopped due to side effects
	ACC-001	In Phase II clinical trials
Anti-amyloid antibodies	IVIg	Failed to meet outcome measures
	Bapineuzumab	Failed to meet outcome measures
	Solanezumab	Shows slowed decline in AD
	Gantenerumab	Ongoing Phase II clinical trials
	Crenezumab	Ongoing Phase II clinical trials
	MABT5102A	Ongoing Phase II clinical trials
	BIIB037	Ongoing Phase II clinical trials

Reducing Amyloid Aggregation

Several agents have been studied that prevent the aggregation of Aβ42 into protein fibrils that form neuritic plaques. Tramiprosate (also known as homotaurine) is a small organic molecule that binds to Aβ and prevents fibrillization, and it may also have anti-inflammatory properties. A 3-month, double-blind, placebo-controlled Phase II trial with a 36-month open label extension of tramiprosate in mild to moderately impaired AD sufferers showed a significant reduction in CSF Aβ42 and a decline in cognitive deterioration, although no clear cognitive improvement on the main outcome measures (Aisen et al., 2007). A larger clinical trial of over 1,000 AD patients also failed to show significant improvement in cognition, although there was a trend toward improvement and less hippocampal volume loss in treated subjects (Aisen et al., 2011). Tramiprosate is no longer in clinical trials but is being sold in Canada and Europe as a therapy for age-associated memory impairment.

Clioquinol (PBT1) and PBT2 are metal protein attenuating compounds that are believed to interfere with Aβ42 aggregation and toxicity by removing extracellular copper and zinc that is coupled to it. Clioquinol has been shown to reduce Aβ deposits in transgenic mice but also to induce myelinopathies in the central nervous system (Zhang et al., 2013). A small Phase II, placebo-controlled trial of clioquinol in 36 AD patients failed to show clinical improvement in cognition, and one patient developed impaired visual acuity and color vision likely due to the medication (Sampson, Jenagaratnam, & McShane, 2012). A similar study of PBT2 indicated that it was well tolerated in mild AD patients and appeared to benefit two tests of executive function, although not a larger outcome measure of cognition (Lannfelt et al., 2008). Additional studies of PBT2 are likely.

Anti-Amyloid Immunotherapy

A treatment strategy for AD being studied in numerous large-scale clinical trials is the use of active and passive immunotherapy to promote clearance of Aβ. Initial optimism began after a vaccine created to treat transgenic mice that develop Aβ42 plaques in their brains was found to not only prevent but also to remove Aβ42 build-up in their brains and restore previous cognitive function. Two clinical trials of the vaccine AN1792 in humans was stopped abruptly in 2002, however, after 6% of the subjects in the second trial developed meningoencephalitis, leading to several deaths.

Despite its premature termination, however, the data revealed that 59% of subjects had an antibody response to Aβ42 in the first trial, and 20% developed high levels of Aβ42 antibodies in the second trial after receiving two of eight planned vaccinations. In addition, antibody responders did better on composite neuropsychological testing and had greater brain volume loss on MRI scans. Later neuropathological studies on a small subset of deceased subjects found decreased cortical Aβ42 loads in antibody responders (Gilman et al., 2005). Long-term follow-up of AN1792 antibody responders showed reduced functional decline (Vellas et al., 2009). ACC-001 is a reformulation of the vaccine currently in clinical trials and has not demonstrated meningoencephalitis to date.

Instead of giving a vaccine containing actual Aβ42, several types of passive immunotherapy are now being studied. One approach involves intravenous infusions of immunoglobulin (IVIg) with high concentrations of human antibodies to Aβ42, while several others involve injections of humanized monoclonal antibodies to Aβ42. Initial data from a six-month clinical trial using IVIg in a small cohort of subjects with AD found that not only were the infusions well tolerated, but they were associated with improvements in cognition and decreasing levels of CSF Aβ42. However, IVIg failed to showed benefit in a more comprehensive trial (Gever, 2013).

There are several monoclonal antibodies in large clinical trials, listed in Table 4.6. Bapineuzumab was the first of this group, but although it showed reductions in CSF levels of Aβ42 and phosphylated tau protein, it failed to demonstrate significant benefit over placebo in individuals with mild to moderate AD (Tayeb, Murray, Price, & Tarazi, 2013). All clinical trials have since been stopped. Solanezumab also failed to showed improvement in cognitive outcome measures in mildly impaired AD patients, but pooled data revealed a slowing of cognitive decline by around 34% (Eli Lilly, 2012). As a result, solanezumab remains in active trials. Both agents have shown a low but clinically relevant incidence of vasogenic edema and cerebral microhemorrhages, believed to be related to the mobilization of Aβ proteins in the brain, particularly in small blood vessels. These occurrences are visualized on MRI scans and typically not associated with clinical symptoms (Tayeb et al., 2013). Vasogenic edema appears to resolve with interruption of treatment and is not usually recurrent when treatment is later resumed. Several other monoclonal antibodies are being studied, listed in Table 4.6. Recently, the FDA has modified its take on these studies, indicating that slowing cognitive decline is a reasonable endpoint in early-stage AD patients as opposed to considering only cognitive improvement (Kozauer & Katz, 2013).

Anti-Tau Therapies

Although the bulk of clinical trials have focused on addressing the role of Aβ in AD, there is also ongoing research into reducing the impact of hyperphosphorylated tau protein or tau_{hp}. These agents, listed in Table 4.7, are aimed at either preventing tau destabilization in the first place or reducing or mitigating its impact once it begins to form neurofibrillary tangles (Desai & Chand, 2009). One approach, for example, involves using lithium to inhibit the kinases (such as glucogen synthase kinase or GSK) that phosphorylate tau. In one study, lithium reduced both the hyperphosphorylation of tau and the aggregation of insoluble tau in the brains of transgenic mice (Noble et al., 2005).

Ongoing clinical trials are investigating methylene blue (methylthionine, or MT) to prevent the aggregation of hyperphosphorylated tau. An initial study suggested that MT could slow cognitive decline in mild to moderate AD (Wischik, Bentham, Wischik, & Seng, 2008; Wischik & Staff, 2009). A stabilized form of MT has been developed and is starting larger clinical trials in mild to moderate AD. A number of other anti-tau strategies are being investigated but without emergent data on efficacy or safety to date. These are all listed in Table 4.7.

Table 4.7 Anti-Tau Strategies

Mechanism	Agents under Investigation
Kinase inhibition	Lithium as inhibitor of glycogen synthase kinase 3 (GSK3)
Tau aggregation inhibition	Heat shock protein 90 (Hsp90) inhibitors Methylene blue (MT; methylthionine) TRx0237 (stabilized, reduced form of MT)
Microtubule stabilization	Paclitaxel AL-108 (divunetide intranasal)
Anti-tau_{hp} antibodies	Phospho-tau derived antibody
Anti-tau vaccine	AADvac1

Other Treatment Strategies

There are many, many other therapies that have been proposed and studied to treat AD, although none of them have generated significant efficacy data. These include anti-oxidant therapy, anti-inflammatory medications, estrogen, statins, and neuroprotective agents. Many of these agents, such as gingko biloba and curcumin, are taken as supplements by patients hoping for clinical benefit. Still, data has either not been forthcoming (as with curcumin) or has failed to show benefit (as with gingko) in AD. Many of these agents are listed in Table 4.8.

There are several other novel treatment approaches for AD that have either failed to show benefit or are currently under study. Several of these have included nerve growth factors and neuroprotectants; neurotransmitter modulators of serotonin, nicotine, histamine, glutamate, and acetylcholine; insulin regulators; neuronal-specific calcium channel blockers; phosphodiesterase inhibitors; anti-androgens; glyconutrients; cannabinoid receptor modulators; and a retinoid receptor agonist—to name just a few. Keep in mind

Table 4.8 Miscellaneous Treatment Strategies for AD

Substance	Comments
Anti-oxidants: Vitamin E (α-tocopherol)	Despite several studies alone and in combination with other medications, Vitamin E has not demonstrated cognitive improvement in AD although high doses might stabilize function. In addition, there was no benefit in reducing the conversion rate of MCI to AD (Petersen et al., 2005).
Curcumin	Curcumin is the principal component of the spice turmeric and is theorized to have antioxidant, antitumor, and anti-inflammatory properties. One study found that curcumin could inhibit the accumulation of beta-amyloid in the brains of transgenic mice (Yang et al., 2005). However, there is no direct evidence indicating a therapeutic role in AD in humans (Begum et al., 2008).
Latrepirdine (Dimebon)	Originally sold as an antihistamine in Russia, latrepridine is believed to be a mitochondrial stabilizer. Initial clinical data showed significant improvement in cognition in AD patients, but a subsequent large multicenter trial failed to show similar efficacy (Doody et al., 2008).
Anti-inflammatory agents: non-steroidal anti-inflammatory drugs (NSAIDS)	Some data indicated a potential AD risk reduction in chronic users of ibuprofen, but there is no prospective data indicating a therapeutic role in AD for that or any other anti-inflammatory agent (Breitner et al., 2011).
Statins	Statins may lower the risk of AD by reducing the risk of comorbid cardio- and cerebrovascular events, as well as by a primary effect on beta-amyloid formation. Several studies have found no benefit in terms of incident AD or cognition over years of follow-up (Arvanitakis et al., 2008; McGuinness et al., 2010).
Estrogen	Although some research indicated a potentially reduced risk of AD, the data is complex and contradictory, indicating no clinical benefit in AD and the potential for increased risk in some women (Henderson, 2013).
Gingko biloba	Extracts of the leaf of the gingko biloba tree may have both antioxidant and anti-inflammatory properties. Gingko biloba 120 mg twice daily versus placebo in $N = 3069$ individuals did not affect the incidence of dementia or AD when followed over approximately six years (DeKosky et al., 2008). Ginkgo biloba has been associated with clotting disturbances and adverse interactions with anesthesia.
DHA	DHA (docosahexa-enoic acid) is an omega-3 fatty acid that is believed to have antioxidant, antiamyloid, and neuroprotective properties. High levels of DHA (from consuming fish 1–3 times/week) is associated with 48%–60% lower risk for AD compared to non–fish eaters (Morris, Evans, & Bienias, 2003). In an 18 month study of patients with mild to moderate AD, DHA did not slow the rate of change on tests of cognition or function (Quinn et al., 2010).
Rosiglitazone	Rosiglitazone is an FDA-approved medication for diabetes mellitus. It increases insulin sensitivity and acts to reduce glucose levels and hyperinsulinemia. Rosiglitazone was shown to improve cognitive function in a small study of patients with AD (Risner et al., 2006), but a larger clinical study failed to demonstrate significant efficacy (Gold et al., 2010).

| Resveratrol | Resveratrol is a naturally occurring polyphenol found in grapes and red wine that has antioxidant and neuroprotective properties. It has been found to lower levels of beta-amyloid in cultured cells (Marambaud, Zhao, & Davies, 2005). Although mild to moderate intake of red wine is associated with a significant reduction in the risk of AD, there is no data indicating clinical benefit for AD specifically from taking resveratrol. |
| Ergoloid mesylates (hydergine) | Ergoloid mesylates consist of several hydrogenated alkaloids of ergot (a rye fungus) and were a popular treatment of dementia in the 1970s. In Europe they are sold in addition to a similar ergot derivative called nicergoline. Although the mechanism of action has never been clarified, it is thought that ergoloid mesylates work as cerebral vasodilators and may also have antioxidant properties. Ergoloid mesylates have been studied in numerous clinical trials, including seven that were double-blind and placebo-controlled. The latter trials demonstrated some degree of improvement in at least 50% of subjects. In patients with AD, the cognitive and behavioral effects of ergoloid mesylates were relatively mild. One critical review notes that much of the research has consisted of small samples without consistent methods of diagnosis (Olin, Schneider, Novit, & Luczak, 2001). |

that just because in vitro data or transgenic mouse data shows effects on AD pathology does not necessarily mean it will show the same in humans with AD. There are many small studies suggesting clinical benefit for a variety of agents, but at the end of the day, even the largest and most sophisticated clinical trials with rigorous selection standards and optimal outcome measures have not shown any consistent benefit from any agent to date. AD is a complex disease with roots extending decades prior to symptom onset, and it will likely require many more years of research and likely revisions of the pathologic model before a major treatment breakthrough occurs.

Cognitive Rehabilitation

Cognitive stimulation can absolutely provide meaningful activities for individuals with AD, but can it actually improve cognition or, in the very least, slow cognitive decline? There is not much evidence to support these latter goals. One notable study randomly assigned 44 individuals with AD into two groups (Loewenstein, Acevedo, Czaja, & Duara, 2004). One group ($N = 25$) received formal cognitive rehabilitation over 24 sessions that focused on problem solving and attention skills, while a second group ($N = 19$) engaged in mentally stimulating activities such as playing games and discussing topics; these activities required memory, concentration, and problem-solving. After the interventions, the cognitive rehabilitation group demonstrated better gains in skills compared to the mental stimulation group, with improvements still evident at the three-month follow up. However, a comprehensive review of nine randomized controlled trials of cognitive interventions for AD found no significant benefit (Clare et al., 2003).

Clinical Tip

Mentally, socially, and physically stimulating activities are important for AD patients. They provide meaning and purpose to the day, dignity, socialization, physical exercise, enhanced well-being, and reduced caregiver burden. Although data from the one study cited above certainly indicates the potential for cognitive improvement in certain AD patients, any gains will be short-lived and are always fighting against the tide of progressive impairment. The best approach, as detailed in Chapter 12, is to identify the unique strengths and interests of each individual with AD, and then try to find activities and programs that engage and leverage these factors.

Treatment Guidelines for AD

Putting everything together in this chapter, the following steps are currently recommended for the treatment of all individuals with AD:

1. They should be engaged in nonpharmacological approaches that can enhance mental and physical health and well-being, including eating a well-balanced diet rich in fruits and vegetables, and participating in mentally and socially stimulating activities and physical exercise appropriate to their level of ability.
2. They should be protected as best as possible from further brain injury by maximizing control of vascular risk factors (e.g., hypertension, diabetes, hyperlipidemia, obesity, and smoking) and reducing the risk of head trauma due to falls or accidents.
3. They should take one of the three commonly prescribed AChE inhibitors (donepezil, rivastigmine, or galantamine) in combination with memantine, all titrated to the optimal doses. Consider the addition of caprylidene to this regimen. Some individuals will not tolerate both an AChE inhibitor and memantine but should at least be on monotherapy with the agent best tolerated.
4. They should consider participating in a clinical trial. Many trials provide state-of-the-art diagnostic techniques (such as the amyloid-based PET scan) for free. Not only is there access to the latest treatments, which carry the potential for slowing the disease, but often there is the opportunity to participate in long-term open-label phases as well. Without research subjects, no treatment will ever be discovered.

Although many individuals with AD take other supplements and "cognitive enhancing" medications, there is simply not enough evidence to recommend anything beyond the guidelines above. Although there is likely no harm to taking multivitamins, antioxidants, Vitamin B12, folate, B vitamins, Vitamin E, or many other other-the-counter and mail-order products that are commonly touted for memory enhancement, there is certainly an economic cost for these products and, again, simply no clear efficacy for any benefit in AD.

References

Ahlskog, J. E., Geda, Y. E., Graff-Radford, N. R., & Petersen, R. C. (2011). Physical exercise as a preventive or disease-modifying treatment of dementia and brain aging. *Mayo Clin Proc, 86*(9), 876–884.

Aisen, P. S. (2002). The potential of anti-inflammatory drugs for the treatment of Alzheimer's disease. *Lancet Neurol, 1*(5), 279–284.

Aisen, P. S., Gauthier, S., Ferris, S. H., et al. (2011). Tramiprosate in mild-to-moderate Alzheimer's disease—A randomized, double-blind, placebo-controlled, multi-centre study (the Alphase Study). *Arch Med Sci, 7*(1), 102–111.

Aisen, P. S., Gauthier, S., Vellas, B., et al. (2007). Alzhemed: a potential treatment for Alzheimer's disease. *Curr Alzheimer Res, 4*(4), 473–478.

Aizenstein, H. J., Nebes, R. D., Saxton, J. A., et al. (2008). Frequent amyloid deposition without significant cognitive impairment among the elderly. *Archives of Neurology, 65*, 1509–1517.

Albert, M. S., DeKosky, S. T., Dickson, D., et al. (2011). The diagnosis of mild cognitive impairment due to Alzheimer's disease: Recommendations from the National Institute on Aging-Alzheimer's Association workgroups on diagnostic guidelines for Alzheimer's disease. *Alz Dem, 7*, 270–279.

Alzheimer's Association (2012). 2012 Alzheimer's disease facts and figures. *Alz Dem, 8*(2), 131–168.

Alzheimer's Disease International. (2010). *World Alzheimer report 2010: The global economic impact of dementia.* London: Alzheimer's Disease International.

American Psychiatric Association. (2000). *Diagnostic and statistical manual of mental disorders* (4th ed., Text Rev.). Washington, DC: Author.

American Psychiatric Association. (2013). *Diagnostic and statistical manual of mental disorders* (5th ed.). Washington, DC: Author.

Anstey, K. J., Mack, H. A., & Cherbuin, N. (2009). Alcohol consumption as a risk factor for dementia and cognitive decline: Meta-analysis of prospective studies. *Am J Geriatr Psychiatry, 17*, 542–555.

Areosa, S. A., Sherriff, F., & McShane, R. (2005). Memantine for dementia. *Cochrane Database Syst Rev, 3*, CD003154.

Arvanitakis, Z., Schneider, J. A., Wilson, R. S., et al. (2008). Statins, incident Alzheimer disease, change in cognitive function, and neuropathology. *Neurol, 70*(19, Pt 2), 1795–1802.

Balasa, M., Gelpi, E., Antonell, A., et al. (2011). Clinical features and APOE genotype of pathologically proven early-onset Alzheimer disease. *Neurol, 76*(20), 1720–1725.

Bateman, R. J., Xiong, C., Benzinger, T.L.S., et al. (2012). Clinical and biomarker changes in dominantly inherited Alzheimer's disease. *N Engl J Med, 367*, 795–804.

Begum, A. N., Jones, M. R., Lim, G. P., et al. (2008). Curcumin structure-function, bioavailability, and efficacy in models of neuroinflammation and Alzheimer's disease. *J Pharmacol Exp Ther, 326*(1), 196–208.

Bertram, L., & Tanzi, R. E. (2008). Thirty years of Alzheimer's disease genetics: The implications of systematic meta-analyses. *Neuroscience, 9*(10), 768–778.

Blennow, K., Hardy, J., & Zetterberg, H. (2012). The neuropathology and neurobiology of traumatic brain injury. *Neuron, 76*(5), 886–899.

Breitner, J. C., Baker, L. D., Montine, T. J., et al., & the ADAPT Research Group. (2011). Extended results of the Alzheimer's disease anti-inflammatory prevention trial. *Alzheimers Dement, 7*(4), 402–411.

Burns, M., & Duff, K. (2002). Cholesterol in Alzheimer's disease and tauopathy. *Ann NY Acad Sci, 977*, 367–375.

Cataldo, J. K., Prochaska, J. J., & Glantz, S. A. (2010). Cigarette smoking is a risk factor for Alzheimer's disease: An analysis controlling for tobacco industry affiliation. *J Alzheimers Dis, 19*, 465–480.

Clare, L., Woods, R. T., Moniz Cook, E. D., et al. (2003). Cognitive rehabilitation and cognitive training for early-stage Alzheimer's disease and vascular dementia. *Cochrane Database Syst Rev, 4*, CD003260.

Clark, C. M., Schneider, J. A., Bedell, B. J., et al. (2011). Use of florbetapir-PET for imaging beta-amyloid pathology. *JAMA, 305*(3), 275–283.

Connor, B., Young, D., Yan, Q., et al. (1997). Brain-derived neurotrophic factor is reduced in Alzheimer's disease. *Brain Res Mol Brain, 49*, 71–81.

Corder, E. H., Saunders, A. M., Strittmatter, W. J., et al. (1993). Gene dose of apolipoprotein E type 4 allele and the risk of Alzheimer's disease in late onset families. *Science, 261*, 921–923.

Corey-Bloom, J., Anand, R., & Veach, J. (1998). ENA 173 B352 study group: A randomized trial evaluating the efficacy and safety of ENA 173 (rivastigmine tartrate), a new acetylcholinesterase inhibitor, in patients with mild to moderately severe Alzheimer's disease. *Int J Geriatr Psychopharmacol, 1*, 55–65.

DeKosky, S. T., Williamson, J. D., Fitzpatrick, A. L, et al., & the Ginkgo Evaluation of Memory (GEM) Study Investigators. (2008). Ginkgo biloba for prevention of dementia: A randomized controlled trial. *JAMA, 300*(19), 2253–2262.

Desai, A. K., & Chand, P. (2009). Tau-based therapies for Alzheimer's disease: Wave of the future? *Prim Psychiatry, 16*(7), 40–46.

Doody, R. S., Gavrilova, S. I., Sano, M., et al. (2008). Effect of dimebon on cognition, activities of daily living, behaviour, and global function in patients with mild-to-moderate Alzheimer's disease: A randomised, double-blind, placebo-controlled study. *Lancet, 372*, 207–215.

Drazkowski, J. F. (2008). Diagnostic tests in the older adult: EEG. In J. I. Sirven & B. L. Malamut (Eds.), *Clinical neurology of the older adult* (2nd ed., pp. 25–32). Philadelphia: Lippincott, Williams and Wilkins.

Eli Lilly. (2012, August 24). Eli Lilly and Company announces top-line results on Solanezumab Phase 3 clinical trials in patients with Alzheimer's disease. (Press release.). Retrieved from http://newsroom.lilly.com/releasedetail.cfm?releaseid=702211

Flacker, J. M., Cummings, V., Mach, J. R. Jr., et al. (1998). The association of serum anticholinergic activity with delirium in elderly medical patients. *Am J Geriatr Psychiatry, 6*(1), 31–41.

Fratiglioni, L., Launer, L. J., Andersen, K., et al. (2000). Incidence of dementia and major subtypes in Europe: A collaborative study of population-based cohorts. Neurologic Diseases in the Elderly Research Group. *Neurology, 54*(11 Suppl. 5), S10–S5.

Freeman, J. M. (2009). The ketogenic diet: Additional information from a crossover study. *J Child Neurol, 24*, 509–512.

Gatz, M., Reynolds, C. A., Fratiglioni, L., et al. (2006). Role of genes and environments for explaining Alzheimer disease. *Arch Gen Psychiatry, 63*(2), 168–174.

Gever, J. (2013, May 7). Alzheimer's disease: IVIG fails in trial. *Medpage Today.* Retrieved from www.medpagetoday.com/Neurology/AlzheimersDisease/38939

Gibson, G. E., & Huang, H-M. (2005). Oxidative stress in Alzheimer's disease. *Neurobiology of Aging, 26*(5), 575–578.

Gilman, S., Koller, M., Black, R. S., et al., & the AN1792(QS-21)-201 Study Team. (2005). Clinical effects of Abeta immunization (AN1792) in patients with AD in an interrupted trial. *Neurol, 64*(9), 1553–1562.

Gold, M., Alderton, C., Zvartau-Hind, M., et al. (2010). Rosiglitazone monotherapy in mild-to-moderate Alzheimer's disease: Results from a randomized, double-blind, placebo-controlled phase III study. *Dement Geriatr Cogn Disord, 30*(2), 131–146.

Green, R. C., Cupples, L. A., Go, R., et al., & the MIRAGE Study Group. (2002). Risk of dementia among white and African American relatives of patients with Alzheimer disease. *JAMA, 287*(3), 329–336.

Gurland, B. J., Wilder, D. E., Lantigua, R., et al. (1999). Rates of dementia in three ethnoracial groups. *Int J Ger Psychiatry, 14*(6), 481–493.

Hauptmann, S., Keil, U., Scherping, I., et al. (2006). Mitochondrial dysfunction in sporadic and genetic Alzheimer's disease. *Exp Gerontol, 41*, 668–673.

Hebert, L., Scherr, P., Bienias, J., et al. (2003). Alzheimer's disease in the US population: Prevalence estimates using the 2000 census. *Arch Neurol, 60*(8), 1119–1122.

Hebert, L. E., Weuve, J., Scherr, P. A., & Evans, D. A. (2013). Alzheimer disease in the United States (2010–2050) estimated using the 2010 census. *Neurol, 80*(19), 1778–1783.

Henderson, S. T., Vogel, J. L., Barr, L. J., et al. (2009). Study of the ketogenic agent AC-1202 in mild to moderate Alzheimer's disease: A randomized, double-blind, placebo-controlled, multicenter trial. *Nutr Metab, 6*, 31.

Henderson, V. W. (2013, May 28). Alzheimer's disease: Review of hormone therapy trials and implications for treatment and prevention after menopause. *J Steroid Biochem Mol Biol.*

Hurd, M. D., Martorelli, P., & Delavande, A. (2013). Monetary costs of dementia in the United States. *N Eng J Med, 368*(14), 1326–1334.

Imbimbo, B. P., & Giardina, G. A. (2011). γ-secretase inhibitors and modulators for the treatment of Alzheimer's disease: Disappointments and hopes. *Curr Top Med Chem, 11*(12), 1555–1570.

Jack, C. R., Knopman, D. S., Jagust, W. J., et al. (2010). Hypothetical model of dynamic biomarkers of the Alzheimer's pathological cascade. *Lancet Neurol, 9*(1), 119–128.

Kaduszkiewicz, H., Zimmermann, T., Beck-Bornholdt, H. P., & van den Bussche, H. (2005). Cholinesterase inhibitors for patients with Alzheimer's disease: Systematic review of randomised clinical trials. *Br Med J, 331*(7512), 321–327.

Köhler, S., van Boxtel, M., Jolles, J., & Verhey, F. (2011). Depressive symptoms and risk for dementia: A 9-year follow-up of the Maastricht Aging Study. *Am J Ger Psychiatry, 19*(10), 902–905.

Koss, E., Attix, D. K., & Story, T. J. (2011). Neuropsychological evaluation. In M. E. Agronin & G. J. Maletta (Eds.), *Principles and practice of geriatric psychiatry* (2nd ed., pp. 119–137). Philadelphia: Lippincott, Williams and Wilkins.

Kozauer, N., & Katz, R. (2013). Regulatory innovation and drug development for early-stage Alzheimer's disease. *N Engl J Med, 368*, 1169–1171.

Lannfelt, L., Blennow, K., Zetterberg, H., PBT2–201-EURO study group, et al. (2008). Safety, efficacy, and biomarker findings of PBT2 in targeting Abeta as a modifying therapy for Alzheimer's disease: A phase IIa, double-blind, randomised, placebo-controlled trial. *Lancet Neurol, 7*(9), 779–786.

Laurin, D., Masaki, K. H., Foley, D. J., et al. (2004). Midlife dietary intake of antioxidants and risk of late-life incident dementia: The Honolulu–Asia Aging Study. *Am J Epidemiol, 159*, 959–967.

Liu, L., Drouet, V., Wu, J. W., Witter, M. P., Small, S. A., et al. (2012) Trans-synaptic spread of tau pathology in vivo. *PLoS ONE, 7*(2), e31302.

Loewenstein, D. A., Acevedo, A., Czaja, S. J., & Duara, R. (2004). Cognitive rehabilitation of mildly impaired Alzheimer disease patients on cholinesterase inhibitors. *Am J Geriatr Psychiatry, 12*(4), 395–402.

Luchsinger, J. A., Tang, M. X., Shea, S., & Mayeux, R. (2003). Antioxidant vitamin intake and risk of Alzheimer disease. *Arch Neurol, 60*, 203–208.

Manly, J. J., & Mayeux, R. (2004). Ethnic differences in dementia and Alzheimer's disease. In N. B. Anderson, R. A. Bulatao, & B. Cohen (Eds.), *Critical perspectives on racial and ethnic differences in health in late life*. Washington, DC: National Academies Press.

Marambaud, P., Zhao, H., & Davies, P. (2005). Resveratrol promotes clearance of Alzheimer's disease amyloid-beta peptides. *J Biol Chem, 280*(45), 37377–37382.

Mayeux, R. (2003). Epidemiology of neurodegeneration. *Annu Rev Neurosci, 26*, 81–104.

McGuinness, B., O'Hare, J., Craig, D., et al. (2010). Statins for the treatment of dementia. *Cochrane Database Syst Rev, 8*, CD007514.

McKhann, G. M., Drachman, D., Folstein, M., et al. (1984). Clinical diagnosis of Alzheimer's disease: Report of the NINCDS–ADRDA work group under the auspices of Department of Health and Human Services Task Force on Alzheimer's Disease. *Neurol, 34*, 939–944.

McKhann, G. M., Knopman, D. S., Chertkow, H., et al. (2011). The diagnosis of dementia due to Alzheimer's disease: Recommendations from the National Institute on Aging-Alzheimer's Association workgroups on diagnostic guidelines for Alzheimer's disease. *Alz Dem, 7*, 263–269.

Menéndez, M. (2005). Down syndrome, Alzheimer's disease and seizures. *Brain & Development, 27*(4), 246–252.

Messier, C., & Teutenberg, K. (2005). The role of insulin, insulin growth factor, and insulin-degrading enzyme in brain aging and Alzheimer's disease. *Neural Plast, 12*, 311–328.

Mok, W., Chow, T. W., Zheng, L., et al. (2004). Clinicopathological concordance of dementia diagnoses by community versus tertiary care clinicians. *Am J Alzheimers Dis Dem, 19*(3), 161–165.

Möller, H. J., & Graeber, M. B. (1998). The case described by Alois Alzheimer in 1911: Historical and conceptual perspectives based on the clinical record and neurohistological sections. *Eur Arch Psychiatry Clin Neurosci, 248*, 111–122.

Morris, J. C., Roe, C. M., Grant, E. A., et al. (2009). Pittsburgh compound B imaging and prediction of progression from cognitive normality to symptomatic Alzheimer disease. *Arch Neurol, 66*(12), 1469–1475.

Morris, M. C., Evans, D.A., & Bienias, J. L. (2003). Consumption of Fish and n-3 fatty acids and risk of incident Alzheimer disease. *Arch Neurol, 60*, 940–946.

Mortimer, J. A., Snowdon, D. A., & Markesbery, W. R. (2003). Head circumference, education and risk of dementia: Findings from the Nun study. *J Clin Exp Neuropsychol, 25*, 671–679.

Mungas, D., Harvey, D., Reed, B. R., et al. (2005). Longitudinal volumetric MRI change and rate of cognitive decline. *Neurol, 65*(4), 565–571.

Murray, M. E., Graff-Radford, N. R., Ross, O. A., et al. (2011). Neuropathologically defined subtypes of Alzheimer's disease with distinct clinical characteristics: A retrospective study. *Lancet, 10*, 785–796.

Noble, W., Planel, E., Zehr, C., et al. (2005). Inhibition of glycogen synthase kinase-3 by lithium correlates with reduced tauopathy and degeneration in vivo. *Proc Natl Acad Sci U S A, 102*(19), 6990–6995.

Olin, J., Schneider, L., Novit, A., & Luczak, S. (2001). Hydergine for dementia. *Cochrane Database Syst Rev, 2*, CD000359.

Petersen, R. C., Smith, G. E., Waring, S. C., et al. (2005). Vitamin E and donepezil for the treatment of mild cognitive impairment. *N Engl J Med, 352*, 2379–2388.

Priller, C., Bauer, T., Mitteregger, G., Krebs, B., Kretschmar, H. A., & Herms, J. (2006). Synapse formation and function is modulated by the amyloid precursor protein. *J Neurosci, 26*(27), 7212–7221.

Profenno, L. A., Porsteinsson, A. P., & Faraone, S. V. (2010). Meta-analysis of Alzheimer's disease risk with obesity, diabetes, and related disorders. *Biol Psychiatry, 67*(6), 505–512.

Querfurth, H. W., & LaFerla, F. M. (2010). Alzheimer's disease. *N Eng J Med, 362*(14), 329–344.

Quinn, J. F., Raman, R., Thomas, R. G., et al. (2010). Docosahexaenoic acid supplementation and cognitive decline in Alzheimer disease: a randomized trial. *JAMA, 304*(17), 1903–1911.

Raber, J., Huang, Y., & Ashford, J. W. (2004). ApoE genotype accounts for the vast majority of AD risk and AD pathology. *Neurobiol Aging, 25*, 641–650.

Rapoport, M., Dawson, H. N., Binder, L. I., Vitek, M. P., & Ferreira, A. (2002). Tau is essential to β-amyloid-induced neurotoxicity. *Proc Natl Acad Sci USA, 99*(9), 6364–6369.

Raskind, M. A., Peskind, E. R., Wessel, T., & Yuan, W. (2000). Galantamine in AD: A 6-month randomized, placebo-controlled trial with a 6-month extension. The Galantamine USA-1 Study Group. *Neurology, 54*(12), 2261–2268.

Reiman, E. M., Chen, K., Alexander, G. E., et al. (2004). Functional brain abnormalities in young adults at genetic risk for late-onset Alzheimer's dementia. *Proc Natl Acad Sci USA, 101*(1), 284–289.

Reitz, C., Brayne, C., & Mayeux, R. (2011). Epidemiology of Alzheimer disease. *Nat Rev Neurol, 7*(3), 137–152.

Risner, M. E., Saunders, A. M., Altman, J. F., et al. (2006). Rosiglitazone in Alzheimer's Disease Study Group: Efficacy of rosiglitazone in a genetically defined population with mild-to-moderate Alzheimer's disease. *Pharmacogenomics J, 6*, 246–254.

Rogaeva, E., Meng, Y., Lee, J. H., et al. (2007). The neuronal sortilin-related receptor SORL1 is genetically associated with Alzheimer disease. *Nat Genet, 39*(2), 168–177.

Rogers, S. L., Doody, R. S., Mohs, R. C., et al. (1998). Donepezil Study Group: Donepezil improves cognition and global function in Alzheimer's disease: A 15-week, double-blind, placebo-controlled study. *Arch Int Med, 158*(9), 1021–1031.

Rountree, S. D., Chan, W., Pavlik, V. N., et al. (2009). Persistent treatment with cholinesterase inhibitors and/or memantine slows clinical progression of Alzheimer's disease. *Alz Res & Ther, 1*, 7.

Sampson, E. L., Jenagaratnam, L., & McShane, R. (2012). Metal protein attenuating compounds for the treatment of Alzheimer's dementia. *Cochrane Database Syst Rev, 5*, CD005380.

Scarmeas, N., Stern, Y., Tang, M. X., et al. (2006). Mediterranean diet and risk for Alzheimer's disease. *Ann Neurol, 59*, 912–921.

Schaefer, E. J., Bongard, V., Beiser, A. S., et al. (2006). Plasma phosphatidylcholine docosahexaenoic acid content and risk of dementia and Alzheimer disease: The Framingham Heart Study. *Arch Neurol, 63*, 1545–1550.

Small, G. W., Bookheimer, S. Y., Thompson, P. M., et al. (2008). Current and future uses of neuroimaging for cognitively impaired patients. *Lancet Neurol, 7*(2), 161–172.

Sperling, R. (2011). Potential of functional MRI as a biomarker in early Alzheimer's disease. *Neurobiol Aging, 32*(Suppl. 1), S37–S43.

Sperling, R. A., Aisen, P. S., Beckett, L. A., et al. (2011). Toward defining the preclinical stages of Alzheimer's disease: Recommendations from the National Institute on Aging-Alzheimer's Association workgroups on diagnostic guidelines for Alzheimer's disease. *Alz Dem, 7*, 280–292.

Swardfager, W., Herrmann, N., Marzolini, S., et al. (2011). Brain derived neurotrophic factor, cardiopulmonary fitness and cognition in patients with coronary artery disease. *Brain Behav Immun, 25*(6), 1264–1271.

Tariot, P. N., Farlow, M. R., Grossberg, G. T., et al. (2004). Memantine treatment in patients with moderate to severe Alzheimer disease already receiving donepezil: A randomized controlled trial. *JAMA, 291*(3), 317–324.

Tayeb, H. O., Murray, E. D., Price, B. H., & Tarazi, F. I. (2013). Bapineuzumab and solanezumab for Alzheimer's disease: Is the "amyloid cascade hypothesis" still alive? *Expert Opin Biol Ther, 13*(7), 1075–1084.

Terry, A. V. Jr., & Buccafusco, J. J. (2003). The cholinergic hypothesis of age and Alzheimer's disease-related cognitive deficits: Recent challenges and their implications for novel drug development. *J Pharmacol Exp Ther, 306*, 821–827.

Vallabhajosula, S. (2011). Positron emission tomography radiopharmaceuticals for imaging brain Beta-amyloid. *Semin Nucl Med, 41*(4), 283–299.

Varvel, N. H., Bhaskar, K., Patil, A. R., et al. (2008). Aβ Oligomers induce neuronal cell cycle events in Alzheimer's disease. *J Neurosci, 28*(43), 10786–10793.

Vellas, B., Black, R., Thal, L. J., et al., & the AN1792 (QS-21)-251 Study Team. (2009). Long-term follow-up of patients immunized with AN1792: Reduced functional decline in antibody responders. *Curr Alzheimer Res, 6*(2), 144–151.

Walsh, D. M., & Selkoe, D. J. (2007). A beta oligomers: A decade of discovery. *J Neurochem, 101*, 1172–1184.

Wang, H.-X., Karp, A., Winblad, B., & Fratiglioni, L. (2002). Late-life engagement in social and leisure activities is associated with a decreased risk of dementia: A longitudinal study from the Kungsholmen Project. *Am J Epidemiol, 155*(12), 1081–1087.

Wilcock, G. K. (2003). Memantine for the treatment of dementia. *Lancet Neurol, 2,* 503–505.

Wischik, C., Bentham, P., Wischik, D. J., & Seng, K. M. (2008, July 29). Tau aggregation inhibitor (TAI) therapy with rember arrests disease progression in mild and moderate Alzheimer's disease over 50 weeks. Abstract presented at the 11th International Conference on Alzheimer's Disease and Related Disorders, Chicago, IL.

Wischik, C., & Staff, R. (2009). Challenges in the conduct of disease-modifying trials in AD: Practical experience from a phase 2 trial of Tau-aggregation inhibitor therapy. *J Nutr Health Aging, 13*(4), 367–369.

Wood, D. F., Rosenberg, P. B., Zhou, Y., et al. (2010). In vivo imaging of amyloid deposition in Alzheimer disease using the radioligand 18F-AV-45 (florbetapir F-18). *J Nucl Med, 51*(6), 913–920.

Yang, F., Lim, G. P., Begum, A. N., et al. (2005). Curcumin inhibits formation of amyloid beta oligomers and fibrils, binds plaques, and reduces amyloid in vivo. *J Biol Chem, 280,* 5892–5901.

Zhang, Y. H., Raymick, J., Sarkar, S., et al. (2013). Efficacy and toxicity of clioquinol treatment and A-beta42 inoculation in the APP/PSI mouse model of Alzheimer's disease. *Curr Alzheimer Res, 10*(5), 494–506.

5 Vascular Dementia

Vascular dementia (VaD), previously known as multi-infarct dementia, is the second most common form of dementia after Alzheimer's disease (AD), affecting 10%–20% of individuals with dementia (Chui, 2007). VaD may resemble AD clinically, but its etiology is distinct. It is caused by focal or diffuse cortical or subcortical brain damage as a result of cerebrovascular disease or injury. Common causes of VaD are embolic strokes resulting from cardiovascular events (i.e., emboli generated during arrhythmias, such as atrial fibrillation) or from carotid artery atheromatous plaques. Given this etiology, the presence of vascular lesions on brain scans represents an essential diagnostic feature of VaD.

The prevalence rates for VaD are tied into the rates of stroke; as a result, the rate of VaD increases nearly 200-fold as one ages from 60 years old to over 90 and includes a significant overlap with AD (Kalaria, 2003). Those individuals with the greatest risk of VaD are those at risk for stroke, with a history of atherosclerosis, hypertension, hyperlipidemia, arrhythmias, diabetes mellitus, and tobacco use (Hébert et al., 2000). Not surprisingly, the prevalence rates of VaD have declined as a result of improvements in stroke prevention and treatment.

Case Study

Mr. A was a 75-year-old advertising executive with diabetes, coronary heart disease, and hypertension who enjoyed smoking cigars. During a ski trip in Utah, he had a stroke that resulted in right-sided hemiparesis and mild aphasia. With aggressive rehabilitation, he was able to walk with a cane and to communicate with only a mild degree of word-finding difficulty. However, four months after the stroke, his wife reported that his short-term memory was poor and that he was prone to fits of anger. Six months after his stroke, Mr. A was forced to retire because he was unable to manage his accounts. Treatment for depression reduced his irritability, but the cognitive impairment persisted. Mr. A was able to control his diet and blood pressure, but he continued to smoke. Two years after his stroke, he had another one that left him severely aphasic and unable to walk. Physical and occupational therapy led to moderate physical improvement, but his cognition remained poor.

The case of Mr. A demonstrates a classic history of VaD in which an individual with multiple risk factors for stroke has a series of events and complications and the subsequent development of dementia. Poor adherence to preventative strategies led to further deterioration.

Diagnostic Criteria

Diagnostic criteria commonly used for VaD come from the *Diagnostic and Statistical Manual of Mental Disorders*, Fourth Edition, Text Revision (DSM-IV-TR; American Psychiatric Association, 2000), the *Diagnostic and Statistical Manual of Mental Disorders*, Fifth Edition (DSM-5; American Psychiatric Association, 2013), and the National Institute of Neurological Disorders and Stroke–Association Internationale pour la Recherche et l'Enseignement en Neurosciences or NINDS–AIREN (Román et al., 1993). All of these criteria sets focus on the relationship between the presence of cerebrovascular disease or the occurrence of strokes and the onset of dementia symptoms. DSM-5 has changed the name of the diagnosis from "vascular dementia" in DSM-IV-TR to "major or minor vascular neurocognitive disorder" and stresses the role of a prominent decline in complex attention, processing speed, and frontal-executive function (American Psychiatric Association, 2013). NINDS–AIREN criteria stress the importance of accounting for the probability of the diagnosis and are summarized in Table 5.1

Table 5.1 National Institute of Neurological Disorders and Stroke–Association Internationale pour la Recherche et l'Enseignement en Neurosciences (NINDS-AIREN) Diagnostic Criteria for Vascular Dementia

Diagnosis	Description
Probable vascular dementia	• Dementia defined by impairment of memory and two or more of the following: orientation, attention, language, visuospatial function, executive function, motor control, and praxis. • Evidence of cerebrovascular disease (CVD), such as focal neurological symptoms or findings on neuroimaging. • Relationship between dementia and CVD is likely given either the onset of dementia within three months after stroke or abrupt cognitive deterioration or a stepwise progression of cognitive deficits. • Clinical features often include gait disturbances and falls, urinary symptoms not explained by urologic disease, personality and mood changes, and subcortical symptoms such as psychomotor retardation and abnormal executive function.
Definite vascular dementia	• Clinical criteria for probable VaD in addition to histopathologic evidence of CVD obtained from biopsy or autopsy, neurofibrillary tangles and presence of neuritic plaques not exceeding those expected for age, and absence of other clinical or pathologic disorders capable of producing dementia.
Possible vascular dementia	• Dementia (as described previously) with focal neurologic signs but without evidence of CVD by neuroimaging or without a temporal relationship to stroke or in patients with subtle onset and variable course of cognitive deficits and evidence of relevant CVD.
Unlikely vascular dementia	• Dementia as described previously but with the absence of focal neurologic signs or focal brain lesions on neuroimaging.

Adapted from Román et al. (1993).

Etiology and Risk Factors

According to data from the Centers for Disease Control, the prevalence of stroke in noninstitutionalized adults 18 years and older in 2010 was 2.7% (Centers for Disease Control, 2012). In this data, the rate of stroke increases significantly from 0.7% at age 18 to 2.9% at ages 45 to 64, and 8.3% at ages 65 and older. Arterial thrombosis and embolisms are the most common causes of strokes. Smaller lacunar infarcts are often silent but do damage in accumulation. Hemorrhagic strokes are less common but often cause severe brain damage.

The impact of any given stroke on cognition is unpredictable. Approximately 25%–30% of individuals develop dementia after stroke. A number of factors will increase the likelihood of post-stroke dementia, including the following: left-sided lesions; tissue death of more than 50–100 cm^3; stroke symptoms, such as dysphagia, gait impairment, and urinary incontinence; stroke complications, such as seizures, arrhythmias, pneumonia, and hypotension; preexisting damage from prior strokes or other brain injury; older age, non-white race/ethnicity, tobacco use, obesity, a family history of dementia; and a medical history of coronary artery disease, atrial fibrillation, hypertension, and diabetes mellitus (Grysiewicz & Gorelick, 2012; Leys, Hénon, Mackowiak-Cordoliani, & Pasquier, 2005). The highest risk group is comprised of individuals with both hypertension and diabetes (Kloppenborg, van den Berg, Kappelle, & Biessels, 2008).

Classification

VaD can be classified in several ways based on the type, location, and time course of the vascular injury. Classification by types of vascular injury includes the following:

- VaD due to large vessel disease: the stroke affects a large tissue area, such as in the distribution of anterior, posterior, or middle cerebral arteries;
- VaD due to small vessel disease: smaller and often multiple strokes, especially lacunar infarcts, that result in accumulating damage.

In one review, half of all cases of VaD were due to small vessel disease, one-fourth of the cases were due to large vessel lesions in both cortical and subcortical areas, and the remainder included elements of both. The most common artery that is affected is the middle cerebral (Román, 2002).

VaD can also be classified by the location of vascular injury, with the two major subtypes being cortical VaD and subcortical VaD. Cortical damage is usually associated with thrombosis and less so with embolic or hemorrhagic events. Less common, non-cerebrovascular accidents that can cause cortical damage include venous thrombosis, hypoperfusion, trauma, and diffuse microinfarcts. Subcortical VaD is usually associated with the presence of multiple lacunar infarcts in the region of the basal ganglia, thalamus, pons, and surrounding white matter tracts. This variant is sometimes referred to as simply a lacunar state.

A third way to classify VaD is by its time course, acute versus subacute. Acute-onset VaD occurs after a clinically evident stroke, and it can include both single or recurrent cortical and subcortical events. Subacute VaD usually refers to subcortical syndromes that involve progressive dementia with a fluctuating course and without an obvious temporal relationship to clinical strokes.

Cortical VaD

Cortical VaD primarily involves memory dysfunction and one or more of the following: apraxia, aphasia, agnosia, and executive dysfunction. The associated neurologic impairment is most often characterized by hemiplegia or paresis contralateral to the lesion. The exact form of cognitive impairment due to cortical injury depends first on whether the dominant or nondominant hemisphere is affected (most individuals are left-hemisphere dominant) and then on the particular lobe(s) affected: frontal, parietal, occipital, and/or temporal. Theoretically, the clinical symptoms of VaD should reflect the site(s) of cerebral injury. The complexity of neural connections in the brain, however, often makes actually correlating the symptoms with the anatomic lesions difficult. Table 5.2 provides a general guide for correlating the clinical symptoms of cortical impairment with known areas of damage (Victor & Ropper, 2009).

Cerebral amyloid angiopathy or CAA represents a group of disorders characterized by the deposition of beta-amyloid protein in cerebral blood vessels, resulting in recurrent lobar hemorrhages, ischemic strokes, and evolving dementia (Weller & Nicoll, 2003). Both cortical and subcortical manifestations are possible. Several different familial forms of CAA exist with autosomal dominant transmission. CAA may account for up to 30% of all lobar hemorrhages and is seen in the majority of individuals with AD (Weller, Boche, & Nicoll, 2009).

Table 5.2 Cognitive Effects of Cortical Stroke

Cortical Lobe	Symptoms from Stroke-Related Damage
Frontal	• Impaired executive functioning • Impaired immediate memory • Slowed cognitive processing and activity; poor concentration • Impairments in judgment, insight, and behavioral control • Personality changes: apathy or inappropriate and disinhibited behaviors • Perseveration of words, sounds, or behaviors • Disinhibited reflexes and/or frontal release signs • Contralateral hemiplegia or paresis • Broca aphasia (nonfluent) from a lesion on the dominant side • Dysprosody (impaired inflection of speech) from lesion on the nondominant side • Impaired coordination of ocular movements • Pseudobulbar palsy (emotional incontinence) due to bilateral lesions • Dorsolateral prefrontal lesions lead to impairment in executive function • Orbitofrontal lesions lead to disinhibition, lability, impulsivity, anosmia (inability to perceive odors), distractibility, and perseveration • Mediofrontal and/or anterior cingulate lesions lead to apathy, personality flattening, akinetic mutism (lack of spontaneous movement and speech), and impaired follow-through on tasks

Temporal	• Impaired memory processing (hippocampus, medial temporal lobe)
	• Impaired cortical hearing (lesions in Heschl's gyrus)
	• Hallucinations (in all sensory modalities)
	• Changes in emotional and behavioral expression (with limbic involvement)
	• Klüver–Bucy syndrome (apathy, placidity, oral exploratory behaviors, hypersexuality, hyperphagia) due to bilateral lesions
	• Visual field cuts (homonymous upper quadrantanopia)
	• Dominant side
	○ Wernicke aphasia (fluent)
	○ Amusia (impaired musical appreciation)
	• Nondominant side
	○ Sound agnosia
	○ Dysprosody (impaired production and interpretation of speech inflection)
Parietal	• Cortical sensory impairment (hemianesthesia with large lesions)
	• Mild hemiparesis
	• Visual field cuts (homonymous hemianopsia)
	• Dominant side
	○ Agraphia (impaired writing ability)
	○ Acalculia (impaired mathematical ability)
	○ Reading impairment and/or dyslexia
	○ Right–left confusion
	○ Aphasia (fluent)
	○ Apraxias (ideomotor, simple tasks; ideational, complex tasks)
	○ Astereognosia (impaired tactile recognition of objects)
	○ Gerstmann's syndrome (agraphia, left–right confusion, finger agnosia, alexia, and acalculia due to a lesion in the dominant posterior parietal and/or angular gyrus)
	• Nondominant
	○ Visuospatial and visuoconstructional impairment and apraxias
	○ Dressing apraxia
	○ Neglect of dominant side (autotopagnosia)
	○ Neglect or denial of illness (anosognosia)
Occipital	• Visual agnosias for objects, colors, and faces (prosopagnosia)
	• Reading impairment and/or dyslexia
	• Panoramic visual impairment
	• Visual field cuts (homonymous hemianopsia)
	• Visual illusions and hallucinations (often of shapes, colors)
	• Visual auras associated with occipital seizures
	• Alexia without agraphia (lesion on the dominant side and adjacent corpus callosum)
	• Bálint's syndrome (visual inattention and poor tracking due to bilateral lesions)
	• Anton's syndrome (visual anosognosia, denial of blindness)
	• Cortical blindness

Subcortical VaD

Subcortical VaD variably affects numerous regions of the brain that lie below the cortex, including the basal ganglia, thalamus, and internal capsule. The basal ganglia serve a central role in the coordination of motor movements, and they include the putamen, globus pallidus, caudate nucleus, and several brainstem nuclei. The thalamus is composed, in part, of several nuclei that integrate both motor and sensory information from the peripheral nervous system, basal ganglia, and cortical regions. The mediodorsal nuclei of the thalamus, along with hippocampal formations, are the key memory-processing centers of the brain. A complex neural feedback loop exists among the frontal cortex, basal ganglia, and thalamus to aid in the integration and regulation of motor movements, cognitive speed, mood, impulse control, and motivation. Because of these connections, subcortical damage directly affects frontal lobe function, as the typical clinical symptoms of subcortical VaD reflect; these include executive dysfunction; memory dysfunction, especially memory retrieval deficits; attentional deficits; slowed thought processing (bradyphrenia); parkinsonism (rigidity, bradykinesia, slowed gait); movement disorders; dysarthria; apathy; and depression (Gold et al., 2007).

Specific injury to the basal ganglia structures may result in various forms of movement disorders, including tremor, rigidity, bradykinesia, postural instability, and involuntary movements (e.g., dystonia, dyskinesia, chorea, athetosis). Thalamic injury may be reflected in dense sensory loss, and it is associated with hemiplegia when concomitant injury to the adjacent cortical motor tracts in the internal capsule occurs. Damage to some thalamic nuclei can also result in memory impairment, including Korsakoff syndrome (or thalamic amnesia), which is characterized by severe anterograde amnesia, a lack of insight, and confabulation.

Clinical Vignette

Mr. L was a 72-year-old taxi driver with a history of hypertension. He reported several episodes of slurred speech and difficulty controlling his hand, each of which lasted only minutes. However, during one episode, he was pulled over by the police due to his erratic driving and was sent to the hospital because he could not articulate his words clearly to the officer. The medical and neurological workup revealed lacunar infarcts. He was forced to give up his job driving a taxi, but he got a part-time job as a dispatcher. However, over the next 12 months, Mr. L demonstrated increased forgetfulness and slowed motor movements. He was increasingly unable to manage his job, so he was let go. At a follow-up appointment, his physician suspected Parkinson's disease, but a trial of levodopa was ineffective. Mr. L became increasingly depressed, and he began spending most of his days sitting at home in front of the television. Antidepressant medication helped to improve his mood, but his wife noted that he lacked motivation to pursue his favorite hobbies, such as bowling and going to baseball games at the nearby stadium.

The presence of parkinsonism or other movement disorders is usually the most helpful symptom for distinguishing between subcortical damage and actual frontal lobe or other cortical dementias. This distinction between cortical and subcortical dementia has been criticized as artificial, however, because of the intimate cortical-subcortical neural connections. The differences between cortical and subcortical dementias are summarized in Table 1.2 in Chapter 1.

There are two subtypes of subcortical VaD that are important to consider. Binswanger's disease, also known as subcortical arteriosclerotic encephalopathy or ischemic periventricular leucoencephalopathy, is a slowly progressive dementia associated with chronic hypertension and manifested by prominent executive impairment. It is characterized by damage to small, penetrating blood vessels in subcortical regions that results in episodic hypoperfusion and white matter degeneration (Libon, Price, Davis Garrett, & Giovannetti, 2004). Cerebral autosomal dominant arteriopathy with subcortical infarcts and leucoencephalopathy or CADASIL is an autosomal dominant disorder mapped to mutations in the Notch 3 gene on chromosome 19, which produces a slowly progressive dementia in adults, usually striking in the mid-40s (Chabriat et al., 2009). It involves a microangiopathic process that affects arterioles and capillaries, resulting in small ischemic infarcts throughout subcortical structures. CADASIL may progress over 20 years and involve transient ischemic attacks and strokes, focal neurologic symptoms, headaches, mood disorders, and seizures, in addition to dementia. The dementia associated with CADASIL is characterized by prominent slowing in mental processing speed and deficits in executive function and attention. In later stages, it closely resembles Binswanger's Disease.

A *mixed dementia* typically refers to an overlap between AD and VaD, in which there is both AD pathology ("plaques and tangle") as well as cerebrovascular lesions. These states can be seen in anywhere from 25% to 80% of individuals with dementia (Jellinger, 2013; Román, 2002). These cases appear to have both a worse prognosis and a faster progression of symptoms (Sheng et al., 2007). Defining these cases is challenging, however, since the presence of one or more small lesions, such as lacunar infarcts, may have occurred years prior to the onset of cognitive impairment or have no bearing on it, suggesting a pure case of AD despite cerebrovascular pathology (Gold et al., 2007).

Clinical Tip

Keep in mind that no part of the brain exists unto itself. Myriad neural connections between brain regions, both cortical and subcortical, mean that damage to any one part will have ramifications for many others. Despite specific findings in neuropsychological testing or the identification of specific lesions on brain scans, a prediction of the subsequent clinical picture can still be difficult.

Assessment

Assessment of VaD follows the procedures outlined in Chapters 1 and 2, although greater diagnostic emphasis is placed on neuroimaging. The distinction between VaD and AD can be difficult, however, because the two entities can appear clinically indistinguishable (and, as noted, they often occur together). Despite the fact that clinicians try to trace the origin of VaD to discrete strokes, a process of accumulated cerebrovascular damage (either due to recurrent small cerebrovascular lesions or progressive atrophy and/or demyelination of white matter tracts) rather than single events may account for many of the cases. Thus, VaD frequently appears to be slowly progressive like AD.

Researchers have increasingly focused on the relationship between the two clinical entities; for example, vascular damage to the brain is associated with a higher risk of AD and a worse course (Sheng et al., 2007), and both VaD and AD likely produce a central cholinergic deficit (Román & Kalaria, 2006). On a gross pathologic level, the brain scans of patients with AD frequently reveal small strokes and white matter lesions; on a microscopic level, senile plaques and neurofibrillary tangles can be found in both disorders, although they do occur with significantly greater density in AD (Gold et al., 2007).

Despite these similarities, several of the following factors point more toward a diagnosis of VaD: focal neurological impairment (including gait disturbances and urinary incontinence), multiple vascular risk factors, brain lesions seen on neuroimaging, a more variable and less progressive course (i.e., fluctuating, stepwise deterioration), greater executive dysfunction, and less prominent memory dysfunction. These differences comprise, in part, the Hachinski Ischemic Scale, shown in Table 5.3, which assigns a score to each variable; higher scores are more consistent with VaD (Hachinski et al., 1975). Much of the information on the Hachinski Ischemic Scale can be obtained by a clinical interview and a neurological examination.

Table 5.3 Hachinski Ischemic Scale

Feature	Number of Points
Abrupt onset	2
Stepwise deterioration	1
Fluctuating course	2
Nocturnal confusion	1
Relative preservation of personality	1
Depression	1
Somatic complaints	1
Emotional incontinence	1
History or presence of hypertension	1
History of strokes	2
Evidence of associated atherosclerosis	1
Focal neurologic symptoms	2
Focal neurologic signs	2

Scoring: The patient receives the number of points indicated for the presence of each feature. Interpretation: 0–4 points indicates a dementia more consistent with AD; with 5–6 points the diagnosis is unclear; a score of 7 or more points is more consistent with VaD.

Modified from Hachinski et al. (1975).

Neuropsychological Testing

A neuropsychological profile may help to identify VaD by revealing patchy deficits, compared with the tendency toward global impairment seen with AD. This is certainly the case in the setting of large, discrete cortical infarcts. However, one comprehensive review of neuropsychological testing found only two areas differentiating VaD from AD—patients with VaD had greater impairment in frontal executive dysfunction and less impairment in verbal long-term memory (Looi & Sachdev, 1999).

Neuroimaging

Neuroimaging studies using computed tomography (CT) or magnetic resonance imaging (MRI) are essential for identifying vascular lesions that have clear causal links to VaD (Guermazi et al., 2007). The frequent presence of cerebral atrophy, ventricular enlargement, and smaller or more diffuse cortical damage can be more difficult to interpret, however, since it can be present without causing cognitive impairment (Gold et al., 2007). White matter hyperintensities are common subcortical findings seen on MRI that appear in the brains of 30%–80% of older individuals, including those with VaD and AD. Their exact nature is controversial, but they are believed to represent small areas of ischemic damage. Even when they are present, however, they are not always associated with cognitive impairment. Findings from positron emission tomography or PET scans that look at cerebral function via glucose utilization tend to reveal more scattered deficits in VaD versus the typical pattern of evolving parietotemporal and cingulate gyrus hypometabolism in AD (Small et al., 2008).

Treatment

As with any form of dementia, early diagnosis and treatment are important, but, in VaD, these may play a greater role because of the possibility of reducing or even arresting further vascular damage to the brain. The risk of recurrent stroke or progressive cerebrovascular damage hangs over patients with VaD, increasing the morbidity and mortality over time. The treatment of VaD involves the following:

- primary prevention of stroke in high-risk patients;
- secondary prevention of recurrent stroke in patients already affected;
- consideration of the use of neuroprotective and neuroenhancing agents;
- use of acetylcholinesterase (AChE) inhibitors; and
- use of the glutamate receptor antagonist memantine.

Primary prevention seeks to reduce the chances of stroke in high-risk individuals. Lifestyle factors that may reduce risk include regular physical exercise, a low-fat diet, and avoidance of smoking. Control of weight, blood pressure (BP), and glucose levels is important for many reasons, although there is no clear information indicating that lowering of blood pressure prevents the development of cognitive impairment in individuals who do not have preexisting cerebrovascular disease (McGuinness, Todd, Passmore, & Bullock, 2009). Many individuals also take an aspirin daily to reduce the risk of myocardial infarction and stroke, as well as a statin medication to reduce cholesterol levels and perhaps to accrue other cardiovascular benefits. Unfortunately, two large studies of over 26,000 individuals taking statin medications did not show clear reductions in the incidence of AD or other forms of dementia (McGuinness, Craig, Bullock, & Passmore, 2009).

Secondary prevention seeks to modify the risk of recurrent stroke after previous events, and it incorporates all the strategies listed for primary prevention (Erkinjuntti et al., 2004). Anticoagulation therapy or cardiac ablation is necessary to reduce the risk of stroke in the setting of chronic arrhythmias such as atrial fibrillation. Carotid endarterectomy may reduce the risk of stroke due to severe carotid stenosis. Another staple of secondary stroke prevention is the use of antiplatelet agents such as aspirin.

Clinical Tip

A review of vascular risk factors should be part of every dementia workup. When VaD is suspected or the individual has multiple risk factors for stroke or an actual history of stroke, involving the patient's internist and/or neurologist is critical for instituting appropriate therapy and recommending lifestyle changes. Watching and waiting in the setting of risk factors such as hypertension, atrial fibrillation, diabetes mellitus, smoking, carotid stenosis, and transient ischemic attacks is never an option.

Neuroprotective and Neuroenhancing Agents

Over the years, several medications considered to have either protective or enhancing effects on cerebral function have been used to treat VaD. Calcium channel blockers such as nimodipine and nicardipine may help improve cerebral blood flow, although they have not been shown to definitively improve symptoms of VaD (López-Arrieta & Birks, 2002; Nimmrich & Eckert, 2013). Ergoloid mesylates and the related ergot derivative nicergoline are believed to work as vasodilators and may also have antioxidant properties. Several studies have shown some benefit for both of these agents, although the studies tended to have small samples and variable definitions of dementia, making it difficult to make efficacy conclusions from the heterogeneous samples (Fioravanti & Flicker, 2001; Olin, Schneider, Novit, & Luczak, 2001).

Ginkgo biloba has a variety of potential mechanisms but has not shown clear efficacy and can also increase the risk of bleeding if taken along with warfarin and antiplatelet agents (DeKosky, Williamson, & Fitzpatrick, 2008). Several nootropic ("acting on the mind") agents include cytidinediphosphocholine (CDP-choline), believed to activate the synthesis of neuronal membrane phospholipids, and a group of amino acid compounds that include piracetam and oxiracetam. Unfortunately, none of these agents have well-established efficacy for enhancing memory and no clear benefit for treating VaD and so are not currently recommended treatment options (Fioravanti & Yanagi, 2005).

Acetylcholinesterase Inhibitors

Recent studies have demonstrated improvement in cognition, function, and even behavior in VaD with the use of the AChE inhibitors, including donepezil (Rockwood et al., 2013; Román et al., 2010), rivastigmine (Ballard et al., 2008; Birks, McGuinness, & Craig, 2013), and galantamine (Auchus et al., 2007). Behavioral indices that improved in VaD patients included apathy, anxiety, irritability, depression, and even psychosis. Donepezil has also shown to significantly improve memory function in patients with Binswanger's disease and executive deficits in CADASIL (Dichgans et al., 2008; Kwon et al., 2009). Given these findings, both AD and VaD likely involve central cholinergic deficits that can be ameliorated with AChE inhibitor therapy (Román & Kalaria, 2006). The mechanism of these agents and the dosing strategies are covered in detail in Chapter 4; see especially Table 4.5.

Glutamate Receptor Antagonists

As described in Chapter 4, memantine is an N-methyl-D-aspartate (NMDA or glutamate)–receptor antagonist that is FDA approved to treat moderate to severe stages of AD. In two clinical trials, VaD patients treated with memantine maintained relative cognitive stability over 28 weeks compared to a placebo group (Orgogozo et al., 2002; Wilcock et al., 2002). In clinical practice, memantine is commonly prescribed in combination with an AChE inhibitor. Memantine is described in more detail in Chapter 4; see Table 4.5 for information about dosing.

References

American Psychiatric Association. (2000). *Diagnostic and statistical manual of mental disorders* (4th ed., Text Rev.). Washington, DC: Author.

American Psychiatric Association. (2013). *Diagnostic and statistical manual of mental disorders* (5th ed.). Washington, DC: Author.

Auchus, A. P., Brashear, H. R., Salloway, S., et al., & the GAL-INT-26 Study Group. (2007). Galantamine treatment of vascular dementia: A randomized trial. *Neurol, 69*(5), 448–458.

Ballard, C., Sauter, M., Scheltens, P., et al. (2008). Efficacy, safety and tolerability of rivastigmine capsules in patients with probable vascular dementia: The VantagE study. *Curr Med Res Opin, 24*(9), 2561–2574.

Birks, J., McGuinness, B., & Craig, D. (2013). Rivastigmine for vascular cognitive impairment. *Cochrane Database Syst Rev, 5*, CD004744.

Centers for Disease Control. (2012). Prevalence of stroke: United States, 2006–2010. *MMWR, 61*(20), 379–382.

Chabriat, H., Joutel, A., Dichgans, M., et al. (2009). CADASIL. *Lancet Neurol, 8*(7), 643–653.

Chui, H. C. (2007). Subcortical ischemic vascular dementia. *Neurol Clin, 25*(3), 717–740.

DeKosky, S. T., Williamson, J. D., & Fitzpatrick, A. L. (2008). Ginkgo biloba for prevention of dementia: A randomized controlled trial. *JAMA, 300*(19), 2253–2262.

Dichgans, M., Markus, H. S., Salloway, S., et al. (2008). Donepezil in patients with subcortical vascular cognitive impairment: A randomised double-blind trial in CADASIL. *Lancet Neurol, 7*(4), 310–318.

Erkinjuntti, T., Román, G., Gauthier, S., et al. (2004). Emerging therapies for vascular dementia and vascular cognitive impairment. *Stroke, 35*(4), 1010–1017.

Fioravanti, M., & Flicker, L. (2001). Efficacy of nicergoline in dementia and other age associated forms of cognitive impairment. *Cochrane Database Syst Rev, 4*, CD003159.

Fioravanti, M., & Yanagi, M. (2005). Cytidinediphosphocholine (CDP-choline) for cognitive and behavioural disturbances associated with chronic cerebral disorders in the elderly. *Cochrane Database Syst Rev, 2*, CD000269.

Gold, G., Kovari, E., Hof, P. R., et al. (2007). Sorting out the clinical consequences of ischemic lesions in brain aging: A clinicopathological approach. *J Neurol Sci, 257*(1–2), 17–22.

Grysiewicz, R., & Gorelick, P. B. (2012). Key neuroanatomical structures for post-stroke cognitive impairment. *Curr Neurol Neurosci Rep, 12*(6), 703–708.

Guermazi, A. Miaux, Y., Rovira-Cùnellas, A., et al. (2007). Neuroradiological findings in vascular dementia. *Neuroradiology, 49*(1), 1–22.

Hachinski, V. C., Iliff, L. D., Zilhka, E., et al. (1975). Cerebral blood flow in dementia. *Arch Neurol, 32*, 632–637.

Hébert, R., Lindsay, J., Verreault, R., et al. (2000). Vascular dementia: Incidence and risk factors in the Canadian study of health and aging. *Stroke, 31*, 1487–1493.

Jellinger, K. A. (2013). Pathology and pathogenesis of vascular cognitive impairment—a critical update. *Front Aging Neurosci, 5*, 17.

Kalaria, R. N. (2003). Comparison between Alzheimer's disease and vascular dementia: Implications for treatment. *Neurol Res, 25*(6), 661–664.

Kloppenborg, R. P., van den Berg, E., Kappelle, L. J., & Biessels, G. J. (2008). Diabetes and other vascular risk factors for dementia: Which factor matters most? A systematic review. *Eur J Pharmacol, 585*(1), 97–108. doi: 10.1016/j.ejphar.2008.02.049

Kwon, J. C., Kim, E. G., Kim, J. W., et al., & the BKVD Study Group. (2009). A multicenter, open-label, 24-week follow-up study for efficacy on cognitive function of donepezil in Binswanger-type subcortical vascular dementia. *Am J Alzheimers Dis Dem, 24*(4), 293–301.

Leys, D., Hénon, H., Mackowiak-Cordoliani, M. A., & Pasquier, F. (2005). Poststroke dementia. *Lancet Neurol, 4*(11), 752–759.

Libon, D. J., Price, C. C., Davis Garrett, K., & Giovannetti, T. (2004). From Binswanger's disease to leukoaraiosis: What we have learned about subcortical vascular dementia. *Clin Neuropsychologist, 18*(1), 83–100.

Looi, J. C. L., & Sachdev, P. S. (1999). Differentiation of vascular dementia from AD on neuropsychological tests. *Neurol, 53*(4), 670–678.

López-Arrieta, J. M., & Birks, J. (2002). Nimodipine for primary degenerative, mixed and vascular dementia. *Cochrane Database Syst Rev, 3*, CD000147.

McGuinness, B., Craig, D., Bullock, R., & Passmore, P. (2009). Statins for the prevention of dementia. *Cochrane Database Syst Rev, 2*, CD003160.

McGuinness, B., Todd, S., Passmore, P., & Bullock, R. (2009). Blood pressure lowering in patients without prior cerebrovascular disease for prevention of cognitive impairment and dementia. *Cochrane Database Syst Rev, 4*, CD004034.

Nimmrich, V., & Eckert, A. (2013). Calcium channel blockers and dementia. *Br J Pharmacol, 169*(6), 1203–1210.

Olin, J., Schneider, L., Novit, A., & Luczak, S. (2001). Hydergine for dementia. *Cochrane Database Syst Rev, 2*, CD000359.

Orgogozo, J. M., Rigaud, A. S., Stöffler, A., et al. (2002). Efficacy and safety of memantine in patients with mild to moderate vascular dementia: a randomized, placebo-controlled trial (MMM 300). *Stroke, 33*(7), 1834–1839.

Rockwood, K., Mitnitski, A., Black, S. E., et al., & The Vaspect Study Investigators. (2013). Cognitive change in donepezil treated patients with vascular or mixed dementia. *Can J Neurol Sci, 40*(4), 564–571.

Román, G. C. (2002). Vascular dementia revisited: diagnosis, pathogenesis, treatment, and prevention. *Med Clin North Am, 86*(3), 477–499.

Román, G. C., & Kalaria, R. N. (2006). Vascular determinants of cholinergic deficits in Alzheimer's disease and vascular dementia. *Neurobiol Aging, 27*, 1769–1785.

Román, G. C., Salloway, S., Black, S. E., et al. (2010). Randomized, placebo-controlled, clinical trial of donepezil in vascular dementia: Differential effects by hippocampal size. *Stroke, 41*(6), 1213–1221.

Román, G. C., Tatemichi, T. K., Erkinjuntti, T., et al. (1993). Vascular dementia: Diagnostic criteria for research studies. Report of the NINDS–AIREN International Workshop. *Neurol, 43,* 250–260.

Sheng, B., Cheng, L. F., Law, C. B., et al. (2007). Coexisting cerebral infarction in Alzheimer's disease is associated with fast dementia progression: Applying the National Institute of Neurological Disorders and Stroke–Association International pour la Recherche et l'Enseignementen Neurosciences neuroimaging criteria in Alzheimer's disease with concomitant cerebral infarction. *J Am Ger Soc, 55*(6), 918–922.

Small, G. W., Bookheimer, S. Y., Thompson, P. M., et al. (2008). Current and future uses of neuroimaging for cognitively impaired patients. *Lancet Neurol, 7*(2), 161–172.

Victor, M. A., & Ropper, A. H. (2009). *Adams and Victor's principles of neurology* (9th ed.). New York: McGraw-Hill Professional.

Weller, R. O., Boche, D., & Nicoll, J. A. (2009). Microvasculature changes and cerebral amyloid angiopathy in Alzheimer's disease and their potential impact on therapy. *Acta Neuropathol, 118*(1), 87–102.

Weller, R. O., & Nicoll, J. A. (2003). Cerebral amyloid angiopathy: pathogenesis and effects on the ageing and Alzheimer brain. *Neurol Res, 25*(6), 611–616.

Wilcock, G., Möbius, H. J., Stöffler, A., & the MMM 500 Group. (2002). A double-blind, placebo-controlled multicentre study of memantine in mild to moderate vascular dementia (MMM500). *Int Clin Psychopharmacol, 17*(6), 297–305.

6 Dementia with Lewy Bodies

Lewy bodies (LBs) are abnormal, spherical intracytoplasmic protein deposits that can appear in both subcortical and cortical neurons. First identified in 1912 by the German neurologist Frederic H. Lewy, these neuronal inclusion bodies were not formally associated with a form of dementia until several seminal case reports appeared in the early 1980s (Kosaka et al., 1984). The clinical picture that has emerged over time often resembles that of both Alzheimer's disease (AD) and vascular dementia (VaD), but there are distinct symptoms that researchers and clinicians have organized into a coherent diagnostic entity known as dementia with Lewy bodies (DLB). Several pathologic studies have found Lewy bodies in the brains of 15%–25% of individuals with dementia, suggesting that DLB may be more common than VaD (Weisman & McKeith, 2007; Zaccai, McCracken, & Brayne, 2005). In one systematic review, however, DLB was found in 4.2% of dementia cases in the community and 7.5% of cases in secondary care settings (Vann Jones & O'Brien, 2013). Although LBs are common findings in aged brains, their presence does not guarantee DLB since 30%–55% of individuals with Lewy body pathology do not show neuropsychiatric symptoms (Jellinger, 2009).

Case Study

Mr. J, a 78-year-old man, was brought to his primary care physician due to the sudden onset of confusion and daytime somnolence. He was sleeping poorly and was complaining of seeing small figures running around the house at night. When his wife was asked about recent events, she reported that they had just returned from a cruise on which Mr. J had had an apparent stomach flu; he had been given an antiemetic agent by the ship's clinic that he took for five days. After thorough physical and mental status examinations, the primary care physician suspected a delirium and hospitalized Mr. J for a medical workup. Because of his increased agitation and hallucinations in the hospital, Mr. J was given several doses of haloperidol intramuscularly. Within 24 hours, he deteriorated precipitously, becoming nearly catatonic. He was taken off all of the medications and rehydrated, and over four weeks his mental status and function slowly improved almost back to his previous baseline. However, three months later, his wife brought him back to the physician with recurrent hallucinations.

Although Mr. J appeared to have a delirium, he was actually in the early stages of DLB, demonstrating the typical pattern of fluctuating decline in cognition and function, accompanied by visual hallucinations. The episode was triggered by an antiemetic medication such as prochlorperazine, which is in the same family as antipsychotic agents, and it was later exacerbated by the administration of haloperidol. Antipsychotic sensitivity is a common feature of DLB.

Diagnostic Criteria

The initial case reports of DLB described patients with a progressive dementia associated with muscle rigidity, fluctuating episodes of decline in function and cognition, and psychotic symptoms. The accumulating literature then reported what has become one of the most challenging aspects of DLB: treatment with antipsychotic medications to control behavioral disturbances and psychotic symptoms often triggered episodes of acute impairment characterized by rigidity, confusion, and sedation. Further clinical observation and research has led to the development of consensus guidelines for DLB, which have been revised several times (McKeith et al., 2005). The core features of DLB, as shown in Table 6.1, are fluctuating symptoms, visual hallucinations, and parkinsonism. The average age at onset is between 50 and 80 years.

Fluctuating cognitive symptoms are seen in 80% of patients with DLB, and these symptoms may involve episodes of reduced attention or alertness, somnolence, and

Table 6.1 Consensus Criteria for the Clinical Diagnosis of Probable and Possible Dementia with Lewy Bodies

- Main criteria: progressive cognitive decline sufficient to interfere with normal social and occupational function. Prominent or persistent memory impairment may not necessarily occur in early stages, but it is evident with disease progression. Prominent neuropsychologic deficits may occur in attention, frontal/subcortical skills, and visuospatial ability.

- Probable DLB requires at least two of the following core features, and possible DLB requires at least one: (1) fluctuating cognition with pronounced variations in attention and alertness, (2) recurrent visual hallucinations that are typically well-formed and detailed, and (3) spontaneous motor features of parkinsonism.

- Features supportive of the diagnosis include repeated falls, syncope, transient loss of consciousness, severe neuroleptic (antipsychotic) sensitivity, systematized delusions, hallucinations in other modalities, depression, REM sleep behavior disorder, and reduced striatal dopamine transporter activity on functional neuroimaging.

- Commonly seen symptoms that support the diagnosis of DLB but are not diagnostic include repeated falls and syncope, transient, unexplained loss of consciousness, severe autonomic dysfunction (e.g., orthostatic hypotension, urinary incontinence), psychotic symptoms other than visual hallucinations (e.g., delusions, auditory hallucinations), depression, abnormal EEG with prominent slow-wave activity and temporal lobe sharp waves, relative preservation of medial temporal lobe structures on CT or MRI, and hypometabolism on PET scans, especially in occipital regions

- A diagnosis of DLB is less likely in the presence of cerebrovascular disease with stroke and when another disorder that can account for the symptoms is present.

Modified from McKeith (2011); McKeith, Perry, and Perry (1999); McKeith et al. (1996, 2005).

decline in function that last from hours to weeks (Del Ser et al., 2000). During these episodes, ruling out other acute causes of mental status changes is critical. Visual hallucinations are seen in approximately 50% of patients with DLB, and these often worsen during periods of decline. The hallucinations are typically recurrent and well-formed, and they may consist of animals or people (Mosimann et al., 2006). They may be associated with visuospatial impairment, visual agnosias, and occipital metabolic disturbances that are evident on positron emission tomography scans. Auditory, olfactory, and tactile hallucinations are less common, but they do have diagnostic importance as well.

The third core feature of DLB is parkinsonism, characterized by muscle rigidity, a stiff and slowed gait, a stooped posture, bradykinesia, masked facies, and resting tremors. In DLB, the onset of dementia is typically within 12 months of the onset of parkinsonism. A history of parkinsonism that predates cognitive impairment by a year or more is suggestive of Parkinson's disease or PD with an associated dementia (McKeith et al., 2005). Other diagnostic features include repeated falls, episodes of syncope, transient loss of consciousness, rapid eye movement or REM sleep behavior disorder, psychosis, and depression. The symptom of repeated falls may be related to the presence of subcortical brain damage that has led to extrapyramidal rigidity and bradykinesia. Extension of LB disease into the brainstem may account for the episodes of syncope. These latter features of DLB are seen in other forms of dementia, however, and are thus of limited diagnostic utility.

Course

Most individuals with DLB have a rather rocky course, facing about a 10% annual decline in both cognitive and motor abilities (McKeith, 2011). The average lifespan from the time of clinical presentation is about eight years, although some individuals succumb much sooner. It has been suggested that DLB patients decline more rapidly than patients with AD, although this is not well-supported (Hanyu et al., 2009). It is possible that any such decline may be due in part to iatrogenic complications from pharmacological agents. In any event, the keys to a better clinical course appear to be judicious management of behavioral disturbances, prevention of injury due to motor symptoms, and caregiver support and education. Caregivers should be referred to both a local branch of the Alzheimer's Association as well as the Lewy Body Dementia Association (www.lewybodydementia.org). See Chapter 12 for more suggestions on helping caregivers.

Etiology and Pathology

Although the exact cause of DLB has not been determined, it is associated with the progressive build-up of LBs in both subcortical and cortical regions of the brain, with ensuing cerebral atrophy. LBs are composed of a core of filamentous protein granules, including alpha-synuclein and ubiquitin, with a surrounding halo of neurofilaments. They are found either around the nucleus of neurons or in the dendrites. Microscopic visualization of LBs is accomplished through immunocytologic staining with antibodies to both ubiquitin and alpha-synuclein. Histopathologic studies have indicated that, in both DLB and PD, heavy concentrations of LBs are present in the subcortical regions, including the hypothalamus and key brainstem nuclei, such as the substantia nigra, the locus coeruleus, and the nucleus basalis of Meynert (Zaccai et al., 2008). In patients with DLB alone, however, LBs are also seen in cortical regions, especially the frontal and temporal lobes, and in associated limbic structures. The cognitive impairment of DLB and concomitant psychiatric symptoms do not necessarily correlate with the density of LBs (Kramer & Schulz-Schaeffer, 2007). As in AD, senile plaques are also seen, but the presence of neurofibrillary tangles is minimal.

Classification

As more has been learned about correlations between clinical symptoms and histopathological findings, some researchers have classified DLB into several subtypes based on the location of the LBs and the degree of dementia (Mrak & Griffin, 2007), including the following:

- Diffuse LBD: LBs are both in the brainstem and cortex; associated with moderate to severe dementia and less prominent parkinsonian features.
- Transitional LBD: LBs mainly in the brainstem; associated with mild to moderate cognitive dysfunction.
- Brainstem LBs: associated with PD with minimal to mild cognitive impairment.
- Cerebral LBs: associated with mild dementia resembling AD.
- Mixed LB and AD or LB variant of AD: LBs, senile plaques, and neurofibrillary tangles in the cerebral cortex; associated with a dementia similar to AD but more pronounced impairments in attention, speech, mood, and visuospatial abilities.

In clinical practice it might not be possible or practical to classify the different types of DLB, as it remains largely a pathologic exercise. But keep in mind that DLB, like AD and VaD, is a heterogeneous disorder with many permutations reflected in clinical symptoms.

Assessment

The assessment of DLB follows the general model outlined for dementia in Chapters 1 and 2. No unique diagnostic tests for DLB exist, and, in general, neither neuroimaging nor electroencephalography is helpful. The first step should be a comparison of the clinical history with the consensus guidelines for diagnosis as given in Table 6.1. Neuropsychological testing can provide more detailed profiles of the cognitive impairment; individuals with DLB demonstrate early impairment in memory retrieval and verbal fluency, attentional performance (e.g., digit span), visuospatial ability, and executive function. Language dysfunction is less prominent in earlier stages (McKeith, 2011).

Despite the very specific core features of DLB, it often resembles AD in both its presentation and course. In general, though, the extrapyramidal features of DLB that are often present, along with recurrent episodes of sensitivity to antipsychotics (and sometimes other psychotropics), should help to distinguish it from the more common presentation of AD. In addition, patients with DLB have been shown to demonstrate greater functional and neuropsychiatric impairment compared to AD patients with similar degrees of cognitive impairment. Unlike the growing use of biomarkers with AD, there are no comparable measurements of LBs or their derivatives in cerebrospinal fluid (CSF) or on positron emission tomography (PET) scans. Neuroimaging may be helpful, however, both in identifying DLB and distinguishing it from AD by showing relative preservation of hippocampal and medial temporal lobe volume on magnetic resonance imaging (MRI) scans (Burton et al., 2009) and loss of cerebral metabolism with marked occipital hypoperfusion on functional scans such as PET or single photon emission computed tomography (Lobotesis et al., 2001). The pronounced functional disability in DLB patients appears directly related to their extrapyramidal symptoms. A more challenging task may be to differentiate between DLB and PD with dementia, as discussed in the next section.

Parkinson's Disease Dementia

PD is a movement disorder caused by the degeneration of a specific dopaminergic subcortical structure called the substantia nigra. The classic symptoms of PD are rigidity, bradykinesia, impaired gait and posture, and resting tremors. Dementia has long been a hallmark of PD, presenting clinically with the subcortical pattern described in Chapters 1 and 5. Parkinson's disease dementia (PDD) eventually afflicts 20% to 45% of patients with PD, with the annual incidence increasing with duration of illness and older age, from 3% per year prior to age 65 to 14% and higher after the age of 70 (Aarsland et al., 2003; Tarawneh & Galvin, 2009). Other risk factors for PDD include a greater severity of motor impairment, visual hallucinations, a history of depression, a poor response to levodopa, and sensitivity to antipsychotics (Aarsland et al., 2005; Emre, Cummings & Lane, 2007). The rates of depression and psychosis associated with PD are as high as 40%. Both hallucinations and delusions commonly result from excessive dopaminergic activity in the mesolimbic pathways, largely as a result of antiparkinsonian medication, such as levodopa.

Twenty-five percent of individuals with PDD are believed to have DLB. The consensus guidelines state that, when parkinsonism precedes symptoms of dementia by 12 months or more, the diagnosis is PDD. When dementia precedes or parallels parkinsonism, the diagnosis is DLB (McKeith et al., 2005). Clinically, distinguishing the symptoms of PDD from DLB can be difficult, with several exceptions. Extrapyramidal symptoms (EPS) in PD tend to be more pronounced, and they respond to levodopa and other anti-Parkinson medications; in contrast, DLB patients respond poorly if at all to levodopa. Individuals with PD do not tend to have the fluctuating symptomatic episodes that are characteristic of DLB, and they do not demonstrate the same type of sensitivity to antipsychotics, aside from the potential for increased EPS with more potent agents. In addition, myoclonus is more common in DLB, whereas tremors are more common in PD.

Other Dementias with Extrapyramidal Features

Other dementias that have a clinical resemblance to DLB due to their prominent extrapyramidal features include progressive supranuclear palsy (PSP), corticobasal degeneration (CBD), and multiple system atrophy (MSA). Because PSP and CBD both involve significant frontal lobe dysfunction, they are described in Chapter 7. MSA is a degenerative neurological disorder that is characterized by parkinsonism, upper motor neuron impairment, cerebellar dysfunction, and dysautonomia (e.g., urinary incontinence, sexual dysfunction, orthostatic hypotension). The average age at onset is in the mid-50s, with a mean survival of 6–7 years (Wenning, Geser, Stampfer-Kountchev, & Tison, 2003). Neuronal loss and gliosis are seen throughout the basal ganglia and brainstem nuclei, with variable involvement of thalamic nuclei, olivopontocerebellar tracts, intermediolateral columns, and pyramidal tracts. The histopathologic findings include glial and, to a lesser extent, neuronal cytoplasmic inclusions that, like LBs, stain positive for the proteins ubiquitin and alpha-synuclein. Mild to moderate dementia with frontal lobe impairment is seen in some individuals with MSA; this typically is less severe than in DLB or AD (Stefanova, Bücke, Duerr, & Wenning, 2009). Although several agents including riluzole, recombinant human growth hormone, and minocycline have been studied, none have shown efficacy in the treatment of MSA (Stefanova et al., 2009).

Treatment

No cure for DLB exists; instead, treatment should focus on ways to improve various clinical symptoms, especially psychosis and behavioral disturbances. Given the clinical complexity of DLB, it is important to promote a multidisciplinary approach to address the variety of cognitive, functional, and behavioral symptoms. In addition, it is critical to educate caregivers about the fluctuating symptoms and sensitivity to medications seen in DLB patients, so that there is added need to vigilantly watch for side effects that could quickly lead to severe loss of function.

Acetycholinesterase Inhibitors

As in AD and VaD, DLB and PDD likely involve central cholinergic deficiencies, a possibility that explains why some individuals with DLB and PDD respond robustly to acetylcholinesterase (AChE) inhibitors (Tiraboschi et al., 2000). Improvements have been seen in all domains, including cognition, behavior, apathy, psychosis, delirium, and sleep disturbances (Aarsland, Mosimann, & McKeith, 2004; Emre et al., 2007; Thomas et al., 2005). PDD patients appear to respond better than DLB patients (Rolinski, Fox, Maidment, & McShane, 2012). The presence of visual hallucinations appear to predict a better response to AChE inhibitors (McKeith, Wesnes, Perry, & Ferrara, 2004). Dosing ranges for the AChE inhibitors donepezil, rivastigmine, and galantamine can be found in Chapter 4 in Table 4.5. In general, individuals with DLB may need to be started at lower doses and be titrated slower than those with AD, in order to monitor for any idiosyncratic reactions. Problematic side effects may include nausea, vomiting, and diarrhea, as well as cholinergic effects such as hypersalivation and rhinorrhea (Thomas et al., 2005).

Glutamate-Receptor Antagonists

A double-blind, placebo-controlled study looking at the use of the glutamate-receptor antagonist memantine in DLB found modest improvement in global improvement and cognition compared to placebo (Aarsland et al., 2009). As with AChE inhibitors, dosing with memantine should start very low (2.5 to 5 mg once a day) and be titrated on a weekly or biweekly basis with close monitoring for paradoxical or idiosyncratic reactions. DLB patients on memantine must be monitored particularly closely for more pronounced symptoms of sedation and confusion than in non-DLB patients, in whom these side effects are typically mild and self-limiting.

Agitation and Psychosis

In all cases of DLB, the clinician faces an immediate challenge in the treatment of agitation and psychosis because nearly 50% of patients with DLB demonstrate sensitivity to antipsychotic medications (McKeith et al., 1992). This sensitivity is characterized by an acute decline in cognition and function, increased parkinsonism, reduced alertness and drowsiness, and a significant increase in mortality over time. These reactions usually occur within several weeks of the initiation of treatment, and they range from mild to severe, with the latter occurring in approximately one-third of sensitive individuals. Conventional antipsychotics cause the highest rate of reactions, and they should be avoided. Atypical antipsychotics including risperidone, olanzapine, clozapine, and quetiapine are preferred because they have a lower risk, although their use must still be monitored closely for acute reactions (Burke, Pfeiffer, & McComb, 1998; Kurlan, Cummings, Raman, & Thal, 2007; Walker et al., 1999). Keep in mind, however, that no one atypical agent has demonstrated clear efficacy in treating the agitation and psychosis associated with DLB; similarly, no specific agent has been shown to offer advantages over the use of any other. With DLB, then, nonpharmacological approaches are always best first-line approaches for behavioral disturbances, and antipsychotics should be avoided if psychotic symptoms are mild and not causing significant distress. See Chapter 9 for more information.

Clinical Tip

Individuals with PDD do not demonstrate the same sensitivity to antipsychotic agents and can often be treated successfully for symptoms of psychosis and agitation without significantly worsening their motor symptoms. Many clinicians prefer to start with a low potency agent such as quetiapine or clozapine, although one can never predict sensitivity ahead of time. It is prudent to administer a test dose of the lowest possible dose of the medication, and then observe for effect, so as to avoid precipitating a catastrophic loss of function due to sensitivity.

Low doses of a mood stabilizer such as valproic acid (125 mg–500 mg range) or benzodiazepines such as lorazepam (0.25 mg–1 mg range) and clonazepam (0.25 mg–1 mg range) can also be used to treat behavioral disturbances, particularly nocturnal ones such as REM sleep behavior disorder, but with the same caution as with any other psychotropic agent (Boeve et al., 2003). The risks of excess sedation and increased falls are of particular concern with these latter medications. Low dose trazodone (25 mg–100 mg range) may be a more benign agent for some DLB patients but not all and can lead to excess sedation. Both behavioral and pharmacological treatment strategies for psychosis and agitation are outlined in Chapter 9, along with more detailed dosing strategies. Approaches for treating apathy, depression, and sleep disturbances are outlined in Chapter 10.

References

Aarsland, D., Andersen, K., Larsen, J. P., et al. (2003). Prevalence and characteristics of dementia in Parkinson disease. *Arch Neurol, 60*(3), 387–392.

Aarsland, D., Ballard, C., Walker, Z., et al. (2009). Memantine in patients with Parkinson's disease dementia or dementia with Lewy bodies: A double-blind placebo-controlled, multicentre trial. *Lancet Neurology, 8*, 613–618.

Aarsland, D., Mosimann, U. P., & McKeith, I. G. (2004). Role of cholinesterase inhibitors in Parkinson's disease and dementia with Lewy bodies. *J Geriatr Psychiatry Neurol, 17*(3), 164–171.

Aarsland, D., Perry, R., Larsen, J. P., et al. (2005). Neuroleptic sensitivity in Parkinson's disease and parkinsonian dementias. *J Clin Psychiatry, 66*(5), 633–637.

Boeve, B. F., Silber, M. H., Parisi, J. E., et al. (2003). Synucleinopathy pathology and REM sleep behavior disorder plus dementia or parkinsonism. *Neurol, 61*, 40–45.

Burke, W. J., Pfeiffer, R. F., & McComb, R. D. (1998). Neuroleptic sensitivity to clozapine in dementia with Lewy bodies. *J Neuropsychiatry Clin Neurosci, 10*(2), 227–229.

Burton, E. J., Barber, R., Mukaetova-Ladinska, E. B., et al. (2009). Medial temporal lobe atrophy on MRI differentiates Alzheimer's disease from in dementia with Lewy bodies and vascular cognitive impairment. *Brain, 132*, 195–203.

Del Ser, T., McKeith, I., Anand, R., Cicin-Sain, A., Ferrara, R., & Spiegel, R. (2000). Dementia with Lewy bodies: Findings from an international multicentre study. *Int J Geriatr Psychiatry, 15*, 1034–1045.

Emre, M., Cummings J. L., & Lane, R. M. (2007). Rivastigmine in dementia associated with Parkinson's disease and Alzheimer's disease: Similarities and differences. *J Alzheimers Dis, 11*(4), 509–519.

Hanyu, H., Sato, T., Hirao, K., et al. (2009). Differences in clinical course between dementia with Lewy bodies and Alzheimer's disease. *Eur J Neurol, 16*(2), 212–217.

Jellinger, K. A. (2009). Formation and development of Lewy pathology: A critical update. *J Neurol, 256*(Suppl. 3), 270–279.

Kosaka, K., Yoshimura, M., Ikeda, K., et al. (1984). Diffuse type of Lewy body disease: progressive dementia with abundant cortical Lewy bodies and senile changes of varying degree: A new disease? *Clin Neuropathol, 3*, 185–192.

Kramer, M. L., & Schulz-Schaeffer, W. J. (2007). Presynaptic alpha-synuclein aggregates, not Lewy bodies, cause neurodegeneration in dementia with Lewy bodies. *J Neurosci, 27*, 1405–1410.

Kurlan, R., Cummings, J., Raman, R., & Thal, L. (2007). Quetiapine for agitation or psychosis in patients with dementia and parkinsonism. *Neurol, 68*(17), 1356–1363.

Lobotesis, K., Fenwick, J. D., Phipps, A., et al. (2001). Occipital hypoperfusion on SPECT in dementia with Lewy bodies but not AD. *Neurol, 56*, 643–649.

McKeith, I. G. (2011). Dementia with Lewy bodies. In M. E. Agronin & G. J. Maletta (Eds.), *Principles and practice of geriatric psychiatry* (2nd ed., pp. 333–341). Philadelphia: Lippincott, Williams and Wilkins.

McKeith, I. G., Dickson, D. W., Lowe, J., et al. (2005). Diagnosis and management of dementia with Lewy bodies: Third report of the DLB Consortium. *Neurol, 65*(12), 1863–1872.

McKeith, I., Fairbairn, A., Perry, R., et al. (1992). Neuroleptic sensitivity in patients with senile dementia of Lewy body type. *Br Med J, 305,* 673–678.

McKeith, I. G., Galasko, D., Kosaka, K., et al. (1996). Consensus guidelines for the clinical and pathologic diagnosis of dementia with Lewy bodies (DLB): Report of the Consortium on DLB International Workshop. *Neurol, 47,* 1113–1124.

McKeith, I. G., Perry, E. K., & Perry, R. H. (1999). Report of the Second Dementia with Lewy Body International Workshop: Diagnosis and treatment. Consortium on Dementia with Lewy Bodies. *Neurol, 53,* 902–905.

McKeith, I. G., Wesnes, K. A., Perry, E., & Ferrara, R. (2004). Hallucinations predict attentional improvements with rivastigmine in dementia with Lewy bodies. *Dement Geriatr Cogn Disord, 18,* 94–100.

Mosimann, U. P., Rowan, EN, Partington, C. E., Collerton, D., Littlewood, E., O'Brien, J. T., et al. (2006). Characteristics of visual hallucinations in Parkinson disease dementia and dementia with Lewy bodies. *Am J Geriat Psychiat, 14*(2), 153–160.

Mrak, R. E., & Griffin, S. T. (2007). Dementia with Lewy bodies: Definition, diagnosis, and pathogenic relationship to Alzheimer's disease. *Neuropsychiatr Dis Treat, 3*(5), 619–625.

Rolinski, M., Fox, C., Maidment, I., & McShane, R. (2012). Cholinesterase inhibitors for dementia with Lewy bodies, Parkinson's disease dementia and cognitive impairment in Parkinson's disease. *Cochrane Database Syst Rev, 14*(3), CD006504.

Stefanova, N., Bücke, P., Duerr, S., & Wenning, G. K. (2009). Multiple system atrophy: An update. *Lancet Neurol, 8*(12), 1172–1178.

Tarawneh, R., & Galvin, J. E. (2009). Dementia with Lewy bodies and other synucleinopathies. In M. F. Weiner & A. M. Lipton (Eds.), *Textbook of Alzheimer disease and other dementias.* Washington, DC: American Psychiatric Publishing.

Thomas, A. J., Burn, D. J., Rowen, E. N., et al. (2005). Efficacy of donepezil in Parkinson's disease with dementia and dementia with Lewy bodies. *Int J Geriatr, 20*(10), 938–944.

Tiraboschi, P., Hansen, L. A., Alford, M., et al. (2000). Cholinergic dysfunction in diseases with Lewy bodies. *Neurology, 54*(2), 407–411.

Vann Jones, S. A., & O'Brien, J. T. (2013). The prevalence and incidence of dementia with Lewy bodies: A systematic review of population and clinical studies. *Psychol Med, 25,* 1–11.

Walker, Z., Grace, J., Overshot, R., et al. (1999). Olanzapine in dementia with Lewy bodies: A clinical study. *Int J Geriatr Psychiatry, 14*(6), 459–466.

Weisman, D., & McKeith, I. (2007). Dementia with Lewy bodies. *Semin Neurol, 27*(1), 42–47.

Wenning, G. K., Geser, F., Stampfer-Kountchev, M., & Tison, F. (2003). Multiple system atrophy: An update. *Mov Disord, 18*(Suppl. 6), S34–S42.

Zaccai, J., Brayne, C., McKeith, I., et al. (2008). Patterns and stages of alpha-synucleinopathy: Relevance in a population-based cohort. *Neurology, 70,* 1042–1048.

Zaccai, J., McCracken, C., & Brayne, C. (2005). A systematic review of prevalence and incidence studies of dementia with Lewy bodies. *Age Ageing, 34*(6), 561–566.

7   Frontotemporal Dementia

The frontal lobes are unique in that they account for nearly one-third of the cerebral cortex and have great anatomic and functional diversity. For this reason, damage to frontal regions (and, by extension, to the temporal lobes as well) produces a spectrum of syndromes with disproportionate effects on executive function, behavioral control, and language. Fronto-temporal dementia (FTD) represents a group of related dementias that have several of the following common elements: focal neuronal loss in the frontal and/or temporal lobes, cognitive impairment, and early disturbances that predominantly affect behavior, language, and personality. Given these characteristics, FTD in its early stages may closely resemble psychiatric disorders with psychotic, obsessive-compulsive, depressive, or manic features. In the middle and later stages, it is often confused with Alzheimer's disease (AD).

FTD is believed to affect 3%–10% of all individuals with dementia (Kertesz, 2005), although, among individuals with early-onset dementia (younger than 65 years of age), the percentage with FTD may be as high as 20% (Snowden et al., 2001). Nearly 80% of individuals with FTD have onset prior to age 65, with a median age of onset around 58 years (Weder, Aziz, Wilkins, & Tampi, 2007). Epidemiologic research suggests that 20%–40% of individuals with FTD may have a family history of the disorder and that having FTD in a first-degree relative may be associated with a 3.5 times greater risk of developing it (McKhann et al., 2001). Although there are no definitive risk factors for FTD, a case-control study found a potential increase in risk associated with head trauma and thyroid disease (Rosso, Landweer, & Houterman, 2003).

Case Study

Mrs. J was a 58-year-old woman with severe dementia who resided in a nursing home. Her clinical history indicated that she had an uneventful childhood, but she was described by her parents as an anxious child. After graduating from college with a degree in biology, she attended nursing school, eventually becoming a registered nurse in a community hospital. She married at the age of 28 and had two children over the course of the next five years. She and her husband began having marital problems shortly after the birth of their second child and divorced after six years of marriage. Mrs. J continued to work, and she got involved with the local Red Cross. Throughout her 30s and 40s, she was in good health, and she enjoyed her roles as a nurse and mother. At the age of 48, Mrs. J began having problems managing her daily schedule. Her children reported that she sometimes forgot to pick them up at school and that she would become uncontrollably upset when they eventually arrived home and expressed anger toward her. Fellow volunteers at the Red Cross noticed that she was quieter and that she seemed to have a hard time expressing herself. At times, she stuttered, and, when she was angry, she had a difficult time articulating her concerns. She also worried incessantly that the blood that she handled at the blood bank was contaminated, and, on several occasions, she expressed paranoid concerns to her supervisor.

At the age of 50, she had a comprehensive dementia workup, the results of which suggested the devastating diagnosis of either AD or FTD. She had already been on leave from work, but, with her mother's assistance, she went on permanent disability. As her behavior became more erratic and her cognition declined, her mother had her move into her home, and her children went to live with their father. Over the next few years, her language function deteriorated to the point where she was unable to produce basic sentences; she would instead use single words or jumbles of words to express herself. She sometimes began screaming incoherently when she could not express particular needs. She also began to demonstrate bizarre behaviors, such as hoarding cereal boxes and eating sugary breakfast cereal for every meal. Along with her progressive cognitive decline, she developed significant gait instability. Her mother became increasingly unable to care for her, largely because of the frequent bouts of agitation that required multiple psychotropic medications. At the age of 56, Mrs. J was admitted to the dementia floor at a nearby nursing home.

The case of Mrs. J demonstrates how FTD often begins with behavioral and language disturbances in relatively young individuals and then progresses inexorably to a more global dementia.

Diagnostic Criteria

Criteria developed by a diagnostic work group define FTD by the development of behavioral or cognitive deficits manifested by either an early and progressive change in personality or early and progressive change in language ability. Such change is gradual and progressive, causes significant social and occupational impairment, and is not attributable to delirium or another medical or psychiatric condition (McKhann et al., 2001). The overall clinical picture varies depending on the exact location of neuronal disease, and reviews of dementia syndromes incorporated under the heading of FTD reveal considerable diversity. As a result, there have been many permutations of FTD described in the literature, with the classic one being Pick's Disease (PiD) which was first described in 1892 by the neurologist Arnold Pick. Currently, however, FTD is characterized by three major clinical subtypes: (1) a frontal lobe variant with prominent behavioral symptoms (FvFTD); (2) a temporal lobe variant with prominent language disturbance (fluent aphasia) called semantic dementia (SD); and (3) a progressive nonfluent aphasia variant (PA). Clinical differences for each variant are summarized in Table 7.1.

Table 7.1 Subtypes of Frontotemporal Dementia

	Frontal Variant FTD	*Semantic Dementia*	*Progressive Aphasia*
Initial symptoms	Personality changes	Language dysfunction	Language dysfunction
Behavioral symptoms	• Apathy • Disinhibition • Impulsivity • Stereotypy • Compulsive behaviors and rituals	• Compulsive behaviors • Personality change including loss of sympathy and empathy • Emotional disturbances • Preoccupations	• Social skills preserved early in course • Late symptoms resemble behavioral changes in FvFTD
Language symptoms	Language impairment when left hemisphere is impaired	Fluent aphasia with word-finding difficulty and loss of word meaning	Nonfluent aphasia with word retrieval impairment and resultant poverty of speech, stuttering, and eventual mutism
Cognitive symptoms	• Executive dysfunction • Attentional deficits • Working memory impairment • Loss of insight	• Poor insight • Agnosia for faces, items, and sensory stimuli • Apraxia for tasks using visual and auditory stimuli	• Alexia • Dysgraphia
Pathology	Variable degeneration of right and/or left orbitobasal, as well as medial and dorsolateral prefrontal cortices	Degeneration of the middle and inferior temporal lobe	Degeneration of left perisylvian cortex

Sources: Weder et al. (2007); Cardarelli, Kertesz, and Knebl (2010).

Frontal Variant FTD

FvFTD involves early onset of progressive, insidious changes in personality and behavior, mediated by variable degeneration in the orbitobasal, medial, and/or dorsolateral regions of the frontal lobes. Orbitobasal atrophy is associated with disinhibited behaviors including inappropriate social behaviors and poor judgment, such as undressing or using profanity in public, unusual dressing, unhygienic grooming or bathroom habits, and verbal or physical agitation. There may also be stereotypical, compulsive, or ritualistic behaviors such as hoarding objects, repetitive hand washing, counting and checking, arranging of objects, inflexible bathroom or hygiene habits, and repetitive gestures, questions, statements, or, later in the disease, vocalizations (Cairns et al., 2007; Mendez & Perryman, 2002).

Medial frontal degeneration is associated with an apathetic syndrome characterized by a lack of spontaneity, flattened affect, social withdrawal, poor insight, and a lack of concern for social etiquette, hygiene, responsibilities, and relationships. These symptoms are often seen in early presentations of FTD and are often mistaken for depression (Kertesz, 2011). Medial frontal degeneration may also be associated with hyperoral behaviors, such as cravings for and/or overeating particular foods for most meals, especially carbohydrates, sweets, condiments, or fast food (Kertesz, 2011; Weder et al., 2007). The latter eating behaviors might also be stereotyped or ritualistic.

Dorsolateral atrophy is most associated with impairments in executive function, including poor planning and organizing, impaired abstract thinking, perseveration, difficulty in set shifting, and attentional deficits (Boxer & Miller, 2005).

Semantic Dementia

Semantic dementia (SD) is associated with degeneration in bilateral middle and inferior regions of the temporal lobes and is characterized by progressive impairment in semantic memory; namely, knowledge of particular words and objects and their meanings. Afflicted individuals initially retain sufficient language skills to carry out a conversation but with progressive loss of word comprehension as well as lack of insight into their language dysfunction. They demonstrate a fluent aphasia in which specific words are often substituted for more general ones (e.g., "animal" used instead of the specific animal intended), and the overall word content lacks meaning (Cardarelli, Kertesz, & Knebl, 2010). There is also lack of recognition or agnosia for well-known faces and objects and their function. Individuals with SD may demonstrate behavioral problems seen in FvFTD but with more compulsive behaviors, preoccupations with ideas, emotional disturbances (e.g., depression, anxiety, irritability, overreactivity to pain), and loss of empathy and sympathy (Boxer & Miller, 2005; McMurtrey et al., 2006).

Progressive Aphasia

The progressive aphasia (PA) subtype of FTD has also been called progressive nonfluent aphasia as well as primary progressive aphasia in previous literature. It is associated with left hemispheric degeneration in the perisylvian cortex (Neary, Snowden, & Mann, 2005) and characterized by an evolving expressive aphasia with slowed, nonfluent speech with marked word-finding difficulty and eventual progression to muteness (Ash et al., 2006). Individuals may also demonstrate stuttering, alexia, and dysgraphia (Cardarelli et al., 2010). Although memory disturbances are not prominent early in the course of PA, many cases progress to a more generalized dementia within several years that may include behavioral symptoms.

Course

FTD and its variants follow a time course similar to that of AD, with progressive deterioration over 2 to 10 years until eventual death. Individuals with SD and PA become severely aphasic and then mute, but behavioral symptoms, severe cognitive impairment, and motor symptoms develop later in the disease course. There may also be an initial presentation of one subtype which then appears to morph to another, such as a presentation of PA looking more like FvFTD with time (Kertesz, 2005). Parkinsonian neurological symptoms including rigidity and slowed movements may evolve with time (Neary et al., 2005).

Etiology and Pathology

There is no known cause of FTD, although it has been linked to mutations on chromosomes 3, 9, and, mainly, 17 (Sikkink, Rollinson, & Pickering-Brown, 2007). Familial FTD has been linked to multiple tau mutations that disrupt microtubule function (Sjogren & Andersen, 2006). FTD may predominantly involve the frontal or temporal lobe, or both, and it may include subcortical and parietal involvement as well. Pathologic changes include atrophy, gliosis, and spongiosis extending from the frontal into anterior temporal regions (Neary et al., 2005). Histopathologic findings are variable and include tau-positive inclusion bodies (composed of hyperphosphorylated tau protein filaments) in approximately 45% of FTD patients and ubiquitin-positive inclusions in the other 55% (Wittenberg et al., 2007). PiD is notable for spherical, tau-positive intracytoplasmic inclusion bodies that are concentrated in neurons in the frontotemporal cortical and hippocampal regions, as well as for swollen or ballooned neurons known as Pick cells. FvFTD appears to involve both a tau- and ubiquitin-positive pathology, whereas PA is more commonly a tauopathy and SD more related to ubiquitin pathology (Cairns et al., 2007; Wittenberg et al., 2007).

Staging

Broe and colleagues (2003) have proposed a pathological staging for FTD based on a series of 24 cases: stage 1 involves mild atrophy in the orbital and superior medial frontal cortices and hippocampus; stage 2 involves progression to the other anterior frontal regions, temporal cortex, and basal ganglia; stage 3 involves progression throughout the remaining frontal and temporal cortices; and stage 4 involves severe atrophy throughout all of these regions of the brain. The researchers noted that these four stages supported the progressive nature of FTD since the stages are correlated with the severity of the dementia symptoms and the duration of the disease.

Assessment

The assessment of FTD follows the general outline presented in Chapters 1 and 2. Although FTD may resemble AD, especially in the later stages, the clinical history and a thorough mental status examination should reveal important differences that help to distinguish the variants of FTD from AD. These are summarized in Table 7.2.

Neurological Evaluation and Neuroimaging

A neurological examination conducted early in the course of FTD may be entirely normal. As the disease progresses, extrapyramidal symptoms (EPS), including bradykinesia and rigidity, commonly emerge, depending on the degree of subcortical involvement and the clinical overlap with corticobasal degeneration, described later in the chapter. Important neurological symptoms that may emerge late in the disease course are as follows: (1) perseveration of both verbal and motor responses, including echolalia (repeating or parroting other individual's words) and echopraxia (mimicking movements) and

Table 7.2 Frontotemporal Dementia versus Alzheimer's Disease

Feature	AD	FTD
Onset	Usually after the age of 65	Usually younger than 65
Language	Evolving aphasia with variable impairment in early and middle stages	Early onset, prominent aphasia, especially in SD and PA, with eventual mutism
Behavior	Agitation, psychosis, and apathy common in middle and late stages	Early changes in personality and behavior, often with compulsive and bizarre behaviors; apathy is common in early stages, and psychosis is less common
Cognition	Early, prominent memory impairment, with slowly evolving, global cognitive decline	Later and less prominent memory changes; early and prominent impairment in executive function
Neurologic exam	Few findings early on; impaired gait in late stages	Parkinsonian symptoms including rigidity and slowed movements in later stages
Neuroimaging	Early atrophy of hippocampus and mesial temporal lobes; evolving hypometabolism most prominent in parietal and cingulate regions	Prominent, evolving frontal and anterior temporal atrophy; evolving hypometabolism most prominent in frontal and anterior temporal regions

(2) primitive reflexes that result from upper motor neuron damage to the frontal lobes and corticobulbar tracts, as seen in pseudobulbar palsy (involuntary, paroxysmal episodes of emotion such as laughter or crying). These abnormal reflexes in adults are referred to as frontal release signs, and they include the snout or pouting reflex, the grasp reflex, the sucking reflex, the jaw-jerk reflex, the palmomental (palm-chin) reflex, and the Babinski sign (or extensor plantar reflex).

Brain neuroimaging reveals frontal and/or temporal lobe atrophy on computed tomography or magnetic resonance imaging scans and selective frontal and/or temporal hypoperfusion or hypometabolism on positron emission tomography (PET) or single photon emission computed tomography scans (Talbot et al., 1995; Weder et al., 2007). Medicare will reimburse for PET scans to differentiate between AD and FTD.

Neuropsychological Testing

As FTD progresses, neuropsychological testing can play a key role in identifying frontal and temporal lobe impairment, especially executive dysfunction as mediated by the dorsolateral regions and language function typically primarily by the left anterior temporal lobe. Discrete neuropsychological tests that can identify impairment in executive dysfunction include word fluency tests: the Wisconsin Card Sorting Test (WCST) and the Trail-Making Test, Part B (TMT-B), and the subtests of the Luria Motor Battery. In word fluency tests, the subject is asked to generate a list of items in particular categories, such as animals or foods. The WCST requires an individual to sort cards in piles based on a specific category that is changed midway through the task. In the TMT-B, an individual is asked to draw lines between alternating, successive letters and numbers scattered on a page. Both the WCST and the TMT-B require subjects to shift their mental set between different rules or categories.

The tasks from the Luria Motor Battery involve having the patient imitate a series of sequential hand movements. Impairment in all these tests is manifested by inflexible mental strategies, inappropriate or disinhibited responses, and perseverated actions. Numerous neuropsychological tests can also identify impairments in other aspects of frontal lobe function, including motor behavior, visual tracking, smell identification, and inhibitory control.

Neuropsychological tests of language function look at skills such as verbal fluency, semantic meaning of words, grammar, syntax, prosody, and articulation (Koss, Attix, & Story, 2011). These skills are examined through spontaneous speech repetition, comprehension, naming, reading, and writing. Some of the main tests used include the Boston Naming Test, in which an individual has to name the objects shown on a series of cards, and the Controlled Oral Word Association Test (COWAT), which tests verbal fluency by asking individuals to name as many words as they can in a finite amount of time in a semantic (e.g., animals) or phonemic (starting with the letter *F*) category.

Two bedside neuropsychological tests that have been developed to assess executive function include the Frontal Assessment Battery or FAB (Dubois, Slachevsky, Litvan, & Pillon, 2000) and the Executive Interview or EXIT (Moorhouse, Gorman, & Rockwood, 2009; Royall, Mahurin, & Gray, 1992). The FAB is a 10-minute test composed of six subtests measuring various skills, such as conceptualization, mental flexibility, motor programming, sensitivity to interference, inhibitory control, and autonomy. The patient is asked to carry out a simple task to assess each skill. Research using the FAB for differential diagnosis among patients with FTD, AD, and VaD has shown limited discrimination and only on one or more subtests but not in terms of total scores (Boban, Malojcić, & Mimica, 2012; Lipton et al., 2005). The EXIT is a 25-item test that takes about 10 minutes and measures skills similar to those the measured on the FAB, but it also incorporates frontal release signs and shortened versions of several neuropsychological tasks. It can serve as an ideal supplement to the MMSE since it highlights dysfunction not well-captured on that instrument. However, it has not been shown to specifically identify FTD versus other forms of dementia. A quick assessment of frontal lobe function using items from a variety of cognitive screens including the FAB and EXIT can be found in Table 7.3.

Kertesz, Davidson, and Fox (1997) developed the Frontal Behavioral Inventory or FBI as a 24-item instrument to distinguish FTD from AD. By looking for behaviors such as apathy, inflexibility, loss of insight, and inattention, the FBI has been able to differentiate FTD from AD in 98% of patients.

Table 7.3 A Quick Clinical Assessment of Executive Function

If one is evaluating a patient in a clinic, the following tests, several of which come from the FAB and the EXIT, can be used to assess frontal lobe function.

Abstracting	• Ask the patient to tell how an apple and a banana are alike. In frontal lobe impairment, look for a failure to determine conceptual similarity (e.g., both are fruits); instead, he or she might deny any similarities or focus on less abstract and more concrete responses (e.g., aspects of shape and color).
Word fluency	• Ask the patient to list as many words beginning with the same letter or animals as he or she can in 60 seconds. Individuals without impairment should be able to list at least 10.
Motor programming	• Luria hand sequence: ask the patient to observe you and to imitate the following three hand movements in their exact order: (1) make a fist and hit it on the table, (2) open the fist and hit the table again with the side of the hand, and (3) slap the table with the hand, palm side down. Look for perseverated movements and a failure to imitate and organize the sequence. • Tap a pattern with your hand and ask the patient to repeat it. • Draw a series of loops and ask the patient to copy it.
Disinhibition	• Check for frontal release signs. Extend your hand to the patient, but ask him or her not to shake it. Look for the patient's inability to inhibit a natural response. Ask the patient to tap only one time after each time you tap twice. Look for perseverated behaviors. • Consider asking a consulting neuropsychologist for a copy of the TMT-B to administer. A short version of the TMT-B (and other frontal tests) can also be found on the Montreal Cognitive Assessment or MOCA.

Treatment

The treatment of FTD itself has not been well-established, in part because of the relatively small size of identified cohorts. The basis of treatment may rest on neurotransmitter deficiencies identified through decreased cholinergic and serotonergic function in the affected cortical regions (Huey, Putnam, & Grafman, 2006). For example, symptoms of FTD, including carbohydrate craving, overeating with weight gain, depression, impulse dyscontrol, and compulsive behaviors may reflect underlying serotonergic dysfunction. Small studies of selective serotonin reuptake inhibitor antidepressants including sertraline, paroxetine, fluoxetine, fluvoxamine, and citalopram have shown improvement in several of these symptoms in FTD (Deakin et al., 2004; Herrmann et al., 2012; Ikeda et al., 2004; Moretti et al., 2003). Trazodone has also been used to treat irritability, aggression, and disinhibition (Lebert, 2006). See Chapter 10 for dosing strategies for these antidepressants.

Although the presence of cholinergic deficits would suggest that use of acetylcholinesterase inhibitors would also benefit patients with FTD, to date, little data support their use. One study of 20 patients with FTD treated with rivastigmine showed improved behaviors and reduced caregiver burden over 12 months (Moretti, Torre, & Antonello, 2004). In a small trial of FTD patients treated with donepezil, no benefit was found, and

4 of 12 patients demonstrated increased disinhibition (Mendez, Shapira, McMurtray, & Licht, 2007). A small 18-week open-label and 8-week placebo-controlled study of 36 FTD patients treated with galantamine did not show any significant benefit overall, although the PA variant patients showed stabilization in global scores and less decline in language scores on galantamine compared to placebo (Kertesz et al., 2008). A randomized, placebo-controlled trial of 81 FTD patients on memantine 20 mg daily did not show any benefit (Boxer, Knopman, & Kaufer, 2013). Antipsychotic medications have also been used to treat behavioral symptoms in FTD, but one study found that 33% of patients developed extrapyramidal symptoms, suggesting a specific vulnerability to this side effect (Pijnenburg, Sampson, & Harvey, 2003).

For more information on both pharmacological and nonpharmacological strategies for dealing with symptoms of agitation, psychosis, depression, and apathy associated with FTD and other dementia types, see Chapters 9 and 10.

Related Tauopathies Associated with Dementia

Three other degenerative neurological conditions share both clinical and pathologic features with FTD and are tauopathies: progressive supranuclear palsy, corticobasal degeneration, and argyrophilic grain disease. These conditions also have pathological involvement of subcortical regions with associated extrapyramidal symptoms, similar to dementia with Lewy bodies.

Progressive Supranuclear Palsy

Progressive supranuclear palsy (PSP; also known as Steele-Richardson-Olszewski syndrome) is a parkinsonian syndrome associated with dementia that is often confused with Parkinson's disease (PD) and other extrapyramidal syndromes. According to the diagnostic criteria developed by the National Institute of Neurological Disorders and Stroke and the Society for PSP, PSP is a gradually progressive disorder that begins after the age of 40 (Litvan, Agid, et al., 1996). It is characterized by prominent symptoms of postural instability and falls in the first year that occur in association with vertical supranuclear gaze palsy and the slowing of vertical eye-tracking movements. One case series of PSP patients found the mean age of onset to be 63 years with a range between 45 and 73 years and an average survival of 5.6 years with a range between 2 and 16.6 years (Litvan, Mangone, et al., 1996). It has been seen in approximately 1–6.5 of 100,000 people in the United Kingdom (Nath et al., 2001). The annual incidence in the United States has been found to be higher in men and to increase with age, from 1.7 per 100,000 people at 50–59 years to 14.7 at 80–99 (Bower, Maraganore, McDonnell, & Rocca, 1997), and it may account for approximately 3% of patients seen for parkinsonian symptoms (Savica et al., 2013). Histopathologic evidence of PSP includes neuronal loss, gliosis, and the presence of tau-positive neurofibrillary tangles in the basal ganglia, diencephalon, and brainstem (Dickson, Rademakers, & Hutton, 2007).

The early clinical symptoms of postural instability, falls, and visual disturbances are commonly followed by the development of rigidity, bradykinesia, dysphagia, and dysarthria (Litvan, Mangone, et al., 1996). Visual disturbances affect 50% of patients with PSP by the end of the first year; the symptoms include diplopia, blurred vision, slowed eye movements, and vertical gaze impairment that progresses to involve all directions. Cognitive impairment associated with PSP is common, affecting 50%–75% of affected individuals, and is characterized primarily by executive dysfunction along with less prominent impairments in memory, language, and visuospatial skills (Brown et al., 2010; Gerstenecker et al., 2013). The dementia eventually affects almost all patients, but it tends to be milder than that seen in dementia with Lewy bodies and AD. The behavioral symptoms are frontal in origin, including apathy, social withdrawal, depression, and pseudobulbar palsy (Bak, Crawford, Berrios, & Hodges, 2010).

Currently, no treatment for PSP exists, although 40%–50% of patients may demonstrate mild, transient improvements in EPS on levodopa. Several case reports have described improvement in motor symptoms, speech, and gaze paresis when treated with the GABA agonist zolpidem (Cotter, Armytage, & Crimmins, 2010; Dash, 2013). One small double-blind placebo-controlled study of donepezil in 21 individuals with PSP showed improvement in memory but significant worsening in motor function, leading the authors to recommend against its use (Litvan et al., 2001). Another small study of open-label donepezil in six patients with PSP did not show any benefit or worsening in symptoms (Fabbrini et al., 2001). A case report of five PSP patients on rivastigmine showed slight cognitive improvement (Liepelt et al., 2010). Physical rehabilitation may also help improve postural instability (Di Pancrazio et al., 2013).

Corticobasal Degeneration

Corticobasal degeneration (CBD), also called cortical-basal ganglionic degeneration, is a neurodegenerative condition characterized by the progressive development of asymmetric parkinsonism with limb rigidity and stiff gait, apraxia, and cortical sensory loss; less common symptoms include the alien hand phenomenon (complex and seemingly purposeful hand movements without cognitive control) and reflex myoclonus (Kouri, Murray, et al., 2011). The extrapyramidal motor symptoms are typically unresponsive to levodopa. Within 2–3 years, most affected individuals go on to demonstrate dementia that is associated with behavioral and language disturbances (Kertesz & McMonagle, 2010). Nearly 50% of affected individuals initially present with frontal lobe dysfunction. In some cases, personality changes and language disturbances may present before the motor symptoms. Given this clinical picture, the differential diagnosis is wide, including PSP, AD, Parkinson's disease, and FTD (Litvan et al., 1999). Because decreased dexterity in a hand is often a presenting symptom in CBD, amyotrophic lateral sclerosis (i.e., Lou Gehrig's disease) is sometimes suspected, and it, in fact, has demonstrated some symptomatic overlap with both CBD and FTD.

More recent attention to the diagnostic criteria for CBD has proposed four clinical subtypes: corticobasal syndrome (CBS), frontal behavioral-spatial syndrome (FBS), nonfluent/agrammatic variant of primary progressive aphasia (naPPA), and progressive supranuclear palsy syndrome (PSPS) (Armstrong et al., 2013). The consensus group also proposed research criteria for probable CBD which includes the following: (1) insidious onset and gradual progression for at least one year; (2) age at onset 50 years or older; (3) no similar family history or known tau mutations; and (4) clinical symptoms consistent with probable CBS or either FBS or naPPA with at least one CBS feature (Armstrong et al., 2013). In this scheme, possible CBD would not have restrictions on age at onset, family history, or the presence of tau mutations, and less adherence to the subtypes but include a PSP syndrome (Armstrong et al., 2013). These proposed changes speak to the strong overlap among these conditions (Wadia & Lang, 2007)

Neuroimaging in CBD typically reveals focal frontal and sometimes parietal atrophy and hypoperfusion, often asymmetrically. Autopsy studies have found asymmetric frontal and parietal neuronal loss, spongiosis, ballooned neurons, gliosis, and tau-positive neurofibrillary tangles in the affected cortical, subcortical, and brainstem regions (Kouri, Whitwell, et al., 2011). No treatment modalities have been identified for CBD, although it is often approached clinically like other similar tauopathies. Specific modalities of physical rehabilitation might help to improve motor function critical for activities of daily living (Kawahira et al., 2009).

Clinical Tip

As noted, there is often significant overlap between the clinical presentations of AD, FTD subtypes, PSP, and CBD. In one case series, several dozen individuals with CBD all developed either FvFTD or PA, most within six months of presenting with either an extrapyramidal movement disorder or a behavioral or language impairment. Distinguishing among these clinical entities can be difficult, and collaboration among neurologists, psychiatrists, and neuropsychologists is required.

Argyrophilic Grain Disease

Argyrophilic grain disease (AGD) is a dementia subtype associated with abnormal tau protein metabolism that primarily affects the limbic system, specifically the hippocampus and amygdala (Ferrer, Santpere, & van Leeuwen, 2008). It is characterized by prominent amnesia and frontal lobe pathology including personality changes, emotional lability (irritability, dysphoria, agitation), apathy, and psychosis (paranoid delusions). The pathologic hallmark of AGD—argyrophilic grains composed of tau protein—has been found in the brains of 5%–10% of late-onset dementia patients (Togo, Cookson, & Dickson, 2002; Tolnay & Clavaguera, 2004). Pure AGD resembles FTD more than AD but involves less prominent neuronal loss and less overall brain atrophy than both FTD and AD. Nonetheless, in one case series approximately two-thirds of individuals found to have AGD on autopsy had comorbid AD, dementia with Lewy bodies, or vascular dementia. More research is needed to further elucidate AGD and determine its place as a distinct disease.

References

Armstrong, M. J., Litvan, I., Lang, A. E., et al. (2013). Criteria for the diagnosis of corticobasal degeneration. *Neurol, 80*(5), 496–503.

Ash, S., Moore, P., Antani, S., et al. (2006). Trying to tell a tale: Discourse impairments in progressive aphasia and frontotemporal dementia. *Neurol, 66*(9), 1405–1413.

Bak, T. H., Crawford, L. M., Berrios, G., & Hodges, J. R. (2010). Behavioural symptoms in progressive supranuclear palsy and frontotemporal dementia. *J NeurolNeurosurg Psychiatry, 81*, 1057–1059.

Boban, M., Malojčić, B., & Mimica, N. (2012). The frontal assessment battery in the differential diagnosis of dementia. *J Geriatr Psychiatry Neurol, 25*(4), 201–207.

Bower, J. H., Maraganore, D. M., McDonnell, S. K., & Rocca, W. A. (1997). Incidence of progressive supranuclear palsy and multiple system atrophy in Olmsted County, Minnesota, 1976 to 1990. *Neurol, 49*(5), 1284–1288.

Boxer, A. L., Knopman, D. S., & Kaufer, D. I. (2013). Memantine in patients with frontotemporal lobar degeneration: A multicentre, randomised, double-blind, placebo-controlled trial. *Lancet Neurol, 12*(2), 149–156.

Boxer, A. L., & Miller, B. L. (2005). Clinical features of frontotemporal dementia. *Alzheimer Dis Assoc Disord, 19*(Suppl. 1), S3–S6.

Broe, M., Hodges, J. R., Schofield, E., et al. (2003). Staging disease severity in pathologically confirmed cases of frontotemporal dementia. *Neurol, 60*(6), 1005–1011.

Brown, R. G., Lacomblez, L., Landwehrmeyer, B. G., Bak, T., et al. (2010). Cognitive impairment in patients with multiple system atrophy and progressive supranuclear palsy. *Brain, 133*, 2382–2393.

Cairns, N. J., Bigio, E. H., Mackenzie, I. R., et al. (2007). Neuropathologic diagnostic and nosologic criteria for frontotemporal lobar degeneration: Consensus of the Consortium for Frontotemporal Lobar Degeneration. *Acta Neuropathol, 114*(1), 5–22.

Cardarelli, R., Kertesz, A., & Knebl, J. A. (2010). Frontotemporal dementia: A review for primary care physicians. *Am Fam Physician, 82*(11), 1372–1377.

Cotter, C., Armytage, T., & Crimmins, D. (2010). The use of zolpidem in the treatment of progressive supranuclear palsy. *J Clin Neurosci, 17*(3), 385–386.

Dash, S. K. (2013). Zolpidem in progressive supranuclear palsy. *Case Rep Neurol Med,* 250865.

Deakin, J. B., Rahman, S., Nestor, P. J., et al. (2004). Paroxetine does not improve symptoms and impairs cognition in frontotemporal dementia: a double-blind randomized controlled trial. *Psychopharmacology, 172*, 400–408.

Dickson, D. W., Rademakers, R., & Hutton, M. L. (2007). Progressive supranuclear palsy: Pathology and genetics. *Brain Pathol, 17*(1), 74–82.

Di Pancrazio, L., Bellomo, R. G., Franciotti, R., et al. (2013). Combined rehabilitation program for postural instability in progressive supranuclear palsy. *NeuroRehabilitation, 32*(4), 855–860.

Dubois, B., Slachevsky, A., Litvan, I., & Pillon, B. (2000). The FAB: A Frontal Assessment Battery at bedside. *Neurol, 55*(11), 1621–1626.

Fabbrini, G., Barbanti, P., Bonifati, V., et al. (2001). Donepezil in the treatment of progressive supranuclear palsy. *Acta Neurol Scand, 103*(2), 123–125.

Ferrer, I., Santpere, G., & van Leeuwen, F. W. (2008). Argyrophilic grain disease. *Brain, 131*(Pt 6), 1416–1432.

Gerstenecker, A., Mast, B., Duff, K., et al. (2013). Executive dysfunction is the primary cognitive impairment in progressive supranuclear palsy. *Arch Clin Neuropsychol, 28*(2), 104–113.

Herrmann, N., Black, S. E., Chow, T., et al. (2012). Serotonergic function and treatment of behavioral and psychological symptoms of frontotemporal dementia. *Am J Geriatr Psychiatry, 20*(9), 789–797.

Huey, A. D., Putnam, K. T., & Grafman, J. (2006). A systematic review of neurotransmitter deficits and treatments in frontotemporal dementia. *Neurol, 66*, 17–22.

Ikeda, M., Shigenobu, K., Fukuhara, R., et al. (2004): Efficacy of fluvoxamine as a treatment for behavioral symptoms in frontotemporal lobar degeneration patients. *Dement Geriatr Cogn Disord, 17*(3), 1117–1121.

Kawahira, K., Noma, T., Iiyama, J., et al. (2009). Improvements in limb kinetic apraxia by repetition of a newly designed facilitation exercise in a patient with corticobasal degeneration. *Int J Rehabil Res, 32*(2), 178–183.

Kertesz, A. (2005). Frontotemporal dementia: one disease, or many? Probably one, possibly two. *Alzheimer Dis Assoc Disord, 19*(Suppl. 1), S19–S24.

Kertesz, A. (2011). Frontotemporal dementia. In M. E. Agronin & G. J. Maletta (Eds.), *Principles and practice of geriatric psychiatry* (2nd ed., pp. 343–358). Philadelphia: Lippincott, Williams and Wilkins.

Kertesz, A., Davidson, W., & Fox, H. (1997). Frontal behavioral inventory: Diagnostic criteria for frontal lobe dementia. *Can J Neurol Sci, 24*(1), 29–36.

Kertesz, A., & McMonagle, P. (2010). Behavior and cognition in corticobasal degeneration and progressive supranuclear palsy. *J Neurol Sci, 289*(1–2), 138–143.

Kertesz, A., Morlog, D., Light, M. et al. (2008). Galantamine in frontotemporal dementia and primary progressive aphasia. *Dement Geriatr Cogn Disord, 25*(2), 178–185.

Koss, E., Attix, D. K., & Story, T. J. (2011). Neuropsychological evaluation. In M. E. Agronin & G. J. Maletta (Eds.), *Principles and practice of geriatric psychiatry* (2nd ed., pp. 119–137). Philadelphia: Lippincott, Williams and Wilkins.

Kouri, N., Murray, M. E., Hassan, A., et al. (2011). Neuropathological features of corticobasal degeneration presenting as corticobasal syndrome or Richardson syndrome. *Brain, 134*(Pt 11), 3264–3275.

Kouri, N., Whitwell, J. L., Josephs, K. A., et al. (2011). Corticobasal degeneration: A pathologically distinct 4R tauopathy. *Nat Rev Neurol, 7*(5), 263–272.

Lebert, F. (2006). Behavioral benefits of trazodone are sustained for the long term in frontotemporal dementia. *Therapy, 3*(1), 93–96.

Liepelt, I., Gaenslen, A., Godau, J., et al. (2010). Rivastigmine for the treatment of dementia in patients with progressive supranuclear palsy: Clinical observations as a basis for power calculations and safety analysis. *Alzheimers Dement, 6*(1), 70–74.

Lipton, A. M., Ohman, K. A., Womack, K. B., et al. (2005). Subscores of the FAB differentiate frontotemporal lobar degeneration from AD. *Neurol, 65*(5), 726–731.

Litvan, I., Agid, Y., Calne, D., et al. (1996). Clinical research criteria for the diagnosis of progressive supranuclear palsy (Steele-Richardson-Olszewski syndrome): Report of the NINDS-SPSP international workshop. *Neurol, 47*(1), 1–9.

Litvan, I., Grimes, D. A., Lang, A. E., et al. (1999). Clinical features differentiating patients with postmortem confirmed progressive supranuclear palsy and corticobasal degeneration. *J Neurol, 246*(Suppl. 2), II1–5.

Litvan, I., Mangone, C. A., McKee, A., et al. (1996). Natural history of progressive supranuclear palsy (Steele-Richardson-Olszewski syndrome) and clinical predictors of survival: A clinicopathological study. *J Neurol Neurosurg Psychiatry, 60*(6), 615–620.

Litvan, I., Phipps, M., Pharr, V. L., et al. (2001). Randomized placebo-controlled trial of donepezil in patients with progressive supranuclear palsy. *Neurol, 57*(3), 467–473.

McKhann, G. M., Albert, M. S., Grossman, M., et al. (2001). Clinical and pathological diagnosis of frontotemporal dementia: report of the Work Group on Frontotemporal Dementia and Pick's Disease. *Arch Neurol, 58*, 1803–1809.

McMurtrey, A. M., Chen, A. K., Shapira, J. S., et al. (2006). Variations in regional SPECT hypoperfusion and clinical features in frontotemporal dementia. *Neurol, 66*, 517–522.

Mendez, M. F., & Perryman, K. M. (2002). Neuropsychiatric features of frontotemporal dementia: Evaluation of consensus criteria and review. *J Neuropsychiatry Clin Neurosci, 14*(4), 424–429.

Mendez, M. F., Shapira, J. S., McMurtray, A., & Licht, E. (2007). Preliminary findings: Behavioral worsening on donepezil in patients with frontotemporal dementia. *Am J Geriatr Psychiatry, 15*(1), 84–87.

Moorhouse, P., Gorman, M., & Rockwood, K. (2009). Comparison of EXIT-25 and the Frontal Assessment Battery for evaluation of executive dysfunction in patients attending a memory clinic. *Dement Geriatr Cogn Disord, 27*(5), 424–428.

Moretti, R., Torre, P., & Antonello, R. M. (2004). Rivastigmine in frontotemporal dementia: An open-label study. *Drugs Aging, 21*(14), 931–937.

Moretti, R., Torre, P., Antonello, R. M., et al. (2003). Frontotemporal dementia: Paroxetine as a possible treatment of behavior symptoms: A randomized, controlled, open 14-month study. *European Neurol, 49*, 13–19.

Nath, U., Ben-Shlomo, Y., Thomson, R. G., et al. (2001). The prevalence of progressive supranuclear palsy (Steele-Richardson-Olszewski syndrome) in the UK. *Brain, 124*(Pt 7), 1438–1449.

Neary, D., Snowden, J., & Mann, D. (2005). Frontotemporal dementia. *Lancet, 4*(11), 771–780.

Pijnenburg, Y. A., Sampson, E. L., & Harvey, R. J. (2003). Vulnerability to neuroleptic side effects in frontotemporal lobar degeneration. *Int J Geriatr Psychiatry, 18*(1), 67–72.

Rosso, S. M., Landweer, E. J., & Houterman, M. (2003). Medical and environmental risk factors for sporadic frontotemporal dementia: a retrospective case-control study. *J Neurol Neurosurg Psychiatry, 74*(11), 1574.

Royall, D. R., Mahurin, R. K., & Gray, K. F. (1992). Bedside assessment of executive cognitive impairment: The executive interview. *J Am Geriatr Soc, 40*(12), 1221–1226.

Savica, R., Grossardt, B. R., Bower, J. H., et al. (2013). Incidence and pathology of synucleinopathies and tauopathies related to parkinsonism. *JAMA Neurol, 70*(7), 859–866.

Sikkink, S., Rollinson, S., & Pickering-Brown, S. M. (2007). The genetics of frontotemporal lobar degeneration. *Curr Opin Neurol, 20*(6), 693–698.

Sjogren, M., & Andersen, C. (2006). Frontotemporal dementia: A brief review. *Mech of Ageing and Development, 127*(2), 180–187.

Snowden, J. S., Bathgate, D., Varma, B., et al. (2001). Distinct behavioral profiles in frontotemporal dementia and semantic dementia. *J Neurol Neurosurg Psychiatry, 70*, 323–332.

Talbot, P. R., Snowden, J. S., Lloyd, J. J., et al. (1995). The contribution of single photon emission tomography to the clinical differentiation of degenerative cortical brain disorders. *J Neurol, 242*, 579–586.

Togo, T., Cookson, N., & Dickson, D. W. (2002). Argyrophilic grain disease: Neuropathology, frequency in a dementia brain bank and lack of relationship with apolipoprotein E. *Brain Pathol, 12*(1), 45–52.

Tolnay, M., & Clavaguera, F. (2004). Argyrophilic grain disease: a late-onset dementia with distinctive features among tauopathies. *Neuropathology, 24*(4), 269–283.

Wadia, P. M., & Lang, A. E. (2007). The many faces of corticobasal degeneration. *Parkinsonism Relat Disord, 13*(Suppl. 3), S336–S340.

Weder, N. D., Aziz, R., Wilkins, K., & Tampi, R. R. (2007). Frontotemporal dementias: A review. *Ann Gen Psychiatry, 6*(15).

Wittenberg, D., Possin, K. L., Rascovsky, K., et al. (2007). The early neuropsychological and behavioral characteristics of frontotemporal dementia. *Neuropsychol Rev, 18*(1), 91–102.

8 Dementia Associated with Medical Conditions

Although many medical conditions can cause transient changes in mental status, a medically induced dementia represents a more enduring condition. In addition to the main dementia subtypes already described in this text, the *Diagnostic and Statistical Manual of Mental Disorders*, Fifth Edition (DSM-5) lists specific major or minor neurocognitive disorders (NCDs) due to traumatic brain injury, HIV infection, Huntington's disease, and prion disease, as well as substance/medication-induced NCD and NCD due to other medical conditions, multiple etiologies, or unspecified causes. The DSM-5 diagnostic criteria for NCD due to another medical condition specifies that there is evidence from the history, physical examination, or laboratory findings that the NCD is the "pathophysiological consequence" of a specified medical condition and is distinct from the other major DSM-5 categories. These and other dementia subtypes will be described in this chapter.

Case Study

Mrs. T was a 93-year-old woman with a six-month history of cognitive decline and behavioral disturbances. She was always considered a relatively bright woman, but now her son described her thinking as "slowed down." In the dining room of the assisted living facility, she would sometimes yell at wait staff and use obscene language. She also fell several times. A routine medical workup was unrevealing, and Mrs. T was tentatively diagnosed with Alzheimer's disease. She was started on an acetylcholinesterase inhibitor and an antidepressant. Her irritability and intermittent agitation continued without improvement. She began to have periods of increased confusion, and she was eventually hospitalized with delirium. In the hospital, Mrs. T was found to have hypercalcemia, and a further workup revealed the source to be a parathyroid adenoma. Despite the risks, she underwent surgery to remove the growth. Her calcium levels normalized, and, over the next three months, her cognition and behavior improved significantly.

In the case of Mrs. T, the clues that pointed to the possibility of an underlying medical cause included the rather precipitous onset of cognitive impairment, the history of falls, and periods of confusion. Unfortunately, a reversible cause of dementia was missed in the initial workup. This mistake is not uncommon, especially when clinicians are so

Table 8.1 Factors Pointing to Higher Likelihood of Dementia Due to a Medical Condition

- Sudden or precipitous onset of dementia
- Rapid progression of cognitive decline
- Young age at onset (younger than 65 years old)
- Recent major medical illness
- Chronic medical illness
- Recent unexplained illness
- Recent cancer chemotherapy or radiation treatment
- Recent surgery
- Family history of dementia subtype
- Head trauma
- Substance abuse (especially alcohol)
- History of occupational exposure to potentially toxic substances
- Prominent frontotemporal and/or subcortical symptoms
- Recent onset of focal neurological symptoms without evidence of stroke (e.g., parkinsonism, ataxia, myoclonus, incontinence, paresthesias, weakness)
- Recent episodes of confusion or delirium

used to seeing Alzheimer's disease (AD) or vascular dementia (VaD) that they assume that every case of cognitive impairment must be caused by one or the other. However, there are several factors in the clinical presentation of a potential dementia that indicate a higher likelihood of an underlying medical cause. These are listed in Table 8.1.

Clinical Tip

There is great risk to making a hasty diagnosis of AD or VaD without a recognition of critical underlying medical conditions that may actually be causative or exacerbating factors of the dementia. Treatment of these conditions can lead to improvement in, or even the reversal of, symptoms. With this in mind, the importance of a complete medical workup in every case of dementia should be obvious.

Dementia Caused by Structural or Traumatic Injury

Structural or traumatic injury to the brain often leads to dementia, and the specific causes are commonly known from the clinical history and confirmed with neuroimaging showing tumors, trauma, bleeding, or strokes.

Neoplastic Tumors

Both primary and metastatic brain tumors can cause dementia. The clinical course is highly variable depending on the location and type of growth and the success of treatment. Neoplastic growths in the brain can arise from the brain parenchyma itself and from surrounding tissues, such as the cerebral vessels and meninges. Benign meningiomas are the most common brain tumor in the elderly, followed by malignant gliomas. Pituitary adenomas and metastatic disease make up a smaller percentage of the cerebral neoplasms encountered.

Cognitive impairment caused by neoplastic growths stems from damage or pressure to regions of the brain that is caused by tumor infiltration and destruction, with subsequent hemorrhaging, occlusion of vessels, compression or mass effect, increased intracranial pressure, and hydrocephalus. The specific symptoms vary by which lobe of the brain is affected; this is reviewed in Table 5.2 in Chapter 5. As a result of a paraneoplastic syndrome, dementia may also be caused by the distant effects of a malignancy that is outside the central nervous system (CNS). Limbic encephalitis is a paraneoplastic syndrome that is associated with a variety of cancers, including small cell lung carcinoma, thymoma, thyroid cancer, and Hodgkin's disease; it is manifested primarily by memory disturbances, seizures, and psychiatric symptoms. It has been associated with antineuronal antibodies and primarily affects the temporal lobes (Tüzün & Dalmau, 2007). It often responds to tumor resection and/or immunotherapy.

Clinical Tip

Dementia associated with neoplasms of the brain can present insidiously, with the symptoms of cognitive and behavioral decline that are seen in many other forms of dementia. This is especially true of benign meningiomas that may grow for periods of years or decades without causing the focal neurological symptoms that would trigger investigation. As every section of this chapter emphasizes, always get a brain scan when conducting an evaluation of dementia.

Depending on the success of treatment, the dementia that is caused by brain neoplasms or paraneoplastic disease is potentially reversible. A small percentage of individuals may, however, develop chronic cognitive impairment from the effects of brain radiation for the treatment of tumors, either acutely or sometime after exposure (Greene-Schloesser & Robbins, 2012).

Traumatic Brain Injury

Traumatic brain injury (TBI) affects at least 1.7 million individuals in the United States each year (Faul, Xu, Wald, & Coronado, 2010), and it is the leading cause of cognitive impairment in young adults. According to DSM-5, the key elements that define a NCD due to TBI include the following:

1. Physical brain injury with one or more of the following: loss or change of consciousness, posttraumatic amnesia, disorientation and confusion, and/or neurological signs (i.e, evidence of trauma on the clinical or physical examination, such as visual field cuts, seizures, anosmia, and hemiparesis).
2. The onset of the NCD immediately after the TBI or after recovery of consciousness with persistence of symptoms beyond the expected post-injury period (American Psychiatric Association, 2013).

Because motor vehicle accidents and falls are the two most common causes of TBI, the following two peaks in prevalence are observed: in young adults 15–19 years old, with a 3:1 male-to-female ratio, and then after the age of 65 (Faul et al., 2010). Motor vehicle accidents are more common than falls in young adults, whereas the reverse is true for the elderly, with falls accounting for 50%–60% of all TBI (Faul et al., 2010; Flanagan et al., 2006) Alcohol intoxication is often a factor in TBI in both young and old.

Mild TBI can result in a postconcussive syndrome that is characterized by short-term memory impairment, slowed cognitive processing, decreased concentration, and neurological symptoms, including headache, blurred vision, and dizziness. Individuals may also experience depression, anxiety, and post-traumatic stress disorder. These symptoms can last for months or years after the injury, but they usually improve with time and appropriate treatment (King, 2003). More severe TBI can result in both focal neurological symptoms and evidence of diffuse neuronal injury, including deficits in memory-processing speed and efficiency, executive dysfunction, language impairment, behavioral disturbances (e.g., impulsivity, agitation, irritability, apathy), and depression (Ryan & O'Jile, 2008). Disruptions in emotional regulation may represent the primary effects of the brain injury or as a psychological reaction to the trauma.

The initial treatment of TBI is devoted to the acute effects of the injury, with the goal of reducing permanent damage. Acute recovery is followed by aggressive physical, occupational, and speech therapy, as well as any appropriate psychiatric or psychological treatment. Cognitive and neurologic impairment often improves with therapy, although, with severe injury, areas of residual impairment are usually present (León-Carrión et al., 2013). Cognitive enhancing medications such as acetylcholinesterase (AChE) inhibitors are recommended to treat cognitive impairment (Neurobehavioral Guidelines Working Group et al., 2006). One study of 111 patients with TBI treated with donepezil, rivastigmine, or galantamine found that these medications were equally tolerated and efficacious, with 61% of the group demonstrating improvement, particularly in attention and overall function (Tenovuo, 2005). Similar results have been found with studies of donepezil and rivastigmine (Silver et al., 2009; Zhang et al., 2004). Methylphenidate and dopaminergic drugs such as amantadine and bromocriptine have shown some benefit for improving arousal, attention, and executive function (Neurobehavioral Guidelines Working Group et al., 2006).

An important TBI syndrome that is seen in the elderly and can be associated with dementia results from a subdural hematoma (SDH). Although SDHs can occur acutely after injury, they can also present chronically, producing fluctuating symptoms of confusion, apathy, lethargy, memory impairment, and executive dysfunction (Ryan & O'Jile, 2008). More than two-thirds of SDHs occur after the age of 60, and nearly one-third of the affected individuals present with no history of trauma. Elderly individuals with gait disturbances, frequent falls, and anticoagulant therapy are at greatest risk for SDHs (Karnath, 2004). The diagnosis is made by MRI or contrast-enhanced brain CT. Some SDHs can resorb over time, but others may persist; these may even become cystic structures, surrounded by fibrous membranes. When chronic SDHs do not resolve quickly and they cause both cognitive decline and/or focal neurological symptoms, the treatment of choice is surgical evacuation.

An increasingly recognized form of TBI is chronic traumatic encephalopathy (CTE), resulting from repeated head injuries in sports such as football, professional wrestling, hockey, and boxing. Characteristic symptoms of CTE develop years after repeated concussive or subconcussive injuries and involve memory impairment, executive dysfunction, mood disturbances (including depression and suicidality), impulsivity, and apathy (Baugh et al., 2012). CTE has classically been called dementia pugilistica, or boxer's encephalopathy and is estimated to effect up to 15% of all professional boxers, on average 16 years after the start of their careers (Clancy, 2006). An associated condition known as post-traumatic parkinsonism or pugilistic parkinsonism has also been described as a form of brain damage associated with boxing. The latter condition's most notable sufferer is former boxing heavyweight champion Muhammad Ali, who was first diagnosed in 1984, three years after his last fight. Brain injury caused by repeated blows to the head during boxing matches is assumed to be the source of the dementia. A boxer's risk of developing dementia pugilistica increases with greater exposure to head blows from sparring, bouts, and knockouts. In addition, the apolipoprotein ε4 allele that confers increased susceptibility to AD also appears to be a risk factor (Jordan et al., 1997).

CTE is only definitively confirmed by postmortem analysis of brain tissue, since neuroimaging of individuals with CTE has not shown any consistent, pathonogmonic findings (Baugh et al., 2012; Jordan et al., 1992). One postmortem study of the brains of 15 former boxers with dementia, each with 400 to over 700 bouts in his career, found a number of pathological features including substantia nigra degeneration, cerebellar scarring, abnormalities of the septum pellucidum, and regional build-up of tau-positive neurofibrillary tangles (Corsellis, Bruton, & Freeman-Browne, 1973). Autopsies of individuals with CTE have shown pronounced atrophy of the frontal and temporal lobes extending into limbic and subcortical structures, and tau deposition (McKee et al., 2009). Functional neuroimaging using PET scans has corroborated these findings by showing increased tau signaling in the brains of retired professional football players (Small et al., 2013).

Normal Pressure Hydrocephalus

Normal pressure hydrocephalus or NPH is characterized by the symptom triad of progressive dementia, gait disturbance, and urinary incontinence (Marmarou et al., 2005). Although this disease has recently received increased press and has been the subject of an award-winning TV ad, it is a rare disease, representing less than 2% of all dementias. It is a diagnosis that the clinician does not want to miss, however, since early intervention may arrest or even reverse its symptoms.

On a neuroanatomical level, NPH represents a chronic, insidious form of hydrocephalus in which a slowly evolving increase in cerebrospinal fluid (CSF) results in dramatic ventricular dilatation and thinning or demyelination of periventricular white matter. This dilatation may also be associated with abnormal ventricular wall compliance. In 50% of cases of NPH there is a known source, such as previous cerebral surgery or trauma that has produced an obstruction, while the remaining cases are idiopathic. Idiopathic NPH (INPH) may evolve slowly over months or years, while NPH due to acute causes has a more rapid onset.

The cognitive impairment seen in INPH is most consistent with a subcortical dementia, characterized by slowed thinking or bradyphrenia, psychomotor slowing (as in fine motor speed and accuracy), inattentiveness, memory encoding and recall problems, and apathy (Hellström et al., 2007). The latter symptoms may result from increased intra-cranial pressure on the frontal lobes, especially the superior frontal gyrus. In terms of the clinical presentation, the abnormal gait is characteristically wide-based with slow, shuffling movements in which the feet barely lift from the ground, as if they are mag-netically attached (hence the term *magnetic gait*). Walking up curbs and steps becomes particularly difficult. Patients may complain of having tired or weak legs. Because the gait disturbance is often an early and prominent manifestation of NPH, the condition is often mistaken for Parkinson's disease. The urinary symptoms begin with frequency and urgency, and eventually progress to frank incontinence.

NPH should be suspected whenever patients present with the symptom triad. The most recent guidelines suggest describing the diagnosis as probable, possible, or unlikely NPH on the basis of the extent of symptoms (Marmarou et al., 2005). The diagnosis should also be designated as either secondary NPH or INPH, depending on whether a specific cause is known. Brain imaging should demonstrate ventricular enlargement out of proportion to sulcal atrophy. Periventricular white matter can appear as thinned and edematous. A spinal tap typically reveals a high normal CSF opening pressure (average 150 mm H_2O, range 60–240 mm H_2O, compared to 120 mm H_2O average in normal adults). An electroencephalogram (EEG) is often normal or may show generalized or focal slow waves. Neuropsychological testing is useful and should evaluate for subcorti-cal impairment.

There are three spinal tap procedures that help to both confirm the diagnosis of NPH as well as predict treatment responsiveness (Walchenbach, Geiger, Thomeer, & Vanneste, 2002; Wikkelsø et al., 2013). The first procedure is to remove 40–50 milliliters of CSF and then look for acute improvement in symptoms. The second test is to calculate CSF out-flow resistance (measured in mm Hg/ml/min) by a small infusion into the subarachnoid space. The third test is conduct external lumbar drainage of 300–500 milliliters of CSF over three days with the patient hospitalized and then look for symptomatic improve-ment. Individuals with probable NPH who demonstrate improvement after CSF removal should be considered for surgery if there are no contraindications, such as comorbid conditions that may increase the already high 30%–40% rate of complications.

Treatment of NPH may involve serial spinal taps to drain CSF but more typically requires placement of a ventriculoperitoneal shunt (Tisell, Tullberg, & Hellström, 2011). Rates of short-term improvement after shunting range from 46% to over 80%, which may decline to slightly under 30% for long-term improvement (Marmarou et al., 2005; Poca et al., 2004). Predictors of shunt responsiveness are listed in Table 8.2.

Table 8.2 Normal Pressure Hydrocephalus: Predictors of Shunt-Responsiveness

- Presence of classic triad and ventriculomegaly
- Secondary NPH (i.e., a known cause)
- Short disease course
- Predominant gait disturbance
- Positive response to CSF tap test and/or external lumbar drainage
- Higher CSF outflow resistance (greater than 13–18 mm Hg/ml/min)

The most common surgical procedure involves placement of a shunt into the lateral ventricle on the nondominant side of the brain, and draining into the peritoneum. Some form of flow restriction device is needed to prevent overdrainage of CSF due to a siphon effect of the shunt. Some shunts contain an adjustable valve that can prevent both over- and underdrainage of CSF. Acute postoperative care after shunting is needed to monitor for various complications, including bleeding, infection, a subdural hematoma, increased intracranial pressure, seizures, shunt malfunction, CSF overdrainage, and death, with mortality rates between 5% and 15%. An endoscopic third ventriculostomy (ETV) is a newer procedure that has also shown clinical benefits and fewer complications than ventriculoperitoneal shunting (Chan et al., 2013; Gangemi et al., 2004). It involves the use of an endoscope placed within the third ventricle to create a drainage hole for CFS into lower regions of the cerebral ventricular system. Ventriculoperitoneal shunt placement has shown better overall results in some but not all studies, but ETV has been recommended as a first-line approach given its similar efficacy and better safety profile (Gangemi et al., 2004; Pinto et al., 2013). Later assessment after either approach should involve repeating the clinical examination, neuroimaging, and neuropsychological testing to look for improvement in previous symptoms.

Dementia Due to Cerebral Anoxia

Both acute and chronic oxygen deprivation to the brain can result in brain damage and a dementia syndrome that is characterized by confusion, impaired memory, apathy, irritability, and somnolence (Lin, 2013). Individuals who survive severe anoxia caused by sustained cardiac or respiratory arrest or other traumatic causes often suffer from profound, permanent neuropsychological impairment. Less severe cognitive impairment can sometimes result from a variety of acute and chronic conditions that produce cerebral hypoxia, including brief cardiopulmonary failure, inadequate surgical ventilation, open heart surgery, sleep apnea, bradycardia, chronic obstructive pulmonary disease, congestive heart failure, anemia, and hyperviscous or hypercoagulable states.

Postoperative Cognitive Dysfunction

Several studies have found that a significant number of older surgical patients suffer from postoperative cognitive dysfunction or POCD both acutely as well as within three to six months of surgery, characterized by discrete declines in attention, verbal and visual memory, language, and executive function. The exact percentages of POCD have varied widely, influenced by age and type of surgery, but have ranged between 5% and over 50% of patients who were evaluated three to six months postoperatively (Evered, Scott, Silbert, & Maruff, 2011; Monk et al., 2008). There has been even greater concern in the medical literature over findings of cognitive impairment associated with coronary-artery bypass grafting or CABG, performed on a half-million Americans every year. Mild impairment in memory processing, mathematical ability, complex planning, attention, and mood regulation have been seen in a significant number of post-CABG individuals, with older and more medically compromised individuals at greatest risk. One longitudinal study found POCD upon discharge in 53% of post-CABG patients, which decreased to 36% at six weeks and 24% at six months, but then rose to 42% when seen for follow-up five years later (Newman et al., 2001). Even taking into consideration the natural rate of dementia, rates in the post-CABG group were two to three times greater than expected.

Risk factors for POCD include advanced age, lower educational level, preoperative cognitive dysfunction, poorer health, longer duration of anesthesia, alcohol abuse, postoperative complications (e.g., infection, respiratory compromise), and depression (Hudetz, Iqbal, & Gandhi, 2007; Monk et al., 2008). There has been much speculation as to the actual causes of POCD, including the following: (1) perioperative cerebral hypotension, (2) perioperative cerebral hypoxia, (3) anesthesia effects (both epidural and general), (4) activation of inflammatory mediators such as complement, cytokines, and others, and (5) use of the cardiopulmonary bypass pump (CBP) during CABG surgery, perhaps due to either inflammatory mediators or cerebral micro-emboli that occur during aortic manipulation and cross-clamping (Baufreton et al., 2005; Crosby & Culley, 2003). In addition, POCD may be influenced by several other surgical factors, including blood and fluid losses, immobility, inflammation, sensory deprivation or overstimulation, pain, sleep disruption, and medication effects. An increased risk of POCD has also been seen in individuals carrying the *APOE*-ε4 allele, normally associated with an increased risk for AD (Tardiff et al., 1997).

The fact that cognitive impairment due to CABG and other types of surgery improves over time in most individuals argues for regular monitoring and aggressive cognitive rehabilitation. Many surgeons have also adopted a more proactive approach by minimizing or eliminating aortic manipulation and clamping, or forgoing the CBP during CABG (Diegeler et al., 2000). For the majority of affected individuals, the deficits will be mild to moderate and will improve within the first year. Cognitive rehabilitation, when available, can benefit memory and other cognitive skills and play a synergistic role with physical, occupational, and speech therapy. Finally, when an individual suffers from POCD that is persistent and seems out of proportion to expected deficits, the clinician should always suspect comorbid depression, medication effects (especially from narcotics and steroids), or an underlying progressive dementia such as AD.

Dementia Caused by Medications, Substances, and Toxins

When an individual is being evaluated for dementia secondary to medications, substance abuse, or toxic exposure, differentiating between the acute effects of overexposure, intoxication, or withdrawal and the chronic effects of exposure is critical. For most individuals, the acute effects remit when the offending substance is withdrawn, but they can return with repeated exposure. The changes in mental status caused by acute overexposure range from mild confusion to frank delirium and psychosis and ultimately to coma and death. Dementia syndromes, conversely, represent the more insidious, often permanent effects of chronic exposure, which sometimes worsen after abstinence. These factors, as well as the general criteria for dementia stated in the introduction, are captured by the DSM-5 diagnostic category of substance- or medication-induced NCD. Table 8.3 contains a list of substances that can cause dementia.

Medications that can cause reversible, transient cognitive impairment come from a range of pharmacologic categories, but a common link among many of them are their

Table 8.3 Medications, Substances, and Toxins Associated with Cognitive Impairment and Dementia

---

- Medications (see Table 2.3 in Chapter 2 for medications that can cause reversible cognitive impairment)
- Alcohol
- Industrial toxins (e.g., solvents, pesticides)
- Toxic metals (e.g., aluminum, arsenic, copper, lead, manganese, mercury)
- Toxic gases (carbon monoxide, carbon disulfide)

---

effects on CNS receptors, including gamma-aminobutyric acid (GABA) agonism and cholinergic (muscarinic) antagonism. GABA receptors have multiple sites of action, and they serve an inhibitory role on cerebral function when they are activated by sedative-hypnotics (e.g., benzodiazepines, barbiturates), anticonvulsants, and alcohol. The therapeutic and eventually intoxicating properties of these substances clearly illustrate their depressive effects on CNS function. Similar degrees of cognitive impairment can result from the potent anticholinergic effects of many commonly used medications, especially when they are used in combination (see Table 2.4 in Chapter 2 for a complete list). The long-term use of any of these agents can produce insidiously disabling impairments in cognition and function, especially in individuals with preexisting dementia.

Alcohol Dementia

Alcohol abuse is a major health problem in the United States, accounting for a variety of medical and psychiatric conditions. Cognitive problems result from the direct toxic effects of alcohol on the liver, brain, and other organs and from the secondary effects of alcohol abuse (e.g., malnutrition, vitamin deficiencies, an increased risk of stroke and head injury). The concept of alcohol dementia is controversial because of the difficulty in separating the role of alcohol from that of other comorbid conditions, and due to the lack of specific neuropathologic findings (Hulse, Lautenschlager, Tait, & Almeida, 2005). Researchers have, however, developed diagnostic criteria to capture the dementia syndrome that has been associated with significant alcohol use (Oslin, Atkinson, Smith, & Hendrie, 1998; Oslin & Cary, 2003). Although moderate use of alcohol has been associated with lower rates of dementia (Solfrizzi et al., 2007), heavy use has been associated with an increased risk of cognitive impairment as well both AD and vascular dementia (Peters et al., 2008; Virtaa et al., 2010; Xu et al., 2009).

The best studied dementia associated with alcohol abuse is Wernicke–Korsakoff's syndrome, which is characterized by two stages: first, the acute onset of confusion, gaze palsy, nystagmus, and ataxia, collectively referred to as Wernicke's encephalopathy; second, progression to a permanent dementia syndrome involving severe retrograde and anterograde amnesia and confabulation, termed Korsakoff's syndrome (Biglan, 2008). Wernicke–Korsakoff's syndrome is attributed to thiamine deficiency and the consequent damage to the cerebral mammillary bodies and adjacent thalamic nuclei (although Korsakoff's syndrome, as a separate entity, can have other causes). Rapid treatment with thiamine supplementation may reverse the symptoms to varying degrees, but a delay in intervention frequently leads to permanent dementia in 80% of individuals (Biglan, 2008).

In contrast to Wernicke–Korsakoff's syndrome, alcohol dementia involves mild to moderate memory impairment, slowed cognitive processing, and executive dysfunction that may resemble frontal lobe impairment (Oslin et al., 1998; Oslin & Cary, 2003). The individual's language function is typically intact. Neuroimaging studies and corresponding pathologic findings demonstrate neuronal atrophy with sulcal widening in the frontal and mediotemporal lobes, ventricular dilation, the loss of hippocampal pyramidal cells, and degeneration of the cerebellar vermis (Oslin et al., 1998; Ridley, Draper, & Withall, 2013). These pathologic changes have not always correlated with the degree of cognitive impairment.

Because some researchers have argued that alcohol dementia and Wernicke–Korsakoff's syndrome may both result from thiamine deficiency and that they vary only in degree, the use of thiamine and multivitamin supplementation are reasonable first steps in the treatment of suspected alcohol dementia. Obviously, abstinence from alcohol is critical, and this goal may necessitate inpatient detoxification, followed by intensive substance abuse treatment. If true abstinence is achieved, the prognosis for both Wernicke–Korsakoff's syndrome and alcohol dementia is variable, but improvement is possible (Oslin & Cary, 2003).

A dementia syndrome associated with alcohol abuse in older men is Marchiafava–Bignami disease, which causes demyelination of the corpus callosum and the adjacent white matter. The associated neurologic symptoms include incontinence, dysarthria, frontal release signs, hemispheric disconnection, seizures, and personality changes with apathy or agitation (Carrilho, Santos, Piasecki, & Jorge, 2013). Cases of Marchiafava–Bignami disease have been treated successfully with intravenous thiamine infusions (Aggarwal, Khandelwal, & Jiloha, 2011).

Exposure to Toxic Industrial Products, Metals, and Gases

Dementia caused by toxic industrial products, metals, and gases requires either massive acute exposure or significant long-term exposure to high levels of dust, fumes, or liquid through inhalation, skin absorption, or ingestion (Liu, Huang, & Huang, 2012). Occupational exposure is one of the most common settings in which this occurs. Acute poisoning can cause neurological symptoms, mental status changes, and organ damage that require emergent intervention, usually as a result of the primary damaging effects of the substance itself. Permanent dementia may also result from such poisoning, often secondary to an anoxic injury, stroke, or head injury associated with the exposure. In general, dementia caused by toxic metal exposure has become rare because of improved occupational safety regulations and the elimination of environmental hazards. Consequently, few dementia workups will hinge on a heavy metal screen.

However, obtaining an employment history and probing for possible occupational exposures to toxic metals or other substances are important. Occupations with the potential for hazardous exposure include mining, smelting, or foundry work; welding; plumbing; construction work; extermination or fumigation; agricultural work involving proximity to pesticides, herbicides, or fungicides; and manufacturing or craftsmanship work with metals, glass, ceramics, paints, varnishes, or stains, dental amalgams, automotive parts, chemicals, or batteries. Metals associated with toxic exposure in these and other settings include lead, mercury, manganese, arsenic, copper, chromium, nickel, tin, iron, zinc, antimony, bismuth, barium, silver, gold, platinum, lithium, thallium, and aluminum. Some of the more common exposures are discussed in this section.

Other toxic substances that can cause neurologic impairment and, more rarely, cognitive disturbances from overexposure include carbon monoxide, carbon disulfide, organophosphate insecticides, and numerous industrial solvents (e.g., toluene, hexacarbons, hydrocarbons). Poisoning can also result from the intentional inhalation or sniffing of vapors from volatile solvents to get "high." Commonly abused solvents include toluene, halogenated hydrocarbons, benzene, and acetone, which are found in common products such as glues, gasoline, spray paints, and cleaning fluids. Brain damage from intentional inhalation results only after significant long-term exposure.

Prolonged exposure to some metals leads to their accumulation in tissues such as the kidney, brain, bone, and liver, with relatively slow rates of metabolic clearance. Initial manifestations of toxicity often include neurological symptoms, such as an ascending peripheral neuropathy, visual disturbances, and weakness. When toxic exposure is suspected, obtain a heavy metal screen but check with the relevant laboratory to determine which metals are included in the screen. Separate blood, urine, and even hair samples are sometimes needed to get a complete screen. The first step in treatment is to identify and to eliminate the route of exposure. If this can be done and the symptoms are not severe, the body will eventually clear the metal. Adjunctive treatment, especially with heavy exposure or severe symptoms such as dementia, involves the administration of chelating agents to bind the metal, forming a more stable, less toxic, and more excretable compound. Common chelating agents include 2, 3-dimercaptosuccinic acid, known as DMSA; calcium ethylenediaminetetraacetic acid, known as EDTA; penicillamine; and dimercaprol.

Chronic lead poisoning, or plumbism, is more of a concern with children who might be exposed to environmental lead, usually in the form of paint chips or dust from old houses. In adults, sources of chronic lead exposure are less common, but they may include contamination from lead-glazed ceramics; lead paint; and occupational work with lead, including metal and ceramic work, construction, and plumbing. Symptoms of lead poisoning in children include cognitive impairment, developmental delay, neurological symptoms, and behavioral disturbances (Soon et al., 1976). These symptoms are less predictable in adults, although associations have been found between elevated bone lead levels in older adults and cognitive decline (Peters et al., 2010; Weuve et al., 2009). Cumulative lead exposure has also been associated with increased cognitive impairment in Parkinson's disease (Weuve et al., 2013)

Mercury is a particularly poisonous metal with numerous industrial uses. It is present in the following three forms: elemental mercury, inorganic mercury salts (e.g., mercuric chloride), and organic mercury compounds (e.g., methylmercury). Exposure can occur through oral ingestion, through the inhalation of vapors, or transdermally (Honda, Hylander, & Sakamoto, 2006). Historically, mercury poisoning was seen in hatmakers, who used mercury to process felt for men's hats in the 19th and early 20th centuries (as illustrated by the character of the Mad Hatter in Lewis Carroll's *Alice in Wonderland*). Chronic exposure to mercury is associated with neurological impairment (headache, fatigue, ataxia, paresthesias, visual and hearing impairment, tremors), skin eruptions, renal toxicity, cognitive impairment, depression, and psychosis (Honda et al., 2006; Hong, Kim, & Lee, 2012). The presence of a mercury-based amalgam in dental fillings has not been associated with dementia or any other medical problems; the concern regarding exposure is for individuals creating or preparing such amalgams (Koral, 2013).

Manganese, a trace element, is an essential mineral in skin, nerve, bone, and cartilage formation. Manganese toxicity is rare, but it may occur from overexposure to industrial or pharmaceutical sources, including manganese dust from welding, mining, or manufacturing metal alloys, batteries, varnish, fungicides, and gasoline additives, or from the use of manganese chemicals used to make designer drugs (Hua & Huang, 1991). Chronic manganese overexposure over several years has been seen mainly in welders and in miners, and it is associated with "manganese madness," which is characterized by cognitive impairment, psychosis, and behavioral disturbances consistent with frontal lobe impairment (e.g., mood lability, compulsive behaviors), followed by extrapyramidal symptoms (Cersosimo & Koller, 2007; Hua & Huang, 1991).

Copper poisoning can occur in the context of Wilson's disease, which is also known as progressive hepatolenticular degeneration. It is an autosomal recessive disease localized to mutations on chromosome 13, and it involves a deficiency of the copper-transporting protein ceruloplasmin (Mak & Lam, 2008). This deficiency leads to copper deposits in tissues throughout the body, especially the liver, brain (specifically, the lenticular formation comprised of the globus pallidus and putamen), kidneys, and corneas (manifested as corneal Kayser–Fleischer rings). Wilson's disease can develop either in childhood or later in life depending on the degree of mutation, but, without early diagnosis and treatment, the condition is slowly progressive until the individual's eventual death within six months to five years (Brewer, Fink, & Hedera, 1999). It typically begins with hepatic dysfunction and progresses to include neurological impairment with ataxia, rigidity, tremor, and dysarthria in over 40% of patients by the second or third decade (Schmitt de Bem et al., 2011). Without treatment, many patients develop a dementia syndrome that includes behavior, mood, and psychotic disturbances.

The diagnosis of Wilson's disease is made based on the clinical symptoms, liver biopsy, and laboratory tests showing low serum ceruloplasmin and copper levels and increased 24-hour urinary copper levels. If treatment begins early, the symptoms can be reversed and controlled with anticopper therapy, including the copper-chelating agents penicillamine and trientine and copper-depleting agents, such as zinc and tetrathiomolybdate. Improvement may take several months, and a recovery to baseline depends on the extent of symptoms (Schmitt de Bem et al., 2011).

Toxic exposure to carbon monoxide is one of the most common causes of poisoning in the United States, typically resulting from prolonged accidental exposure to excessive fumes from vehicles or home heating devices without adequate ventilation. Carbon monoxide poisoning is also seen in suicide attempts, in which intentional exposure to vehicle exhaust occurs in a closed space. Individuals who survive carbon monoxide poisoning usually make a full recovery, although a significant percentage may develop sequelae, including cognitive impairment, extrapyramidal symptoms, and other focal neurological symptoms (Hsiao, Kuo, & Huang, 2004). A less common gas causing poisoning involves carbon disulfide, which is used in the manufacture of rayon and as a grain fumigant. Long-term exposure has been associated with behavioral and cognitive disturbances, ataxia, peripheral neuropathy, and parkinsonism (Chuang et al., 2007; Liu et al., 2012).

Dementia Caused by Vitamin Deficiencies

Vitamin deficiencies in older individuals have many causes, including a lack of income to buy food, physical disability that limits the ability to purchase and/or prepare food, poor appetite, lack of education, unusual diets, eating disorders, alcoholism, apathy, dementia, dental problems, dysphagia, gastrointestinal disease, and malabsorption syndromes. Deficiencies of several key vitamins including vitamin B12 (cobalamin), folate, niacin (vitamin B3; deficiency known as pellagra), and thiamine (vitamin B1; deficiency known as beri beri) have been associated with various symptoms of cognitive impairment, apathy, mood disturbances, psychosis, and peripheral neuropathies (Lanska, 2010; Sadighi, Butler, & Koenig, 2012; Werder, 2010). A more severe condition associated with a vitamin B12 deficiency is subacute combined degeneration, a demyelinating disorder associated with peripheral neuropathy, depression, and dementia (Vasconcelos et al., 2006).

These conditions are less commonly encountered in Western countries because of the generally adequate nutrition and vitamin supplementation of many food products. A routine dementia workup should always include attention to the individual's typical diet; medical conditions and any medications that may affect his or her eating, digestion, and appetite; and the social and financial resources required to maintain adequate nutrition. For some individuals, vitamin supplementation may be an important part of dementia care.

Dementia Associated with Infectious Diseases

Historically, infectious diseases have represented a significant cause of dementia; epidemics of neurosyphilis date back to the 16th century, and encephalitis lethargica affected millions of individuals in the decade that followed World War I. The advent of antibiotics in the 1940s virtually eliminated neurosyphilis, and the further development of antimicrobial, antifungal, and, more recently, antiviral agents has blunted the potential impact of other infectious diseases. These medical developments have also contributed greatly to longer life spans, meaning that most individuals in developed countries live to the stages of life at highest risk of both AD and VaD. Consequently, the surge in prevalence of these dementia types in the past 50 years has eclipsed that of dementia caused by infectious sources.

Acute infection of the CNS can result in either a meningitis or an encephalitis characterized by fever, meningeal signs (headache, stiff neck, photophobia), focal neurological signs, seizures, and mental status changes consistent with delirium (see Chapter 9 for more details). These emergent states require rapid medical intervention, but, even with aggressive treatment, they can sometimes lead to permanent neurological symptoms, dementia, or death. Immunocompromised, older, and medically ill individuals are at greatest risk of developing encephalitis and its sequelae. Chronic infections of the CNS present more insidiously, and they may produce a dementia in which no clear evidence of the underlying source is obvious. Brain damage from infections can result from several of the following mechanisms: (a) the direct toxic effects of the pathogen and its products, (b) inflammatory responses, (c) opportunistic and secondary infections, and (d) immune-mediated postinfectious encephalitic states.

Clinical Tip

Several clues in the dementia workup that may suggest an underlying infectious encephalitis include a recent viral or other unexplained illness or rash; seasonal or geographic proximity to epidemic or endemic illnesses (e.g., overseas travel); an acute onset of symptoms, seizures, extrapyramidal symptoms; and HIV infection. A thorough physical examination may reveal unrecognized sites of infections that can seed the CNS, such as tooth abscesses, cardiac valvular vegetations, and sinus infections. Neuroimaging may reveal occult abscesses in the CNS.

Infectious pathogens that can cause encephalitis and subsequent dementia include bacteria, viruses, spirochetes, fungi, and parasites. Also included in this category are the infectious proteinaceous particles, or prions, that cause the transmissible spongiform encephalopathies. Potential infectious sources are listed in Table 8.4. The requisite laboratory tests include a complete blood count, blood cultures, and an analysis of CSF. In viral encephalitis, CSF analysis typically shows a mild lymphocytosis with normal glucose and increased protein levels. In most cases of presumed viral illness, however, the source is never isolated, even with serologic investigation. CSF analysis for bacterial and fungal infections of the CNS is usually more revealing, with findings of gross lymphocytosis and elevated protein levels. CSF culture and staining can isolate bacteria and most fungi, but serologic studies, including immunologic markers, are needed for spirochetes and some fungi. Brain scans are typically normal for acute meningoencephalitis, but, in chronic infections, scans may demonstrate abscesses or focal neuronal loss or demyelination, especially in the basal ganglia. Electroencephalography (EEG) may demonstrate diffuse slowing with abnormal frontal and temporal rhythms across all types of infections (Drazkowski, 2008).

Bacterial infections of the CNS are uncommon causes of dementia by their very nature; they are usually rapidly emergent and result in either recovery or death. However, undiagnosed bacterial brain abscesses and postinfectious processes may cause cognitive and behavioral disturbances, as well as seizures and other neurological symptoms. The aggressive use of intravenous antibiotics is curative in many cases of acute bacterial encephalitis and in most cases of subacute or chronic infections. The most common causes of bacterial encephalitis in older individuals include *Streptococcus pneumoniae, Neisseria meningitides, Listeria monocytogenes,* and *Haemophilus influenzae* Type b (Roos, 2008). Other bacterial sources are listed in Table 8.4.

Viral infections are the most common cause of both acute and chronic encephalitis, with HIV representing the source of the most cases. The next most commonly reported viral sources include herpes simplex, influenza, measles, and Epstein–Barr virus. Herpes simplex encephalitis presents as an acute viral syndrome, and more than half of all

Table 8.4 Infectious Sources of Encephalitis and Dementia

Bacterial Meningoencephalitides and Brain Abscesses

Streptococcus pneumoniae, Neisseria meningitides, Listeria monocytogenes, Haemophilus influenzae Type b, gram-negative bacilli (*Eschrichia coli*, Klebsiella, *Pseudomonas aeruginosa*, Enterobacter), *Mycoplasma pneumonia, Mycobacterium tuberculosis, Legionella pneumophila* (Legionnaire's disease), *Rochalimaea henselae* (catscratch disease), brucellosis, *Tropheryma whippelii* (Whipple's disease)

Viral Meningoencephalitides

Human immunodeficiency virus 1; herpes simplex virus, types 1 and 2; Epstein–Barr virus; cytomegalovirus; mumps; influenza; coxsackie; rabies; flaviviruses (West Nile virus, yellow fever, dengue fever); arboviruses (St. Louis encephalitis, western and eastern equine encephalitis); papovavirus (JC virus)

Spirochetal Encephalopathies

Neurosyphilis (*Treponema pallidum*), Lyme disease (*Borrelia burgdorferi*)

Fungal Meningoencephalitides and Brain Abscesses

Cryptococcus, Coccidioides, Histoplasma, Aspergillus, Candida, Blastomyces, Actinomyces, Mucor, Sporothrix, Nocardia

Parasitic Diseases and Brain Abscesses

Rickettsial diseases (Q fever, typhus, Rocky Mountain spotted fever), toxoplasmosis, cysticercosis, amebic meningoencephalitis, malaria (*Plasmodium falciparum* and others), trypanosomiasis, trichinosis, strongyloidiasis, visceral larva migrans, schistosomiasis

Prion Diseases

Creutzfeldt–Jakob disease, variant Creutzfeldt–Jakob disease, kuru, Gertsmann–Sträussler–Scheinker syndrome, fatal familiar insomnia

Postinfectious Dementias

Subacute sclerosing panencephalitis (measles sequelae), encephalitis lethargica

cases occur in the elderly (Stahl et al., 2012). The infection has a predilection for the mediotemporal and orbitofrontal cortices, and it is associated with frontal lobe symptoms. Dementia that is characterized by amnesia and aphasia is a possible postinfectious consequence. Damage to the mediotemporal lobes may result in Klüver–Bucy syndrome. Aggressive antiviral treatment and supportive care are critical to decreasing the morbidity and mortality associated with herpes simplex encephalitis and many other viral encephalitides (Stahl et al., 2012; Vachalová, Kyavar, & Heckmann, 2013).

Progressive multifocal leukoencephalopathy (PML) is a cerebral demyelinating disorder that results from infection with the John Cunningham or JC virus, a ubiquitous human polyomavirus (formerly called papovavirus). The virus apparently leaves its dormant state and begins active replication in susceptible individuals who are either elderly, have a hematologic cancer, are taking certain chemotherapeutic or other drugs alone or in combination (e.g., brentuximab for Hodgkin's Lymphoma, natalizumab for multiple sclerosis, tacrolimus for immunosuppression, or efalizumab for psoriasis), or are otherwise immunocompromised, particularly patients with AIDS; the latter currently comprise 85% of all cases of PML (Bellizzi, Anzivino, & Rodio, 2013; Mateen et al.,

2011). The clinical symptoms of PML include a rapid onset of dementia, personality changes, and focal neurological symptoms, including hemiparesis progressing to quadriparesis, aphasia, ataxia, visual disturbances, and dysarthria. Brain imaging reveals demyelinating lesions of various sizes. Death occurs within three to six months, although the use of antiretroviral therapy has led to variable outcomes in patients with AIDS. The antiviral medication cidofovir (Segarra-Newnham & Vodolo, 2001) and the antimalarial drug mefloquine (Gofton et al., 2010) have been used successfully to treat PML in several cases.

Several rare dementing conditions, which are believed to represent chronic infection or an immune-mediated postinfectious condition, occur months to years after an acute viral infectious episode. Subacute sclerosing panencephalitis can occur in children and occasionally in young adults 6–8 years after a bout of measles and involves the progressive onset of neurological impairment and dementia that usually culminates in death within one to three years (Faivre, Souraud, & McGonigal, 2009; Schönberger, Ludwig, & Wildner, 2013). It is rarely seen today because of the use of the measles vaccine. Encephalitis lethargica, which is also known as von Economo disease or sleeping sickness, affected nearly five million people in the decade after the influenza pandemic of 1917, but it has rarely been seen since 1930. This acute cortical and subcortical syndrome was characterized by profound lethargy ("sleeping"), ophthalmoplegia, parkinsonism, psychosis, and a fatal encephalitis in 20% to 30% of patients. Recovery from the acute syndrome was followed by the development of a parkinsonian syndrome months or years later and an ensuing subcortical dementia. The exact cause of encephalitis lethargica is not known, although it has been ascribed to an immunologic reaction to the influenza virus of the 1918 pandemic or some other pathogen, an autoimmune reaction, or an enterovirus infection (Dourmashkin, Dunn, Castano, & McCall, 2013; McCall, Vilensky, Gilman, & Taubenberger, 2008).

Spirochetes are motile microorganisms that cause CNS infections, including syphilis caused by *Treponema pallidum*, Lyme disease caused by *Borrelia burgdorferi*, and leptospirosis caused by *Leptospira interrogans*. Both syphilis and Lyme disease are described in detail later in the chapter.

Fungal CNS infections associated with encephalitis have become more common in the past 20 years as opportunistic infections occurring in the setting of HIV infection and other immunocompromised states. The range of fungal culprits includes Cryptococcus, Coccidioides, Histoplasma, Aspergillus, Candida, Blastomyces, Actinomyces, Mucor, Nocardia, and Sporothrix organisms. Fungal meningitis generally develops insidiously over weeks or months, producing classic meningeal signs. The complications can include cranial neuropathies, strokes, brain abscesses, and hydrocephalus (Roos, 2008). A diagnosis is usually made on the basis of CSF staining, cultures, or fungal antigen titers. Traditionally, antifungal treatment relied on intravenous or even intrathecal amphotericin B with its associated toxicity, but several newer and less toxic triazole antifungal agents are now available for use. Cryptococcal meningitis, the most common fungal CNS infection (especially in HIV patients), can produce focal neurological symptoms and delirium, as well as a dementia with waxing and waning symptoms over months or years. The overall mortality rate approaches 40% (Park et al., 2009).

Parasitic infections of the CNS are rare, but, like fungal infections, they are now seen more commonly in the setting of HIV infection and other immunocompromised states.

These infections include organisms such as rickettsias (intracellular bacterial parasites), protozoa, and worms (cestodes, nematodes, and trematodes). Several other parasitic diseases are listed in Table 8.4. One of the more common parasitic infections of the brain associated with dementia is neurocysticercois, caused by ingesting eggs of the pork tapeworm Taenia solium (García et al., 2002). CNS involvement by each of these parasites can include meningoencephalitis, cerebral cysts, seizures, and hydrocephalus. Treatment involves the use of antiparasitic agents along with treatment of cerebral complications such as increased intracranial pressure and seizures (White, 2009).

HIV-Associated Neurocognitive Disorders

Infection with HIV is associated with direct viral damage to the CNS, which, in turn, leads to increasing degrees of neuropsychiatric impairment. *HIV-associated neurocognitive disorder* (HAND) is the term used to encompass three subtypes: asymptomatic neurocognitive impairment, mild neurocognitive disorder, and HIV-associated dementia or HAD (Giunta et al., 2013); the latter term is also known as HIV encephalopathy or AIDS dementia complex. HAD is characterized by the development of impaired attention or concentration, memory impairment, mental or motor slowing, incoordination, poor balance, and tremors. Language dysfunction is less common, and overall the clinical picture resembles a subcortical dementia (American Psychiatric Association, 2013). Common psychiatric symptoms include sleep disturbances, sexual dysfunction, apathy, agitation, and psychosis.

The diagnosis of HAND is based on clinical symptoms because no specific diagnostic laboratory tests or neuroimaging findings have been identified. However, a greater degree of cognitive impairment and risk for progression is associated with increased serum and/or CSF viral load as well as increased microglial activation (Kaul et al., 2005). Previously, up to 50% of all AIDS patients developed HAND, but its incidence has decreased significantly because of the widespread use of highly active antiretroviral therapy or HAART (Sacktor, 2002; Ances, Benzinger, & Christensen, 2012), which itself can sometimes be a cause of transitory cognitive impairment, confusion, lethargy, and even agitation and psychosis. Older age is a risk factor, and HAND may be seen as an initial manifestation of AIDS in nearly 20% of older patients (Valcour, Shikuma, Watters, & Sacktor, 2004).

The presence of HAND has been associated with increased mortality, and its identification should prompt aggressive management. In addition to antiretroviral therapy (Tan & McArthur, 2012), therapeutic agents that have shown promise in treating symptoms of HAND include minocycline, memantine, and selegiline (Lindl, Marks, & Kolson, 2010; Schifitto et al., 2007, 2009). Psychostimulants such as methylphenidate and modafinil have been used with some success to treat the cognitive slowing and lethargy associated with HAND (McElhiney, Rabkin, Van Gorp, & Rabkin, 2010).

Neurosyphilis

Syphilis is a communicable disease caused by the spirochete Treponema pallidum, a spiral-shaped motile microorganism. It is primarily transmitted via the skin and mucous membranes during sexual contact, but it can also be spread by blood transfusions and perinatal contact. Primary syphilis presents as follows: development of a chancre at the site of infection within several weeks, followed by spontaneous resolution. Secondary syphilis presents as follows: development of a red maculopapular rash on the body, followed by spontaneous resolution. Thirty percent of infected individuals have no further manifestations after the primary or secondary stages, and another 30% have latent disease, or tertiary syphilis, which may not manifest for years or decades after the primary infection. This latter stage can cause granulomatous lesions in the skin, bones, and liver; cardiac and ophthalmologic problems; and CNS infection or neurosyphilis.

Neurosyphilis is characterized by meningeal inflammation, frontal and temporal lobe demyelination, and cortical atrophy (Zetola, Engelman, Jensen, & Klausner, 2007). Clinical symptoms include progressive dementia; frontal lobe symptoms, such as personality change, apathy, and poor judgment; psychosis; mood disturbances; and various neurologic symptoms including tabes dorsalis, a peripheral neuropathy that manifests as pain in the extremities, ataxia, and incontinence.

Syphilis may be suspected based on clinical symptoms, but arriving at a definitive diagnosis relies on nontreponemal antigenic tests (including a Venereal Disease Research Laboratories or VDRL test; a rapid plasma reagin test (RPR); treponemal detection via a fluorescent treponemal antibody absorption test or FTA-ABS). The standard treatment for primary or secondary stage syphilis is 2.4 million units of penicillin G given intramuscularly. The symptoms of neurosyphilis can be reversed to variable degrees with successful treatment involving at least 10 days of intravenous penicillin (Kent & Romanelli, 2008). Alternative antibiotics include ceftriaxone, doxycycline, and tetracycline.

Clinical Tip

Testing for syphilis with an RPR or a VDRL test has always been a routine part of dementia workups, even though the infection has become quite uncommon as an actual cause of dementia. Even when syphilis does occur, seeing a case that has progressed to the tertiary stage is rare. Recent outbreaks of syphilis, however, should prompt all clinicians to include syphilis in the differential diagnosis, especially in individuals with known HIV infection or HIV risk factors (Zetola et al., 2007).

Lyme Encephalopathy

Lyme disease is a tick-transmitted disease in humans that is caused by the spirochete *B. burgdorferi*. The disease is the most common vector-borne illness in the United States, and it has been associated with neurologic and psychiatric symptoms in up to 15% of infected individuals (Halperin, 2008). Although Lyme disease had been clinically described for decades, it was first identified and classified serologically after an outbreak of arthritis in a group of infected children in Lyme, Connecticut, in 1977.

The initial stage of Lyme disease is a localized, target-shaped rash, called erythema migrans, at the site of a tick bite; its appearance is sometimes associated with the subsequent development of flulike symptoms. Early disseminated infection may then occur acutely days or weeks after infection or as a later stage months or years later; it is characterized by fever, fatigue, headache, migrating joint and tendon pain, and lymphadenopathy. CNS involvement may occur as cranial or peripheral neuropathies and a meningoencephalitis. Lyme encephalopathy or dementia can be seen in late-stage disease and is characterized by mild to severe impairment in short-term memory, bradyphrenia, word-finding and reading difficulties, visuospatial impairment, depression, and emotional lability (Halperin, 2013)

When conducting a dementia workup, always inquire about tick bites or exposure to wooded areas endemic to ticks and Lyme disease. The standard blood test is a Lyme titer, which may give a false negative result in the first month after infection. In cases with a negative titer but a high index of suspicion, conducting an enzyme-linked immunosorbent assay or a Western blot test may be necessary. In addition to serum titers, an analysis of the CSF should be considered when neurological symptoms are present. The treatment of choice for Lyme disease is antibiotic therapy; with therapy, the prognosis is generally good for all symptoms (Halperin, 2013).

Human Prion Diseases

Human prion diseases, also known as transmissible spongiform encephalopathies, are rapidly progressive neurodegenerative disorders that are believed to be caused by nonviral/nonbacterial agents known as proteinaceous infectious particles or prions. Prion diseases are seen in both human and certain mammalian species and share several common features: (1) they are caused by abnormal prion proteins, (2) they arise de novo or as a result of genetic mutations, (3) they can result from exposure to prion-infected tissue, and (4) they cause spongiform degeneration of the brain. Human prion diseases can be categorized as sporadic, hereditary, or acquired. A complete list can be found in Table 8.5.

The most widely known is Creutzfeldt–Jakob disease (CJD). Scrapie is the classic animal prion disease and is seen in sheep and goats; it spurred much of the initial research. Other mammalian prion diseases include chronic wasting disease (CWD), found in deer and elk; transmissible mink encephalopathy, found in mink; and bovine spongiform encephalopathy (BSE), found in cattle, also known as "mad cow disease." BSE was seen widely among the cattle population in the United Kingdom in the late 1980s and early 1990s, leading to massive culling.

The concept of infectious proteinaceous particles was first proposed in 1982 by Dr. Stanley Prusiner and was greeted by much controversy (Prusiner, 1982). Historically, both CJD and scrapie were believed to be caused by some form of a slow virus, and the idea of a nonviral/nonbacterial infectious agent without nucleic acid was seen as heretical. Accumulating evidence did not, however, point to any known form of infectious agent, especially one that was found to be resistant to common methods of sterilization such as boiling, formalin, and ultraviolet light, and instead required the use of either bleach or pressure autoclaving. Prusiner proposed that the true cause of CJD and related diseases was a proteinaceous, infectious particle which lacked nucleic acid and was derived from a normal cellular prion protein, labeled PrPc, which is present in neurons but with an unknown role. In prion diseases, this normal isoform of the prion protein is changed to an abnormal form labeled PrPsc (which was initially isolated from

Table 8.5 Dementias Due to Human Prion Diseases

Sporadic	
Creutzfeldt–Jakob Disease (CJD)	• Unknown trigger of abnormal prions
	• Age of onset, older than 50 years old
	• Prevalence, 1:1 million (200–300 cases/year in U.S.)
	• Represents 85% of all CJD cases
	• Rapid course until death (less than 12 months)
	• Five subtypes based on genetic polymorphism
Inherited	
• Familial CJD	• Autosomal dominant conditions caused by mutations in prion protein gene (more than 24 different mutations)
• Gerstmann-Straüssler-Scheinker syndrome	
• Fatal familial insomnia	• Represent up to 15% of all cases of CJD
	• Variable presentations, even in same family
	• Age of onset in middle age
Acquired	
• Iatrogenic CJD	• Several cases of iatrogenic CJD acquired through contamination of surgical instruments, corneal or dura mater transplants, and human growth hormone, with an incubation period of 19–46 months
• Kuru	
• Variant CJD (vCJD)	
	• Kuru seen in Fore Tribe in New Guinea, associated with ritual cannibalism of brain matter, with an incubation period of 3–40 years
	• vCJD seen in less than 200 cases, mainly in United Kingdom; likely related to ingestion of beef products from cows with bovine spongiform encephalopathy; average age of onset is 28 years

scrapie samples). When PrPc is changed to PrPsc, the alpha-helical content of the protein decreases while the beta-sheet content increases, resulting in a pathologic, insoluble form that causes rapid brain damage associated with vacuoles and in some cases plaques composed of prion fibrils (Prusiner, 1998). Mutations in the prion protein gene have been localized mainly to codon 129, where a methionine is substituted for a valine. Homo- versus heterozygous combinations of alleles produce various disease phenotypes.

Creutzfeldt–Jakob disease is a rare form of dementia, seen sporadically in individuals between the ages of 50 and 70 years. Between 5% and 15% of all cases are familial, with autosomal dominant transmission and typically a younger age at onset. Iatrogenic cases of CJD have been seen in individuals exposed to infected brain tissue, such as from inadequately sterilized surgical instruments or growth hormone made from infected pituitary glands. Similar transmission is seen with the prion disease kuru, found among members of one particular New Guinea tribe that practiced cannibalism of brain tissue as part of its burial rites. Kuru has almost disappeared along with the abandonment of ritual cannibalism.

The clinical picture of CJD, from initial symptoms through rapidly progressive decline and then death, takes an average of 6–12 months. Early symptoms may include fatigue, insomnia, anorexia, mood swings, apathy, and behavioral disturbances (Roos, 2008). Depression and psychosis are seen in approximately 10% of cases and may include detailed delusions and hallucinations. As the disease progresses, memory impairment, speech disturbances, visual impairment, gait ataxia, and cerebellar dysfunction become more prominent. Many individuals display prominent myoclonic jerks, incontinence, and hallucinations. In the terminal phase, patients develop akinetic mutism: they cannot move, speak, swallow, or respond to stimulation. MRI scans of the brain may show basal ganglia hyperintensities in T2-weighted images (Cambier et al., 2003). In 80% of cases, EEGs show periodic bursts of characteristic bifrontal sharp waves or triphasic waves, set against a slowed background rhythm (Drazkowski, 2008). The 14-3-3 protein is a biomarker for CJD seen in the cerebrospinal fluid of over 90% of individuals with CJD (Hsich et al., 1996). As with Alzheimer's disease, the only way to make a 100% accurate diagnosis of CJD is to examine brain tissue via biopsy or autopsy and look for spongiform changes. In addition to microscopic examination, brain tissue (and with variant CJD some researchers have looked at tonsillar tissue) can be stained with antibodies to prion proteins.

Two other human prion diseases similar to CJD are Gerstmann-Straüssler-Scheinker (GSS) syndrome and fatal familial insomnia (FFI). Both GSS and FFI are rare disorders that strike middle-age adults and are associated with genetic mutations in the prion protein gene. GSS is an autosomal dominant disorder characterized by dementia with pyramidal, extrapyramidal, and cerebellar symptoms, while FFI is a rapidly progressive disease of thalamic nuclei that is characterized by multiple neurologic disturbances, a frontal lobe-type dementia, insomnia, and dysautonomia (Roos, 2008).

Many of the persistent questions regarding the etiology of prion diseases came to the forefront during the epidemic of BSE in the United Kingdom (UK) in the late 1980s and early 1990s. At its peak, nearly 40,000 cases of BSE occurred, required the mass slaughter and cremation of a large portion of the UK's cattle herd in order to stop the spread of the disease. The cause of BSE was believed to be due to cows being given feed with infected neural tissue from other animals and was traced to the removal of specific sterilization procedures in the production of feed in the 1970s. In 1988, the UK banned the use of animal proteins in cattle feed. However, subsequent to the BSE epidemic, there have been nearly 140 cases of spongiform dementias in humans, presumably due to the consumption of meat products that contained infected neural tissue from cows with BSE. This new dementia was labeled variant CJD.

Unlike CJD, variant CJD strikes young individuals, after an estimated incubation period of six years from the time of ingesting the tainted beef. Early manifestations of variant CJD almost always include psychiatric disturbances such as personality changes, social withdrawal, depression, anxiety, and psychosis with complex delusions and hallucinations. Other symptoms include insomnia, excessive somnolence during the day, and anorexia, progressing to include neurological symptoms such as myclonus, ataxia, and pain and paresthesias in the extremities, head, and neck. Progressive dementia results in a mute, rigid state, with death occurring after an average course of 14 months (Belay & Schonberger, 2002). Although variant CJD is presumed to result from contact with tissue from cattle with BSE, the exact method of transmission has not been confirmed, since it is not possible to know with certainty whether someone had contact with such products. In addition, the sporadic nature of variant CJD among thousands of individuals who likely ingested the same contaminated meat products raises questions about why certain younger individuals were disproportionately affected. Ongoing research is investigating whether mutations in the prion protein gene might confer a genetic susceptibility to developing variant CJD. Of great concern is the specter of dormant cases that may emerge in the coming years.

Unfortunately, there are no effective treatments for any human prion diseases, and clinicians become involved mainly for diagnosis and palliation of symptoms. Clinical trials have not found clear efficacy for several drugs used to treat CJD, including the antimalarial drug quinacrine (Collinge et al., 2009) and intraventricular infusions of pentosan polysulfate (Rainov et al., 2009). Future treatment approaches may seek to prevent the conversion of PrPc to PrPsc or to destabilize or destroy PrPsc once it has been formed, perhaps by using a vaccine. Both benzodiazepines (e.g., clonazepam) and anticonvulsants (e.g., valproic acid) have been used to reduce myoclonic jerks. Antidepressants and antipsychotics can treat associated mood and behavior disturbances.

Dementia Due to Renal and Hepatic Failure

More than 300,000 individuals in the United States have been diagnosed with chronic renal failure, and two-thirds are receiving hemodialysis. Chronic renal failure can cause a state of impaired cognitive functioning that is known as uremic encephalopathy. This state is best characterized as a form of delirium rather than as dementia. The early symptoms of headache, weakness, poor concentration, apathy, and irritability can progress to a more pronounced state of confusion, memory impairment, psychosis, agitation, and insomnia (Seifter & Samuels, 2011). Hepatic encephalopathy is characterized by confusion, asterixis, ataxia, hyperreflexia, mood disturbances, and psychosis (Cash et al., 2010). Both neuropsychological testing and positron emission tomography studies suggest the presence of predominantly bifrontal and biparietal impairment in hepatic encephalopathy, including declines in executive dysfunction and fine motor skills. The most common causes in adults and the elderly are alcohol-induced cirrhosis and chronic infectious hepatitis.

Dementia Associated with Endocrine Disease

Endocrine diseases, which represent some of the most common late-life medical disorders, are associated with significant morbidity, including the potential for dementia. Diabetes mellitus is the most common endocrine disorder, with the adult-onset or type II form affecting 20% of individuals older than the age of 80. The chronic hyperglycemia of diabetes mellitus causes both microvascular and macrovascular damage throughout the body, resulting in a significantly increased risk of peripheral vascular disease, myocardial infarction, and stroke. Not surprisingly, diabetes mellitus is found in nearly 50% of individuals with VaD, and it has been shown to nearly double the risk of both AD and VaD (Profenno, Porsteinsson, & Faraone, 2010). Chronic episodes of hypoglycemia can also cause cognitive impairment, including memory impairment and behavioral disturbances (Flicker & Ames, 2005).

Hypothyroidism, the second most common endocrine disease after diabetes mellitus, is characterized by a variety of neuropsychiatric symptoms, including lethargy, depression, apathy, slowed thinking (bradyphrenia), and dementia (Flicker & Ames, 2005; Shanker, 2008). However, improved surveillance by physicians has significantly reduced the risk of active disease reaching that point. The mood disturbances and mild cognitive impairment usually improve with treatment, but they can persist in as many as 10% of patients.

Hyperparathyroidism causes the excessive production of parathyroid hormone, which can result in hypercalcemia with resultant bone resorption and an increased risk of fracture, urinary calculi, gastrointestinal disturbances, and peptic ulcer disease. The most common cause of hyperparathyroidism is a parathyroid adenoma. The neuropsychiatric symptoms of this condition include depression, impaired memory, paranoid psychosis, agitation, confusion, personality changes, and apathy (Duque, Segal, Wise, & Bianco, 2005; Roman & Sosa, 2007). Hypocalcemia can also lead to confusion, cognitive impairment, and personality changes (Shanker, 2008).

Cushing's syndrome is associated with hypercortisolemia, and it results from adrenocortical hyperfunction. The most common cause of Cushing's syndrome is excess production of the adrenocorticotropic hormone in the anterior pituitary gland (Cushing's disease), but adrenocortical hyperplasia can also be a cause. Hypercortisolemia can lead to numerous neuropsychiatric symptoms, including memory impairment, poor concentration and attention, bradyphrenia, impaired abstract thinking, and depression (Belanoff, Gross, Yager, & Schatzberg, 2001). Addison's disease, or adrenocortical insufficiency, can also produce a slowly progressive dementia that is characterized by memory impairment, bradyphrenia, depression, and psychosis (Ten, New, & Maclaren, 2001). Mental status changes in both Cushing's syndrome and Addison's disease can be reversed with appropriate treatment.

Dementia Associated with Chronic Neurological Disease

Regardless of the cause, a common pathologic end point in many cases of dementia is demyelination. Demyelinating disorders are characterized by the progressive loss of the myelin sheath or physiologic insulation on neurons, which leads to slowing and the disruption of axonal transmission. Myriad causes exist for the various demyelinating disorders, and these disorders can occur at any age.

Multiple Sclerosis

Multiple sclerosis (MS) is the most common demyelinating disorder seen in adults. MS is an autoimmune disorder that produces multiple areas of focal white matter demyelination in the CNS (Compton & Coles, 2008). It typically presents in early adulthood, with less than 1% of cases seen after the age of 60. MS is more prevalent in women and in northern latitudes. The initial presentations of MS are extremely variable, ranging from obvious pathognomonic symptoms to subtle and fluctuating ones that elude diagnosis.

MS may follow one of several courses, ranging from a relapsing and/or remitting pattern of symptoms to a slowly or rapidly progressive course. A slowly progressive course is more common in older patients.

Acute symptoms include fatigue in 75% of patients, impaired motor function, gait disturbances and ataxia, spastic weakness, incontinence, optic neuritis, gaze palsies, and paresthesias. Neuropsychiatric symptoms include sexual dysfunction, sleep disturbances, apathy, depression, euphoria, and mania. Eventually, cognitive impairment is seen in 30% to 50% of patients with MS; this has frontal-subcortical characteristics, including memory impairment, slowed information processing, and executive dysfunction (Bobholz & Rao, 2003). The cognitive impairment can evolve into a clear dementia in 5% of patients (Amato, Ponziani, Siracusa, & Sorbi, 2001).

Three other rare demyelinating disorders that have been associated with cognitive impairment include adrenoleukodystrophy, an X-linked demyelinating disorder of the cerebral white matter that is caused by a deficiency of a peroxidase enzyme (Moser et al., 2004); metachromatic leukodystrophy, an inherited autosomal recessive demyelinating disorder that is related to a deficiency of arylsulfatase A (Shapiro, Lockman, Knopman, & Krivit, 1994); and cerebrotendinous xanthomatosis, an autosomal recessive disorder that causes increased levels of cholestanol because of the impaired hepatic synthesis of bile salts (Guyant-Maréchal, Verrips, & Girard, 2005).

Huntington's Disease

Huntington's disease is a progressive neurodegenerative genetic disease that is associated with a dyskinetic movement disorder, dementia, and psychiatric disturbances. It is transmitted in an autosomal dominant manner, meaning that at least 50% of all offspring will be affected, and is caused by excess trinucleatide (CAG) sequences coding for the huntingtin protein on chromosome 4 (Myers, 2004; Walker, 2007). The key pathologic feature is atrophy of the striatum (caudate and putamen), followed by eventual cerebral atrophy and ventricular dilation. The clinical symptoms of Huntington's disease typically begin in the late 30s to early 40s; they include changes in personality (e.g., apathy, impulsivity) and behavior, as well as slowly evolving involuntary dyskinetic movements. The initial fidgeting movements in the hands and extremities progress to more general dyskinetic movements, including chorea and athetosis. Gaze palsies, dysarthria, decreased coordination with an abnormal and unsteady gait, orolingual apraxias, and increasing rigidity and dystonias are some of the associated neurologic symptoms that develop (Anderson & Marder, 2006). Psychiatric disturbances, including depression, mania, suicidality, irritability, aggression, psychosis, and apathy are seen in 10% to over 50% of patients with Huntington's disease (Anderson & Marder, 2006; Fiedorowicz, Mills, & Ruggle, 2011).

The dementia associated with Huntington's disease begins with memory deficits and progresses over the course of the disease to encompass more global impairment, including visuospatial impairment, apraxias, dyscalculia, language disturbances, and executive dysfunction (Paulsen, 2011). No effective treatment exists for Huntington's disease, and it progresses over 15 to 20 years until eventual death. Antipsychotic medications have been used to treat the behavioral disturbances, psychosis, and dyskinetic movements.

Dementia Caused by Inflammatory Disease

Several inflammatory diseases, including collagen vascular diseases and vasculitides, can cause dementia (Biglan, 2008). The mechanism of cognitive impairment is typically the immune-mediated destruction of small blood vessels, leading to tissue micro-infarcts throughout the body. In general, these diseases are rare, and dementia is the result of severe and long-standing illness. Consequently, most individuals who present for a dementia workup generally have a longstanding history of symptoms and often a confirmed diagnosis. However, in the absence of a diagnosis, the clinician should obtain an erythrocyte sedimentation rate, which is a nonspecific marker for systemic inflammation. Although more specific tests are indicated for various diagnoses, rheumatologic and/or neurological consultation is advised when an inflammatory disease is suspected.

The systemic symptoms common to most inflammatory diseases are fever, weight loss, headache, arthritis, and skin lesions. CNS involvement is seen in one-third to two-thirds of the affected individuals, including cranial neuropathies, dysarthria, ataxia, ocular movement disturbances, corticospinal tract signs (e.g., paresis, spasticity), myelopathy, seizures, stroke-like attacks, delirium, and dementia. Dementia caused by inflammatory diseases usually involves the frontotemporal lobe, with memory and language impairment, executive dysfunction, and personality changes (e.g., apathy or disinhibition), as well as psychiatric symptoms such as psychosis and mood disturbances. The treatment varies with each disease, but, in general, corticosteroids, anti-inflammatory agents, cytotoxic agents, and immunosuppressive therapy are used (Biglan, 2008).

The main collagen vascular diseases that can cause cognitive impairment include Behçet syndrome, Sjögren syndrome, and systemic lupus erythematosus. Of the three, systemic lupus erythematosus is the most common, with CNS involvement including seizures, strokes, delirium, myelopathy, optic neuritis, and acute psychosis in 5% to nearly 40% of cases (Hanly et al., 2004; Kampylafka et al., 2013).

Vasculitides that can have CNS involvement include granulomatous angiitis, lymphomatoid granulomatosis, polyarteritis nodosa, Wegener's granulomatosis (Churg–Strauss syndrome), microscopic angiitis, and primary angiitis of the central nervous system (Biglan, 2008; Berlit, 2010). All of these have the potential to produce encephalopathy in 20%–30% of patients (Bae et al, 1991; Koo & Massey, 1988; Nishino et al., 1993).

References

Aggarwal, A., Khandelwal, A., & Jiloha, R. C. (2011). A case of marchiafava bignami disease: Complete recovery with thiamine. *J Neuropsychiatry Clin Neurosci, 23*(2), E28.

Amato, M. P., Ponziani, G., Siracusa, G., & Sorbi, S. (2001). Cognitive dysfunction in early-onset multiple sclerosis: A reappraisal after 10 years. *Arch. Neurol, 58*(10), 1602–1606.

American Psychiatric Association. (2013). *Diagnostic and statistical manual of mental disorders* (5th ed.). Washington, DC: Author.

Ances, B. M., Benzinger, T. L., & Christensen, J. J. (2012). HIV Associated Neurocognitive Disorder (HAND) is not associated with increased fibrillar amyloid deposits using 11C-PiB in middle-aged HIV+ participants. *Arch Neurol, 69*(1), 72–77.

Anderson, K. E., & Marder, K. S. (2006). Huntington's disease. In D. V. Jeste & J. H. Friedman (Eds.), *Current clinical neurology: Psychiatry for neurologists* (pp. 227–240). Totowa, NJ: Humana Press.

Bae, W. K., Lee, K. S., Kim, P. N., et al. (1991). Lymphomatoid granulomatosis with isolated involvement of the brain: Case report. *J Korean Med Sci, 6*(3), 255–259.

Baufreton, C., Allain, P., Chevailler, A., et al. (2005). Brain injury and neuropsychological outcome after coronary artery surgery are affected by complement activation. *Ann Thorac Surg, 79,* 1597–1605.

Baugh, C. M., Stamm, J. M., Riley, D. O., et al. (2012). Chronic traumatic encephalopathy: Neurodegeneration following repetitive concussive and subconcussive brain trauma. *Brain Imaging Behav, 6*(2), 244–254.

Belanoff, J. K., Gross, K., Yager, A., & Schatzberg, A. F. (2001). Corticosteroids and cognition. *J Psychiatr Res, 35*(3), 127–145.

Belay, E. D., & Schonberger, L. B. (2002). Variant Creutzfeldt–Jakob disease and bovine spongiform encephalopathy. *Clin. Lab. Med, 22*(4), 849–862.

Bellizzi, A., Anzivino, E., & Rodio, D. M. (2013). New insights on Human Polyomavirus JC and pathogenesis of Progressive Multifocal Leukoencephalopathy. *Clin Dev Immunol, 839719.* Published online April 17, 2013.

Berlit, P. (2010). Diagnosis and treatment of cerebral vasculitis. *Ther Adv Neurol Disord, 3*(1), 29–42.

Biglan, K. M. (2008). Neurologic manifestations of systemic disease: disturbances of the kidneys, electrolytes, water balance, rheumatology, hematology/oncology, alcohol, and iatrogenic conditions. In J. I. Sirven & B. L. Malamut (Eds.), *Clinical neurology of the older adult* (2nd ed., pp. 499–528). Philadelphia: Lippincott, Williams and Wilkins.

Bobholz, J., & Rao, S. (2003). Cognitive dysfunction in multiple sclerosis: A review of recent developments. *Curr Opin Neurol, 16*(3), 283–288.

Brewer, G. J., Fink, J. K., & Hedera, P. (1999). Diagnosis and treatment of Wilson's disease. *Semin Neurol, 19*(3), 261–270.

Cambier, D. M., Kantarci, K., Worrell, G. A., et al. (2003). Lateralized and focal clinical, EEG, and FLAIR MRI abnormalities in Creutzfeldt-Jakob disease. *Clin Neurophysiol, 114*(9), 1724–1728.

Carrilho, P. E., Santos, M. B., Piasecki, L., & Jorge, A. C. (2013). Marchiafava-Bignami disease: A rare entity with a poor outcome. *Rev Bras Ter Intensiva, 25*(1), 68–72.

Cash, W. J., McConville, P., McDermott, E., et al. (2010). Current concepts in the assessment and treatment of hepatic encephalopathy. *QJM, 103*(1), 9–16.

Cersosimo, M. G., & Koller, W. C. (2007). The diagnosis of manganese-induced parkinsonism. *NeuroToxicology, 27*(3), 340–346.

Chan, A. K., McGovern, R. A., Zacharia, B. E., et al. (2013). Inferior short-term safety profile of endoscopic third ventriculostomy as compared to ventriculoperitoneal shunt placement for idiopathic normal pressure hydrocephalus: a population-based study. *Neurosurgery,* August 5.

Chuang, W. L., Huang, C. C., Chen, C. J., et al. (2007). Carbon disulfide encephalopathy: Cerebral microangiopathy. *Neurotoxicology, 28*(2), 387–393.

Clancy, F. (2006). The bitter science. *Neurology Now, 2*(2), 24–25.

Collinge, J., Gorham, M., Hudson, F., et al. (2009). Safety and efficacy of quinacrine in human prion disease (PRION-1 study): A patient-preference trial. *Lancet neurology, 8*(4), 334–344.

Compton, A., & Coles, A. (2008). Multiple sclerosis. *Lancet, 372*(9648), 1502–1517.

Corsellis, J. A., Bruton, C. J., & Freeman-Browne, D. (1973). The aftermath of boxing. *Psychol Med, 3,* 270–303.

Crosby, G., & Culley, D. J. (2003). Anesthesia, the aging brain, and the surgical patient. *Can J Anesthesia, 50,* R12.

Diegeler, A., Hirsch, R., Schneider, F., et al. (2000). Neuromonitoring and neurocognitive outcome in off-pump versus conventional coronary bypass operation. *Ann Thorac Surg, 69,* 1162–1166.

Dourmashkin, R. R., Dunn, G., Castano, V., & McCall, S. A. (2013). Evidence for an enterovirus as the cause of encephalitis lethargica. *BMC Infect Dis, 12,* 136.

Drazkowski, J. F. (2008). Diagnostic tests in the older adult: EEG. In J. I. Sirven & B. L. Malamut (Eds.), *Clinical neurology of the older adult* (2nd ed., pp. 25–32). Philadelphia: Lippincott, Williams and Wilkins.

Duque, G., Segal, R., Wise, F., & Bianco, J. (2005). Chronic hypercalcemia as a reversible cause of cognitive impairment: Improvement after a single administration of pamidronate. *J Am Geriatr Soc, 53*(9), 1633–1634.

Evered, L., Scott, D. A., Silbert, B., & Maruff, P. (2011). Postoperative cognitive dysfunction is independent of type of surgery and anesthetic. *Anesth Analg, 112*(5), 1179–1185.

Faivre, A., Souraud, J-B., & McGonigal, A. (2009). Rare disease: Fulminant adult-onset subacute sclerosing panencephalitis: a case report. *BMJ Case Rep.* doi: 10.1136/bcr.09.2008.0922

Faul, M., Xu, L., Wald, M. M., & Coronado, V.G. (2010). *Traumatic brain injury in the United States: Emergency department visits, hospitalizations, and deaths.* Atlanta: Centers for Disease Control and Prevention, National Center for Injury Prevention and Control.

Fiedorowicz, J. G., Mills, J. A., & Ruggle, R. (2011). Suicidal behavior in prodromal Huntington disease. *Neurodegener Dis, 8*(6), 483–490.

Flanagan, S. R., Hibbard, M. R., Reardon, B., et al. (2006). Traumatic brain injury in the elderly: Diagnostic and treatment challenges. *Clin Geriatr Med, 22,* 449–468.

Flicker, L., & Ames, D. (2005). Metabolic and endocrinological causes of dementia. *Int Psychogeriatr, 17*(Suppl. 1), S79–S92.

Gangemi, M., Maiuri, F., Buonamassa, S., et al. (2004). Endoscopic third ventriculostomy in idiopathic normal pressure hydrocephalus. *Neurosurg, 55*(1), 129–134.

García, H. H., Evans, C. A., Nash, T. E., et al. (2002). Current consensus guidelines for treatment of neurocysticercosis. *Clin Microbiol Rev, 15*(4), 747–756.

Giunta, B., Hervey, W., Klippel, C., et al. (2013). Psychiatric complications of HIV infection: An overview. *Pychiatr Ann, 43*(5), 199–203.

Gofton, T. E., Al-Khotani1, A., O'Farrell, B., et al. (2010). Mefloquine in the treatment of progressive multifocal leukoencephalopathy. *J Neurol Neurosurg Psychiatry, 82*(4), 452–455.

Greene-Schloesser, D., & Robbins, M. E. (2012). Radiation-induced cognitive impairment: From bench to bedside. *Neuro Oncol, 14*(Suppl. 4), 37–44.

Guyant-Maréchal, L., Verrips, A., & Girard, C. (2005). Unusual cerebrotendinous xanthomatosis with fronto-temporal dementia phenotype. *Am J Med Genet A, 139A*(2), 114–117.

Halperin, J. J. (2008). Nervous system Lyme disease. *Infect. Dis. Clin. North Am., 22*(2), 261–274.

Halperin, J. J. (2013). Nervous system Lyme disease: diagnosis and treatment. *Curr Treat Options Neurol, 15*(4), 454–464.

Hanly, J. G., McCurdy, G., Fougere, L., et al. (2004). Neuropsychiatric events in systemic lupus erythematosus: Attribution and clinical significance. *J Rheumatol, 31*(11), 2156–2162.

Hellström, P., Edsbagge, M., Archer, T., et al. (2007). The neuropsychology of patients with clinically diagnosed idiopathic normal pressure hydrocephalus. *Neurosurgery, 61*(6), 1219–1226; discussion 1227–1228.

Honda, S., Hylander, L., & Sakamoto, M. (2006). Recent advances in evaluation of health effects on mercury with special reference to methylmercury-A minireview. *Environ Health Prev Med, 11*(4), 171–176.

Hong, Y. S., Kim, Y. M., & Lee, K. E. (2012). Methylmercury exposure and health effects. *J Prev Med Public Health, 45*(6), 353–363.

Hsiao, C. L., Kuo, H. C., & Huang, C. C. (2004). Delayed encephalopathy after carbon monoxide intoxication: Long-term prognosis and correlation of clinical manifestations and neuroimages. *Acta Neurol Taiwan, 13*(2), 64–70.

Hsich, G., Kenney, K., Gibbs, C. J., et al. (1996). The 14-3-3 brain protein in cerebrospinal fluid as a marker for transmissible spongioform encephalopathies. *N Eng J Med, 335,* 924–930.

Hua, M. S., & Huang, C. C. (1991). Chronic occupational exposure to manganese and neurobehavioral function. *J Clin Exp Neuropsychol, 13*(4), 495–507.

Hudetz, J. A., Iqbal, Z., & Gandhi, S. D. (2007). Postoperative cognitive dysfunction in older patients with a history of alcohol abuse. *Anesthesiology, 106*(3), 423–430.

Hulse, G. K., Lautenschlager, N. T., Tait, R. J., & Almeida, O. P. (2005). Dementia associated with alcohol and other drug use. *Int Psychogeriatr, 17*(Suppl. 1), S109–S127.

Jordan, B. D., Jahre, C., Hauser, W. A., et al. (1992). CT of 338 active professional boxers. *Radiology, 185*(2), 509–512.

Jordan, B. D., Relkin, N. R., Ravdin, L. D., et al. (1997). Apolipoprotein E epsilon4 associated with chronic traumatic brain injury in boxing. *JAMA, 278*(2), 136–140.

Kampylafka, E. I., Alexopoulos, H., Kosmidis, M. L., et al. (2013). Incidence and prevalence of major central nervous system involvement in systemic lupus erythematosus: A 3-year prospective study of 370 patients. *PLoS One, 8*(2), e55843.

Karnath, B. (2004). Subdural hematoma: Presentation and management in older adults. *Geriatrics, 59*(7), 18–23.

Kaul, M., Zheng, J., Okamoto, S., et al. (2005). Review HIV-1 infection and AIDS: Consequences for the central nervous system. *Cell Death Differ, 12*(Suppl. 1), 878–892.

Kent, M. E., & Romanelli, F. (2008). Reexamining syphilis: An update on epidemiology, clinical manifestations, and management. *Ann Pharmacother, 42*(2), 226–236.

King, N. S. (2003). Post-concussion syndrome: clarity amid the controversy? *Brit J of Psychiatry, 183*, 276–278.

Koo, E. H., & Massey, E. W. (1988). Granulomatous angiitis of the central nervous system: Protean manifestations and response to treatment. *J Neurol Neurosurg Psychiatry, 51*(9), 1126–1133.

Koral, S. M. (2013). Mercury from dental amalgam: exposure and risk assessment. *Compend Contin Educ Dent, 34*(2), 138–140, 142, 144 passim.

Lanska, D. J. (2010). Historical aspects of the major neurological vitamin deficiency disorders: The water-soluble B vitamins. *Handb Clin Neurol, 95*, 445–476.

León-Carrión, J., Machuca-Murga, F., Solís-Marcos, I., et al. (2013). The sooner patients begin neurorehabilitation, the better their functional outcome. *Brain Inj, 27*(10), 1119–1123.

Lin, B. (2013). Encephalopathy: A vicious cascade following forebrain ischemia and hypoxia. *Cent Nerv Syst Agents Med Chem, 13*(1), 57–70.

Lindl, K. A., Marks, D. R., & Kolson, D. L. (2010). HIV-Associated Neurocognitive Disorder: Pathogenesis and therapeutic opportunities. *J Neuroimmune Pharmacol, 5*(3), 294–309.

Liu, C-H., Huang, C-Y., & Huang, C-C. (2012). Occupational neurotoxic diseases in Taiwan. *Saf Health Work, 3*(4), 257–267.

Mak, C. M., & Lam, C. W. (2008). Diagnosis of Wilson's disease: A comprehensive review. *Crit Rev Clin Lab Sci, 45*(3), 263–290.

Marmarou, A., Bergsneider, M., Relkin, N., et al. (2005). Idiopathic normal-pressure hydrocephalus guidelines, part 1–5. *Neurosurgery, 57*(3, Suppl.), S1–S52.

Mateen, F. J., Muralidharan, R., Carone, M., et al. (2011). Progressive multifocal leukoencephalopathy in transplant recipients. *Ann Neurol, 70*(2), 305–322.

McCall, S., Vilensky, J. A., Gilman, S., & Taubenberger, J. K. (2008). The relationship between encephalitis lethargica and influenza: A critical analysis. *J Neurovirol, 14*(3), 177–185.

McElhiney, M., Rabkin, J., Van Gorp, W., & Rabkin, R. (2010). Modafinil effects on cognitive function in HIV+ patients treated for fatigue: a placebo controlled study. *J Clin Exp Neuropsychol, 32*(5), 474–480.

McKee, A. C., Cantu, R. C., Nowinski, C. J., et al. (2009). Chronic traumatic encephalopathy in athletes: Progressive tauopathy after repetitive head injury. *J Neuropathol Exp Neurol, 68*(7), 709–735.

Monk, T. G., Weldon, B. C., Garvan, C. W., et al. (2008). Predictors of cognitive dysfunction after major noncardiac surgery. *Anesthesiology, 108*(1), 18–30.

Moser, H. W., Smith, K. D., Watkins, P. A., et al. (2004). X-linked adrenoleukodystrophy. In C. W. Scriver, A. L. Beaudet, W. A. Sly, et al. (Eds.), *Metabolic and molecular bases of inherited disease* (8th ed.). New York: McGraw Hill.

Myers, R. H. (2004). Review Huntington's disease genetics. *NeuroRx, 1*(2), 255–262.

Neurobehavioral Guidelines Working Group, Warden, D. L., Gordon, B., et al. (2006). Guidelines for the pharmacologic treatment of neurobehavioral sequelae of traumatic brain injury. *J Neurotrauma, 23*(10), 1468–1501.

Newman, M. F., Kirchner, J. L., Phillips-Bute, B., et al. (2001). Longitudinal assessment of neuro-cognitive function after coronary-artery bypass surgery. *N Engl J Med, 344*(6), 395–402.

Nishino, H., Rubino, F. A., DeRemee, R. A., et al. (1993).Neurological involvement in Wegener's granulomatosis: An analysis of 324 consecutive patients at the Mayo Clinic. *Ann Neurol, 33*(1), 4–9.

Oslin, D., Atkinson, R. M., Smith, D. M., & Hendrie, H. (1998). Alcohol related dementia: Proposed clinical criteria. *Int J Geriatr Psychiatry, 13*(4), 203–212.

Oslin, D. W., & Cary, M. S. (2003). Alcohol-related dementia: Validation of diagnostic criteria. *Am J Geriatr Psychiatry, 11*(4), 441–447.

Park, B. J., Wannemuehler, K. A., Marston, B. J., et al. (2009). Review estimation of the current global burden of cryptococcal meningitis among persons living with HIV/AIDS. *AIDS, 23*(4), 525–530.

Paulsen, J. S. (2011). Cognitive impairment in Huntington disease: Diagnosis and treatment. *Curr Neurol Neurosci Rep, 11*(5), 474–483.

Peters, J. L., Weisskopf, M. G., Spiro, A.. III, et al. (2010). Interaction of stress, lead burden, and age on cognition in older men: The VA Normative Aging Study. *Environ Health Perspect, 118*(4), 505–510.

Peters, R., Peters, J., Warner, J., et al. (2008). Alcohol, dementia and cognitive decline in the elderly: A systematic review. *Age Ageing, 37*(5), 505–512.

Pinto, F. C., Saad, F., Oliveira, M. F., et al. (2013). Role of endoscopic third ventriculostomy and ventriculoperitoneal shunt in idiopathic normal pressure hydrocephalus: Preliminary results of a randomized clinical trial. *Neurosurgery, 72*(5), 845–853; discussion 853–854.

Poca, M. A., Mataró, M., Del Mar Matarín, M., et al. (2004). Is the placement of shunts in patients with idiopathic normal-pressure hydrocephalus worth the risk? Results of a study based on continuous monitoring of intracranial pressure. *J Neurosurg, 100*(5), 855–866.

Profenno, L. A., Porsteinsson, A. P., & Faraone, S. V. (2010). Meta-analysis of Alzheimer's disease risk with obesity, diabetes, and related disorders. *Biol Psychiatry, 67*(6), 505–512.

Prusiner, S. B. (1982). Novel proteinaceous infectious particles cause scrapie. *Science, 216*, 136–144.

Prusiner, S. B. (1998). Prions. *Proc Natl Acad Sci U S A, 95*(23), 13363–13383.

Rainov, N. G., Tsuboi, Y., Krolak-Salmon, P., et al. (2009). Experimental treatments for human transmissible spongiform encephalopathies: Is there a role for pentosan polysulfate? *Expert Opin Biol Ther, 7*(5), 713–726.

Ridley, N. J., Draper, B., & Withall, A. (2013). Alcohol-related dementia: An update of the evidence. *Alzheimers Res Ther, 5*(1), 3.

Roman, S., & Sosa, J. A. (2007). Psychiatric and cognitive aspects of primary hyperparathyroidism. *Curr Opin Oncol, 19*(1), 1–5.

Roos, K. L. (2008). Nonviral infectious diseases of the nervous system. In J. I. Sirven & B. L. Malamut (Eds.), *Clinical neurology of the older adult* (2nd ed., pp. 433–447). Philadelphia: Lippincott, Williams and Wilkins.

Ryan, L. M., & O'Jile, J. R. (2008). Cognitive effects of head trauma in the older adult. In J. I. Sirven & B. L. Malamut (Eds.), *Clinical neurology of the older adult* (2nd ed., pp. 284–295). Philadelphia: Lippincott, Williams and Wilkins.

Sacktor, N. (2002). The epidemiology of human immunodeficiency virus-associated neurological disease in the era of highly active antiretroviral therapy. *J Neurovirol, 8*(Suppl. 2), 115–121.

Sadighi, Z., Butler, I. J., & Koenig, M .K. (2012). Adult-onset cerebral folate deficiency. *Arch Neurol, 69*(6), 778–779.

Schifitto, G., Navia, B. A., Yiannoutsos, C. T., et al. (2007). Memantine and HIV-associated cognitive impairment: A neuropsychological and proton magnetic resonance spectroscopy study. *AIDS, 21*(14), 1877–1886.

Schifitto, G., Yiannoutsos, C. T., Ernst, T., et al. (2009). Selegiline and oxidative stress in HIV-associated cognitive impairment. *Neurology, 73*(23), 1975–1981.

Schmitt de Bem, R., Muzzillo, D. A., Deguti, M. M., et al. (2011). Wilson's disease in southern Brazil: A 40-year follow-up study. *Clinics, 66*(3), 411–416.

Schönberger, K., Ludwig, M-S., & Wildner, M. (2013). Epidemiology of subacute sclerosing panencephalitis (SSPE) in Germany from 2003 to 2009: A risk estimation. *PLoS One, 8*(7), e68909.

Segarra-Newnham, M., & Vodolo, K. M. (2001). Use of cidofovir in progressive multifocal leukoencephalopathy. *Ann Pharmacother, 35*(6), 741–744.

Seifter, J. L., & Samuels, M. A. (2011). Uremic encephalopathy and other brain disorders associated with renal failure. *Semin Neurol, 31*(2), 139–143.

Shanker, V. L. (2008). Neurologic manifestations of systemic disease: GI and endocrine. In J. I. Sirven & B. L. Malamut (Eds.), *Clinical neurology of the older adult* (2nd ed., pp. 484–498). Philadelphia: Lippincott, Williams and Wilkins.

Shapiro, E. G., Lockman, L. A., Knopman, D., & Krivit, W. (1994). Characteristics of the dementia in late-onset metachromatic leukodystrophy. *Neurology, 44*(4), 662.

Silver, J. M., Koumaras, B., Meng, X., et al. (2009). Long-term effects of rivastigmine capsules in patients with traumatic brain injury. *Brain Inj, 23*(2), 123–132.

Small, G. W., Kepe, V., Siddarth, P, et al. (2013). PET scanning of brain tau in retired National Football League players: Preliminary findings. *Am J Geriatr Psychiatry, 21*(2), 138–144.

Solfrizzi, V., D'Introno, A., Colacicco, A. M., et al. (2007). Alcohol consumption, mild cognitive impairment, and progression to dementia. *Neurology, 68*(21), 1790–1799.

Soon, W. T., Tang, K. L., Chen, R. C., et al. (1976). Lead encephalopathy in adults. *Bull Chin Soc Neurol Psychiatry, 2*, 16–20.

Stahl, J. P., Mailles, A., De Broucker, T., & Steering Committee and Investigators Group. (2012). Herpes simplex encephalitis and management of acyclovir in encephalitis patients in France. *Epidemiol Infect, 140*(2), 372–381.

Tan, I. L., & McArthur, J. C. (2012). HIV-associated neurological disorders: A guide to pharmacotherapy. *CNS Drugs, 26*(2), 123–134.

Tardiff, B. E., Newman, M. F., Saunders, A. M., et al. (1997). Preliminary report of a genetic basis for cognitive decline after cardiac operations. *Ann Thorac Surg, 64*, 715–720.

Ten, S., New, M., & Maclaren, N. (2001). Clinical review 130: Addison's disease 2001. *J Clin Endocrin Metab, 86*(7), 2909–2922.

Tenovuo, O. (2005). Central acetylcholinesterase inhibitors in the treatment of chronic traumatic brain injury-clinical experience in 111 patients. *Prog Neuropsychopharmacol Biol Psychiatry, 29*(1), 61–67.

Tisell, M., Tullberg, M., & Hellström, P. (2011). Shunt surgery in patients with hydrocephalus and white matter changes. *J Neurosurg, 114*(5), 1432–1438.

Tüzün, E., & Dalmau, J. (2007). Limbic encephalitis and variants: Classification, diagnosis and treatment. *Neurologist, 13*(5), 261–271.

Vachalová, I., Kyavar, L., & Heckmann, J. G. (2013). Pitfalls associated with the diagnosis of herpes simplex encephalitis. *J Neurosci Rural Pract, 4*(2), 176–179.

Valcour, V. G., Shikuma, C. M., Watters, M. R., & Sacktor, N.C. (2004). Review cognitive impairment in older HIV-1-seropositive individuals: Prevalence and potential mechanisms. *AIDS, 18*(Suppl. 1), S79–S86.

Vasconcelos, O. M., Poehm, E. H., McCarter, R. J., et al. (2006). Potential outcome factors in subacute combined degeneration: review of observational studies. *J Gen Intern Med, 21*(10), 1063–1068.

Virtaa, J. J., Järvenpää, T., Heikkilä, K., et al. (2010). Midlife alcohol consumption and later risk of cognitive impairment: A twin follow-up study. *J Alzheimers Dis, 22*(3), 939–948.

Walchenbach, R., Geiger, E., Thomeer, R. T., & Vanneste, J. A. (2002). The value of temporary external lumbar CSF drainage in predicting the outcome of shunting on normal pressure hydrocephalus. *J Neurol Neurosurg Psychiatry, 72*(4), 503–506.

Walker, F. O. (2007). Huntington's disease. *Lancet, 369*(9557), 218–228.

Werder, S. F. (2010). Cobalamin deficiency, hyperhomocysteinemia, and dementia. *Neuropsychiatr Dis Treat, 6*, 159–195.

Weuve, J., Korrick, S. A., Weisskopf, M. G., et al. (2009). Cumulative exposure to lead in relation to cognitive function in older women. *Environ Health Perspect, 117*(4), 574–580.

Weuve, J., Press, D. Z., Grodstein, F., et al. (2013). Cumulative exposure to lead and cognition in persons with Parkinson's disease. *Mov Disord, 28*(2), 176–182.

White, Jr., A. C. (2009). New developments in the management of neurocysticercosis. *J Infectious Dis, 199*(9), 1261–1262.

Wikkelsø, C., Hellström, P., Klinge, P. M., et al. (2013). The European iNPH Multicentre Study on the predictive values of resistance to CSF outflow and the CSF Tap Test in patients with idiopathic normal pressure hydrocephalus. *J Neurol Neurosurg Psychiatry, 84*(5), 562–568.

Xu, G., Liu, X., Yin, Q., et al. (2009). Alcohol consumption and transition of mild cognitive impairment to dementia. *Psychiatry Clin Neurosci, 63*(1), 43–49.

Zetola, N. M., Engelman, J., Jensen, T. P., & Klausner, J. D. (2007). Syphilis in the United States: An update for clinicians with an emphasis on HIV coinfection. *Mayo Clin Proc, 82*(9), 1091–1102.

Zhang, L., Plotkin, R. C., Wang, G., et al. (2004). Cholinergic augmentation with donepezil enhances recovery in short-term memory and sustained attention after traumatic brain injury. *Arch Phys Med Rehabil, 85*(7), 1050–1055.

Part III

Psychiatric Conditions Associated with Dementia

9 Agitation and Psychosis

All forms of dementia have a strong association with the psychiatric symptoms of agitation and psychosis. Various forms of agitation are seen in 80% to 90% of dementia patients over the course of the underlying illness, with higher rates seen in more severe dementia and in nursing home populations (Ballard et al., 2001; International Psychogeriatric Association, 2000). One study, which looked at dementia patients over five years, found point prevalence rates for aggression between 13% and 24% (Steinberg et al., 2008). Psychotic symptoms overlap considerably with agitated behaviors and often generate them. These symptoms include delusions, with paranoid delusions and misidentifications being most common, and hallucinations, with visual and auditory components being most common. Psychotic symptoms are seen in an estimated 30% to 50% of dementia patients, across various subtypes (Jeste & Finkel, 2000).

Although these symptoms may be present early in the course of a dementia, their frequency and intensity usually peak during the moderate stages of the dementia and then begin to decline as an individual enters the more severe stages. Agitation and psychosis are particularly disruptive to the lives of the affected individuals and their caregivers, and, frequently, they give rise to excess disability, threats to both personal health and the safety of others, emergent medical visits, acute hospitalization, and, ultimately, long-term institutionalization. The early recognition and treatment of these symptoms can mitigate these consequences, however, thus reducing the stress to the patients and the burden on their caregivers.

Case Study

Mrs. D was an 82-year-old woman with a four-year history of moderate vascular dementia and a long-standing history of a paranoid personality. She lived with her daughter, son-in-law, and two young grandchildren. A home health aide visited weekly to help with bathing Mrs. D after her daughter began a part-time job. However, Mrs. D was suspicious of the aide, and she frequently refused care due to paranoid concerns that the aide was trying to hurt her. After noticing that the aide was pregnant, Mrs. D told her daughter that the aide must have had an affair with her son-in-law and that she was trying to break up the family. The daughter tried to dispel her mother's concerns, but she did not intervene further. A week later Mrs. D became acutely agitated when the aide visited, and she began screaming at her not to touch her and to leave her family alone. When the aide attempted to approach Mrs. D. to calm her, she lunged at the aide with her walker, threatening to kill the baby. The aide fled the house in tears and lodged a complaint with the agency. Her daughter returned home to find several police cars in front of her home; they had come in response to a hysterical call to 911 that Mrs. D had made, saying that someone was trying to kill her. Mrs. D began screaming and swearing at her daughter and the police, accusing them of leaving her alone to be killed. The two young grandchildren were terrified of the scene, and they began crying hysterically. Mrs. D was taken to an emergency department for evaluation and was subsequently hospitalized on a geriatric psychiatry unit. Given the severity of her episode of psychosis and agitation, the family decided to admit Mrs. D to a nearby nursing home.

This case is not at all uncommon. Unfortunately, the family did not fully appreciate the risk of behavioral problems that could result when Mrs. D began reporting her paranoid delusions. Earlier intervention might have prevented this terrible episode. Because the severity of the episode was so upsetting to the family, Mrs. D's continued residence at their home was no longer safe or appropriate. She needed a more structured and secure environment.

Definitions

The term *agitation* is used throughout the chapter to describe a variety of inappropriate verbal, vocal, and/or motor behaviors that are seen in association with dementia, including the following: (1) verbal or physical aggression, assaultiveness, or abuse (e.g., screaming, cursing, hitting, combativeness); (2) repetitive or hyperactive verbalizations, vocalizations, or motor behaviors; and (3) disinhibited or inappropriate behaviors or verbalizations. Psychosis is defined as a mental state that is out of touch with reality because of false beliefs, perceptions, or disorganization. Common manifestations include the following:

- Delusions (false, fixed ideas)
  - paranoid type ("someone is trying to kill me")
  - grandiose type ("I am leading a platoon of men to hunt terrorists")
  - jealous type ("my wife is having an affair with other residents")
  - misidentification ("that is not the nurse, that is my mother")
- Hallucinations (false sensory percepts): most often auditory or visual
- Formal Thought Disorder (distinct from cognitive impairment)
  - disorganized thought process (e.g., loose associations)
  - bizarre or unusual use of language (e.g., clanging) or mannerisms

Agitation is easier to detect because it is observable, whereas a diagnosis of psychosis often relies on patient reports, which can be confusing, unreliable, and reflective of non-psychotic experiences. The latter point is especially valid when the clinician is trying to distinguish a formal thought disorder from the disturbances in thinking and language that define the dementia.

Causes

Agitation and psychosis are multidetermined phenomena, meaning that several factors occur and interact simultaneously to trigger them. The major causes include the following:

- dementia itself
- medical illness
- delirium
- medications
- pain and/or physical discomfort
- psychiatric illness
- sleep problems
- stress (psychologic and environmental).

The dementia itself is sufficient to cause agitation or psychosis simply as a result of underlying impairment in brain circuits or neurochemistry critical to the control and expression of behavior. For example, aggression has been associated with frontal and temporal hypometabolism in brain regions with significant cholinergic deficits (Sultzer et al., 1995; Tekin et al., 2001). It is less likely in individuals with better preservation of cortical serotonergic neurons (Proctor, Francis, Stratmann, & Bowen, 1992). The type, prevalence, and pattern of agitation or psychosis will be shaped in part by the type of dementia, described in previous chapters.

Medical symptoms and illnesses are common causes of agitation, either directly through impairment of brain function from infection, organ dysfunction, or metabolic disturbances, or indirectly from associated pain, immobility, medication effects, or equipment such as an intravenous line or a cast. The clinician should bear in mind that the demented brain is especially vulnerable to metabolic changes that would not normally cause problems in the nondemented brain. The risk of compromised brain function is particularly high with any medical condition that impairs the flow of oxygen or blood to the brain, which often results in a state of delirium. Common medications that have been associated with agitation include stimulants, oral steroids, opioid analgesics, anticholinergics, and dopaminergic agents; agitation has also been seen in paradoxical responses to psychotropics such as antidepressants or benzodiazepines (Kotlyar, Gray, Maher, & Hanlon, 2011).

Clinical Tip

The mechanism by which infection and other illnesses cause agitation or psychosis is not always clear, and the clinical symptoms of underlying medical illness are not always obvious. The rule of thumb for evaluating acute behavioral or mental status changes is that one should always obtain a urinalysis and urine culture and then a medical consultation. The first step is important because urinary tract infections are the most common cause of delirium in nursing home populations and, by extension, in older individuals with dementia.

Delirium is defined as an acute, transient, reversible brain syndrome that is characterized by fluctuating disturbances of consciousness, attention, perception, cognition, and neuropsychiatric function (e.g., sleep, appetite, psychomotor activity). Clinicians sometimes fail to diagnose delirium because it fluctuates over time, and it can be confused with preexisting symptoms of dementia. Table 9.1 lists some of the main features for distinguishing between dementia and delirium. Delirium is an especially dangerous condition because it typically lasts for weeks to months, and it is associated with mortality rates as high as 40% in the first year (Inouye, 2006). Although delirium is considered reversible, it can severely disrupt medical and rehabilitative recovery, it can unmask or even cause enduring cognitive impairment, and it can lead to long-standing functional decline.

Delirium always has a medical cause. The method by which medical problems trigger delirium is unclear, but one avenue may be through the disruption of cholinergic function. In individuals with dementia, the risk factors for delirium include advancing age, infection, fractures, malnutrition, low albumin levels, sensory deprivation, physical restraints, and bladder catheters (Inouye, 2006). In long-term care settings, urinary tract infections are the most common cause of delirium. Delirium is particularly common in postoperative states, and it is seen in 30%–40% of older individuals after hip and other orthopedic surgeries due to factors such as anesthesia, dehydration, anemia, and narcotic

Table 9.1 Distinguishing Between Dementia and Delirium

Clinical Feature	Delirium	Dementia
Onset	Acute, over days to weeks	Chronic, over months to years
Course	Fluctuating symptoms	Stable symptoms with progressive decline
Duration	Days to weeks or months	Years until inevitable death
Awareness	Reduced	Clear
Attention	Impaired, fluctuating, distractable	Normal or mild impairments in mild to moderate stage AD; able to focus on short, discrete tasks
Alertness	Fluctuates; lethargic or hypervigilant at times	Usually normal
Orientation	Impaired	Impaired
Memory	Immediate and recent memory impaired, remote memory intact	Recent and remote memory impaired
Perception	Hallucinations are common	Intact
Thinking	Fragmented, disorganized, with transient paranoid and other delusions	Impaired abstract thinking, vague or impoverished content; agnosia.
Language	Speech slow or rapid, sometimes incoherent	Word-finding difficulty, aphasia
Psychomotor	Variable: hyper- or hypokinetic	Apraxia as dementia progresses; slowed in subcortical dementia
Sleep-Wake Cycle	Disrupted, reversed	Reversed or fragmented

analgesics (Meagher, Norton, & Trzepacz, 2011). Medications, especially those with anticholinergic (see Table 2.4, in Chapter 2), narcotic, antihistaminic, and sedative effects are often the cause of delirium. Some individuals also show a particular sensitivity to steroids and some antibiotics.

Physical pain or discomfort associated with medical conditions can precipitate both agitation and psychosis. Even seemingly innocuous states such as constipation, pruritus, and excess hunger or thirst can trigger behavioral problems in those individuals who cannot adequately communicate their discomfort because of aphasia or disorganized thinking. These individuals may act out their pain, often in a manner that does not give a clear indication to caregivers of the true problem. Identifying this underlying discomfort is crucial so that patients are not given medication to calm them while the true cause of their suffering is missed. When pain is suspected, a test dose of an analgesic, such as acetaminophen, may be warranted.

Psychiatric illness can cause and shape agitation and psychosis through the influence of comorbid symptoms or the rekindling of past disorders. The common psychiatric disorders that give rise to behavioral problems include psychotic disorders (e.g., schizophrenia, delusional disorder), mood disorders (e.g., major depression, bipolar disorder), anxiety disorders (e.g., generalized anxiety disorder, specific phobias, panic disorder, post-traumatic stress disorder), substance use disorders, somatoform disorders, and sleep disorders. The detection of psychiatric symptoms requires a consideration of how the effects of aging and dementia may obscure or change the ways in which they present, compared with their presentation in younger individuals or those without dementia. For example, depression in dementia may manifest as pain, somatic complaints, social withdrawal, irritability, or preoccupation with deceased relatives. Mania might present as repetitive vocalizations, lack of sleep, and restless motor activity, while panic attacks may manifest in paroxysmal screaming and motor restlessness but without subjective reports of intense fear.

Sleep disturbances such as insomnia and rapid eye movement or REM sleep behavior disorder are also causes of agitation. These disorders often result from the disruptive effects of both aging and progressive brain damage on normal sleep architecture. Individuals with dementia tend to have less efficient sleep because of increased nighttime arousals, a loss of rapid eye movement sleep, and the breakdown of the circadian rhythms that previously enabled them to maintain a normal sleep–wake cycle (Endeshaw & Bliwise, 2011). Moreover, older individuals with dementia rarely receive comprehensive sleep evaluations; instead, they are often treated with increasing doses of sedative-hypnotics that then compound the problem. The result can be irritability, poor daytime function, and agitation. Sundowning is one type of agitation occurring in the early evening or nighttime, perhaps as a result of accumulated fatigue or the inability to recognize time cues.

Environmental stress is often a cause or, at the very least, a contributing factor to agitation and psychosis. Common environmental stresses include unfamiliar or uncomfortable surroundings (e.g., excess heat, cold, or noise), moves from familiar to unfamiliar settings (e.g., nursing home placement, room changes), and disruptive caregivers or roommates. Hearing and/or visual loss can limit an individual's ability to perceive and to adjust to the changes occurring around him or her. The sense of confusion and increased disorientation after moves can be so frightening and threatening to individuals with poor memory and insight that they strike out in what they perceive to be self-defense. This fight-or-flight response, which is hardwired into the human brain, remains intact well into the later stages of a progressive dementia. The individual's baseline personality characteristics—to the extent that the personality remains intact— partially determine the manner in which the patient with dementia copes with stress. Individuals with inflexible personality traits are particularly prone to stress-induced behavioral problems.

Clinical Tip

One major stress for many individuals with dementia is living in an environment with excessive social and functional demands. When such individuals are unable to keep up with daily needs and they feel uncomfortable interacting in socially appropriate and competent ways with people without dementia, the result may be frustration, anger, anxiety, uncertainty, social withdrawal, or even disruptive behaviors in an attempt to cope with such an environment. Sometimes, the individuals themselves or their families force them into such situations because of pride, stubbornness, ignorance, or poor judgment. They are often motivated by a fear of nursing home placement.

Assessment

The assessment of agitation and psychosis involves the following basic steps: (1) establishing a clear description of the problematic behaviors and (2) identifying their potential causes. The necessary information that should be obtained is summarized with the mnemonic ABC's.

Antecedents

- What was occurring right before the problematic behaviors?
- Is there anything occurring that seems to trigger the behaviors?
- Do they occur at a particular time of day?
- Are they associated with a particular person?
- Have any recent changes been made to the affected individual's schedule, location, or medications?

Behaviors

- What is reported as the specific problem by the patient and by caregivers?
- Have actual or threatened injuries to the patient or others occurred?
- Are the observed behaviors consistent with the reports? If not, how are they different?
- Are problematic behaviors new or recurrent?

- If they are recurrent, are they similar or different from past behaviors?
- Who is bothered by the behaviors (patient, staff, other residents)?

Concurrent/Comorbid Stresses

- Are there concurrent environmental stresses that may be relevant?
- Does the patient have comorbid medical or psychiatric disorders?

Consequences

- What results from the behaviors?
- Are they reinforced in any way (i.e., something happens that increases their frequency)?

Clinical Tip

During an evaluation, keep in mind that most problematic behaviors are intermittent and often situational, and they often will not present during a clinical interview. In addition, records and caregiver reports are not always accurate or reliable. You may hear different, and sometimes contradictory, descriptions from various staff members on a unit, such as being told about a woman's terrible behavioral problems and then meeting a "sweet little old lady" whom you cannot imagine misbehaving. Caregivers may minimize or exaggerate their concerns. Do not rush to judgment; gather information from a variety of sources, corroborate these reports, and inquire about possible explanations. Careful investigation and observation help the clinician avoid unnecessary or misguided treatment.

Antecedent factors may include specific caregiving activities, individual contacts, and a time of day. For example, an individual with dementia and paranoia may react to being bathed or dressed as if he or she were being harmed. Such individuals may appear nervous and suspicious of their caregivers, and they may demonstrate overt paranoid ideation and physical resistance to care. The reasons behind these reactions may not be apparent or logical, but the association is important to notice. Taking note of the consequences of the behaviors is also essential. Do caregivers or staff react in such a manner as to reinforce the behaviors? Laughing at obscene comments or gestures or giving excessive attention to repetitive demands or aggressive movements may, in those patients with sufficient memory capacity, actually increase the frequency of the behavior. With any potential behavioral problem, check to ensure that the complaints that are reported are consistent with what is actually taking place and that innocuous behaviors are not being misinterpreted or that, conversely, worrisome behaviors are not being dismissed.

Clinical Vignette

Nurses reported that Mr. W was acting in a sexually inappropriate way on the unit. A review of the chart indicated that he was seen walking down the hallway while exposing his genitals. Further discussion with staff members revealed that Mr. W had severe dementia and that he did not know how to fasten his pants after using the bathroom. As a result, he frequently wandered into the hallway with his pants down, trying to get assistance.

In the case of Mr. W, a behavior was misinterpreted as representing sexual disinhibition when it really represented confusion, apraxia, and an attempt to communicate nonverbally. This case illustrates how some behaviors can be considered "normal" in the context of dementia, instead of being labeled as forms of agitation that warrant treatment. Examples of such "normal" behaviors in dementia include wandering, reaching out toward others, incoherent vocalizations, and unintentional incontinence or disrobing. This case also reinforces the importance of establishing a clear description of the problematic behaviors, including an operational definition. Simply stating that someone is "agitated" would not be sufficient, since that can mean so many different things and will obscure the ability to track progress over time. A better description might be something like "the patient is an 80-year-old man with Alzheimer's disease who is hitting nurses with his hands during attempts to bathe him in the morning," or "the patient is a 75-year-old woman with dementia due to a stroke who is screaming incoherently after mealtimes." These examples enable the second goal of the workup, which is to identify potential causes of the agitation. Thus, the first example might suggest the possibility of anxiety, fear, or discomfort during caregiving, while the second example raises the possibility of a postprandial issue such as heartburn or constipation, which may lie at the root of the behaviors.

Psychotic symptoms can range from subtle to obvious, and they can easily be confused with nonpsychotic symptoms. For example, when a patient insists that he or she saw a deceased loved one, this can reflect an actual visual hallucination, a delusion of misidentification (i.e., the false, fixed belief that another person is the deceased loved one), or simply agnosia (impaired recognition) associated with the dementia itself (e.g., an unfamiliar person is mistaken for a familiar one, perhaps because of similar physical characteristics or because the misidentified person's death was forgotten). Hallucinations can occur in all sensory modalities, but they are usually auditory or visual. Hallucinations reported by a person with dementia can be difficult to distinguish from confused descriptions of sensory input, images from dreams, and illusions (i.e., misinterpretations of sensory stimuli). The presence of psychotic symptoms should always prompt a search for medications that can induce them, especially in Parkinson's disease or dementia with Lewy bodies.

Medical Workup

A medical workup is always indicated for the following: (1) suspicion of delirium, (2) sudden changes in behavior, and (3) treatment-resistant problems (Bharucha & Pollack, 2011). For these acute changes, the obvious goal of this workup is to identify an etiology that can be treated to resolve the behavioral problems or delirium. The medical workup should always include the following:

- physical and neurologic examinations
- a review of all medications and supplements being taken
- basic laboratory tests including a urinalysis.

Depending on the patient's presentation, history, and test results, additional tests may be performed, including liver and thyroid function tests, a toxicology screen, bacterial cultures, cerebrospinal fluid analysis and culture, electrocardiography, brain computed tomography or magnetic resonance imaging, and other relevant radiographs. The older patient will typically have numerous medical conditions, both acute and chronic, and will be taking multiple medications, so determining a causal relationship is not always clear. Medical consultation will be critical to weigh the relative contributions of these elements.

Treatment

One way to approach treatment for agitation and psychosis is summarized by the mnemonic TREAT:

Target: define target symptoms.
Reversible: treat reversible causes.
Environment: optimize the environment and implement a behavior plan.
Agents: select, when necessary, an appropriate psychopharmacologic agent.
Try again: try again, if the improvement is insufficient.

Target Symptoms

The clinician must know what problems other than just "agitation" or "psychosis" he or she is treating. The exact description of the problematic behaviors—the operational definition described earlier—that is gained during the assessment allows treatment to be directed toward the source of the problem. For example, an individual's agitation may consist of repetitive screaming, hitting, and resistance to bathing, and each of these three target behaviors may require a different approach. Each behavior can then be tracked individually to assess whether improvement is occurring. Sometimes, an improvement in only one or two of the multiple target behaviors is sufficient to decrease the overall level of acuity. For example, treatment of a man who is screaming and hitting because he is paranoid may produce a response of less screaming and hitting but persistent paranoia. However, the overall reduction in his agitation may be a sufficient goal.

Reversible Causes

The importance of identifying the reversible causes of agitation and psychosis is covered earlier in the chapter. During treatment or palliation of the reversible causes, the use of behavioral and pharmacologic treatment strategies may still be indicated while waiting for the source of the behaviors to remit.

Environment

Environmental, behavioral, or nonpharmacologic approaches should always be considered and implemented. These interventions, as will be described, may consist of individualized behavioral approaches or may be part of larger therapeutic activities. Many of these interventions speak to the multidisciplinary aspect of treatment since they are typically carried out by long-term care staff and other caregivers rather than by individual clinicians. Such interventions may involve enhanced group activities or therapeutic programming and caregiver training (Femia et al., 2007; Meeks et al., 2008). Examples include music and pet therapy and exercise groups, as well as sensory activities such as aromatherapy or massage, arts and crafts, simulated presence, and structured walks, to name a few (Cohen-Mansfield, 2001). In long-term care facilities, staff in-services to provide an understanding of agitation and behavioral analysis, cultivate empathy, and teach protective strategies have been associated with reduced agitation and medication use (Fitzwater & Gates, 2002). Several meta-analyses have found a moderate degree of efficacy for various therapeutic activities, including aromatherapy, music therapy, multisensory stimulation, physical exercise, and caregiver training (Kong, Evans, & Guevara, 2009; Kverno et al., 2009; Olazarán et al., 2010).

Common barriers to nonpharmacologic approaches include patient unwillingness, unavailability, and unresponsiveness, and family and staff resistance. However, anticipating these barriers can help with optimal planning (Cohen-Mansfield et al., 2011). In addition, Jiska Cohen-Mansfied has emphasized using a team approach and focusing on individualized behavioral interventions based on the patient's unique background, including his or her cognitive, sensory, and physical abilities (Cohen-Mansfield, Libin, & Marx, 2007). Thus, pet therapy might be ideal for one person while music therapy is best for another.

In terms of more specific behavioral approaches, there are two levels of intervention. The first strategies are employed in the moment, often involving a single caregiver at a time for implementation, and are aimed at immediate reduction of the intensity and frequency of the behavioral disturbance. Several of these strategies are listed in Table 9.2. More in-depth behavioral approaches can be based on principles of applied behavior analysis (ABA) therapy, which is commonly used for children and adolescents with behavioral disturbances associated with pervasive developmental disorders.

Table 9.2 Basic Behavioral Strategies for Agitation

- Distract and redirect behavior
  - Assist and compliment individuals on their strengths ("Can I help you?"; "You are doing great") rather than commanding or insisting they do things or point out weaknesses ("Stop doing that!"; "I can't understand you!")
  - Be flexible on the timing of requests and caregiving, expecting more in the morning and less in the evening, but do not let this flexibility lead to neglect of needs
  - Distract the individual with stimulating, relaxing, pleasant, or fun activities, depending on the situation or on his or her preferences
- Provide for unmet needs (e.g., hunger, thirst, toileting)
- Address environmental stresses (e.g., excessive noise, excessive heat or cold, disruptive roommates)

A premise underlying the ABA approach is that dementia reduces a person's repertoire of behaviors, and adaptive responses to this change often produce behaviors that are viewed as disruptive (Ayalon, Gum, Feliciano, & Areán, 2006). ABA uses interviews, instruments, and direct observation to examine the context in which the behavior occurs in order to determine its function. This is called a functional assessment. The acronym PASTE summarizes the five main functions that disruptive behaviors may serve: (1) pain attenuation, (2) attention, (3) stimulation, (4) tangibles (e.g., food), and (5) escape. The overall goal of ABA is to prevent the behavior rather than simply to react to it. This can be accomplished either through changing the environment so the individual gets his or her needs met another way or by substituting the disruptive behavior for a more adaptive one. The ABA therapist will try to achieve this by developing an ongoing plan to modify the antecedents or consequences of the behavior or to differentially reinforce other more adaptive behaviors (LeBlanc, Raetz, & Feliciano, 2011). This model is well developed for children, but there are very few ABA therapists who are trained to work with the elderly. However, the process of functional assessment can be extremely informative to the team in terms of understanding the roots and consequences of agitated behaviors and then shaping a treatment plan.

Individual psychotherapy as part of the behavioral plan can be helpful, depending on the degree of dementia. Severe short-term memory impairment will limit an individual's ability to acquire insight and cognitive skills and to carry them into future sessions. A more practical approach involves supportive psychotherapy in the here and now to provide socialization, anxiety reduction, and rudimentary problem solving. Neuropsychological testing helps determine the feasibility and best approach to individual psychotherapy.

Finally, a behavioral approach should consider providing the caregiver with respite time as well as education and even hands-on training in caregiver skills. A rested, relaxed, competent, and more hopeful caregiver will certainly have a positive impact on decreasing behavioral disturbances in the demented person. More information and clinical tips on working with caregivers can be found in Chapter 12.

Several examples of behavioral approaches are illustrated in the following clinical vignettes.

Clinical Vignettes

Problem: Resistance to Care and Abusive Language
Mr. G resisted attempts by the staff to dress him in the morning. He would become combative and verbally abusive when the aides attempted to get him ready for breakfast. Otherwise, he was relatively calm. The staff identified early morning as a particularly difficult time for him, and the decision was made to postpone attempts to dress him until after breakfast. This change reduced the morning struggle. The staff ignored his abusive language and praised him when he spoke more reasonably. Mr. G's family members later told the staff that, before developing dementia, Mr. G always enjoyed spending several hours in the morning drinking coffee and reading

the paper before getting ready for work. The staff started to provide Mr. G with a cup of decaffeinated coffee and a paper with breakfast. His resistance to care improved markedly because the behavioral approach was replicating what was once a very familiar and relaxing routine for Mr. G.

Problem: Intrusive Wandering, Agitation, and Physical Aggression

Ms. A was constantly going into the nursing station and attempting to take things from the front desk. She would ask questions repeatedly despite being provided with answers. When the staff shooed her away, she became furious and would begin cursing the staff and damaging items. The staff members then learned that Ms. A was an executive secretary at a prestigious corporation, and they wondered whether her behaviors were an attempt to "work." To accommodate Ms. A, they designated a corner of the desk at the nursing station as Ms. A's workspace and stocked it with extra papers, tape dispensers, envelopes, and magazines. Whenever Ms. A approached the desk, she would be "asked" by staff to help with some work by sitting in her "desk." This request mollified Ms. A, who seemed to enjoy moving papers around and making suggestions to the unit secretary. She also enjoyed the verbal banter with the nurses and the other staff members who frequently stopped by the desk.

In each of these vignettes, the behavioral plan took into account each patient's previous lifestyle and personality characteristics, and it attempted to provide a more accommodating schedule or environment to decrease triggers, to increase structure, and to redirect behaviors into a more stimulating and productive direction. Behavioral plans require a great deal of creativity, flexibility, and patience on the part of staff. They require an understanding of the unique aspects of the individual's personality; social, cultural and religious background; personal history; needs; and preference. Several examples of environmental and behavioral strategies for specific behaviors are listed in Table 9.3. Keep in mind that when repeated behavioral plans fail, the surrounding environment may not be safe or sufficiently structured for a particular person, and a move must be considered.

Clinical Tip

Although the use of behavioral techniques can seem quite involved, always begin by using your common sense. Think about the patient and the situation, and ask yourself several of the following basic questions: What does the patient need? What is bothering him or her? What might make him or her feel better? The best environmental and behavioral plans are often based on the practical, intuitive, and empathic ways in which clinicians can comfort and care for troubled patients.

Table 9.3 Environmental and Behavioral Strategies for Common Target Behaviors

Target Behavior	Strategies
Agitation during caregiving	• Use a calm, nonthreatening manner • Select an optimal time • Provide soothing or relaxing stimulation beforehand
Repetitive screaming, yelling, or vocalizations	• Identify unmet needs (e.g., pain, needs, requests, or for toileting) • Provide increased socialization • Reduce overstimulation in environment
Intrusive wandering	• Provide safe and stimulating areas to wander • Distract with meaningful activities and socialization • Enhance personal space with familiar photographs or other items
Verbally abusive behavior	• Redirect to other topics and activities • Reinforce nonabusive language with praise • Provide meaningful activities and socialization
Inappropriate touching	• Set limits and redirect to other activities • Provide adequate, appropriate physical stimulation
Paranoid ideation	• Interact in nonthreatening manner • Avoid challenging the paranoid beliefs, but empathize with the fear experienced • Redirect onto less threatening topics
Repetitive somatic complaints	• Identify unmet needs (e.g., is there adequate pain control?) • Provide positive sensory stimulation • Give one-to-one contact to reassure and reduce anxiety

Psychopharmacologic Approaches

The use of psychopharmacology to treat agitation and psychosis ideally occurs after a thorough assessment has been completed, any reversible problems have been addressed, and environmental and behavioral strategies have been implemented. The selection of an appropriate pharmacologic agent is guided by several initial questions:

- What are the target symptoms?
- Is a comorbid psychiatric disorder present?
- Has any particular agent worked well or not worked in the past?
- Is the patient taking other medications that pose risks for drug interactions?
- What side effects should be avoided?

Of particular importance is the presence of a psychiatric disorder or symptom cluster that underlies the agitation or psychosis. For example, psychotic symptoms almost always necessitate the use of an antipsychotic agent, whereas depressive features that are associated with agitation or psychosis suggest the use of an antidepressant. Not every case will fit neatly into one of these categories, but they provide a means for approaching a clinical presentation initially and then a method for reevaluating it if the symptoms persist.

With respect to using pharmacologic agents, there is no universally recognized FDA-designated definition to encompass agitation and other behavioral disturbances, and thus there are no FDA approved agents for individuals with dementia. Many studies that have examined various agents are of short duration, often show a high placebo response, and use small samples and multiple assessment instruments (Kindermann, Dolder, Bailey, Katz, & Jeste, 2002). In addition, the use of antipsychotics in patients with dementia and in long-term care settings has come under attack from various sources, triggered in part by boxed warnings about potential increases in mortality along with other potent side effects. Prompted by these concerns, a 2011 report from the Office of the Inspector General evaluated the use of antipsychotics in nursing homes due to concerns about off-label use and found that despite the boxed warning about increased mortality, 83% of Medicare claims were for off-label indications, and 88% of residents using them had dementia (Office of the Inspector General, 2011). The fact that there is no FDA-approved medication was somewhat lost in the argument, however, since the growing concern about the use of antipsychotic medications for agitation has at times overshadowed the fact that there are no other alternatives with clearly established safety or efficacy.

Nearly every type of psychopharmacologic agent has been used to treat agitation, whereas only antipsychotic agents are used to treat psychosis. A clinical presentation that involves both agitation and psychosis requires, at the very least, the use of an antipsychotic. When the clinician is selecting a first-line agent, he or she should always determine whether anything the individual has taken in the past has worked well, has failed to work, or has caused side effects. The clinician should also anticipate the likely side effects for each potential agent and should consider the impact on the patient. For example, a more stimulating medication may not be desirable in a hyperactive patient, whereas a more sedating agent may be hazardous for a patient with an unsteady gait and a high risk of falls. Medications that strongly induce or inhibit key hepatic isoenzymes can disrupt the effectiveness of, or can cause toxicity with, medications such as warfarin, anticonvulsants, and tricyclic antidepressants. In patients with brittle diabetes, medications that cause a risk of glucose intolerance should be used only with extra caution and close monitoring; in patients with severe cardiac disease, medications that can significantly elevate the heart rate, alter blood pressure, slow cardiac conduction, or elevate triglyceride levels should not be prescribed.

The spectrum of potential psychopharmacologic agents is broad, including the following:

- anxiolytics
- antidepressants
- beta-blockers
- cognitive enhancers
- mood stabilizers
- antipsychotics

Although each category is reviewed here, the most broad-spectrum and efficacious choices are the atypical antipsychotics. Table 9.4 contains a list of the main psychopharmacologic medications and dosing strategies used to treat agitation and psychosis (dosing for cognitive enhancers is presented in Chapter 4, Table 4.5, and antidepressants, in Chapter 10, Table 10.1). The reader should keep in mind that this table provides guidelines for dosing based on common practice, but higher or lower doses may be used clinically, depending on the situation. Only the pharmacologic agents that have published efficacy data are included in the prescribing guidelines in this chapter.

Table 9.4 Recommended Psychopharmacologic Agents for Agitation Associated with Dementia

Name	Starting Dose (mg)	Dose Range (mg/day)
*Antipsychotics**		
Risperidone	0.25–0.5 mg	0.25–2 mg/day
Olanzapine	2.5–5 mg	2.5–20 mg / day
Quetiapine	25–50 mg	25–400 mg/day
Aripiprazole	2–5 mg	2–10 mg/day
Clozapine	6.25–12 mg	6.25–200 mg/day
Haloperidol	0.25–0.5 mg	0.25–2 mg/day
Anxiolytics		
Lorazepam	0.25–0.5 mg	0.25–2 mg/day
Clonazepam	0.25–0.5 mg	0.25–2 mg/day
Alprazolam	0.125–0.25 mg	0.125–1.5 mg/day
Oxazepam	7.5–10 mg	7.5–45 mg/day
Buspirone	5–10 mg	10–45 mg/day
Mood Stabilizers		
Valproic acid	125–250 mg twice daily	250–1500 mg/day in divided doses or extended release
Carbamazepine	50 mg twice daily	100–500 mg/day
Lithium carbonate (or citrate)	150 mg once or twice daily	150–900 mg daily titrated to level 0.4–1.0 ng/ml
Antidepressants		
Trazodone	25–50 mg once or twice daily standing order or on an as-needed (PRN) basis	25–200 mg daily
Serotonin selective reuptake inhibitors; Serotonin norephinephrine reuptake inhibitors; buproprion	See Chapter 10, Table 10.1 for dosing strategies	See Chapter 10, Table 10.1 for dosing strategies
Cognitive Enhancers		
Donepezil; rivastigmine; galantamine; memantine	See Chapter 4, Table 4.5 for dosing strategies	See Chapter 4, Table 4.5 for dosing strategies
Other Agents		
Prazosin	1 mg once daily or twice daily with blood pressure monitoring	1–6 mg/day in divided doses
Propranolol	10 mg once or twice daily with pulse and blood pressure monitoring	10–120 mg daily in 2–3 divided doses or once daily using long-acting form

* Antipsychotics can also be used for psychotic symptoms.

Clinical Tip

The goal of medication management for agitation or psychosis is to achieve symptom remission at a given dose of an agent that is tolerated by the patient. After the initial doses are given, an improvement in agitation ideally should occur within hours to days, depending on the agent. Antipsychotic effects can take several weeks, however. After symptomatic improvement begins, further titration may be needed to maximize this benefit without causing side effects, or the dose may need to be adjusted because of side effects. This process can take several weeks.

Antipsychotic Medications

Antipsychotic agents including both older conventional agents and newer atypical agents are often the mainstay of treatment due to their ability to treat comorbid psychosis and the fact that they are rapidly acting, potent, come in versatile preparations, and have a moderate amount of data on both efficacy and dosing strategies. Studies have shown limited efficacy in the treatment of agitation and psychosis associated with dementia for haloperidol (Devanand et al., 1998), risperidone (Brodaty et al., 2003; Katz et al., 1999), olanzapine (De Deyn et al., 2004; Street et al., 2000), quetiapine (Tariot et al., 2000), and aripiprazole (De Deyn, Jeste, & Mintzer, 2003), although these findings have been called into question by numerous other studies (Jin et al., 2013; Schneider et al., 2006). For individuals with good responses, though, withdrawal from antipsychotics has been associated with significant relapse (Devanand et al., 2012).

There are strong clinical concerns, however, about side effects associated with antipsychotics. A number of studies have found that elderly individuals and those with dementia or other forms of brain damage have a greater risk of extrapyramidal symptoms, particularly tardive dyskinesia (Jeste et al., 1999, 2000). For example, Jeste and colleagues found rates of tardive dyskinesia to be over 30% in older individuals exposed to 1 milligram of haloperidol over nine months (Jeste et al., 1999).

Accumulating evidence of diabetes mellitus associated with atypical antipsychotics (Newcomer et al., 2002; Sernyak et al., 2002) prompted the FDA in 2004 to require all manufacturers of these agents to include a warning in their package insert for potential diabetes and even diabetic ketoacidosis in individuals under treatment. A consensus statement on antipsychotic drugs and obesity and diabetes issued in 2004 by several national organizations including the American Diabetic Association summarized existing evidence on the issue and recommended that clinicians prescribing antipsychotic medications obtain baseline levels and routine measurements of weight, fasting glucose, and lipids (American Diabetes Association, 2004).

Perhaps no other safety issue has generated more concern among clinicians than the FDA warnings regarding the potential for cerebrovascular adverse events and increased mortality in individuals with dementia-related psychosis being treated with antipsychotics. Index studies for risperidone, olanzapine, and aripiprazole in individuals with dementia and psychosis found slightly higher rates of cerebrovascular adverse events—defined as strokes, transient ischemic attacks, or stroke-like events—in those on active drug versus placebo ("Atypical Antipsychotics in the Elderly," 2005). A review of the data is complicated by the fact that the studies themselves were not designed to look for cerebrovascular adverse events, many of the affected individuals had preexisting vascular risk factors, and no specific cardiovascular or other mechanism could be identified. Nonetheless, the FDA mandated a warning be placed in the package inserts of the relevant drugs. In addition, later research suggested a 1.3- to 2-fold increased probability of cerebrovascular accidents in elderly patients on antipsychotics (Sacchetti, Turrina, & Valsecchi, 2010).

In addition to the warning about cerebrovascular events, an FDA review of 17 studies of atypical antipsychotic agents in individuals with dementia and psychosis found that the overall mortality rate was between 1.6 and 1.7 times greater in drug-treated patients than in those on placebo in 15 of the 17 studies, or an average of 4.5% compared to 2.6% (Kuehn, 2005). Although the differences were not statistically significant in any study, the trend was consistent in nearly every study. Most of the deaths were cardiovascular or infectious in nature, and no specific mechanism was identified. Subsequent studies of antipsychotic use in patients with dementia have raised similar safety concerns, finding increased rates of injury, hospitalization, and mortality related to falls, hip fractures, stroke, and pneumonia (Kennedy et al., 2008; Pratt, Roughead, Salter, & Ryan, 2012; Trifirò et al., 2010).

If an antipsychotic medication is prescribed for agitation or psychosis, it is important to document the exact reason for its use and to conduct an informed consent discussion with the patient and/or the next of kin, which includes consideration of risks versus benefits. It is important prior to treatment to record the patient's baseline weight, fasting glucose level, and lipid panel. These levels should be rechecked several times during the first three months of treatment and then three to four times per year thereafter. Significant metabolic changes during therapy must be addressed, sometimes by dose reduction or switching to another agent if the antipsychotic appears to be the cause.

Clinical Tip

If you are going to elect an antipsychotic medication, is there a preferred agent? There are pluses and minuses to each agent, but selection is most often guided by potential side effects. Risperidone is one of the least sedating of the atypical agents but carries a risk of EPS. Olanzapine is associated with sedation, weight gain, anticholinergic effects, and diabetes. Two of the more common side effects for quetiapine are sedation and dizziness. Aripiprazole carries some risk of EPS but minimal weight gain or risk of diabetes. Clozapine can produce strong sedative effects, significant weight gain, anticholinergic effects, glucose dysregulation, diabetes, and agranulocytosis. These side effects, as well as the need to perform a complete blood count every two weeks, limit its use in older individuals with dementia.

Anxiolytics

Benzodiazepines such as lorazepam, alprazolam, and clonazepam are typical first-line agents since they have a quick onset of action, are relatively easy to dose, are familiar to most nurses, can be given in oral or intramuscular forms, and have excellent short-term effectiveness (Meehan, Wang, & David, 2002). However, they carry increased risks for dizziness, ataxia, confusion, and falls, and the possibility of paradoxical effects, rebound symptoms, withdrawal symptoms, and, over time, physical dependence. Buspirone, a novel antianxiety medication that works as a partial serotonin agonist, has an onset of action that is similar to that of antidepressants, requiring from 10 days to 2 weeks or longer for improvement to occur. Therefore, it cannot be used like benzodiazepines on an as-needed basis. It has mainly been used to treat generalized anxiety disorder, but it can also augment other antidepressants in the treatment of depression and obsessive-compulsive disorder. In general, it is well tolerated, and its common side effects include nausea, vomiting, headache, and dizziness. Buspirone is best when used in patients with mild to moderate agitation who have a clear anxiety component underlying their symptoms (Cantillon, Brunswick, Molina, & Bahro, 1996; Desai & Grossberg, 2003).

Clinical Tip

Be cautious when adding benzodiazepines to a regimen that already includes sleeping pills such as temazepam or zolpidem or the antihistamine diphenhydramine, which is found in many over-the-counter (OTC) sleeping pills, as the combination might cause excess sedation and mental status changes. Potentially safer alternatives for insomnia include the use of sleep hygiene techniques, herbal teas, and other similar preparations, as well as medications such as trazodone, mirtazapine, ramelteon, and OTC melatonin. Additional information on sleep hygiene and dosing strategies for these medications can be found in Chapter 10.

Antidepressant Medications

Antidepressants are commonly used to treat agitation with depressive features (e.g., irritability, negativity, weepiness, impaired sleep and appetite). The mechanism of action may be their ability to address the serotonergic dysfunction noted earlier in the chapter (McLoughlin, Lucey, & Dinan, 1994; Sukonick et al., 2001). Several studies have found limited efficacy for antidepressants such as the serotonin selective reuptake inhibitors and trazodone in the treatment of agitation in dementia, sometimes related to the treatment of underlying depression (Barak et al., 2011; Henry, Williamson, & Tampi, 2011; Seitz et al., 2011). Because of its sedating properties, trazodone is often used as a treatment for agitation both in standing doses and on an as-needed or PRN basis.

Compared to more rapidly acting anti-agitation medications, antidepressants can take several weeks or longer to achieve a therapeutic dose and have a clinical effect. In addition, the risk of actually triggering agitation and psychosis because of excess stimulation must be considered, especially when dopaminergic activity is increased. As a result, clinicians should always monitor patients closely for increased agitation and restlessness in the first few weeks of treatment, especially with stimulating antidepressants such as SSRIs and bupropion, as well as psychostimulants, which are sometimes used to treat apathy, excess fatigue, and failure to thrive (see Chapter 10). Several antidepressants can have important interactions with drugs commonly prescribed to elderly patients such as coumadin, tramadol, and many anticonvulsants. High doses of trazodone can lead to dizziness, headache, orthostasis, cardiac irritability, and, rarely, priapism.

Mood Stabilizers

Mood stabilizers have been used to treat bipolar disorder, recurrent depression, impulse control disorders, and aggression associated with brain impairment. Lithium was the first mood stabilizer, and it has been a staple of psychiatric care for more than four decades. Several anticonvulsants, in addition to being used to treat seizure disorders, neuropathic pain, and migraine headaches, are used as mood stabilizers. Mood stabilizers have also been used to treat agitation in dementia but with significant data establishing their efficacy. Several case studies and randomly controlled trials using valproic acid have shown limited to no benefit (Gauthier, et al., 2010) while two small randomly controlled trials with carbamazepine suggest modest efficacy for aggression and hostility (Olin et al., 2001; Tariot et al., 1998). The data for gabapentin (Sommer, Fenn, & Ketter, 2007; Kim, Wilkins, & Tampi, 2008), lamotrigine (Ng et al., 2009), oxcarbazepine (Sommer et al., 2007), and topiramate (Sommer et al., 2007) is not strong enough to support their use. All mood stabilizers take weeks to have an effect, have limited data on dosing, and require monitoring for critical side effects including sedation, confusion, ataxia, and increased risk of falls, as well as hepatic, hematologic, and dermatologic toxicity.

Because of its side effects and narrow therapeutic window, lithium carbonate (or lithium citrate) is often not used in agitated elderly individuals with dementia. Checking blood levels routinely is imperative, especially after dose changes or the addition of medications known to affect lithium levels. Common side effects of lithium include sedation, tremor, and diarrhea. Renal and thyroid tests should be checked before the medication is begun to establish a baseline and then every four to six months thereafter because of the risk of damage to both organs. Many medications, especially nonsteroidal anti-inflammatory drugs, can affect lithium levels, usually by increasing them.

Valproic acid, which is dispensed as divalproex sodium, comes in a variety of preparations, including enterically coated and extended-release tablets, sprinkles, and syrup. The extended-release form is dosed once daily and at a dose 20% higher when converting from an immediate-release preparation. Five to six days after each dose increase, a trough blood level should be drawn at least 12 hours after the last dose and before the next dose; the aim should be for levels in the range of 40–90 milligrams per milliliter. Valproic acid levels should be checked every four months once an individual is stable. The most common side effects include gastrointestinal intolerance, sedation, and ataxia. Hepatotoxicity, thrombocytopenia, and pancreatitis are less common but important side effects. For this reason, the clinician should be sure to obtain baseline liver function tests, an amylase level, and a complete blood count and then to monitor these levels every 4–6 months while the patient continues on treatment with valproic acid. A rare but possible side effect may involve muscle rigidity and abnormal movements.

Carbamazepine, like valproic acid, should be titrated to clinical effect, not to blood level, although safe levels for elderly individuals with dementia are in the range of 3–8 milligrams per milliliter. Some common side effects are sedation, ataxia, gastro-intestinal intolerance, and tremor; less common but important side effects include the syndrome of inappropriate secretion of antidiuretic hormone (SIADH), hepatotoxic-ity, bone marrow suppression, and Stevens–Johnson syndrome. In addition to checking carbamazepine levels every 1–2 weeks during the first 6–8 weeks of treatment and every four months once the patient is stable, liver function tests and a complete blood count should be checked at baseline and then every six months thereafter. Carbamazepine can strongly induce its own hepatic metabolism and those of numerous other medica-tions, such as warfarin and valproic acid, thereby reducing the therapeutic effect of itself or of the other agents. On the flipside, carbamazepine plasma levels can be increased by oral antifungal medications, macrolide antibiotics, calcium channel blockers, fluoxetine, cimetidine, and other medications, leading to an increased risk of drug toxicity. Extra monitoring of blood levels is required with all of these combinations.

Cognitive Enhancing Medications

As noted earlier, behavioral problems in Alzheimer's disease and other dementias may be related to cholinergic deficits, suggesting a role for acetylcholinesterase (AChE) inhibi-tors (Sultzer et al., 1995; Tekin et al., 2001). The role of excess glutamate activity in causing behavioral problems is less clear. In fact, studies of both AChE inhibitors and memantine appear to show a lower incidence of behavioral disturbances compared to placebo, although they have not shown clear efficacy in terms of improving agitation in dementia (Lockhart et al., 2011; Maidment et al., 2008; Rodda, Morgan, & Walker, 2009). The exceptions may be dementia with Lewy bodies and Parkinson's disease dementia in which AChE inhibitors have been shown to improve both behavior and psychosis (Mori et al., 2012; Rolinski et al., 2012). Despite these findings, the data do not indicate a very potent effect of any cognitive enhancing medication on behavioral disturbances and cer-tainly not on psychotic symptoms. Lacking these data, cognitive enhancing medications should not be used as first-line agents for moderate to severe agitation or for psychosis. Rather, they may be helpful for mild agitation or in combination with other psychophar-macologic agents, particularly antipsychotics. The limiting factor is that it takes weeks to get to a therapeutic dose of any cognitive enhancing medication, and such medication will not be helpful when symptoms have an acute onset and pose more immediate risk of harm to self or others.

Other Agents

Beta-blockers such as propranolol are sometimes used to reduce agitation and aggres-sion in patients with dementia and brain injury, and have shown some efficacy when augmenting other psychotropics (Peskind et al., 2005). The rationale for their use is based on the belief that aggression is associated with a heightened reactivity to noradrenergic stimulation. Beta-blockers can also be used to treat akathisia (motor restlessness), which is a side effect of antipsychotics and, if left untreated, can cause agitation. Other pharmacologic agents that have been used to treat agitation include the alpha-1 antagonist prazosin (Wang et al., 2009), and estrogen and anti-androgens for both agitation and sexually inappropriate behaviors (Hall, Keks, & O'Connor, 2005; Tucker, 2010). There is, however, limited data on both efficacy and safety for all of these agents and no clear guidelines on when they may be preferred over antipsychotics or benzodiazepines.

Addressing the Behavioral Crisis

A behavioral crisis involves an individual who is engaging in physically assaultive, suicidal, or extremely unsafe behaviors that represent an immediate threat to the safety of the patient or others. Such behaviors are especially dangerous when the individual is living at home with minimal supervision or when the surrounding home environment or neighborhood is not safe. When these situations occur, remember that acutely agitated patients with dementia are often reacting to feelings of fear or neglect, so the clinician should try to help them feel safe and cared for. He or she should avoid responding to the crisis in an overly reactive manner, which can result in patients being overmedicated or inappropriately hospitalized.

The approach to behavioral emergencies represents an accelerated, more intense version of the normal assessment and treatment of agitation and psychosis. Behavioral emergencies can be addressed using the mnemonic CALM as follows:

Calm the individual
Assess the environment
Limit access to unsafe places or situations
Medicate as necessary

Immediate intervention is required in behavioral emergencies, and it should initially be aimed at calming the individual and eliminating the situation that is producing the crisis. If the clinician is on the scene, he or she should approach the individual with a concerned expression and a friendly demeanor, speaking calmly with a soothing but firm tone. He or she should then try to distract the individual and redirect him or her into a safer area and situation or instruct a caregiver or staff member to do so. In the appropriate situations, food or drink should be offered or the individual's other needs should be addressed. Noxious triggers in the environment, such as loud or annoying voices or noises, uncomfortable physical stimuli (e.g., soiled clothes or bedding, insufficient or excessive light or heat), unpleasant odors, other agitated individuals, or even angry or stressed caregivers, should be identified and eliminated.

Then, the clinician should make sure that the individual cannot return to the unsafe situation. This may involve removing sharp objects or potential weapons when suicidal or homicidal threats have been made and limiting access to doors or windows when

Table 9.5 Medications for Behavioral Emergencies

Strategy	Dose Range	Comments
Lorazepam	0.5–1 mg PO or IM	May repeat one time and then every 4–12 hours as needed; may combine with other agents for severe agitation
Risperidone	0.25–0.5 mg PO as pill, rapidly dissolving tablet, or liquid	May repeat one time and then every 6–12 hours as needed
Olazapine	2.5–5 mg PO as pill, rapidly dissolving tablet, or IM injection	May repeat one time and then every 6–12 hours as needed
Quetiapine	25–50 mg PO	May repeat one time and then every 6–12 hours as needed
Haloperidol	0.5–1 mg PO as tablet, liquid, or IM injection	May repeat one time and then every 6–12 hours as needed
Trazodone	25–100 mg	May repeat one time and then every 4–12 hours as necessary

escape is a risk. In a home environment, the intervention can be more challenging because the caregiver may lack assistance, or the patient may live in an unsafe neighborhood, area of high traffic, or near bodies of water, which can be hazardous if the patient wanders away. In life-threatening situations, emergency personnel should be called for assistance in transporting the individual to an emergency department or a psychiatric facility.

When behavioral approaches do not quickly resolve the crisis, psychopharmacologic agents as listed in Table 9.5 can be used to calm the individual quickly and safely. Lorazepam may be the best choice in terms of a fast-acting benzodiazepine because it is simple to metabolize and has a reasonable duration of action; additionally, it is a familiar and accessible medication in most settings. Both short-acting and long-acting benzodiazepines can be associated with unwanted side effects. For example, diazepam has an extremely quick onset of action, but it stays in the body for a long time, increasing the risk of side effect accumulation. Alprazolam also works quickly and relatively well, but there is a risk of paradoxical agitation and rebound symptoms due to its short half-life. Despite these admonitions, selecting a benzodiazepine that the patient is already taking or has responded to in the past is always best.

When intramuscular preparations are needed, lorazepam or haloperidol are often used since they are typically readily available and familiar to many nurses. Of the atypical antipsychotics, olanzapine, ziprasidone, and aripiprazole have injectable preparations. If intramuscular haloperidol or another conventional antipsychotic is used, however, the patient should be switched to an atypical agent when an oral dose can be given in order to reduce the longer-term risk of movement disorders. Consider combining a benzodiazepine with an antipsychotic agent for severe or resistant agitation. Avoid use of triazolam, diphenhydramine, hydroxyzine, chloral hydrate, chlorpromazine, thioridazine, or narcotic analgesics due to risk of oversedation, dizziness, ataxia, falls, and confusion.

Clinical Vignette

Mrs. H, an 86-year-old woman with Alzheimer's disease, lived with her daughter. The daughter paged her mother's psychiatrist one evening. When the psychiatrist returned her call, she was in tears. She reported that her mother attacked her with a cane and then smashed the window in the front door, trying to leave the house. Mrs. H was paranoid and agitated, accusing her daughter of trying to keep her in a jail.

The psychiatrist instructed the daughter over the phone to ask her mother calmly to sit down and then to offer her a favorite snack or drink. She then tried to give her mother an extra 0.5-milligram dose of risperidone. Mrs. H calmed down over the next hour, sat quietly in front of the television, and then fell asleep for the night. In the follow-up phone call, the psychiatrist advised the daughter to increase Mrs. H's daily risperidone dose to 0.5 milligrams twice daily.

Sexual Aggression

Sexually aggressive or inappropriate behaviors include obscene sexual comments or requests; public nudity or masturbation; and aggressive fondling, groping, or forced sexual activity. Such behaviors are present in 2%–7% of individuals with dementia (Guay, 2008; Hajjar & Kamel, 2003), although the rates in dementia units may be as high as 25% (Hashmi, Krady, Qayum, & Grossberg, 2000). Such behaviors in dementia are more common in men and often associated with frontal and temporal lobe impairment, mania, psychosis, stroke, head trauma, and premorbid sexual aggression (Agronin & Westheimer, 2011; Guay, 2008; Hashmi et al., 2000). Although these behaviors create a disproportionate amount of concern and anxiety among caregivers, they can be approached and treated in the same manner as other agitated behaviors. The assessment tries to determine whether the behavior is due to excess libido, disinhibited sexual impulses, unmet sexual needs, or confusion. For example, a man with dementia who is reported to have groped a staff member may simply have been reaching out or grabbing for attention from the level of a wheelchair, thus hitting the staff member in the waist or chest area, or he may have actually been trying to satisfy a sexual urge.

The treatment of these behaviors should begin with behavioral techniques that set limits and redirect the individual into more appropriate behaviors. Eliminating the inadvertent reinforcement of these behaviors (e.g., when staff members laugh at obscene comments) is also important. In some situations, the individual may be expressing unmet needs for physical stimulation or intimacy that can be gratified by partners. For example, an individual with dementia who attempts to fondle other residents could be provided with increased physical stimulation through hugs and massages during visits with his or her spouse. Problematic behaviors that appear associated with excess or disinhibited libido may respond to antidepressants that have sexual side effects, such as the SSRIs. Rarely, clinicians use estrogen or an antiandrogen steroid hormone, such as medroxyprogesterone, to reduce sexual urges (Hall et al., 2005; Tucker, 2010).

Aggressive, disinhibited, hyperactive, or hypersexual behaviors often respond well to atypical antipsychotics and mood stabilizers.

When Treatment Fails

At times, behavioral disturbances or psychotic symptoms may persist or even worsen despite everyone's best efforts; such situations are frustrating for any caregiver or clinician. Consider the following situations.

Clinical Vignettes

Mr. S, a 78-year-old man with Wernicke–Korsakoff's encephalopathy, was a pleasant but confused individual who, most of the time, spent his days wandering up and down the hallway of the special care unit. However, one or two times a month, he would suddenly and unpredictably strike out at another resident or staff member. On one occasion, he pushed over a female resident who was using a walker, nearly causing a hip fracture. Another time, he slapped an aide in the face and attempted to push her to the ground. He had no memory of these episodes afterward and denied that he would ever do such a thing. Multiple trials of psychotropics, including benzodiazepines, mood stabilizers, antipsychotics, and combinations, resulted in sedation, but they did not extinguish these episodic behaviors.

Ms. W, a 102-year-old nursing home resident with Alzheimer's disease, spent her days sitting in a wheelchair in front of the nursing station, calling out her son Johnny's name repeatedly. Other times, she would repeat, "Johnny, I need help" or "oh, oh, oh" for hours. She would stop briefly when she was asked a question, but she would then start again. Her cognitive impairment was so severe that she had no insight into her behaviors, and nothing seemed to stop them. Staff members were conflicted over whether her vocalizations warranted treatment with medications, but they felt pressured to respond to the multiple complaints from other residents, families, and staff about how disruptive the verbalizations were. Trials of lorazepam, an SSRI antidepressant, and an antipsychotic medication were ineffective.

These cases illustrate some of the barriers involved in treatment-resistant symptoms. Sometimes, the symptoms are episodic but severe, and their unpredictability limits an environmental or behavioral plan. Other behaviors, such as repetitive verbalizations or vocalizations, intrusive wandering, and refusal to take medications or to cooperate with therapy or institutional rules, may not cause harm to the patient or others, but they can be extremely annoying to the other residents, caregivers, or staff. In such cases, staff members are often unsure about whether the use of psychotropic medications is justified. Other circumstances require the use of lengthy legal proceedings and family cooperation and resources to obtain a guardianship and mandated treatment plan. Behaviors that are particularly difficult to treat with medications include episodic, impulsive, aggressive behaviors; repetitive disruptive vocalizations; and isolated delusions. When the clinician is facing treatment-resistant symptoms, several steps may be taken.

- Reassess for underlying medical problems, especially medication side effects or pain that may be triggering the problems.
- Reassess the diagnosis. Is there underlying depression, panic disorder, or mania that is not being treated with the appropriate medication?
- Reassess the environment for unseen triggers.
- Reassess the environmental or behavioral plan. Perhaps elements need to be added or changed.
- Reassess the safety and appropriateness of the living setting. Consider moving the patient to a more structured setting (e.g., from home to a long-term care facility or from an open unit to a locked unit) where staff have behavioral training.
- Reassess the capabilities or appropriateness of the caregiver; perhaps he or she is poorly trained, exhausted, depressed, or abusive. No medication can resolve that.
- Reassess the medication trials. Were adequate doses used for sufficient lengths of time? Was the patient compliant with the medication(s)? Was the caregiver dispensing it correctly? Some patients will falsely claim to be taking medications; check blood levels when possible.
- Always consider a paradoxical effect of a psychotropic medication. Is it actually exacerbating the symptoms?
- Obtain more information about the patient's underlying personality characteristics. A long-standing history of dysfunctional traits can cause persistent problems that were not fully appreciated during earlier assessments.

Augmentation Strategies

Several of the following pharmacologic augmentation strategies can be considered for treating agitation or psychosis when single agents are not working:

- AChE inhibitors and/or memantine
- antipsychotic plus a benzodiazepine
- antipsychotic plus an antidepressant or trazodone
- antipsychotic plus a mood stabilizer
- antidepressant plus antidepressant with different receptor profile (e.g., SSRI plus mirtazapine)
- antidepressant plus buspirone
- mood stabilizer plus other mood stabilizer (e.g., divalproex plus lithium)
- mood stabilizer plus antidepressant

Sometimes three or more agents are used. Combining two or more antipsychotics or multiple benzodiazepines should be avoided because of the increased risk of side effects. Clozapine is usually the medication of last resort (Lee et al., 2007). In intensive care settings, intravenous haloperidol has also been used with success. However, a dose-related risk of ventricular arrhythmias, specifically torsade de pointes, must be kept in mind, and it may necessitate the use of cardiac monitoring (Meyer-Massetti et al., 2010). Electroconvulsive therapy is indicated when the presence of treatment-resistant mania or psychotic depression is suspected, but it may also be considered for severe agitation that does not clearly fit into any category (Ujkaj et al., 2012). When all other strategies have failed to control severe agitation, the clinician should consider moving the individual to a more structured setting, such as a dementia unit or a psychiatric hospital, for more intensive behavioral and pharmacologic management.

The clinician should remember that, even in the best medication trials, response rates are never 100%; in fact, they are rarely even 80%. Realistically, 20%–40% of patients with agitation and/or psychosis do not respond to initial medication trials, even under the best of circumstances. Thus, a reassessment of the diagnosis, environment, and behavioral plans as well as team involvement is critical to making progress. Over time, with all of the parties working together, significant improvement can usually be achieved. Whatever the outcome, the clinician should never give up!

References

Agronin, M. E., & Westheimer, R. K. (2011). Sexuality and sexual disorders in late life. In M. E. Agronin & G. J. Maletta (Eds.), *Principles and practice of geriatric psychiatry* (2nd ed., pp. 603–626). Philadelphia: Lippincott, Williams and Wilkins.

American Diabetes Association. (2004). Consensus development conference on antipsychotic drugs and obesity and diabetes. *J Clin Psychiatry, 65*(2), 267–272.

Atypical antipsychotics in the elderly. (2005). *The Medical Letter on Drugs and Therapeutics, 47*(1214), 61–62.

Ayalon, L., Gum, A., Feliciano, L., & Areán, P. A. (2006). The effectiveness of nonpharmacological interventions for the management of neuropsychiatric symptoms in patients with dementia: A systematic review. *Arch Int Med, 166,* 2182–2188.

Ballard, C. G., Margallo-Lana, M., Fossey, J., et al. (2001). A 1-year follow-up study of behavioral and psychological symptoms in dementia among people in care environments. *J Clin Psychiatry, 62,* 631–636.

Barak, Y., Polpski, I., Tadger, S., et al. (2011). Escitalopram versus risperidone for the treatment of behavioral and psychotic symptoms associated with Alzheimer's disease: A randomized double-blind pilot study. *Int Psychogeriatr, 23,* 1515–1519.

Bharucha, A. J., & Pollack, B. G. (2011). Agitation and psychosis associated with dementia. In M. E. Agronin & G. J. Maletta (Eds.), *Principles and practice of geriatric psychiatry* (2nd ed., pp. 675–704). Philadelphia: Lippincott, Williams and Wilkins.

Brodaty, H., Ames, D., Snowdon, J., et al. (2003). A randomized placebo-controlled trial of risperidone for the treatment of aggression, agitation, and psychosis of dementia. *J Clin Psychiatry, 64,* 134–143.

Cantillon, M., Brunswick, R., Molina, D., & Bahro, M. (1996). Buspirone vs. haloperidol: A double-blind trial for agitation in a nursing home population with Alzheimer's disease. *Am J Ger Psychiatry, 4*(3), 263–267.

Cohen-Mansfield, J. (2001). Nonpharmacologic interventions for inappropriate behaviors in dementia: A review, summary, and critique. *Am J Geriatr Psychiatry, 9,* 361–381.

Cohen-Mansfield, J., Libin, A., & Marx, M. S. (2007). Nonpharmacological treatment of agitation: A controlled trial of systematic individualized intervention. *J Gerontol A Biol Sci Med Sci, 62,* 908–916.

Cohen-Mansfield, J., Thein, K., Marx, M. S., et al. (2011). What are the barriers to performing nonpharmacogical interventions for behavioral symptoms in the nursing home? *J Am Med Dir Assoc, 13*(4), 400–405.

De Deyn, P. P., Carrasco, M. M., Deberdt, W., et al. (2004). Olanzapine versus placebo in the treatment of psychosis with or without associated behavioral disturbances in patients with Alzheimer's disease. *Int J Geriatr Psychiatry, 19*, 115–126.

De Deyn, P. P., Jeste, D., & Mintzer, J. (2003, March 1–4). Aripiprazole in dementia of the Alzheimer's type. Presented at the 16th Annual Meeting of the American Association for Geriatric Psychiatry, Honolulu, Hawaii.

Desai, A. K., & Grossberg, G. T. (2003). Buspirone in Alzheimer's disease. *Exp Rev Neurother, 3*, 19–28.

Devanand, D. P., Marder, K., Michaels, K. S., et al. (1998). A randomized, placebo-controlled dose-comparison trial of haloperidol for psychosis and disruptive behaviors in Alzheimer's disease. *Am J Psychiatry, 155*, 1512–1520.

Devanand, D. P., Mintzer, J., Schultz, S. K., et al. (2012). Relapse risk after discontinuation of risperidone in Alzheimer's disease. *N Eng J Med, 367*(16), 1497–1507.

Endeshaw, Y., & Bliwise, D. L. (2011). Sleep disorders in the elderly. In M. E. Agronin & G .J. Maletta (Eds.), *Principles and practice of geriatric psychiatry* (2nd ed., pp. 583–601). Philadelphia: Lippincott, Williams and Wilkins.

Femia, E. E., Zarit, S. H., Stephens, M. A., et al. (2007). Impact of adult day services on behavioral and psychological symptoms of dementia. *Gerontologist, 47*, 775–788.

Fitzwater, E. L., & Gates, D. M. (2002). Testing an intervention to reduce assaults on nursing assistants in nursing homes: A pilot study. *Geriatric Nursing, 23*, 18–23.

Gauthier, S., Cummings, J., Ballard, C., et al. (2010). Management of behavioral problems in Alzheimer's disease. *Int Psychogeriatr, 22*, 346–372.

Guay, D. R. (2008). Inappropriate sexual behaviors in cognitively impaired older individuals. *Am J Geriatr Pharmacother, 6*(5), 269–288.

Hajjar, R. R., & Kamel, H. K. (2003). Sexuality in the nursing home, part 2: Managing abnormal behaviour-legal and ethical issues. *J Am Med Dir Assoc, 5*(Suppl. 2), 203–206.

Hall, K. A., Keks, N. A., & O'Connor, D. W. (2005). Transdermal estrogen patches for aggressive behavior in male patients with dementia: A randomized, controlled clinical trial. *Int Pychogeriatr, 17*, 165–178.

Hashmi, F. H., Krady, A. I., Qayum, F., & Grossberg, G. T. (2000). Sexually disinhibited behavior in the cognitively impaired elderly. *Clin Geriatr, 8*(11), 61–68.

Henry, G., Williamson, D., & Tampi, R. R. (2011). Efficacy and tolerability of antidepressants in the treatment of behavioral and psychological symptoms of dementia: A literature review of evidence. *Am J Alzheimers Dis Other Demen, 26*, 169–183.

Inouye, S. K. (2006). Delirium in older persons. *N Engl J Med, 354*(11), 1157–1165.

International Psychogeriatric Association. (2000). Behavioral and psychological symptoms of dementia (BPSD): A clinical and research update. *Int Psychogeriatr, 12*(Suppl. 1), 1–424.

Jeste, D. V., & Finkel, S. I. (2000). Psychosis of Alzheimer's disease and related dementias: Diagnostic criteria for a distinct syndrome. *Am J Geriatr Psychiatry, 8*(1), 29–34.

Jeste, D. V., Lacro, J. P., Bailey, A., et al. (1999). Lower incidence of tardive dyskinesia with risperidone compared with haloperidol in older patients. *J Am Ger Soc, 47*, 716–719.

Jeste, D. V., Okamoto, A., Napolitano, J., et al. (2000). Low incidence of persistent tardive dyskinesia in elderly patients with dementia treated with risperidone. *Am J Psychiatry, 157*(7), 1150–1155.

Jin, H., Pei-an, B. S., Golshan, S., et al. (2013). Comparison of longer-term safety and effectiveness of 4 atypical antipsychotics in patients over age 40: A trial using equipoise-stratified randomization. *J Clin Psychiatry, 74*(1), 10–18.

Katz, I. R., Jeste, D. V., Mintzer, J. E., et al. (1999). Comparison of risperidone and placebo for psychosis and behavioral disturbances associated with dementia: A randomized, double-blind trial. *J Clin Psychiatry, 60,* 107–115.

Kennedy, J., Tien, Y. Y., et al. (2008). The association between class of antipsychotic and rates of hospitalization. *Clin Psychopharmacol, 28*(5), 532–535.

Kim, Y., Wilkins, K. M., & Tampi, R. R. (2008). Use of gabapentin in the treatment of behavioral and psychological symptoms of dementia: A review of the evidence. *Drug Aging, 25,* 187–196.

Kindermann, S. S., Dolder, C. R., Bailey, A., Katz, I. R., & Jeste, D. V. (2002). Pharmacological treatment of psychosis and agitation in elderly patients with dementia: Four decades of experience. *Drugs Aging, 19,* 257–276.

Kong, E. H., Evans, L. K., & Guevara, J. P. (2009). Nonpharmacological intervention for agitation in dementia: A systematic review and meta-analysis. *Aging & Mental Health, 4*(13), 512–520.

Kotlyar, M., Gray, S. L., Maher, R. L., & Hanlon, J. T. (2011). Psychiatric manifestations of medications in the elderly. In M. E. Agronin & G. J. Maletta (Eds.), *Principles and practice of geriatric psychiatry* (2nd ed., pp. 721–733). Philadelphia: Lippincott, Williams and Wilkins.

Kuehn B. M. (2005). FDA warns antipsychotic drugs may be risky for elderly. *JAMA, 293,* 2562.

Kverno, K. S., Black, B. S., Nolan, M. T., et al. (2009). Research on treating neuropsychiatric symptoms of advanced dementia with non-pharmacological strategies, 1998–2008: A systematic literature review. *Int Psychogeriatr, 21,* 825–843.

LeBlanc, L. A., Raetz, P., & Feliciano, L. (2011). Behavioral gerontology. In W. W. Fisher, C. C. Piazza, & H. Roane (Eds.), *Handbook of applied behavior analysis* (pp. 472–486). New York: Guilford Press.

Lee, H. B., Hanner, J. A., Yokley, J. L., et al. (2007). Clozapine for treatment-resistant agitation in dementia. *J Geriatr Psychiatry Neurol, 20*(3), 178–182.

Lockhart, I. A., Radcliffe, J., Molchan, S. A., et al. (2011). The efficacy of licensed-indication use of donepezil and memantine monotherapies for treating behavioral and psychological symptoms of dementia in patients with Alzheimer's disease: Systematic review and meta-analysis. *Dement Geriatr Cogn Dis Extra, 1*(1), 212–227.

Maidment, I. D., Fox, C. G., Boustani, M., et al. (2008). Efficacy of memantine on behavioral and psychological symptoms related to dementia: A systematic meta-analysis. *Ann Pharmacother, 42,* 32–38.

McLoughlin, D. M., Lucey, J. V., & Dinan, T. G. (1994). Role of serotonin in the behavioral and psychological symptoms of dementia. *Am J Psychiatry, 151,* 1701–1703.

Meagher, D. J., Norton, J. W., & Trzepacz, P. T. (2011). Delirium in the elderly. In M. E. Agronin & G. J. Maletta (Eds.), *Principles and practice of geriatric psychiatry* (2nd ed., pp. 383–403). Philadelphia: Lippincott, Williams and Wilkins.

Meehan, K. M., Wang, H., & David, S. R. (2002). Comparison of rapidly acting intramuscular olanzapine, lorazepam, and placebo: A double-blind, randomized study in acutely agitated patients with dementia. *Neurospychopharmacology, 26,* 494–504.

Meeks, S., Looney, S. W., Van, H. K., et al. (2008). BE-ACTIV: A staff-assisted behavioral intervention for depression in nursing homes. *Gerontologist, 48,* 105–114.

Meyer-Massetti, C., Cheng, C. M., Sharpe, B. A., et al. (2010). The FDA extended warning for intravenous haloperidol and torsades de pointes: How should institutions respond? *J Hosp Med, 5*(4), E8–E16.

Mori, E., Ikeda, M., Kosaka, K., et al. (2012). Donepezil for dementia with Lewy bodies: A randomized placebo-controlled trial. *Ann Neurol, 72,* 41–52.

Newcomer, J. W., Haupt, D. W., Fucetola, R., et al. (2002). Abnormalities in glucose regulation during antipsychotic treatment of schizophrenia. *Arch Gen Psychiatry, 59,* 337–345.

Ng, B., Camacho, A., Bardwell, W., et al. (2009). Lamotrigine for agitation in older patients with dementia. *Int Psychogeriatr, 21*, 207–208.

Office of the Inspector General. (2011, May). Medicare atypical antipsychotic drug claims for elderly nursing home residents. Retrieved from https://oig.hhs.gov/oei/reports/oei-07–08–00150.pdf

Olazarán, J., Reisberg, B., Clare, L., et al. (2010). Nonpharmacological therapies in Alzheimer's disease: A systematic review of efficacy. *Dement Geriatr Cogn Disord, 30*, 161–178.

Olin, J. T., Fox, L. S., Pawluczyk, S., et al. (2001). A pilot randomized trial of carbamazepine for behavioral symptoms in treatment-resistant outpatients with Alzheimer disease. *Am J Geriatr Psychiatry, 9*(4), 400–405.

Peskind, E. R., Tsuang, D. W., Bonner, L. T., et al. (2005). Propranolol for disruptive behaviors in nursing home residents with probable or possible Alzheimer disease: A placebo-controlled study. *Alzheimer Dis Assoc Disord, 19*, 23–28.

Pratt, N., Roughead, E. E., Salter, A., & Ryan, P. (2012). Choice of observational study design impacts on measurement of antipsychotic risks in the elderly: A systematic review. *Biomed Central Med Res Methodol, 12*, 72.

Proctor, A.W., Francis, P.T., Stratmann, G.C., & Bowen, D.M. (1992). Serotonergic pathology is not widespread in Alzheimer patients without prominent aggressive symptoms. *Neurochem Res, 17*, 917–922.

Rodda, J., Morgan, S., & Walker, Z. (2009). Are cholinesterase inhibitors effective in the management of the behavioral and psychological symptoms of dementia in Alzheimer's disease? A systematic review of randomized, placebo-controlled trials of donepezil, rivastigmine and galantamine. *Int Psycohogeriatr, 21*(5), 813–824.

Rolinski, M., Fox, C., Maidment, I., et al. (2012). Colinesterase inhibitors for dementia with Lewy bodies, Parikinson's disease dementia and cognitive impairment in Parkinson's disease. *Cochrane Database Syst Rev, 14*(3), CD006504.

Sacchetti, E., Turrina, C., & Valsecchi, P. (2010). Cerebrovascular accidents in elderly people treatment with antipsychotic drugs: a systematic review. *Drug Saf, 33*(4), 273–288.

Schneider, L., Tariot, P., Dageman, N., et al. (2006). Effectiveness of atypical antipsychotic drugs in patients with Alzheimer's disease. *N Eng J Med, 355*(15), 1525–1538.

Seitz, D. P., Adunuri, N., Gill, S. S., et al. (2011). Antidepressants for agitation and psychosis in dementia. *Cochrane Database Syst Rev, 2*, CD008191.

Sernyak, M. J., Leslie, D. L., Alarcon, R. D., et al. (2002). Association of diabetes mellitus with use of atypical neuroleptics in the treatment of schizophrenia. *Am J Psychiatry, 159*(4), 561–566.

Sommer, B. R., Fenn, H. H., & Ketter, T. A. (2007). Safety and efficacy of anticonvulsants in elderly patients with psychiatric disorders. *Expert Opin Drug Saf, 6*, 133–145.

Steinberg, M., Shao, H., Zandi, P., et al. (2008). Point and 5-year period prevalence of neuropsychiatric symptoms in dementia: The Cache County Study. *International Journal of Geriatric Psychiatry, 23*(2), 170–177.

Street, J. S., Clark, W. S., Gannon, K. S., et al. (2000). Olanzapine treatment of psychotic and behavioral symptoms in patients with Alzheimer disease in nursing care facilities: A double-blind, randomized, placebo-controlled trial. *Arch Gen Psychiatry, 57*, 968–976.

Sukonick, D.L., Pollack, B.G., Sweet, R.A. et al. (2001). The 5-HTTPR*S/*L polymorphism and aggressive behavior in Alzheimer disease. *Arch Neurol, 58*, 1425–1428.

Sultzer, D. L., Mahler, M. E., Mandelkern, M. A., et al. (1995). The relationship between psychiatric symptoms and regional cortical metabolism in Alzheimer's disease. *J Neuropsychiatry Clin Neurosci, 7*, 476–484.

Tariot, P. N., Erb, R., Podgorski, C. A., et al. (1998). Efficacy and tolerability of carbamazepine for agitation and aggression in dementia. *Am J Psychiatry, 155*, 54–61.

Tariot, P. N., Salzman, C., Yeung, P. P., et al. (2000). Long-term use of quetiapine in elderly patients with psychotic disorders. *Clin Ther, 22*, 1068–1084.

Tekin, S., Mega, M. S., Mastermann, D., et al. (2001). Orbitofrontal and anterior cingulate cortex neurofibrillary tangle burden is associated with agitation in Alzheimer disease. *Ann Neurol, 49*, 355–361.

Trifirò, G., Gambassi, G., Sen, E. F., et al. (2010). Association of community-acquired pneumonia with antipsychotic drug use in elderly patients: a nested case-control study. *Ann Intern Med, 152*(7), 418–425.

Tucker, I. (2010), Management of inappropriate sexual behaviors in dementia: A literature review. *Int Psychogeriatrics, 22*(5), 683–692.

Ujkaj, M., Davidoff, D. A., Seiner, S. J., et al. (2012). Safety and efficacy of electroconvulsive therapy for the treatment of agitation and aggression in patients with dementia. *Am J Geriatr Psychiatry, 20*(1), 61–72.

Wang, L. Y., Shofer, J. B., Rohde, K., et al. (2009). Prazosin for the treatment of behavioral symptoms in Alzheimer's disease patients with agitation and aggression. *Am J Ger Psychiatry, 17*, 744–751.

10 Depression, Anxiety, and Apathy

Depression, anxiety, and apathy are some of the most significant psychiatric problems associated with dementia. They are diagnosed both as primary illnesses in individuals with dementia and in association with the states of agitation and psychosis described in Chapter 9. In this chapter, each of these conditions will be reviewed within the context of dementia.

Depression

Although some have argued that it is normal to be depressed in late life, research argues otherwise, finding that not only do older individuals report higher levels of well-being than middle aged adults (Stone, Schwartz, Broderick, & Deaton, 2010), but rates of major depressive disorder (MDD) in the community are lower in late life. In the hospital or outpatient medical setting, however, rates of MDD and less severe minor or subsyndromal depressive states are seen with increased frequency in older individuals (Blazer, Steffens, & Koenig, 2009). In addition, substance abuse, chronic pain, and various forms of dementia are associated with higher rates of depression (Blazer, 2003; Wong et al., 2011). MDD and other states of depression are estimated to affect between 20% and 55% of all individuals with various forms of dementia (van Asch et al., 2013; Zubenko et al., 2003). These rates lie at the higher end of this range in individuals with Parkinson's disease and in those who have had a recent stroke (Lindén, Blomstrand, & Skoog, 2007; Reijnders et al., 2008; Robinson, Starr, Kubos, & Price, 1983).

These relatively high rates reflect the fact that brain damage from all types of dementia creates a vulnerability to depression. In addition, depression itself is a risk factor for Alzheimer's disease (AD), perhaps due to damage to the hippocampus from chronically elevated glucocorticoid levels (Sachs-Ericsson & Blazer, 2011). Finally, depressive symptoms might represent prodromal signs of dementia. The link between depression and dementia might stem from both age-related and dementia-related factors, including neuronal loss to key brain regions involved in mood regulation and serotonergic dysfunction (McKinney & Sibille, 2013). In vascular dementia, depression is more common after damage to left frontal and right parietal regions of the brain (Robinson et al., 1983). In addition, an association between small vessel cerebrovascular disease and depression has led to the suggested diagnosis of *vascular depression*, especially in individuals with an older age at onset, subcortical symptoms, white matter hyperintensities seen on brain scans, and executive dysfunction (Taylor, Aizenstein, & Alexopoulos, 2013).

The role of subcortical vascular damage may contribute to the fact that depression is a core symptom of cerebral autosomal dominant arteriopathy with subcortical infarcts and leukoencephalopathy or CADASIL (Chabriat et al., 2009). Depression has also been associated with many of the medical conditions that afflict individuals with dementia and with numerous medications, including anti-hypertensives, anti-Parkinson's, beta-blockers, corticosteroids, hypoglycemic agents, narcotic analgesics, and sedative-hypnotics. Despite these associations, establishing a clear, causative link between a particular illness or medication and depression is difficult because so many other factors can be present simultaneously.

Definition and Diagnostic Criteria

When the term *depression* is used within the context of dementia, it may refer to MDD or to the atypical or less severe forms of depression often included under the labels "minor depression," "subsyndromal depression," or "depressive disorder, not otherwise specified." Other relevant syndromes involving depressive symptoms include dysthymic disorder, adjustment disorder, depressive personality disorder, bereavement, and bipolar disorder. To diagnose an individual with a major depressive episode according to criteria from either the *Diagnostic and Statistical Manual of Mental Disorders*, Fourth Edition, Text Revision (DSM-IV-TR; American Psychiatric Association, 2000) or the *Diagnostic and Statistical Manual of Mental Disorders*, Fifth Edition (DSM-5; American Psychiatric Association, 2013), an individual must have a sad or depressed mood and/or a significant decrease in interest or pleasure in almost all activities, nearly every day for most of the day, for at least two weeks, as well as four or more of the following features:

- significant change in weight or appetite;
- insomnia or hypersomnia nearly every day;
- psychomotor agitation or retardation;
- fatigue or loss of energy nearly every day;
- feelings of worthlessness or excessive or inappropriate guilt;
- diminished ability to think or concentrate; or
- recurrent thoughts of death or suicidal ideation or suicidal plan or attempt.

As will be noted in the section on assessment, there is significant overlap between symptoms of depression and dementia (e.g., poor concentration is a symptom of both entities), and depression within dementia can look different from the basic criteria of MDD. Because of these factors, researchers have proposed diagnostic entities of both vascular depression (Taylor et al., 2013) and depression of AD (Lyketsos & Olin, 2002). The latter diagnosis includes existing depressive criteria but adds symptoms of irritability and social isolation or withdrawal.

Pseudodementia refers to a syndrome of cognitive deficits that are associated with depression and that improve with treatment. The cognitive impairment is usually mild, involving problems with attention, recall, motor speed, and syntactic complexity. Compared with major depression without cognitive impairment, depression with pseudodementia tends to be more severe. Additionally, it is often recurrent, and it involves more motor retardation, hopelessness, helplessness, and psychosis. Aphasia and apraxia are typically not seen, but a previous history of depression is often present. The increased risk of developing a true dementia in individuals with pseudodementia is impressive—in one study of individuals hospitalized for depression, 43% with pseudodementia later developed irreversible dementia, compared with 12% of those who had depression alone (Alexopoulos et al., 1993).

Manic symptoms can be seen in dementia, ranging in severity from mild hyperactivity and pressured speech to gross impulsivity, disinhibition, agitation, and psychosis. These symptoms can represent either the recurrence of previous bipolar disorder or a new onset secondary to a host of medical conditions or medications. Secondary mania has been reported in association with both AD and vascular dementia, although the exact nature of this connection has yet to be elucidated (Forester, Antognini, & Kim, 2011).

Failure to thrive is characterized by poor appetite and weight loss and is a frequent problem encountered in patients with moderate to severe dementia, especially in those with depression. These problems trigger the following cascade of events: dehydration, malnutrition, decreased renal function, suppressed immune response, worsening medical problems, infection, delayed healing of skin ulcers, and, ultimately, premature death. Failure to thrive may range from mild to severe, and it is more common among institutionalized or hospitalized older individuals, especially after they have sustained a hip fracture. Although depression associated with dementia is often an obvious cause of this deadly syndrome, aggressive antidepressant treatment for these individuals is frequently overlooked because their caregivers and clinicians adopt a fatalistic attitude, believing that a terminal phase of dementia has begun. Several strategies may be helpful to address failure to thrive:

- Evaluate for difficulty chewing, swallowing (dysphagia), or digesting.
- Evaluate for comorbid medical causes of anorexia, including medications.
- Consider empirical treatment for depression with an antidepressant medication.
- Consider treatment for apathy with a stimulating antidepressant or psychostimulant.
- Consider the use mirtazapine or megestrol acetate.

As is indicated in the last recommendation, megestrol acetate 400 to 800 milligrams daily has been found to improve appetite and to cause weight gain in older individuals with physical wasting or cachexia, whether due to dementia, cancer, or AIDS (Yeh, Lovitt, & Schuster, 2009). Nutritional consults are always important in these situations, to help evaluate the cause as well as to make suggestions on oral supplements. Dosing guidelines for antidepressants can be found in the treatment section of this chapter in Table 10.1.

Assessment

The assessment of depressive symptoms usually begins with the following key question: Is this truly depression or merely dementia? Differentiating among dementia, depression, or dementia with depression can be difficult due to symptom overlap since all three entities may involve apathy, agitation, social withdrawal, impaired concentration, cognitive impairment, weight loss, and sleep disturbances. Even more complicated is the presence of pseudodementia, since it must be distinguished from an actual dementia so that the appropriate therapy can be implemented. There are two major steps to identify depression and distinguish it from pseudodementia.

Step 1: re-examine the history to determine whether the current cognitive impairment existed before the depressive symptoms (as in dementia associated with depression) or presented more precipitously after the onset of depressive symptoms (as in pseudodementia). Depressive symptoms can also be associated with the recurrence of other psychiatric disorders, including anxiety disorders, personality disorders, and substance abuse.

Step 2: look for clues in the mental status examination. Depressive symptoms associated with dementia often look different from the typical symptoms seen in younger individuals or in those without dementia. Consider the following areas.

Affect and mood: many individuals with dementia and depression do not always present with overt sadness; instead, they demonstrate uncharacteristic irritability, unreasonableness, or passivity.

Clinical Tip

Verbal reports of affect may be inconsistent in later stages of dementia. For example, some individuals express that they feel sad at one moment, but an hour later, they do not report feeling that way. Some individuals become irritable on and off because of a temporary annoyance, but they then return to their baseline after hours or days. Although truly depressive symptoms may also fluctuate, over time, they continue to manifest with a clearly negative impact on daily function and care.

Response style and attitude: individuals with dementia alone often attempt to answer questions and may confabulate when they do not know an answer. Severely depressed individuals (including those with pseudodementia) make poor attempts at even providing answers.

Thought content: depressive symptoms may include any of the following: preoccupation with somatic symptoms or pain despite treatment with analgesics; excessive thoughts and comments about deceased relatives, personal losses, or death; and somatic delusions.

Behaviors: the presence of agitation or physical aggression should always prompt a search for underlying depression. The clinician should also look for isolative behaviors (e.g., staying in his or her room all day, refusing social contacts); noncompliance with caregiving; slow progress in rehabilitation; failure to thrive; and indirect life-threatening behaviors, such as refusing to eat or refusing critical medications or procedures.

Clinical Vignette

Mrs. V, an 82-year-old woman with moderate to severe vascular dementia and aphasia, lived in a long-term care facility. She was wheelchair-bound, nearly nonverbal, and totally dependent on the staff for care. She had a feeding tube due to poor swallowing. Staff members asked for a psychiatric evaluation after they noticed that she had stopped smiling at them during bathing and that she had begun to have episodes of crying. At times, they heard her moaning in her room for no apparent reason. Mrs. V was unable to communicate her feelings, and her cognitive impairment prevented her from even fully understanding them. A clinical interview could yield little information because she was nonverbal. However, changes in behavior and episodes of crying suggested underlying depression. The proof came when these episodes ceased following the use of antidepressant medication.

Clinical Tip

Individuals with sudden and frequent fits of crying or laughter may have underlying brain damage that has disrupted their control of emotional expression. This condition has several names, including pseudobulbar affect (PBA) and emotional incontinence, and is commonly seen in individuals with dementia, stroke, multiple sclerosis, amyotrophic lateral sclerosis, and other neurodegenerative conditions. Although many affected individuals are mislabeled as depressed, the paroxysmal nature of these crying attacks, sometimes in response to being startled, along with the frequent absence of other depressive symptoms should point toward PBA.

Suicidality

The potential for suicidality in depression associated with dementia must be one of the most serious concerns for all clinicians. Older white men, especially those 80 years and older, represent the group at highest risk of suicide in the United States, with rates that are four to five times greater than those for younger individuals (American Association of Suicidality, 2010). Older men commit 80% of all suicides in individuals older than 65 years of age, with firearms being the most common method. Depression represents the most significant cause of suicide in this group, but other important risk factors for suicidality in late life include previous suicide attempts, a family history of suicide, depression, substance abuse, widowhood, physical illness, pain, and disability (Duberstein, Heisel, & Conwell, 2011).

Suicide risk should be of particular concern with individuals who are newly diagnosed with dementia and who have some insight into the diagnosis. The risk of suicide decreases in individuals with more severe dementia who lack the cognitive or physical ability to carry out a suicide plan and in residents of long-term care facilities. However, such individuals may instead demonstrate indirect life-threatening behaviors, such as refusing food, water, medications, or critical medical tests or treatments.

Regardless of the stage of dementia, the occurrence of suicidal threats, gestures, attempts, or indirect life-threatening behaviors should prompt immediate clinical assessment, suicide precautions, and the aggressive treatment of depression. Suicide precautions include the removal of sharp or other potentially dangerous objects, safekeeping of medications, and 24-hour monitoring, until a clinician has indicated that the risk has abated. Severe situations should always prompt immediate assessment, followed by hospitalization in a secure psychiatric facility.

Assessment Tools

Although the differential diagnosis for depression and dementia relies mostly on the mental status examination, several assessment tools can be useful. On the one hand, neuropsychological tests will often show similar deficits in dementia and depression, although with more pronounced findings in dementia (Sachs-Ericsson & Blazer, 2011). Structural brain scans are not particularly useful for distinguishing AD from late-life depression because both may involve similar findings, such as diffuse atrophy, ventricular enlargement, and leukoariosis. However, AD patients with depression have been found to have a greater volume of right parietal white matter changes (Starkstein et al., 2009). Positron emission tomography scans may demonstrate increased cerebral glucose metabolism in frontal and parietal hemispheres in depression, while parietal lobe hypometabolism is observed in AD (Gunning & Smith, 2011; Smith, Kramer, & Hermann, 2009.

The Geriatric Depression Scale is a 15- or 30-item self-report instrument that can be helpful in early stages of disease when the individual is still a relatively reliable historian (Marc, Raue, & Bruce, 2008). In the moderate to severe stages of dementia, however, the Cornell Scale for Depression in Dementia is more practical because it is based on the clinical interview plus observation and caregiver input (Kørner et al., 2006).

Treatment

Several unique challenges are encountered when one is treating depression associated with dementia. The degree of cognitive impairment poses an immediate limitation to the efficacy of various forms of psychotherapy. Insight-oriented therapy becomes impossible if an individual cannot retain insights from one appointment to the next (Agronin, 2010). Progressive aphasia makes communication with the therapist increasingly difficult. Even overlearned coping skills can be compromised by impairment in executive function. As a result, the psychological skills that are required for talk therapy to overcome depression fade away over time. However, adapting cognitive and/or behavioral techniques to benefit individuals with mild to moderate dementia are possible. In addition, improving the problem-solving skills of their caregivers may benefit depressed individuals with dementia. Some other beneficial forms of psychotherapy are supportive individual and group therapy, structured activities, recreational therapy, music therapy, and increased caregiver support.

Clinical Vignette

Mr. J, a 78-year-old man with dementia who lived in a nursing home, suffered from chronic loneliness that evolved into a depressive state that was characterized by episodes of crying, loss of appetite, and social isolation. His poor memory made remembering his weekly meetings with the social worker impossible. Knowing that he loved jazz and used to play in a small band, the staff arranged for him to meet with the music therapist. Although he could not remember the therapist between sessions, he clearly responded to the music and the opportunity to play several percussion instruments. His family also made arrangements to visit him more often. Mr. J improved moderately over the course of several weeks.

Such therapeutic approaches have variable results, but they should always be incorporated into the treatment. Patients with severe dementia live in the present, and they do not retain memories or new skills from activity to activity. Instead, therapy provides comfort and support, as well as social, physical, and sensory stimulation to gratify their basic needs and to tap into long-held interests and personality strengths.

Antidepressant Therapy

When depressive symptoms do not respond adequately to nonpharmacologic approaches or when the symptoms are severe and potentially life-threatening, antidepressant medications are needed. The same medications used in younger individuals and in those without dementia are used to treat patients with dementia, with the same adage as with all elderly patients: start low, go slow, but go. As with all geriatric patients, it may take several weeks to titrate to a therapeutic dose and six to eight weeks to achieve a full therapeutic response. In addition, different medications may bring very different results, in terms of both efficacy and side effects. It is critical for caregivers and physicians to identify these side effects early in the course of treatment because they can decrease compliance and can even worsen the cognitive impairment. Dosing strategies for each type of recommended antidepressant are listed in Table 10.1.

Overall, there is empirical evidence to support the efficacy of a range of antidepressant strategies for older patients, although a limited number of studies have looked specifically at patients with dementia. A meta-analysis by Nelson and colleagues of older depressed individuals (without dementia) age 60 and higher in the community found remission rates that were generally similar across all antidepressant categories, with a slight advantage for the serotonin-norepinephrine reuptake inhibitors such as venlafaxine and mirtazapine (Nelson, Delucchi, & Schneider, 2008).

Antidepressants that have demonstrated some degree of efficacy in treating depression associated with AD include sertraline (Banerjee, Hellier, & Dewey, 2011; Lyketsos et al., 2000; Rosenberg et al., 2010), imipramine (Reifler et al., 1989), clomipramine (Petracca et al., 1996), fluoxetine (Petracca, Chemerinski, & Starkstein, 2001), and mirtazapine (Banerjee et al., 2011). Sertraline was studied in individuals with vascular depression and resulted in a remission rate of 33% (Sheline, Pieper, & Barch, 2010). A

Table 10.1 Dosing for Recommended Antidepressants in Dementia

Antidepressant	Starting Dose	Range
SSRIs		
Fluoxetine	5–10 mg/day	5–40 mg/day
Sertraline	25–50 mg/day	25–200 mg/day
Paroxetine	5–10 mg/day 12.5 mg/day (controlled release)	10–40 mg/day 12.5–50 mg/day (controlled release)
Citalopram	5–10 mg/day	10–40 mg/day
Escitalopram	5 mg/day	5–20 mg/day
SNRIs		
Mirtazapine	7.5–15 mg/day	7.5–45 mg/day
Venlafaxine	25 mg twice daily 37.5 mg/day (extended release)	50–225 mg/day 37.5–225 mg/day
Other Antidepressants		
Bupropion	37.5–50 mg twice daily 100 mg (sustained release) 150 mg (extended release)	100–300 mg/day
Duloxetine	20 mg/day	20–60 mg/day
Vilazodone	10 mg/day	10–40 mg/day
Tricyclics	See restrictions in text	
Nortriptyline	10–25 mg/day	50–150 mg/day Blood level: 50–150 ng/ml
Desipramine	10–25 mg/day	50–200 mg/day Blood levels: 115–200 ng/ml

SSRIs = selective serotonin reuptake inhibitors; SNRIs = serotonin norepinephrine reuptake inhibitors.

meta-analysis by Nelson and Devanand (2011), however, looked at response rates across seven double-blind placebo-controlled studies of antidepressant treatment for depression and dementia and found that the data suggested but did not confirm efficacy. Keep in mind, then, that all of these research findings do not support one antidepressant over another, as there are so many potential variables that would support or contraindicate specific agents for each individual older patient.

Common wisdom has held that older patients tend to respond slower and with less robustness to antidepressants compared to younger patients. These beliefs are not supported, however, by research by Sackeim, Roose, and Lavori (2006), who found no significant difference in rates of response, remission, and time to remission between young and old cohorts of depressed individuals treated with antidepressants. Rates of response increase with study length, and specific rates of antidepressant response in older adults may vary by the study site (Roose et al., 2004) and whether or not the medication is being compared to an active control or placebo, with active comparator trials generally eliciting greater overall response (Sneed et al., 2008). Older individuals with vascular damage and executive dysfunction, however, do not respond as well to antidepressant therapy and have shorter times to relapse (Alexopoulos et al., 2000; Alexopoulos et al., 2004; Kalayam & Alexopoulos, 1999).

Specific Antidepressants

The selective serotonin reuptake inhibitors (SSRIs) are considered first-line agents for treating depression associated with dementia and include fluoxetine, sertraline, paroxetine, citalopram, and escitalopram. As their name indicates, SSRIs work by blocking the reuptake of serotonin. They are the most widely used antidepressants in geriatric populations. No SSRI has been demonstrated to have an efficacy that is superior to that of another for treating depression associated with dementia. SSRIs are typically dosed once daily in the morning because of their stimulating effects. Common side effects of all SSRIs include insomnia, anorexia, weight loss, diarrhea, and agitation, and some individuals experience sedation and weight gain.

Both venlafaxine and mirtazapine stimulate serotonin and norepinephrine activity. Mirtazapine also has antagonistic properties at the $5\text{-}HT_{2A}$, $5\text{-}HT_{2C}$, and $5\text{-}HT_3$ serotonin receptors, allowing it to enhance serotonergic function while potentially avoiding the common SSRI side effects of anxiety, irritability, sexual dysfunction, nausea, and vomiting. Because of its selective profile, mirtazapine is often used to target symptoms of insomnia, poor appetite, and weight loss associated with depression. Mirtazapine is also used to augment other antidepressants, particularly the SSRIs and venlafaxine, and sometimes to reverse the common SSRI side effects previously mentioned. Mirtazapine tends to be well-tolerated, with common side effects of sedation and weight gain. Mirtazapine also comes in an orally dissolving tablet.

Venlafaxine's main side effects include sedation, headache, nausea, insomnia, and increased blood pressure. The patient's blood pressure should be monitored daily for a week after both the initiation of treatment and each dose increase. Although the typical increase in blood pressure is usually small (5–10 mm Hg on average) and may be partially mitigated by the extended release formula, it can be higher in some individuals; therefore, it should be closely tracked in individuals with underlying hypertension. Venlafaxine is often used to augment mirtazapine and bupropion.

Bupropion is believed to enhance both noradrenergic and dopaminergic transmission, although the exact mechanism is not known. Given its dopaminergic properties, bupropion often has stimulating effects that are useful for treating apathy and depressive states associated with fatigue. However, this stimulating effect may also precipitate anxiety and agitation in patients with dementia. Common side effects include agitation, insomnia, and muscle weakness, especially in the legs. A small increase in the risk of seizures has been reported and may be especially relevant if the patient has a history of seizures or a potential seizure focus, such as that due to a stroke. To avoid increasing this risk, single doses of immediate release bupropion should be limited to no more than 150 milligrams.

Duloxetine is a dual serotonin and norepinephrine reuptake inhibitor. It has an indication for treating both major depression and pain associated with diabetic peripheral neuropathy. The most common side effects include nausea, dry mouth, constipation, decreased appetite, fatigue, sedation, and increased sweating.

Tricyclic antidepressants (TCAs) were once the mainstay of antidepressant treatment. Today, however, their use has decreased dramatically in the elderly because other, newer medication choices have equal efficacy with increased safety and better side effect profiles. The current Omnibus Budget Reconciliation Act of 1987 guidelines for long-term care and the Beers Criteria discourage use of the TCAs because of their common side effect profile, including the following: orthostatic hypotension, sedation, strong anticholinergic effects, and slowed cardiac conduction. Neurologists sometimes use TCAs in low doses to treat neuropathic pain and migraine headaches, but, even at low doses, they can cause sedation, anticholinergic effects, and confusion. TCA use in the elderly with dementia is commonly restricted to nortriptyline and desipramine because of their lower risk of problematic side effects compared with the other TCAs. However, they are not recommended for older patients with dementia primarily due to their anticholinergic effects.

Although the monoamine oxidase inhibitors (MAOIs) are excellent antidepressants, they are infrequently used in the elderly because of their potential to cause debilitating side effects and life-threatening drug–drug and drug–food interactions. Given the medical complexity of MAOIs and the use of multiple medications in the typical patient with dementia, the use of MAOIs is not recommended.

Psychostimulants are sometimes used alone or to augment antidepressants for older individuals with depression, narcolepsy, low energy, medication-induced fatigue, failure to thrive, and apathy. They consist of forms of amphetamine, and they work by increasing dopaminergic function. The most commonly prescribed stimulant in the elderly is methylphenidate. The literature on stimulant use in dementia has been variable, but several studies have found that methylphenidate is beneficial in treating depressive symptoms in older, medically ill patients (Hardy, 2009). Although stimulants were once a popular treatment for these individuals, they have largely been replaced by the SSRIs and bupropion because these latter medications show proven efficacy in the treatment of depression, stimulating properties, and relative safety.

Methylphenidate has a rapid onset of action, short half-life, and a brief duration of action. For example, onset of action is observed within one hour of administration, and its effects last three to six hours. In the elderly, dosing is begun at 2.5 to 5 milligrams in the morning. Look for a positive effect in two to four hours, and titrate to 5 to 10 milligrams at morning and noon. Doses given later in the day can lead to insomnia. Pulse and blood pressure should be monitored during the first week of titration, although changes are usually minimal. Aside from immediate release methylphenidate, there are several controlled-release methylphenidate and amphetamine preparations that provide stimulant action throughout an entire day, but these are only indicated for individuals with attention deficit hyperactivity disorder (ADHD) and have not been studied in individuals with late-life depression or in individuals with dementia. Similarly, neither the noradrenergic agent atomoxetine (an FDA-approved treatment for ADHD) nor the stimulants modafinil and its R-enantiomer armodafinil (FDA-approved medications to treat narcolepsy, shift work sleep disorder, and excessive daytime sleepiness associated with obstructive sleep apnea) have been studied in individuals with late-life depression or dementia.

The potential side effects of psychostimulants include insomnia, anxiety, irritability, anorexia, weight loss, dizziness, headache, and increased heart rate and blood pressure.

Less common, but important, side effects are agitation and psychosis. Stimulants may increase the serum levels of warfarin, anticonvulsants, and TCAs and may potentiate the effects of some narcotics. Although, historically, amphetamines have been drugs of abuse, the potential for physical dependence is extremely low with geriatric dosing.

Treatment Resistance

If an individual has responded partially or not at all after a first-line agent has been started and its dose has been maximized and continued for a 6- to 8-week trial, several strategies may be considered. First, the clinician should reevaluate the diagnosis (e.g., is this actually apathy instead of depression?) and look for untreated comorbid medical and psychiatric conditions, such as pain, medication side effects, and substance abuse. The environment should also be reevaluated: Is there ongoing stress, abuse, neglect, or lack of structure that is perpetuating the depressive symptoms? Also, the clinician and caregivers should consider whether a move to a more structured setting is warranted. Consider adding some form of therapeutic activity if not done already, ranging from individual or group psychotherapy (in early stages of dementia) to therapeutic activities, as outlined earlier in this chapter.

In terms of pharmacologic approaches to treatment resistance, the first strategy is to switch to another antidepressant, either in the same class (e.g., from one SSRI to another) or in an entirely different class (e.g., SSRI to SNRI such as mirtazapine or venlafaxine). Next, augmenting the antidepressant with another agent should be considered. Frequent combinations include SSRIs plus mirtazapine, venlafaxine, or bupropion; mirtazapine plus venlafaxine; or an SSRI plus an atypical antipsychotic or mood stabilizer. Older strategies, such as adding lithium, beta-blockers, TCAs, or thyroid hormone to an existing antidepressant, can be considered, but the risk of side effects must be weighed carefully. For medication-resistant symptoms, life-threatening depressive symptoms (especially with severe psychosis), or intractable mania, the treatment of choice is electroconvulsive therapy, regardless of age.

Anxiety

Anxiety disorders are actually more common than mood disorders in late life, affecting an estimated 8% of elders in the community, with specific phobias being the most common anxiety disorder (Byers, Yaffe, & Covinsky, 2010). Other anxiety disorders include generalized anxiety disorder, panic disorder, social phobia, obsessive-compulsive disorder, and post-traumatic stress disorder (PTSD). Anxiety symptoms in dementia are often difficult to identify because they frequently coexist with states of depression, agitation, or psychosis, and may involve primary and longstanding anxiety disorders or symptom clusters. These symptoms may involve classic symptoms of subjective worry and tension and physiologic signs of muscle tension, hypervigilance, sweating, hyperventilation, and gastrointestinal discomfort. In individuals with dementia who are unable to process and/or express their anxiety, however, signs of anxiety or even panic may include restlessness, hyperactivity, pained facial expressions, irritability, insomnia, physical resistance or aggression, repetitive behaviors or mannerisms, moaning, yelling, or screaming. Anxiety symptoms are often more common in earlier stages of dementia and may be particularly frequent in the presence of cerebrovascular disease due to more pronounced frontal deficits (Porter et al., 2003). Managing patients with anxiety (as well with comorbid depression and agitation) can be extremely challenging, especially since they tend to become less sociable and more dependent (Bartels et al., 2003; Porter et al., 2003).

In terms of assessment, a good clinical history should ask about previous anxiety disorders and not merely symptoms. Knowing that an individual had a history of chronic, generalized anxiety, panic attacks, phobias, obsessive thoughts, compulsive behaviors and rituals, or PTSD (e.g., a war survivor) will enable the clinician to both anticipate symptoms as well as look for dementia-related permutations of anxiety. Consider the following case.

Clinical Vignette

Mr. M was a 65-year-old man with vascular dementia who was admitted to a nursing home after he suffered another stroke and was left with right-sided hemiparesis and expressive aphasia. Staff reported that every morning he would begin screaming and thrashing in his room around the same time. He began pushing chairs and other objects in his room against the door, trying to barricade himself in. When the social worker spoke to Mr. M's sister, she learned that he was a highly decorated combat veteran from the Vietnam War and had struggled with PTSD symptoms for years. With this in mind, staff took a closer look at the timing and context of Mr. M's agitation and noticed that it appeared to be triggered by the banging noises during the morning from the kitchen that was nearby his room. The noises were evidently causing either flashbacks or panic symptoms in Mr. M that he could not express but that he acted out through his screaming and attempts to barricade himself in his room. Mr. M was moved to a quieter room at the other end of the unit where he could not hear the banging noises in the morning. His agitation improved, but he remained hypervigilant and would rapidly startle at noises on the unit. An antidepressant was added, which helped to reduce these PTSD symptoms.

In the case of Mr. M, knowing that he had PTSD was critical to understanding his symptoms and providing some relief. It is also important to look for recent or ongoing stresses that may be reactivating anxiety or panic. Rule out any medical conditions (e.g., hyperthyroidism, sensory impairment), symptoms (e.g., pain, shortness of breath), or medications (e.g., psychostimulants, caffeine, corticosteroids, thyroid hormone, bronchodilators, dopaminergic agents) that may be increasing anxiety.

The most effective treatment for anxiety disorders will use the same antidepressants described in the preceding section and detailed in Table 10.1. In addition, many individuals will need occasional symptomatic relief or augmentation with anxiolytic medications such as the benzodiazepines. Dosing guidelines for the recommended agents can be found in Chapter 9 in Table 9.4. Individual counseling or therapy can also be helpful in early stages of dementia if the individual can retain insights or strategies from one session to another. Otherwise, routine use of relaxation techniques that the individual is guided through (e.g. deep breathing relaxation) can help in the moment to relieve anxiety.

Sleep Disorders

Common sleep disorders in late life include sleep apnea, restless legs syndrome, circadian rhythm disorder, periodic limb movement disorder, and rapid eye movement (REM) behavior disorder (Endeshaw & Bliwise, 2011). Unfortunately, these conditions are often overlooked, despite the fact that they can result in significant morbidity and mortality. Sleep disturbances are particularly common in dementia, in which they sometimes manifest as a core symptom of depression or anxiety. In the latter situations, the symptoms typically include difficulty falling asleep and frequent middle of the night or early morning awakenings. As an individual's depression or anxiety improves, his or her sleep should improve as well, unless the underlying problem is due more to the dementia or to a primary sleep disorder. Sleep disturbances can also result from medications; for instance, insomnia can result from dopaminergic agents and many antidepressants, and nightmares can result from acetylcholinesterase inhibitors. Unfortunately, these disturbances are not always readily diagnosed in individuals with dementia, given the challenges of obtaining a description from the individual or caregiver or a formal sleep study (including overnight polysomnography), especially when the individual has a history of agitation. Sometimes, a physician can make a diagnosis based on the observations of a caregiver or nurse.

The first step in treatment is to improve sleep hygiene in order to facilitate the normal neurophysiologic process of sleep. Sleep hygiene involves both the sleep environment and sleep habits. Several strategies are listed in Table 10.2. These strategies are straightforward, they have no side effects, and they often improve sleep without further intervention.

Table 10.2 Strategies for Improving Sleep Hygiene in Dementia

- Avoid stimulants in the afternoon or evening (e.g., coffee, tea, or other substances with caffeine; stimulating antidepressants; dopaminergic agents)
- Avoid the use of nicotine and alcohol before sleep
- Avoid heavy meals or snacks before bedtime
- Maintain a consistent, relaxing evening and bedtime routine
- Minimize excess lighting and noise during evening and nighttime hours
- Avoid waking the patient to dispense medications
- Use bed for sleep only; avoid activities in bed, such as reading and watching television
- Minimize daytime napping
- Maximize daytime exposure to sunlight
- Provide adequate daytime activity, including physical exercise
- Promote bladder emptying before bedtime and bladder control during sleep
- Avoid excess use of diuretics, especially before bedtime

Table 10.3 Dosing for Recommended Hypnotics in Dementia

Agent	Starting Dose	Range
Zolpidem	5 mg 6.25 mg (controlled release)	5–10 mg 6.25–12.5 mg (controlled release)*
Zaleplon	5 mg	5–10 mg
Eszopiclone	1 mg	1–3 mg
Trazodone	25–50 mg	25–200 mg
Temazepam	7.5 mg	7.5–30 mg
Ramelteon	4 mg	4–8 mg
Melatonin	1 mg	1–6 mg
Mirtazapine	7.5 mg	7.5–45 mg

* The FDA recommends zolpidem dosing to be limited to 5 mg (or 6.25 controlled release), especially for women, due to hangover effects in the morning. For individuals with early stage dementia who are still driving, these limits should be strictly enforced.

In addition to the focus on sleep hygiene, medications are often needed to restore adequate sleep. Within the setting of depression, a sedating antidepressant such as mirtazapine may be sufficient. The clinician should bear in mind, however, that other antidepressants, particularly the SSRIs, can sometimes cause insomnia. Otherwise, the mainstay of treating dementia-associated sleep disturbances involves the use of a sedative-hypnotic agent. Keep in mind that individuals with dementia can sometimes suffer from excess sedation, confusion, falls, and unexpected or even paradoxical reactions to several of these agents, especially in the presence of dementia with Lewy bodies. With all of these agents, the lowest possible dose should be used, with frequent attempts at dose reduction and discontinuation.

It is generally wise to avoid use of both short-acting benzodiazepines such as triazolam and alprazolam due to their potential for paradoxical effects. Diphenhydramine should also be avoided in light of its problematic anticholinergic and antihistaminic side effects, including excess sedation, dizziness, and confusion. A safer over-the-counter agent is melatonin, which has shown efficacy and minimal side effects in treating insomnia in elderly subjects (Wade, Ford, & Crawford, 2007). There is also the melatonin-receptor agonist ramelteon, which can take several weeks to have a full effect. Low dose doxepin is also being marketed as a sleeping pill, although there is a risk for anticholinergic effects since it is a TCA. Recommended dosing for all of these agents appears in Table 10.3.

Clinical Tip

Sleeping pills are some of the most frequently prescribed medications in the elderly, and they are often taken in excessive doses, for excessive periods, and without proper indication. The clinician must not forget to emphasize sleep hygiene and sleep studies, especially for individuals with resistant symptoms. Daytime function should be examined to gauge the true impact of a sleep disturbance. A patient who complains about insomnia but who is functioning well during the day without excess sedation may actually be receiving adequate sleep. When a sleeping pill is needed for longer than 10–14 days, as well as for individuals with chronic insomnia who have taken a particular agent for months or even years, the physician should reevaluate its use periodically and consider regular attempts at tapering the dose.

Apathy

Apathy is a syndrome characterized by diminished goal-directed activity due to a lack of motivation. In contrast, depression is a disorder of mood, not just motivation. The presence of apathy does not imply an underlying diagnosis of depression, although the two can occur together. Apathy is actually the most common behavioral problem in dementia, as it is seen in 20% to nearly 40% of individuals with AD and other forms of dementia (Hölttä, Laakkonen, & Laurila, 2012; Vilalta-Franch, Calvó-Perxas, & Garre-Olmo, 2013). It is of great importance to caregivers and clinicians because it interferes with patient care, limits patient participation in social and therapeutic activities, and even appears to increase rates of mortality (Hölttä et al., 2012). Apathy is particularly common in Parkinson's disease, affecting approximately 30% of individuals (Starkstein, 2012).

Apathy can result from strokes or other damage to one or more areas of the brain, including the frontal cortex (especially the dorsolateral regions), thalamus, striatum, and amygdala. Direct damage to the frontal lobes or to subcortical nuclei that have white matter connections to the frontal lobes is perhaps the most common setting in which apathy is seen (Orr, 2011). Apathy can also result from functional impairment to any of these brain structures, such as that seen in psychiatric disease or as a result of medications or metabolic disturbances. Two of the more common pharmacologic causes are beta-blockers and antipsychotics.

Apathy and depression can seem clinically indistinguishable. Many caregivers complain that their loved one is stubborn or perhaps even depressed because the patient has no interests or motivation, because he or she does not start conversations or answer questions with much detail, or because he or she is less sociable and is unwilling to participate in activities. The caregivers can become overly frustrated and angry with the affected person, causing them to constantly complain and nag. The caregivers do not realize, however, that, when apathy is the cause, no amount of cajoling will motivate the affected person.

Several clinical keys can help to determine whether an individual is depressed or merely apathetic. When the clinician is evaluating a person's recent psychiatric history, he or she should look for some of the following symptoms, which are common with depression but rare with apathy: suicidal ideation, somatic complaints, anxious or depressive ruminations, and hallucinations or delusions. Affect also can differentiate the two states: in depression, affect may appear as overtly sad or depressed, weepy, labile, irritable, angry, or anxious; in apathy, affect tends to be placid or neutral, flat, and blunted. During the mental status examination, depressed individuals with dementia may become upset, impatient, or irritable with the questioning, sometimes refusing to answer. Individuals with apathy, conversely, often sit and stare contentedly during the mental status examination, demonstrating minimal spontaneous speech or motor movements. Responses to questions often consist only of one or two words, and even persistent questioning will not evoke more detail. The apathetic individual rarely confabulates because motivation is required for that.

Treatment of a reversible cause of apathy often results in clinical improvement. Apathy due to the specific brain damage associated with dementia is more difficult to treat, since it responds poorly to environmental, behavioral, or psychotherapeutic intervention. The individual simply does not have enough motivation to engage in such therapy. Instead, psychopharmacologic treatment must often be used to attempt some improvement. Stimulating antidepressants, such as bupropion or the SSRIs, are usually the treatment of choice, particularly bupropion because of its dopaminergic properties. In addition, the psychostimulant methylphenidate (in doses between 5 mg and 20 mg daily) has been shown to increase motivation and activity levels in individuals with apathy associated with AD (Padala et al., 2010), stroke (Spiegel et al., 2009), and Parkinson's disease (Chatterjee & Fahn, 2002).

Like methylphenidate, modafinil (in doses between 100 mg to 400 mg daily) has been studied in apathy, showing some benefit in case studies with elderly individuals (Camargos & Quintas, 2011; Padala, Burke, & Bhatia, 2007) but no clear efficacy in a double-blind placebo-controlled trial of individuals with apathy associated with AD (Frakey, Salloway, & Buelow, 2012). Acetylcholinesterase inhibitors and memantine (in therapeutic dosing ranges; see, in Chapter 4, Table 4.5) alone and in combination have also been shown in clinical trials to improve symptoms of apathy (Berman, Brodaty, Withall, & Seeher, 2012; Gauthier et al., 2010; Waldemar, Gauthier, & Jones, 2011). Dopaminergic agents, including bromocriptine, amantadine, and pergolide are used infrequently because of the lack of convincing evidence of their efficacy and their multiple potential side effects (e.g., hypotension, dry mouth, nausea and vomiting, sleep disruptions, psychosis).

References

Agronin, M. E. (2010). *Therapy with older clients: Key strategies for success.* New York: W. W. Norton.

Alexopoulos, G. S., Kiosses, D. N., Murphy, C., & Moonseong, H. (2004). Executive function, heart disease burden, and remission of geriatric depression. *Neuropsychopharmacology, 29*(12), 2278–2284.

Alexopoulos, G. S., Meyers, B. S., Young, R. C., et al. (1993). The course of geriatric depression with "reversible dementia": A controlled study. *Am J Psychiatry, 150*(11), 1693–1699.

Alexopoulos, G. S., Meyers, B. S., Young, R. C., et al. (2000). Executive dysfunction and long-term outcomes of geriatric depression. *Arch Gen Psychiatry, 57*(3), 285–290.

American Association of Suicidology. (2010). *Elderly suicide fact sheet.* Retrieved from www.suicidology.org/c/document_library/get_file?folderId=262&name=DLFE-624.pdf

American Psychiatric Association. (2000). *Diagnostic and statistical manual of mental disorders* (4th ed., Text Rev.). Washington, DC: Author.

American Psychiatric Association. (2013). *Diagnostic and statistical manual of mental disorders* (5th ed.). Washington, DC: Author.

Banerjee, S., Hellier, J., & Dewey, M. (2011). Sertraline or mirtazapine for depression in dementia (HTA-SADD): A randomised, multicentre, double-blind, placebo-controlled trial. *Lancet, 378*(9789), 403–411.

Bartels, S. J., Horn, S. D., Smout, R. J., et al. (2003). Agitation and depression in frail nursing home elderly patients with dementia: Treatment characteristics and service use. *Am J Ger Psychiatry, 11*(2), 231–238.

Berman, K., Brodaty, H., Withall, A., & Seeher, K. (2012). Pharmacologic treatment of apathy in dementia. *Am J Geriatr Psychiatry, 20*(2), 104–122.

Blazer, D. G. (2003). Depression in late life: Review and commentary. *J Gerontol, 58A*(3), 249–265.

Blazer, D. G., Steffens, D. C., & Koenig, H. G. (2009). Mood disorders. In D. G. Blazer & D. C. Steffens (Eds.), *Textbook of geriatric psychiatry* (4th ed., pp. 275–299). Washington, DC: American Psychiatric Publishing.

Byers, A. L., Yaffe, K., & Covinsky, K. E. (2010). High occurrence of mood and anxiety disorders among older adults: The national comorbidity survey replication. *Arch Gen Psychiatry, 67*(5), 489–496.

Camargos, E. F., & Quintas, J. L. (2011). Apathy syndrome treated successfully with modafinil. *BMJ Case Rep,* ii: bcr0820114652.

Chabriat, H., Joutel, A., Dichgans, M., et al. (2009). Cadasil. *Lancet Neurol, 8*(7), 643–653.

Chatterjee, A., & Fahn, S. (2002). Methylphenidate treats apathy in Parkinson's disease. *J Neuropsychiatry Clin Neurosci, 14*(4), 461–462.

Duberstein, P. R., Heisel, M. J., & Conwell, Y. (2011). Suicide in older adults. In M. E. Agronin & G. J. Maletta (Eds.), *Principles and practice of geriatric psychiatry* (2nd ed., pp. 451–463). Philadelphia: Lippincott, Williams and Wilkins.

Endeshaw, Y., & Bliwise, D. L. (2011). Sleep disorders in the elderly. In M. E. Agronin & G. J. Maletta (Eds.), *Principles and practice of geriatric psychiatry* (2nd ed., pp. 583–601). Philadelphia: Lippincott, Williams and Wilkins.

Forester, B., Antognini, F. C., & Kim, S. (2011). Geriatric bipolar disorder. In M. E. Agronin & G. J. Maletta (Eds.), *Principles and practice of geriatric psychiatry* (2nd ed., pp. 423–449). Philadelphia: Lippincott, Williams and Wilkins.

Frakey, L. L., Salloway, S., & Buelow, M. (2012). A randomized, double-blind, placebo-controlled trial of modafinil for the treatment of apathy in individuals with mild-to-moderate Alzheimer's disease. *J Clin Psychiatry, 73*(6), 796–801.

Gauthier, S., Juby, A., Dalziel, W., et al., & the EXPLORE Investigators. (2010). Effects of rivastigmine on common symptomatology of Alzheimer's disease (EXPLORE). *Curr Med Res Opin, 26*(5), 1149–1160.

Gunning, F. M., & Smith, G. S. (2011). Functional neuroimaging in geriatric depression. *Psychiatr Clin North Am, 34*(2), 403–422, viii.

Hardy, S. E. (2009). Methylphenidate for the treatment of depressive symptoms, including fatigue and apathy, in medically ill older adults and terminally ill adults. *Am J Geriatr Pharmacother, 7*(1), 34–59.

Hölttä, E. H., Laakkonen, M. L., & Laurila, J. V. (2012). Apathy: Prevalence, associated factors, and prognostic value among frail, older inpatients. *J Am Med Dir Assoc, 13*(6), 541–545.

Kalayam, B., & Alexopoulos, G. S. (1999). Prefrontal dysfunction and treatment response in geriatric depression. *Arch Gen Psychiatry, 56*(8), 713–718.

Kørner, A., Lauritzen, L., Abelskov, K., et al. (2006). The Geriatric Depression Scale and the Cornell Scale for Depression in Dementia: A validity study. *Nord J Psychiatry, 60*(5), 360–364.

Lindén, T., Blomstrand, C., & Skoog, I. (2007). Depressive disorders after 20 months in elderly stroke patients: A case-control study. *Stroke, 38*(6), 1860–1863.

Lyketsos, C. G., & Olin, J. (2002). Depression in Alzheimer's disease: Overview and treatment. *Biol Psychiatry, 52*(3), 243–252.

Lyketsos, C. G., Sheppard, J. M., Steele, C. D., et al. (2000). Randomized, placebo-controlled, double-blind clinical trial of sertraline in the treatment of depression complicating Alzheimer's disease: Initial results from the Depression in Alzheimer's Disease study. *Am J Psychiatry, 157*(10), 1686–1689.

Marc, L. G., Raue, P. J., & Bruce, M. L. (2008). Screening performance of the 15-item geriatric depression scale in a diverse elderly home care population. *Am J Geriatr Psychiatry, 16*(11), 914–921.

McKinney, B. C., & Sibille, E. (2013). The age-by-disease interaction hypothesis of late-life depression. *Am J Geriatr Psychiatry, 21*(5), 418–432.

Nelson, J. C., Delucchi, K., & Schneider, L. S. (2008). Efficacy of second generation antidepressants in late-life depression: A meta-analysis of the evidence. *Am J Ger Psychiatry, 16*(7), 558–567.

Nelson, J. C., & Devanand, D. P. (2011). A systematic review and meta-analysis of placebo-controlled antidepressant studies in people with depression and dementia. *J Am Ger Soc, 59*(4), 577–585.

Orr, W. B. (2011). Executive dysfunction in the elderly: From apathy to agitation. In M. E. Agronin & G. J. Maletta (Eds.), *Principles and practice of geriatric psychiatry* (2nd ed., pp. 659–673). Philadelphia: Lippincott, Williams and Wilkins.

Padala, P. R., Burke, W. J., & Bhatia, S. C. (2007). Modafinil therapy for apathy in an elderly patient. *Ann Pharmacother, 41*(2), 346–349.

Padala, P. R., Burke, W. J., Shostrom, V. K., et al. (2010). Methylphenidate for apathy and functional status in dementia of the Alzheimer type. *Am J Geriatr Psychiatry, 18*(4), 371–374.

Petracca, G. M., Chemerinski, E., & Starkstein, S. E. (2001). A double-blind, placebo-controlled study of fluoxetine in depressed patients with Alzheimer's disease. *Int Psychogeriatr, 13*(2), 233–240.

Petracca, G., Teson, A., Chemerinski, E., et al. (1996). A double-blind placebo-controlled study of clomipramine in depressed patients with Alzheimer's disease. *J Neuropsychiatry Clin Neurosci, 8*(3), 270–275.

Porter, V. R., Buxton, W. G., Fairbanks, L. A., et al. (2003). Frequency and characteristics of anxiety among patients with Alzheimer's disease and related dementias. *J Neuropsychiatry Clin Neurosci, 15*(2), 180–186.

Reifler, B. V., Teri, L., Raskind, M., et al. (1989). Double-blind trial of imipramine in Alzheimer's disease patients with and without depression. *Am J Psychiatry, 146*(1), 45–49.

Reijnders, J. S., Ehrt, U., Weber, W. E., et al. (2008). A systematic review of prevalence studies of depression in Parkinson's disease. *Mov Disord, 23*(2), 183–189.

Robinson, R. G., Starr, L. B., Kubos, K. L., & Price, T. R. (1983). A two-year longitudinal study of post-stroke mood disorders: Findings during the initial evaluation. *Stroke, 14*(5), 736–741.

Roose, S. P., Sackeim, H. A., Krishnan, K.R.R., et al. (2004). Antidepressant pharmacotherapy in the treatment of depression in the very old: A randomized, placebo-controlled trial. *Am J Psychiatry, 161*(11), 2050–2059.

Rosenberg, P. B., Drye, L. T., Martin, B. K., et al. (2010). Sertraline for the treatment of depression in Alzheimer disease. *Am J Geriatr Psychiatry, 18*(2), 136–145.

Sachs-Ericsson, N., & Blazer, D. G. (2011). Depression and anxiety associated with dementia. In M. E. Agronin & G. J. Maletta (Eds.), *Principles and practice of geriatric psychiatry* (2nd ed., pp. 705–719). Philadelphia: Lippincott, Williams and Wilkins.

Sackeim, H. A., Roose, S. P., & Lavori, P. W. (2006). Determining the duration of antidepressant treatment: Application of signal detection methodology and the need for duration adaptive designs (DAD). *Biol Psychiatry, 59*(6), 483–492.

Sheline, Y. I, Pieper, C. F., & Barch, D. M. (2010). Support for the vascular depression hypothesis in late life depression: Results from a two site prospective antidepressant treatment trial. *Arch Gen Psychiatry, 67*(3), 277–285.

Smith, G. S., Kramer, E., & Hermann, C. (2009). Serotonin modulation of cerebral glucose metabolism in depressed older adults. *Biol Psychiatry, 66*(3), 259–266.

Sneed J. R., Rutherford B. R., Rindskopf, D., et al. (2008). Design makes a difference: A meta-analysis of antidepressant response rates in placebo-controlled versus comparator trials in late-life depression. *Am J Ger Psychiatry, 16*(1), 65–73.

Spiegel, D. R., Kim, J., Greene, K., et al. (2009). Apathy due to cerebrovascular accidents successfully treated with methylphenidate: A case series. *J Neuropsychiatry Clin Neurosci, 21*(2), 216–219.

Starkstein, S. E. (2012). Apathy in Parkinson's disease: Diagnostic and etiological dilemmas. *Mov Disord, 27*(2), 174–178.

Starkstein, S. E., Mizrahi, R., Capizzano, A. A., et al. (2009). Neuroimaging correlates of apathy and depression in Alzheimer's disease. *J Neuropsychiatry Clin Neurosci, 21*(3), 259–265.

Stone, A. A., Schwartz, J. E., Broderick, J. E., & Deaton, A. (2010). A snapshot of the age distribution of psychological well-being in the United States. *Proc Natl Acad Sci USA, 107*(22), 9985–9990.

Taylor, W. D., Aizenstein, H. J., & Alexopoulos, G. S. (2013). The vascular depression hypothesis: Mechanisms linking vascular disease with depression. *Mol Psychiatry, 18*(9), 963–974.

van Asch, I. F., Nuyen, J., Veerbeek, M. A., et al. (2013). The diagnosis of depression and use of antidepressants in nursing home residents with and without dementia. *Int J Geriat Psychiatry, 28*(3), 312–318.

Vilalta-Franch, J., Calvó-Perxas, L., & Garre-Olmo, J. (2013). Apathy syndrome in Alzheimer's disease epidemiology: Prevalence, incidence, persistence, and risk and mortality factors. *J Alzheimers Dis, 33*(2), 535–543.

Wade, A. G., Ford, I., & Crawford, G. (2007). Efficacy of prolonged release melatonin in insomnia patients aged 55–80 years: Quality of sleep and next-day alertness outcomes. *Curr Med Res Opin, 23*(10), 2597–2605.

Waldemar, G., Gauthier, S., & Jones, R. (2011). Effect of donepezil on emergence of apathy in mild to moderate Alzheimer's disease. *Int J Geriatr Psychiatry, 26*(2), 150–157.

Wong, W. S., Chen, P. P., et al. (2011). Chronic pain and psychiatric morbidity: A comparison between patients attending specialist orthopedics clinic and multidisciplinary pain clinic. *Pain Med, 12*(2), 246–259.

Yeh, S. S., Lovitt, S., & Schuster, M. W. (2009). Usage of megestrol acetate in the treatment of anorexia-cachexia syndrome in the elderly. *J Nutr Health Aging, 13*(5), 448–454.

Zubenko, G. S., Zubenko, W. N., McPherson, S., et al. (2003). A collaborative study of the emergence and clinical features of the major depressive syndrome of Alzheimer's disease. *Am J Psychiatry, 160*(5), 857–866.

Part IV

Psychosocial Issues in Dementia Care

11 Legal and Ethical Issues

From the very first signs and symptoms of dementia, clinicians, caregivers, and patients must face unique and important legal and ethical issues. These issues arise because the disease, in whatever form it takes, impairs an individual's capacity to make decisions and to function independently. End-of-life issues, in particular, have become more prominent and more complex in the past few decades because the practice of medicine has increasingly achieved the ability to prolong the lives of individuals with dementia, despite their severe physical and mental incapacity. The ability of a clinician to understand these issues and to intervene effectively and appropriately depends upon conducting a thorough assessment to determine a diagnosis of dementia and its stage; an awareness of the religious, cultural, and philosophic factors that influence decision-making for both the patient and family; and personal involvement with the patient, family, and other surrogate decision-makers.

Principles of Ethics

Any discussion of medical-legal issues should be rooted in several basic ethical principles, including autonomy, beneficence, justice, and confidentiality (Anfang & Appelbaum, 2011; Beauchamp & Childress, 2008). Autonomy or self-determination refers to an individual's right to make his or her own decisions and have those decisions respected by others. With dementia patients, autonomy may be restricted by a diminished capacity to understand the decision at hand and the ramifications of each choice. This issue will be discussed further within the context of capacity evaluations. Beneficence refers to the responsibility of all clinicians to act for the good of the patient. The corollary to beneficence is nonmaleficence—meaning "to do no harm" to the patient. Both concepts are based in part upon various religious, cultural, and ethical belief systems with respect to the value or sanctity of human life. With dementia patients, clinicians have a key responsibility to ensure that all decision-making is truly is in line with what would be best according to the impaired individual's own values or previously stated wishes. Such an approach will be highlighted when discussing the role of advance directives.

The principle of justice mandates that clinicians and health care institutions should treat all patients fairly when administering care and allocating resources. Issues of justice often arise when discussing the allocation of medical resources for individuals in the last few weeks or days of life, when medical crises often require enormous expenditures.

Hospice and palliative care are often utilized to refocus care on comfort rather than on futile life-saving interventions.

A final major ethical principle is confidentiality. Clinicians have a responsibility to ensure the integrity and confidentiality of all medical records and communication. This principle has received increased attention in the last few years as a result of privacy provisions for health care in the Health Insurance Portability and Accountability Act or HIPAA, enacted in 1996 (U.S. Department of Health and Human Services, 2012). Clinical work with dementia patients often requires contacts with other caregivers, but any such contact must be based on the explicit permission of the impaired individual if he or she is capable of providing such, or on the decision of a legally authorized representative.

Several key virtues help implement and safeguard these fundamental ethical principles, including honesty, empathy, respect for dignity, discretion, and a commitment to mutual communication. Attention to these virtues when working with vulnerable populations helps to infuse an ethical approach with one that is simultaneously kind and compassionate (Agronin, 2011; Oakley & Cocking, 2001).

Capacity and Competence

When working with individuals suffering from dementia, nearly every ethical dilemma will be shaped by the capacity of an individual to make his or her own decisions. Capacity is the clinical term for an individual's relative cognitive ability to understand or do something, while competency refers to a judge's determination of this ability in an individual (Anfang & Appelbaum, 2011). Although the two terms are often used interchangeably, their legal distinction should be understood. Both terms should always be invoked with respect to a specific purpose, including the following:

1. Making health care decisions; for example, seeking or refusing treatment, enrolling in research, and so on.
2. Making financial or estate decisions; for example, managing property, giving gifts of money, making a will, and so on.
3. Living independently and managing personal obligations; for example, choosing one's own residence, feeding and clothing oneself, taking medications, driving, voting, and so on.
4. Participating in legal proceedings; for example, entering into a contract, suing or being sued, standing trial or testifying at one, serving on a jury, marrying, and so on.

All individuals are assumed legally competent unless they are proven otherwise, and a diagnosis of dementia does not automatically imply that someone is incompetent. An individual may retain capacity in one sphere but not in another. Struggles ensue when a clinician, caregiver, or another involved party questions an individual's mental capacity, thus prompting further investigation. The clinician must bear in mind, however, that, even with a diagnosis of dementia, individuals can be competent yet still be indecisive, resistant to help, and able to make bad decisions. Sorting through these various possibilities and making a determination of an individual's decision-making ability is the first step in all legal and ethical questions.

Both capacity and competency require that an individual's ability to make his or her own decisions includes the following features:

- an understanding or knowledge of the relevant facts involved in the decision;
- an appreciation of the fact that he or she has a choice, what the consequences of different choices could be in terms of risks and benefits, and the significance of various facts;
- the ability to think rationally about the choices and to consider, compare, and weigh facts and options in an organized manner; and
- the ability to make and express a decision in actuality.

All of these abilities must be present and brought to bear on a specific domain in a consistent manner. A person who can weigh choices one day but not the next cannot consistently make competent decisions. However, an individual could have the capacity to think about and to express a choice about giving a gift to someone but not to drive safely or to serve on a jury. Similarly, an individual may have a limited ability to make choices, such as to whom to give a gift of money, but he or she may rely on others to help clarify and implement the decision, such as how much money to give and in what manner.

Determination of capacity occurs informally all the time, as clinicians advise patients and their families on what they can or cannot do, with variable compliance. A formal capacity evaluation will involve the components listed in Table 11.1 (Anfang & Appelbaum, 2011).

A legal determination of competence can only be decided by a judge, but this decision is based, in part, on the clinician's assessment of mental capacity. If someone is found incompetent in one or more spheres, he or she is assigned a surrogate to make decisions for him or her. Depending on the state, various legal terms are used for this surrogate

Table 11.1 The Capacity Evaluation

- Obtain psychiatric and medical history from patient and informants
- Conduct a mental status examination
- Query the patient with respect to the issue at hand and include the following questions:
  - Can he or she tell you the basic facts of the situation?
  - Can he or she describe what his or her choices are?
  - Does he or she appreciate his or her ability to make a choice, as well as the risks and benefits of each choice?
  - Does he or she know the consequences of not making a choice?
  - Can he or she describe their reasoning in an organized, appropriate, and consistent manner?
  - Is he or she able to express a choice?
- Administer a brief cognitive screen to test for memory and other cognitive abilities
- Conduct a brief functional assessment relative to the issue at hand; for example, for financial issues ask the patient to describe how he or she would access and manipulate his or her assets
- Make a determination of the capacity to make decisions in an autonomous and reasonable manner relevant to the specific domains involved

decision-maker, including *guardian, conservator,* and *fiduciary.* Surrogate decision-makers can also be designated by individuals themselves before they become incapacitated. Typically, individuals (with the help of an attorney) prepare a durable power of attorney to designate someone to handle health care decisions or financial matters when they are unable to do so.

Clinical Vignette

Mr. N is a 78-year-old man who was involved in a motor vehicle accident in which he ran a stoplight and hit another car, injuring three people. He acted erratically afterward, sitting down on the ground when police tried to question him. He was arrested but managed to contact a friend to bail him out. A home visit by his attorney revealed a cluttered, unkempt house that was a clear fire hazard. Mr. N insisted on remaining in his home and resuming driving. His attorney wondered whether Mr. N could live alone anymore, drive, or even stand trial. When he was brought before the judge for an initial hearing, a psychiatric evaluation was ordered.

Dr. S, the psychiatrist appointed by the court, interviewed Mr. N, his primary care physician, and a distant cousin. During the interview, Mr. N demonstrated poor short-term memory, and his factual account of the car accident was vague at best. He was unable to summarize what happened afterward, and he did not appreciate the severity of the charges against him. He reported that he was able to live alone, and he was oblivious to the poor condition of his house and his malnutrition. He scored 20 of a possible 30 points on the Mini-Mental State Examination. When Dr. S asked Mr. N what would happen if he were to be convicted, he was unable to make a rational connection between the facts of the case and the potential legal consequences. Based on the forensic report, the judge declared Mr. N incompetent to stand trial and ordered that a guardian be appointed for him. He also mandated further evaluation in a geriatric psychiatry hospital unit. After a four-week stay in which a diagnosis of probable Alzheimer's disease was made, Mr. N's guardian moved him into a nursing home.

Diagnostic Truth Telling

Because of its prognosis, families do not always want loved ones to know that they have dementia, especially Alzheimer's disease (AD). They may also choose not to tell the individual with dementia about a diagnosis of a terminal illness or a family crisis or tragedy. Some of the reasons to withhold such information are a desire to protect the individual from severe emotional reactions, as well as the belief that nothing can be gained by imparting information that the individual does not fully understand.

Whether to provide or withhold information depends on the degree of dementia, especially with respect to the individual's short-term memory and insight. Because individuals in early-stage dementia retain some degree of memory and insight into the diagnosis, most clinicians and dementia organizations recommend being truthful about a diagnosis, and they suggest that information on the nature of the disease, its prognosis, and the available treatments and support should be provided (Pinner, 2000; Post & Whitehouse, 1995). Similarly, most clinicians encourage family members to be honest with individuals with early-stage dementia when there are important family crises or tragedies. Being truthful has the following advantages.

- It may relieve the individual's anxiety and confusion over his or her symptoms of dementia or over the emotional reactions that he or she sees in other loved ones.
- It allows an individual to make important decisions about health care, estate planning, and life plans before he or she loses the capacity to do so.
- It affords the person the opportunity to make decisions about treatment options, including support groups and research studies.
- It enables the person to grieve the loss of a loved one or to provide support to those in crisis or grief.

As an individual's dementia increases, all of these advantages recede. The clinician must then make a judgment call about what is appropriate to tell the patient, including how much he or she needs to know. But clinicians should be reassured by the fact that studies have shown that individuals do not tend to have catastrophic emotional reactions when learning about a diagnosis of dementia (Carpenter et al., 2008).

Imparting Bad News

Imparting information about a dementia diagnosis, a terminal disease, or a family crisis or tragedy must be done in a sensitive, humane, and thoughtful manner. The clinician should know ahead of time the individual's relative cognitive abilities so that he or she can make a judgment call about how much the individual can understand and at what level of detail. The clinician should never assume that, even in the advanced stages of dementia, the individual will not have an emotional reaction. Supportive family, friends, and staff should be present or immediately available. If the clinician anticipates a traumatic reaction from the individual, such as that which may occur in an individual with a history of depression or suicidality or when the loss is quite severe (e.g., the loss of an only child who was a primary support), he or she should have a mental health clinician available for consultation within hours. The clinician must also choose an appropriate time and location to meet so that privacy, confidentiality, and adequate time to relate the information, process it, and deal with the repercussions are ensured. The necessary details should be given without any excessive elaboration that the patient will neither understand nor request; instead, the clinician should be prepared to provide additional details in response to questions that the individual may ask (Agronin, 2011).

If the information is not imparted to the individual with dementia, he or she is potentially robbed of his or her autonomy to participate in personal and family decisions, as well as his or her right to prepare for death or to grieve a loss. Even in the advanced stages of dementia, an individual may retain the capacity to react to news and to grieve, although clinicians and family members may question whether any inherent good exists in putting someone through such pain if he or she does not truly understand nor retain the information. Under those circumstances, providing upsetting information to someone who cannot retain it only risks retraumatizing them with each telling. It is important, then, to make certain that all caregivers respond in consistent ways when an individual with poor short-term memory asks repeatedly about a missing loved one.

Informed Consent for Treatment and Research

Informed consent is one of the foundations of the doctor–patient relationship. The responsibility of the clinician is to inform the patient of his or her condition and the risks and benefits of various treatment options as honestly and completely as possible and to obtain voluntary consent for treatment on that basis. Adequate information includes the name and characteristics of the diagnosis, its prognosis, the consequences of no treatment, and the various treatment options including their duration, risks, and benefits. In addition, informed consent is frequently sought for patient participation in research studies looking at dementia and its associated conditions.

For those individuals who have some capacity to understand their situation, regardless of whether they are making a treatment decision, it is important to discuss the diagnosis, treatment, and/or study protocol at their level of cognitive ability, without excessive detail that may confuse or frighten them (Karlawish & Casarett, 2001). This responsibility cannot always be discharged with patients with dementia, who may lack the capacity to understand, to appreciate, and to think rationally about their condition or treatment options. For these individuals, then, a surrogate is needed to make the decision. Ideally, the potential subject would have a living will that stipulates both treatment and research directives as well as a surrogate. Unfortunately, it is rare to find individuals who have such complete advance directives. In most states, consent for research is preferably provided by a legal guardian or an individual with durable power of attorney for health care, but it can also be given by an undesignated surrogate, such as a spouse or child, followed by a sibling or a close friend who serves as next of kin. Informed consent on the part of the surrogate requires that he or she fully understands the reason for the study, its risks and benefits, and the right to refuse or withdraw consent at any point without fear that the patient would be denied alternate treatment.

Not every study is appropriate for every patient with dementia. In general, if the study involves a minimal risk of harm to subjects, regardless of whether it may benefit them specifically, all patients with dementia can ethically be considered. When a risk of harm is present, however, the decision to enroll should weigh the potential benefit to the subject. Enrollment is obviously considered more preferable when such a benefit exists, but, when it is unclear, the enrollment should be restricted to those individuals who can either consent themselves or who have executed a research-specific advance directive (International Conference on Harmonisation of Technical Requirements for Registration of Pharmaceuticals for Human Use [ICH], 1996; Karlawish & Casarett, 2001).

Driving

As the population ages, the number of older drivers has increased significantly. Although older drivers tend to be safer divers, they also have more fatalities per mile than younger drivers, except for young men ages 16 to 19 (Centers for Disease Control and Prevention, 2013). Given the declines in cognitive skills essential for safe driving, older drivers with dementia pose a particular hazard above and beyond that posed by individuals with the normal age-related risk factors for motor vehicle accidents. Clinical predictors of impaired driving include declines in an individual's short-term memory and decreases in his or her Mini-Mental State Examination scores (Iverson et al., 2010). Neuropsychological deficits in visuospatial processing and frontal lobe function are particularly worrisome as regards driving, since they will impair an individual's ability to quickly and accurately identify and attend to the most important elements in their visual field (Mathias & Lucas, 2009).

Signs of impaired driving in individuals with dementia include driving too slowly; difficulty in making turns, lane changes, or exits; failing to observe traffic signs and rules of the road; becoming lost in familiar areas; slowed reaction to objects, other vehicles, or pedestrians in the road; leaving the car running or the keys in the ignition after stopping; forgetting to turn on the headlights at night or to fill up the gas tank; improper or poor parking; and a history of crashes and citations (Dobbs, Heller, & Schopflocher, 1998; Iverson et al., 2010).

Despite these risk factors, after an individual has been licensed to drive, retesting is not obligatory in most states (aside from visual acuity testing). In addition, older individuals are typically reluctant to give up driving even when they are told to do so, although many do moderate their driving anyway by driving less frequently at night, on freeways, or on unfamiliar roads. Giving up driving voluntarily or under duress can be devastating for an older individual because it harms his or her self-worth, robs the individual of his or her independence, increases his or her dependence on others, and makes going places and running errands difficult.

A diagnosis of dementia does not automatically disqualify someone from driving, but it does strongly indicate the need for limits, supervision, and alternate means of transportation. Ultimately, the individual must stop driving. When a clinician is concerned about a patient's capacity to drive, he or she should ask the patient and a reliable informant about the pattern of driving, including usual frequency, time of day, weather and road conditions, destinations, type and condition of the vehicle, and passengers; additionally, he or she should ask for a history of the patient's violations and accidents. At the very least, the clinician should always recommend some form of functional assessment, such as a computerized test offered by some memory centers or an on-road test by a qualified representative of the state's Department of Motor Vehicles. Some states require physicians to report impaired drivers for retesting. The problem is that this provision requires the physician to break patient–doctor confidentiality, so that the patient may no longer trust the physician or return for follow-up. Even worse, the individual may no longer be honest about his or her limitations. Regardless, the goal of intervention is to ensure the safety of the patient and others since the consequences of not intervening when an individual has become an impaired driver could be catastrophic.

The American Academy of Neurology recommends that drivers with early-stage dementia undergo on-road retesting and regular reassessment every six months at a minimum, given the likely progression of the disease (Iverson et al., 2010). Individuals with moderate to severe dementia (including a rating of one or above on the Clinical Dementia Rating Scale [CDR]) should not be driving at all, given their significant impairment in driving performance and the increases in accident rates. Unfortunately, many patients with dementia ignore these and other clinician recommendations and continue to drive in all circumstances. Even more alarming is the fact that many of these individuals and their caregivers believe that they can continue to drive throughout the course of their disease. As a result, the clinician's recommendations for a driver evaluation or for the patient to stop driving altogether frequently causes conflicts among clinicians, caregivers, and patients.

To deal with potential conflict with patients and caregivers, clinicians should arm themselves with as much supporting data as possible, and they should document their recommendations carefully for the sake of risk management. Impaired individuals should be reported to the state's Department of Motor Vehicles, especially when this is mandated by state law. In many cases, caregivers may need to be instructed to take away the individual's car keys. For individuals with mild impairment, the clinician should always consider compromises, such as restricting driving to daylight hours in good weather and road conditions and only on well-recognized, less congested roads. Clinicians and caregivers should also take an active role in arranging alternative transportation for the patient so as not to leave him or her stranded. If the individual continues to drive, he or she should not be allowed to transport anyone (especially children), except for a caregiver who is aware of potential limitations.

The same concerns about driving apply to many other potentially hazardous activities that an individual with dementia may engage in, including possessing and using firearms, caring for children, some athletics (e.g., biking, skiing), driving boats and other recreational vehicles, and using power tools and yard equipment. All of these activities may require limitations and supervision in the early stages of dementia and prohibition later in the course of the illness.

Sexual Relationships

Individuals with dementia have the right to engage in sexual relationships with a partner, assuming both individuals have the capacity to understand the nature of the relationship and to provide consent. This issue often arises in relationships when a spouse or partner questions the ability of the other partner to provide consent or, in a long-term care setting, when two individuals with dementia are engaging in sexual activity (Agronin & Westheimer, 2011). The latter situation often creates considerable anxiety, especially if one or more of the individuals have a spouse. In such situations, a psychiatric or psychological consultation can help to determine the individuals' relative capacity to provide consent. Even though the individual may lack capacity in many other areas, he or she may still be able to consent to sex. When concerns arise, the clinician should question the individual to determine whether he or she knows the sexual partner and understands the nature of the relationship, including its risks, and whether he or she is able to refuse unwanted intimacy (Lichtenberg & Strzepek, 1990). In addition, the individual's current sexual behaviors should be compared with his or her past behaviors and known personal values.

Advance Directives

Advance directives are legal documents that are prepared and signed by individuals to indicate how medical decisions should be made for them if and when they become mentally incapacitated. They must be executed when an individual is still competent to make decisions. Advance directives are not unique to patients with dementia, and, since the enactment of the Patient Self-Determination Act in 1990, health care organizations are mandated to provide all patients with information on them (Rempusheski & Hurley, 2000). Advances directives may consist of the following: (1) a proxy directive, which designates a surrogate to make decisions for an individual in case he or she develops mental incapacity. The surrogate can be designated as a durable power of attorney for heath care or a health care proxy. Spouses and adult children are the individuals most commonly designated to serve as proxies, followed by parents, siblings, and other relatives; and (2) a living will, which specifies an individual's wishes with respect to health care decisions when he or she lacks the mental capacity to make them. Some of the medical issues that may be discussed in a living will include the following:

• statement of religious principles or personal philosophy to guide medical decisions;
• use of cardiopulmonary resuscitation and artificial respiration in case of cardiopulmonary arrest;
• use of intravenous hydration and feeding tubes if the individual is unable to eat or drink;
• use of artificial life support in case of a coma or persistent vegetative state;
• participation in research studies; and
• permissibility of organ or tissue donation and autopsy.

Ideally, all individuals should prepare a document that includes a living will and designates a proxy to make health care decisions based on its guidelines. Without a living will, a designated proxy may make decisions inconsistent with the wishes of the patient. Without a designated proxy, a living will must be interpreted by the next of kin, who may or may not choose to honor its guidelines.

When an individual has no advance directives and he or she either has no next of kin or the family is unsure of what to do, medical decisions for the individual may be made based on his or her known values or religious beliefs, on previous statements made with respect to end-of-life care, or ultimately on what appears to be the most reasonable approach.

Clinical Vignette

Mrs. E, a 75-year-old woman with mild memory loss, had told her daughter that she was afraid of being kept alive "like a vegetable" and that she would like her to prevent unnecessary interventions when she could no longer make decisions. She did not want her son to make decisions for her because he had recently sustained a head injury, and she did not trust his judgment. The son, however, told his sister that he was the oldest child and that he therefore had the right to make decisions for his mother. Mrs. E signed a living will that specified her desire not to be put on artificial life support if she were in a terminal state. She also designated her daughter as her durable power of attorney for health care decisions.

End-of-Life Care

Despite their long courses, AD and other progressive dementias are terminal illnesses. In the last 6 to 12 months of life, patients with AD steadily enter a vegetative state as they lose their ability to communicate, ambulate, and swallow. Death often results from infection and malnutrition. However, medical technology has advanced considerably in the past few decades, and various interventions can now prolong this end stage for months. Although clinicians and caregivers seek to prevent pain and suffering during this stage, many question the value of prolonging the dying process when the individual has little perceived quality of life. Other individuals believe that the sanctity of life is paramount and that all efforts to prolong life should be exerted.

Advance directives play a key role in these situations, and all long-term care institutions request that families make decisions about do not resuscitate or DNR orders in the setting of end-stage dementia because the chances of recovery from cardiopulmonary arrest are slim. Caregivers need to understand, however, that DNR orders only apply to the use of cardiopulmonary resuscitation in emergent situations and that the use of other medical interventions can still be provided. Physicians still need to discuss with caregivers how aggressively to treat superimposed medical conditions, such as infections, injuries (e.g., hip fracture), and malignancies.

The most common approach in end-stage dementia is to provide definitive treatment for minor problems that may otherwise cause undue pain or discomfort (e.g., coughs, small wounds or lacerations, constipation, diarrhea, and skin eruptions) as well as for more serious acute problems that cause significant suffering but that can be relieved with straightforward treatment (e.g., using a diuretic for pulmonary edema or a nebulizer treatment for an asthma attack). With more serious problems that require invasive treatment or surgery, such as fractures, malignancies, and myocardial infarction, the treatment approach is more often palliative, meaning that its aim is to relieve pain and to provide comfort without curing the problem. The issue becomes more controversial with an acute infection, such as pneumonia, that can be cured with a moderate degree of intervention but that otherwise may result in death within days. Even with advance directives, the emotional reactions to such situations can complicate decision-making.

A similar ethical issue arises when an individual with dementia has dysphagia, putting him or her at risk of choking and developing aspiration pneumonia. In the past, oral feeding was attempted as long as possible and was sometimes temporarily supplemented with nasogastric or intravenous nutrition. Since the 1980s, however, the placement of permanent feeding tubes directly through the abdominal wall and into the stomach has become more commonplace because of the development of percutaneous endoscopic gastrostomy or PEG tubes. These tubes allow indefinite nutritional supplementation. For many individuals without end-stage dementia, tube feeding can prolong life and can even provide a bridge of survival during recovery from a stroke or another illness that makes eating impossible.

For individuals with end-stage dementia, however, the survival benefit is less clear. The idea of not feeding someone and thus allowing him or her to die makes many clinicians and caregivers quite uncomfortable. Research suggests, however, that tube feeding in end-stage dementia does not necessarily enhance the individual's quality of life nor prolong his or her survival (Candy, Sampson, & Jones, 2009; Finucane, Christmas, & Travis, 1999). It can be associated with uncomfortable but manageable symptoms, such as abdominal distention and cramping, aspiration, pain and infections at the tube site, nausea and vomiting, diarrhea, and agitation (Schrag, Sharma, & Jaik, 2007). Without artificial hydration and nutrition from tube feeding, death usually results within days. Although starvation is imagined to be painful, this is not necessarily true, perhaps in part because of the production of natural endorphins and the availability of supplemental morphine. Increasingly, hospice and palliative care have been playing a role in end-stage dementia, with the recognition that the goals of most families are palliation of pain and suffering and optimal comfort during the final days of life (Hughes, Jolley, Jordan, & Sampson, 2007).

A Guide to Legal Protection

Based on the information in this presentation, all individuals should consider executing several of the following precautionary legal steps before the potential onset of dementia or, at the latest, during the early stages of disease, with the assistance of a caregiver:

1. Advance directives: an individual should prepare a living will and should designate a durable power of attorney for health care decisions and research. He or she should specify that the power of attorney should follow the guidelines of the living will.
2. Financial and estate planning: the individual should prepare a will and should consider including a statement of capacity (with a videotape) if he or she is in the early stages of dementia. He or she should set up joint bank accounts with a spouse or a designated individual, who then serves as a surrogate for the management of financial assets, and the individual should arrange for the direct deposit of pensions and other sources of income. He or she should designate a representative payee, if necessary, to manage his or her government benefits. These steps may prevent exploitation.
3. Personal values and philosophy: the individual should review his or her wishes with family members and designated proxies so that they understand his or her philosophy and can express any reservations about discharging them. If an individual distrusts a particular person, he or she should take the steps necessary to limit his or her involvement in decision-making.

As regards advance directives and estate planning, an individual should consider consulting with competent, professional individuals with expertise in these areas. The Alzheimer's Association is a good first stop. For legal issues, the National Academy of Elder Law Attorneys can provide information and referrals by telephone or through its website at www.naela.com. The website for Caring Connections at www.caringinfo.org and its hotline can provide more information on advance directives.

The three steps listed are rapidly becoming standard for all adults, especially because health care institutions now provide information on advance directives every time someone is hospitalized. It is important for individuals to keep in mind that decision-making during times of crisis or at the end of life may be influenced by strong emotions, family disputes, and situations that were not previously anticipated. Advance directives that include a living will and a designation of proxies can steer caregivers through these rough straits, but they must be coupled with open and honest communication between family members and clinicians and an appeal to personal values and ethics that encompass the particulars of the situation.

References

Agronin, M. E. (2011). *How we age: A doctor's journey into the heart of growing old.* Boston: Da Capo.

Agronin, M. E., & Westheimer, R. K. (2011). Sexuality and sexual disorders in late life. In M. E. Agronin & G. J. Maletta (Eds.), *Principles and practice of geriatric psychiatry* (2nd ed., pp. 523–546). Philadelphia: Lippincott, Williams and Wilkins.

Anfang, S. A., & Appelbaum, P. S. (2011). Forensic evaluation of the older patient. In M. E. Agronin & G. J. Maletta (Eds.), *Principles and practice of geriatric psychiatry* (2nd ed., pp. 163–176). Philadelphia: Lippincott, Williams and Wilkins.

Beauchamp, T. L., & Childress, J. F. (2008). *Principles of biomedical ethics* (6th ed.). New York: Oxford University Press.

Candy, B., Sampson, E. L., & Jones, L. (2009). Enteral tube feeding in older people with advanced dementia: Findings from a Cochrane systematic review. *Int J Palliat Nurs, 15*(8), 396–404.

Carpenter, B. D., Xiong, C., Porensky, E. K., et al. (2008). Reaction to a dementia diagnosis in individuals with Alzheimer's disease and mild cognitive impairment. *JAGS, 55*(3), 405–412.

Centers for Disease Control and Prevention. (2013). *Older adult drivers data & statistics.* Retrieved from www.cdc.gov/Motorvehiclesafety/Older_Adult_Drivers/data.html

Dobbs, A. R., Heller, R. B., & Schopflocher, D. (1998). A comparative approach to identify unsafe older drivers. *Accid Anal Prev, 30*(3), 363–370.

Finucane, T. E., Christmas, C., & Travis, K. (1999). Tube feeding in patients with advanced dementia: A review of the evidence. *JAMA, 282*(14), 1365–1370.

Hughes, J. C., Jolley, D., Jordan, A., & Sampson, E. L. (2007). Palliative care in dementia: Issues and evidence. *Advances in Psychiatric Treatment, 13*, 251–260.

International Conference on Harmonisation of Technical Requirements for Registration of Pharmaceuticals for Human Use (ICH). (1996). *Guideline for good clinical practice E6(R1).* Retrieved from http://ichgcp.net

Iverson, D. J., Gronseth, G. S., Reger, M. A., et al. (2010). Practice parameter update: Evaluation and management of driving risk in dementia. Report of the Quality Standards Subcommittee of the American Academy of Neurology. *Neurol, 74*(16), 1316–1324.

Karlawish, J. H., & Casarett, D. (2001). Addressing the ethical challenges of clinical trials that involve patients with dementia. *J Geriatr Psychiatry Neurol, 14*(4), 222–228.

Lichtenberg, P. A., & Strzepek, D. M. (1990). Assessments of institutionalized dementia patients' competencies to participate in intimate relationships. *Gerontologist, 30*, 117–120.

Mathias, J. L., & Lucas, J. K. (2009). Cognitive predictors of unsafe driving in older drivers: A meta-analysis. *Int Psychogeriatr, 21*(4), 637–653.

Oakley, J., & Cocking, D. (2001). *Virtue ethics and professional roles.* Cambridge: Cambridge University Press.

Pinner, G. (2000). Truth-telling and the diagnosis of dementia. *Br J Psychiatry, 176*, 514–515.

Post, S. G., & Whitehouse, P. J. (1995). Fairhill guidelines on the ethics of the care of people with Alzheimer's disease: A clinician's summary. *JAGS, 43*, 1423–1429.

Rempusheski, V. F., & Hurley, A. C. (2000). Advance directives and dementia. *J Gerontol Nurs, 26*(10), 27–34.

Schrag, S. P., Sharma, R., & Jaik, N. P. (2007). Complications related to percutaneous endoscopic gastrostomy (PEG) tubes: A comprehensive clinical review. *J Gastrointestin Liver Dis, 16*(4), 407–418.

U.S. Department of Health and Human Services. (2012). *A patient's guide to the HIPAA Privacy Rule: When health care provides may communicate about you with your family, friends or others involved in your care.* Retrieved from www.hhs.gov/ocr/privacy/hipaa/understanding/consumers/consumer_ffg.pdf

12   Caring for the Caregiver

The main focus of every preceding chapter in this book has been on the individual with dementia. However, emphasizing the necessity of dementia workup, diagnosis, and treatment without discussing a critical component—the caregiver—would be incomplete. Every individual with dementia requires some degree of assistance with daily living. The degree of assistance varies depending on the type and stage of dementia, but all individuals with a progressive dementia eventually require total care. As of 2000 there were 4 to 5 million Americans suffering from Alzheimer's disease (AD) alone; now that number is around 5.4 million—a 10% to 20% increase in the last 10 years—and it will likely triple by 2050 (Alzheimer's Association, 2012; Hebert et al., 2003). For every individual with AD, there are one or more caregivers who must assume enormous responsibilities day in and day out for years. They must spend time with the affected individual to prepare meals, insure adequate hygiene, administer medications, take them to places and appointments, engage them in activities, monitor their whereabouts and safety—and the list goes on and on.

The term *caregiver burden* has been used widely to describe the resulting physical, emotional, and financial toll. AD caregivers have to spend more time with hands-on care and face more behavioral resistance than non-AD caregivers (Depp, Romero, Thompson, & Gallagher-Thompson, 2011). Even after an individual is placed in a long-term care institution, the former caregiver can be left with feelings of guilt, sadness, and depression, and be affected by the ongoing struggle of watching a loved one succumb to a tragic illness. This chapter describes these caregivers and the incredible burden that they face, and it provides numerous tips on how the clinician can help them cope with dementia and optimize dementia care.

Clinical Vignette

The following is based on a social worker's interview of the 76-year-old wife of Mr. A, a 78-year-old man with a six-year history of AD. He had lived at home with Mrs. A until four months ago, when he was admitted to a long-term care facility. Mrs. A continues to live at home, and she visits him five or six days a week (SW, social worker; Mrs. A, caregiver).

SW: Tell me what it was like when your husband developed Alzheimer's disease.

MRS. A: It was just terrible. At first, he began to forget to do things around the house, but then he began wandering off. We were once on a vacation in Las Vegas, and I told him to wait by the bathroom in the casino while I went in. He wandered off, and I couldn't find him for hours, even with the help of the police. It was a ruined vacation.

SW: How were you able to care for him?

MRS. A: In the early stages, I could leave him alone for short periods of time. After the wandering incident, however, I had to stay with him 24 hours a day. My daughter sometimes came over to help, but I felt guilty every time I left the house. I would try to go out to lunch with a girlfriend, but then I would get this unsettling guilty feeling, like I was abandoning him. I never really enjoyed time away, although it did help. As he got worse, I had to hire a girl to come in and bathe him several times a week. He would fight me when I tried to shave him, and once he gave me a black eye. He would go to the bathroom in his pants but refuse to let me change him. The worst was when he would wake up at night and wander around the house, sometimes making a racket in the kitchen. He fell several times, once breaking his arm. I slept with one eye open and was exhausted most days. Finally, my daughter said that enough was enough.

SW: Since he was admitted to the nursing home, have things been better?

MRS. A: Things are better because I can finally sleep at night. It is easier physically, but I still feel badly emotionally. I feel guilty when I'm not here. He always asked me never to put him away, and now ... [crying] ... I can't believe what life has dealt us. We've been married 55 years. I try to come every day. I make sure that he is taken care of, and I help feed him. He used to be such a fun, vibrant person, but now he is just a shell. He doesn't speak anymore—that is one of the toughest things; I can't talk with him.

Mrs. A described many common themes for caregivers, including the following: endless hours of exhausting tasks, episodes of frightening and humiliating behavioral disturbances, and strong feelings of guilt and grief that last for years. Caregivers often suffer in silence, feeling too embarrassed or too isolated to confide in others, including clinicians, until the situation becomes unbearable.

Caregivers and Caregiver Burden

A caregiver is any individual who assumes the primary responsibility of caring for an individual suffering from dementia. The term *informal caregiver* refers to individuals who take on this role as an obligation rather than for pay or as part of a profession. It has been estimated that 70% to 80% of all individuals with dementia are cared for at home, with most care provided by family members (Parks, 2000). The typical caregiver is an older woman caring for a husband with dementia; in fact, 80%–90% of all caregivers are women, and 40%–50% of those are spouses. Daughters and daughters-in-law account for another 40% of caregivers, and sons and other individuals account for less than 10% (Depp et al., 2011). On average, home caregivers spend up to 70 hours a week assisting a moderately to severely demented individual.

As noted, the term *burden* reflects the negative impact of caregiving on physical and emotional functioning and on financial resources. Burden is affected by both disease-related factors such as functional loss, agitation, and poor safety awareness and caregiver issues such as financial resources, hours required, gender, housing, and coping strategies (Kim, Chang, Rose, & Kim, 2012). The physical and emotional toll on caregivers is clear: compared to noncaregivers, they suffer from higher rates of medical illness and use significantly more prescription drugs; they have rates of depression two to three times greater than the general population; and they even have higher mortality rates (Depp et al., 2011; Taylor et al., 2008). Depression tends to amplify burden and decrease quality of life for caregivers.

The financial toll is significant. As of 2012, the total annual cost of caring for an individual in the United States with AD or other dementias was estimated at around $48,000, of which nearly $18,000 represented informal caregiving (Alzheimer's Disease International, 2010). There are an estimated 15 million unpaid caregivers providing 17.4 billion hours of care equivalent to $210 billion (Alzheimer's Association, 2012). It is likely that caregivers spend upwards of $10,000 per year for unreimbursable services and supplies for the individual with dementia (Hurd, Martorelli, & Delavande, 2013). In addition, long-term care placement for the individual with dementia can quickly deplete one's life savings.

Assessment of Burden

Every clinical visit with an individual with dementia should include attention to the caregiver, with questions about how he or she is coping with his or her loved one's illness and whether he or she has sufficient help. It is wise to interview the caregiver alone to allow him or her to be more open without worrying about upsetting the patient. Signs of caregiver stress include feelings of exhaustion, guilt, anger, and anxiety; social withdrawal and isolation; impaired sleep and concentration; increased health problems; and a decline in caregiving, which sometimes is reflected in the condition of the individual with dementia. Two brief measures for caregiver burden are the Caregiver Self-Assessment Questionnaire, which was developed by the American Medical Association and available for free on the Internet in both English and Spanish (American Medical Association, 2013), and the Zarit Burden Interview, which comes in 4- and 12-item self-report versions (Zarit, Reever, & Bach-Peterson, 1980; Bédard, Molloy, & Squire, 2001). A brief, practical burden interview that can be used in clinical practice can be found in Table 12.1. Regardless of the outward signs, the caregiver's perceived burden is ultimately the most important factor (Zarit, Todd, & Zarit, 1986). Caregivers who perceive themselves as being under more stress tend to fare worse; caregivers with positive perceptions who are bolstered by active coping styles, family support, and spirituality do better.

Table 12.1 A Brief Screen for Caregiver Burden

Perceptions and Experience of Burden

1. Do you feel you are under significant stress? If yes, describe.
2. Do you feel depressed? Anxious? To what degree?
3. Have you had difficulty sleeping? Eating?
4. Do you have more medical problems than before?
5. Do you constantly feel exhausted?
6. Have you felt that life is not worth living? Suicidal?
7. Have you ever felt like hitting or even ending the life of your loved one with dementia?

Potential Causes of Burden

1. Do you need more visitors? More assistance? More time for yourself?
2. Does your loved one have behavioral problems? Paranoia?
3. Is he or she depressed? Apathetic?

The greater the number of "yes" responses to these questions, the greater the likelihood of increased burden and the need for active intervention.

Clinical Tip

If a caregiver admits to feelings of depression, hopelessness, or helplessness, the clinician should always inquire about suicidal and homicidal thoughts. The intensity of the burden can be so overwhelming for some caregivers that they consider ending their own life and the life of the individual with dementia. Suicide-homicides are a small but growing problem; they are more common in elderly couples in which the husband is the primary caregiver. Caregiver risk factors for suicide-homicide include social isolation, higher socioeconomic status, medical problems, depression, and a controlling personality (Cohen, 2004).

Conflict with Caregivers

A particular subset of caregivers can be difficult to assess and help, and this group may prove disruptive to the doctor–patient relationship and to long-term care settings. Such caregivers struggle with both informal and formal supports, including their friends and family, professionals, and staff members at supportive agencies, programs, and institutions. These struggles often stem from inflexible or even pathologic coping styles, behavioral patterns, or personalities. They are fueled by the stress and strong emotions inherent to the caregiver role. For example, a caregiver may feel deep anger at his or her loved one for being ill, but, instead, he or she directs it at those trying to help. He or she may feel inadequate as a caregiver or guilty about having to place the loved one in an institution, and he or she then projects these feelings onto external supports. The resulting anger, accusations, and demands can create turmoil in the caregiving setting, leaving the caregiver isolated from those who want to help.

Clinical Vignette

Mr. R is a retired physician who visits his wife daily at the nursing home and spends five to six hours helping to care for her. His obsessive-compulsive personality drives him to keep meticulous records of his wife's care, down to the daily temperature readings and bowel movement characteristics. He frequently berates staff members for minor mistakes and demands that custodial staff and nursing aides be available whenever he calls. He has had numerous fights with both the administrative and clinical staff because he tries to dictate details of his wife's care.

When a clinician has had a difficult encounter with a caregiver, he or she should not jump to "diagnose" the caregiver or to assign blame to him or her. Instead, the clinician must recognize the role of clinical staff or other factors that may be causing part of the problem. Remaining an empathic and open listener to the caregiver and providing timely and honest communication are essential. At the same time, however, the clinician may need to educate the caregiver on the limits of his or her own role and to provide the caregiver with relevant referrals to other professionals. The clinician should always consider involving other team members whose specialties may be of help for specific aspects of the conflict. In institutions, the administrative and legal staff may need to be involved.

Caring for the Caregiver

The following basic rules will enable every clinician to help caregivers to cope with their situation and reduce stress: be available and supportive; listen; communicate; and guide them to available resources. The clinician must bear in mind the fact that caregivers are undergoing a tremendous change in their life, having to shift their previous roles and responsibilities to take on difficult new tasks. For example, the spouse of the adult patient with dementia finds himself or herself assuming responsibilities that are reminiscent of past parenting with young children, including constant monitoring, toileting, feeding, and bathing. Gender roles can be reversed as a husband or wife has to assume the unfamiliar tasks once handled by the spouse, such as managing household finances, routine cleaning and maintenance of the home and yard, and grocery shopping. In addition, a spouse may lose his or her main source of communication and support. An older caregiver also must struggle to maintain adequate levels of energy, enthusiasm, and concentration for meeting the needs of his or her loved one, despite being beset by his or her own physical and emotional problems.

Adult children who serve as caregivers face similar physical and emotional demands, but their perspective is different. Many women, in particular, are faced with the dual roles of caring both for children and teenagers and for an aged parent with dementia, leaving little time for other interests, a situation that has led to them being aptly described by the term *sandwich generation*. The adult children also face the emotional burden of having to reverse the parent–child role, especially when they are dealing with the toileting, bathing, and behavioral problems of a parent. Sons who have relied on their wives to provide most of the hands-on child care in their own household may be particularly perplexed and frustrated by such caregiving; they may instead defer the assumption of many responsibilities to a sister, wife, or hired aide.

Grief, loss, confusion, anger, and frustration—all of which are emotional reactions to seeing a loved one suffer from dementia—can trigger previous unresolved feelings toward, or conflicts with, the individual with dementia. The reactions of caregivers vary widely, and they are unpredictable. Some caregivers act out with inappropriate and excessive behaviors, accounting for some of the reactions of difficult caregivers that were described earlier. A son or daughter who never got much attention from the parent may now feel even angrier as the dementia robs them of a chance to make up for lost time, or he or she may plunge into caregiving with excessive zeal to try to heal this emotional wound. Previously abusive parents who now have dementia may be neglected by family members who feel freed of their domination or who seek "revenge" for years of abuse. Fortunately, most individuals who are unable to cope with past unresolved conflicts benefit from support groups and therapy. The clinician's understanding of these dynamics helps him or her to provide the best care and to select the most relevant resources (Parker, Mills, & Abbey, 2008).

Key Strategies: The Six E's

With all of these factors in mind, clinicians should be aware of the effectiveness of many strategies and interventions for helping caregivers best meet the care demands of an individual with dementia (Parker et al., 2008; Van Mierlo, Meiland, Van der Roest, & Dröes, 2012). These approaches can be represented by a mnemonic labeled "The Six E's," which includes the following:

- *educate* caregivers about the diagnosis, disease course, and available resources;
- *empower* the strengths of the caregiver and the abilities of the patient with dementia;
- *environmental* comfort, stimulation, and safety serve to organize caregiving, protect the individual with dementia, and optimize his or her course;
- *engage* both caregivers and patients in stimulating, comfortable, and structured activities;
- *energize* the caregiver by taking care of his or her needs and providing respite time;
- *endpoints* are long-term care placement and hospice care; they help caregivers to foster realistic attitudes, and be proactive toward the inevitabilities of dementia without becoming excessively pessimistic.

Educate

Fear and confusion are two of the greatest barriers for caregivers, and each can take a significant toll. Most caregivers do not fully understand the exact diagnosis and course of the disease, and, thus, they have difficulty understanding and making decisions about events that take place along the way. Clinicians have the responsibility of reviewing all this information with caregivers. They must teach them what to expect along the way without unduly frightening them and guide them toward organizations, websites, books, and other resources that can help (see the lists at the end of this chapter).

Empower

Although caregivers face significant burdens, they also have a wellspring of strengths that sustain them from day to day. These strengths include their physical and psychological abilities, their intellectual skills, their social supports, their financial resources, and their spiritual or religious inclinations. Clinicians can help caregivers recognize and optimize their strengths. Table 12.2 lists a variety of tips to help empower caregivers in order to actively enhance dementia care.

Table 12.2 Tips on Enhancing Dementia Care

Enhance communication

- Use simple, direct language, and repeat it as needed
- Use friendly and engaging nonverbal cues (e.g., eye contact, smiles, touches)
- Compensate for sensory limitations (e.g., glasses, hearing aids)
- Limit distractions, such as excessive noise or commotion

Enhance memory

- Provide daily orientation with large-print calendars and lists
- Label drawers, closets, and other places with explanatory words or pictures
- Post a list of important phone contacts near the phone
- Always introduce visitors by name and relationship

Enhance daily caregiving

- Structure daily caregiving but allow some flexibility
- Break up caregiving into easier, quicker, and more tolerable tasks
- Get assistance from aides, nurses, friends, and family
- Prepare the room and needed accessories ahead of time
- Encourage the dementia patient to exercise as much control as possible
- Ensure dignity and privacy during bathing, toileting, grooming, and dressing

Environment

An assessment of the caregiving environment, which focuses on identifying potentially unsafe situations, is outlined in Chapter 2. The home environment can be adapted to optimize the safety and function of the individual with dementia. Potentially hazardous substances, medications, and items such as power tools and firearms should be locked away. Exits should be safeguarded to prevent an individual with dementia from wandering away from the house.

Clinical Tip

If the individual with dementia is at risk of wandering away from his or her living situation, there are several safeguards that can be put in place. One is the MedicAlert + Alzheimer's Association Safe Return program, which provides 24-hour emergency response for individuals with dementia who go missing. To sign up someone and receive an ID bracelet and emergency response information, go to www.alz.org/care/dementia-medic-alert-safe-return.aspto or call 1-888-572-8566. The Alzheimer's Association also offers enhanced systems called Comfort Zone and Comfort Zone Check-In to provide GPS tracking for individuals with dementia. You can learn more about these programs at www.alz.org/comfortzone/.

To improve ambulation and minimize the risk of falls, the environment can be enhanced by removing excess furniture and clutter and installing proper lighting, non-slip rugs and mats, and assist bars in the bathroom. Caregivers should keep up the regular maintenance of the home, yard, car, major appliances, and utilities, and they should have a list of repair services and emergency contacts handy.

The most unsafe situation is that of an individual with dementia who is living alone without sufficient monitoring and assistance. When a situation involving compromised safety, neglect, abuse, or exploitation is suspected, necessary interventions may include consulting with a social worker or case manager and contacting the local agency that investigates potential abuse. Sometimes, the police must be contacted when an imminent threat is suspected.

Engage

Even in later stages of progressive dementia, individuals retain the ability to respond to sensory stimulation in positive ways. At any stage in dementia, such stimulation can be critical for the individual with dementia to maintain engagement with his or her surroundings, attachment to loved ones, a sense of identity and integrity, and dignity. Unfortunately, family members sometimes react out of depression, anger, guilt, disgust, or grief and disengage from the individual with dementia, either actively through staying away or passively by visiting in body but not in mind or spirit. Caregivers who see no meaning to the life of a person with dementia may discourage visits from loved ones, or the loved ones may feel unsure about what to do during visits other than sit and count the minutes.

A counterpoint to these attitudes emphasizes that individuals in every stage of dementia retain key strengths that can be engaged and enhanced. To identify these strengths, the clinician should ask caregivers the following questions about the individual with dementia:

• What is he or she still able to do currently?
• What did he or she love to do earlier in life?

- What held great meaning for him or her?
- Are cultural or religious items, rituals, foods, music, languages, or individuals that held great meaning for him or her present?
- What forms of sensory stimulation can he or she still enjoy?

The clinician should make a list of the impaired individual's retained capabilities as the first step toward generating ideas for ongoing vital involvement in life. In long-term care facilities, the social workers and recreational therapists rely on these strengths to plan appropriate activities and programs. For individuals with dementia who are living at home, caregivers must find resources in the community to help. Such resources may include programs at religious or cultural centers and houses of worship, senior centers, adult day care programs, support groups, and friendly visitor programs.

Table 12.3 Suggested Activities with an Individual with Dementia

Sensory stimulation

- Prepare and eat a favorite food together
- Take a walk through a serene garden or park
- Hand massage with scented oils or lotions
- Hugging, holding hands
- Bring soft objects and stuffed animals to hold
- Listen to music

Reminiscing

- Look at old photograph albums together
- Listen to music from an earlier period in the patient's life
- Ask about early memories that may be retained
- Visit an old friend
- Converse in a first language together

Intergenerational activities with younger family or volunteers

- Look at old photographs and take new ones
- Decorate room, wheelchair, and/or walker together
- Participate in arts and crafts
- Watch movies together
- Plant something that will grow, continually reminding children of the visit

Physical activities

- Do household chores together
- Engage in mild exercise, such as stretching or walks
- Participate in simple sports (fishing, horseshoes, catching a ball)

Religious/spiritual activities

- Attend religious service together
- Have the clergy visit
- Read religious texts and pray together
- Celebrate holidays and conduct rituals together

Table 12.3 contains a list of suggested activities. Several of the books listed at the end of the chapter also contain suggestions.

Children and teenagers who have a loved one suffering from dementia may sometimes react to the situation with confusion, fear, and anger. They may not understand why their grandparent forgets things, does not recognize them at times, or acts differently. They may fear that they or their parents will get dementia, or they may be afraid of particular behaviors, especially when the individual displays psychosis or agitation. They may be angry if the affected person or the caregiver spends less time with them. Sometimes, these reactions are clearly stated; at other times, they are acted out indirectly, perhaps at school or with friends. The clinician should recognize the importance of both identifying these reactions and helping the family to engage children and teenagers with their loved one with dementia. The clinician should also educate children and teens about dementia, speaking at their level of understanding and using examples rather than technical descriptions. It is important to ask younger individuals about their feelings or find constructive ways for them to be expressed. The caregiver should not expect, nor ask, a child or adolescent to help with caregiving responsibilities, especially bathing and hygiene. If they offer to help with some tasks, the caregiver should find easy, nonthreatening things for them to do with the person with dementia, such as simple physical activity or games, arts and crafts, and reminiscing (see Table 12.3).

Clinical Vignette

Mrs. P, a 78-year-old Haitian woman, was admitted to a nursing home due to severe dementia and associated agitation at home. In the first month, she continued to be agitated, and she often refused to eat. The staff had difficulty understanding her because she only spoke Creole. Her three daughters were distraught over her condition, and they felt guilty and angry about putting her in the facility. The social worker, Mrs. T, convened a family meeting and asked the family members to tell her about their mother. Words and tears flowed for more than an hour as the family described a strong matriarch who had brought them from Haiti to the United States and had worked several jobs to put them all through school. They described her loves as preparing Haitian foods, sewing, and spending time with her young grandchildren. Mrs. T asked the family to work with the dietitian to bring in some of Mrs. P's favorite foods. They arranged for a Creole-speaking aide to visit her daily and to bring her to arts and crafts for sewing. The daughters also were encouraged to visit and to bring along the grandchildren on a regular basis. Mrs. P reacted well to these changes and quickly regained the lost weight.

Energize

Caregivers need to take care of themselves and reenergize on a regular basis in order to avoid burnout. One of the best ways to reenergize is simply to have a break from caregiving. Caregivers should be encouraged on their own to visit friends and family, to eat out, to see a movie, to attend a concert, to experience a sporting event, to have beauty treatments, and to engage in relaxing and aesthetically pleasing activities. Caregivers should also tend to their own physical and mental health by engaging in exercise, maintaining a healthy diet, and getting adequate sleep. For the majority of caregivers, religious and spiritual connections play a vital role in finding some meaning to their burden and in receiving support from clergy and the community. Although a caregiver may want to and should include the demented individual in these activities, he or she should be given permission (or even a prescription!) to be away from the loved one as well. Life cannot stop entirely for the caregiver; otherwise, he or she is guaranteed to suffer from excess burden that ultimately will impair his or her caregiving ability.

Sexuality in Dementia

Despite a diagnosis of dementia, sexuality may continue to be an important factor in the lives of many individuals and their partners. For these couples, sexual intimacy can provide a nonverbal means of communication and connection. As dementia progresses into more severe stages, however, the ability to initiate sexual activity, to provide consent, and to sustain performance may become impaired (Davies et al., 2010; Rosen, Lachs, & Pillemer, 2010). Caregivers may face other difficulties as well, including sexually aggressive or inappropriate behaviors (Guay, 2008) and ethical issues regarding extramarital relationships and competency to consent to sexual activity (See Chapters 9 and 11). Despite the centrality of all of these issues for caregivers, health care professionals often fail to inquire about them.

Dementia can affect sexuality in several ways. In general, research indicates that sexual activity is decreased by more than 50% in couples with a partner with AD (Eloniemi-Sulkava et al., 2002). Many possible explanations for this exist. Caregivers may be turned off and may have less sexual desire for a partner with dementia who does not always recognize them, who is less physically attractive (i.e., due to poor hygiene, incontinence, loss of motor or language functions), or who requests sex repeatedly because he or she cannot remember when they last had it. Caregivers may be confused by their conflicting feelings of love and fidelity for their spouse with dementia and guilt over their desires for extramarital intimacy (Agronin & Westheimer, 2011). The depression experienced by both caregivers and patients with dementia can also be associated with a loss of sexual desire. The dementia process itself may be a culprit because the cognitive impairment may reduce the individual's attentional capacity during sex, as well as the ability to initiate and sequence components of lovemaking (Rosen et al., 2010). Despite all of these factors, sexual dysfunction is not the rule in dementia, and sexual desire may remain strong or it may even increase as previously held inhibitions are reduced by cognitive impairment.

When assessing a couple in which one partner has dementia, clinicians should inquire about sexual problems, such as loss of desire, erectile dysfunction, or other problems that interfere with lovemaking. The clinician should not let his or her own discomfort in discussing sexual topics get in the way of helping the couple (Agronin & Westheimer, 2011). The following simple recommendations can help many couples with sexual problems.

- Shift the focus from sexual intercourse to physical intimacy and foreplay.
- Rule out causes of sexual dysfunction, such as medical problems or medications.
- Encourage gynecologic or urologic consultation when necessary.

In long-term care facilities, the staff has the responsibility of ensuring privacy for conjugal visits. With more severe stages of dementia, however, the cognitively intact partner may question whether the patient with dementia retains the capacity to consent to sexual activity (Lichtenberg & Strzepek, 1990). The issue of an individual's capacity to consent to sex is covered in Chapter 11.

Endpoints

A major endpoint occurs in the later stages of dementia when the individual is no longer able to live in his or her current environment and must be placed in a more structured one. Although this usually means a move from home to a long-term care facility, it can also refer to moves from an independent to an assisted-living facility or from an open to a closed dementia or behavioral unit within a facility. How does the clinician know when the patient has reached an endpoint with respect to the environment? Signs may include the following:

- recurrent accidents or behavioral problems by the person with dementia;
- the caregiver is physically or psychologically incapacitated;
- the environment is always unsafe or unkempt;
- the person with dementia is being neglected or abused;
- the caregiver is not able to meet the needs of the person with dementia.

Caregivers often agonize over long-term care placement because of a view that such facilities are unpleasant and impersonal places that warehouse elders in their remaining days. They may object to a move to a more structured unit because they view its residents as "more impaired" than their loved one or because they see the move as a harbinger of impending death. Patients often resist moving for similar reasons. Being proactive is always better because it allows the caregiver more time to explore possibilities and to make a choice without a crisis looming.

Sometimes, additional resources, such as visiting nurses, aides, or companions, can improve the situation and buy the caregiver time. Cognition, function, and behavior in the existing environment should be optimized through appropriate treatment of any underlying medical and psychiatric problems. When problems persist, however, the clinician should advise the caregivers to visit several potential facilities to learn about their options. He or she may suggest a transitional admission to a hospital when this is appropriate, such as when the individual with dementia has significant behavioral problems that warrant a geriatric psychiatry evaluation before placement can even be considered.

Easing the Transition to Long-Term Care

To smooth the process of admission to a long-term care facility, the clinician should encourage the caregivers to prepare the person and the new environment for the move. This may include making visits ahead of time, speaking with staff about the person's background and special needs, and preparing the new room ahead of time with photographs, personal items, and other touches of home and comfort (e.g., a colorful quilt, a working radio and television). Residents or caregivers should not bring in heirlooms or expensive or irreplaceable items whose damage or disappearance may devastate them. Instead, they should bring in copies of old photographs, costume jewelry, and inexpensive appliances that can easily be replaced. Caregivers should plan to spend time with the individual on the day of admission, and friends and family should be encouraged to call or to visit frequently. They should make personal contact with the nursing and social work staff and should supply them with an accurate medical and psychiatric history and medication lists.

The Final Endpoint: Hospice and Palliative Care

The endpoint occurs when an individual with a progressive dementia enters a terminal state, which is usually characterized by a severe decline in function in which the individual can no longer walk, swallow, or communicate verbally. Ethical issues, such as advance directives, tube feeding, and do not resuscitate status, are discussed in Chapter 11. From the standpoint of both the caregiver and palliative care, the goal is to maximize the comfort of the patient in a dignified and compassionate way. Hospice care with dementia involves the control and palliation of pain and discomfort for the patient and counseling and spiritual guidance for both the patient and caregiver. This does not mean that anything is done to hasten the patient's death, but it does recognize the limitations of care, the inevitability of death, and the value of comfort and dignity. Several resources on hospice care are listed at the end of the chapter.

Clinical Tip

Even in severe stages of dementia, affected individuals are often still capable of receiving and giving affection, warmth, and personal communication. Caregivers are sometimes the best teachers for clinicians with respect to this point as they persist in providing love and affection for individuals who seem incapable of engaging with it. The health care profession demands that we persist in our efforts to treat individuals with dementia in a compassionate and dignified manner throughout the entire progression of disease.

Caregiver Resources

All the following organizations and websites can provide information, resources, and referrals for caregivers and individuals with dementia.

Alzheimer's Association

The website for the Alzheimer's Association contains comprehensive access to information and news on AD, as well as patient and caregiver resources and advocacy. The "carefinder" website has detailed information on identifying, choosing, and coordinating care.

Website: www.alz.org. Also: www.alz.org/carefinder
Phone: 800-272-3900 (24-hour hotline)

Alzheimer's Disease Education and Referral Center (ADEAR)

The ADEAR Center is a service provided by the National Institute on Aging to provide patients and families with the latest news and information on AD. You can access a number of useful fact sheets and caregiver guides, as well as the latest on research trials.

Website: www.nia.nih.gov/alzheimers
Phone: 800-438-4380

Alzheimer's Foundation of America (AFA)

The AFA provides information, resources, education, and support for individuals suffering from dementia, and their caregivers and loved ones.

Website: www.alzfdn.org
Phone: 866-AFA-8484

The Alzheimer's Store

The Alzheimer's Store is a website with articles, tips, news, links, and an online store for dementia-related books and products.

Website: www.alzstore.com
Phone: 800-752-3238

American Association for Geriatric Psychiatry (AAGP)

The AAGP provides news and education on dementia and related psychiatric conditions and can help patients and caregivers locate referrals for local geriatric psychiatrists.

Website: www.aagponline.org
Phone: 301-654-7850

Bright Focus Foundation

The Bright Focus Foundation, formerly called the American Health Assistance Foundation, offers news, education fact sheets and publications, and guides to resources for caregivers.

Website: www.brightfocus.org
Phone: 800-437-2423

Caregiver Action Network

Formerly called the National Family Caregivers Association, the Caregiver Action Network bills itself as "the nation's leading family caregiver organization working to improve the quality of life for the more than 65 million Americans who care for loved ones with chronic conditions, disabilities, disease, or the frailties of old age." This includes AD.

> Website: www.caregiveraction.org
> Phone: 800-896-3650

Children of Aging Parents (CAPS)

CAPS provides support and resources for caregivers in general.

> Website: www.caps4caregivers.org
> Phone: 800-227-7294

Elderweb Locator

The Elderweb is a website for caregivers to research home care, long-term care, legal and financial issues, housing options, and medical issues.

> Website: www.elderweb.com

Family Caregiver Alliance

The Family Caregiver Alliance provides education, research, advocacy, and resources on caregiving and long-term care.

> Website: www.caregiver.org

GeriCareFinder

This website is a useful resource to locate advisors such as attorneys and accountants as well as a variety of community resources (e.g., hospitals, transportation), products, and services for elderly individuals.

> Website: www.gericarefinder.com

National Association of Area Agencies on Aging (AAA)

The National Association of AAA provides older individuals and those with disabilities information on community resources.

> Website: www.n4a.org

A wide variety of resources can be found on the Eldercare Locator by going to www.eldercare.gov./Eldercare.NET/Public/Index.aspx or by calling 800-677-1116.

National Association for Home Care & Hospice (NAHC)

The NAHC provides education, support, and advocacy for individuals and caregivers who need in-home care, as well as for those with needs for hospice.

Website: www.nahc.org
Phone: 202-547-7424

Well Spouse Association

This organization advocates for and provides resources and support for spouses and partners of individuals who are chronically ill or disabled.

Website: www.wellspouse.org
Phone: 800-838-0879

Books for Caregivers

The Alzheimer's Action Plan: What You Need to Know—and What You Can Do—about Memory Problems, from Prevention to Early Intervention and Care, by P. Murali Doraiswamy, Lisa P. Gwyther, and Tina Adler. St. Martin's Griffin, 2009.

Alzheimer's Activities: Hundreds of Activities for Men and Women with Alzheimer's Disease and Related Disorders, by B. J. Fitzray. Rayve Productions, 2001.

Alzheimer's Disease and Other Dementias: The Caregiver's Complete Survival Guide, by Nataly Rubinstein. Two Harbors Press, 2011.

The Alzheimer's Prevention Program: Keep Your Brain Healthy for the Rest of Your Life, by Gary Small and Gigi Vorgan. Workman Publishing Company, 2012.

Alzheimer's Treatment, Alzheimer's Prevention: A Patient and Family Guide, 2012 Edition, by Richard S. Isaacson. A. D. Consultants, 2012.

Learning to Speak Alzheimer's: A Groundbreaking Approach for Everyone Dealing with the Disease, by Joanne Koenig Coste. Mariner Books, 2004.

Talking to Alzheimer's: Simple Ways to Connect When You Visit a Family Member or Friend, by Claudia J. Strauss. New Harbinger Publications, 2002.

The 36-Hour Day: A Family Guide to Caring for People Who Have Alzheimer Disease, Related Dementias, and Memory Loss, 5th ed., by Nancy Mace and Peter Rabins. Grand Central Life & Style, 2012.

References

Agronin, M. E., & Westheimer, R. K. (2011). Sexuality and sexual disorders in late life. In M. E. Agronin & G. J. Maletta (Eds.), *Principles and practice of geriatric psychiatry* (2nd ed., pp. 523–546). Philadelphia: Lippincott, Williams and Wilkins.

Alzheimer's Association. (2012). 2012 Alzheimer's disease facts and figures. *Alz Dem, 8*(2), 131–168.

Alzheimer's Disease International. (2010). *World Alzheimer report 2010: The global impact of dementia.* London: Author.

American Medical Association. (2013). Caregiver self-assessment questionnaire. Retrieved from www.ama-assn.org/resources/doc/public-health/caregiver_english.pdf

Bédard, M., Molloy, D. W., & Squire, L. (2001). The Zarit Burden Interview: A new short version and screening version. *Gerontologist, 41*(5), 652–657.

Cohen, D. (2004). Behind the looking glass: Dementia caregivers who kill. *J Ment Health Aging, 10*, 147–150.

Davies, H. D., Newkirk, L. A., Pitts, C. B., et al. (2010). The impact of dementia and mild memory impairment (MMI) on intimacy and sexuality in spousal relationships. *Int Psychogeriatr, 4*, 618–628.

Depp, C. A., Romero, R., Thompson, L. W., & Gallagher-Thompson, D. (2011). The geriatric caregiver. In M. E. Agronin & G. J. Maletta (Eds.), *Principles and practice of geriatric psychiatry* (2nd ed., pp. 43–58). Philadelphia: Lippincott, Williams and Wilkins.

Eloniemi-Sulkava, U., Notkola, I. L., Hämäläinen, K., et al. (2002). Spouse caregivers' perceptions of influence of dementia on marriage. *Psychogeriatrics, 14*(1), 47–58.

Guay, D. R. (2008). Inappropriate sexual behaviors in cognitively impaired older individuals. *American Journal of Geriatric Pharmacotherapy, 6*(5), 269–288.

Hebert, L., Scherr, P., Bienias, J., et al. (2003). Alzheimer's disease in the US population: Prevalence estimates using the 2000 census. *Arch Neurol, 60*(8), 1119–1122.

Hurd, M.D., Martorelli, P., & Delavande, A. (2013). Monetary costs of dementia in the United States. *N Eng J Med, 368*(14), 1326–1334.

Kim, H., Chang, M., Rose, K., & Kim, S. (2012). Predictors of caregiver burden in caregivers of individuals with dementia. *J Adv Nurs, 68*(4), 846–855.

Lichtenberg, P. A., & Strzepek, D. M. (1990). Assessments of institutionalized dementia patients' competencies to participate in intimate relationships. *Gerontologist, 30*, 117–120.

Parker, D., Mills, S., & Abbey, J. (2008). Effectiveness of interventions that assist caregivers to support people with dementia living in the community: A systematic review. *Int J Evid Based Healthc, 6*(2), 137–172.

Parks, S. M. (2000). A practical guide to caring for caregivers. *Am Fam Phy, 62*(12), 2613–2622.

Rosen, T., Lachs, M. S., & Pillemer, K. (2010). Sexual aggression between residents in nursing homes: Literature synthesis of an underrecognized problem. *JAGS, 58*(10), 1970–1979.

Taylor, D. H., Ezell, M., Kuchibhatla, M., et al. (2008). Identifying the trajectories of depressive symptoms for women caring for their husbands with dementia. *JAGS, 56*(2), 322–327.

Van Mierlo, L. D., Meiland, F. J., Van der Roest, H. G., & Dröes, R. M. (2012). Personalised caregiver support: Effectiveness of psychosocial interventions in subgroups of caregivers of people with dementia. *Int J Geriatr Psychiatry, 27*(1), 1–14.

Zarit, S. H., Reever, K. E., & Bach-Peterson, J. (1980). Relatives of the impaired elderly: Correlates of feelings of burden. *Gerontologist, 20*(6), 649–655.

Zarit, S. H., Todd, P. A., & Zarit, J. M. (1986). Subjective burden of husbands and wives caregivers: A longitudinal study. *Gerontologist, 26*(3), 260–266.

Index

Page numbers followed by an "f" indicate figures; those followed by a "t" indicate tables.